Praise for *The Generational Wealth Code*

"Most financial books tell you to save and invest. John Vento invites readers to think about how what they've built may be preserved and passed on. With four decades as a CPA and CFP®, he understands what advisors often miss: most investment decisions are tax decisions. Anyone serious about building lasting wealth for the next generation needs to read this."

—**Michael Sincere**, Author of Understanding Stocks and Understanding Options

"The Generational Wealth Code masterfully translates decades of tax-smart planning into a practical blueprint that every family can use. It's rare to find a book that is equally empowering to first-time savers, seasoned investors, and professionals guiding clients toward real financial independence."

—**Gene F. Goldman**, CFA, Chief Investment Officer, Cetera Financial Group

"The Generational Wealth Code is a must-read for anyone serious about meaningfully and reliably reducing their tax burden. Backed by real-world credibility as CPAs, CFP®s and investment advisors, the authors offer a rare multigenerational perspective on how to implement tax-smart financial planning and investment strategies that build lasting family wealth."

—**Michael K. Deluke**, DDS, MDS, ABO, Host of *The DOC Podcast*

"This is essential reading for hardworking individuals who want to sustain financial independence throughout their lives while building and protecting generational wealth. Widely regarded as a benchmark in financial planning, the book delivers practical, tax-smart strategies designed to help readers reach their financial goals faster and with greater confidence."

—**Dr. Satjit Bhusri**, MD, Founder of Upper East Side Cardiology & Vein Institute, and Fellow of the American College of Cardiology

The Generational Wealth Code

The Generational Wealth Code

A TAX-SMART ROADMAP TO FINANCIAL INDEPENDENCE

John J. Vento, CPA, MBA, CFP®

John J. Vento Jr., CPA, CFP®

Nicole Vento, CPA, CFP®

Christine Vento Conway, CPA

WILEY

Published by John Wiley & Sons, Inc., Hoboken, New Jersey.

For general information on our other products and services or for technical support, please contact our Customer Care Department within the United States at (800) 762-2974, outside the United States at (317) 572-3993 or fax (317) 572-4002.

Wiley also publishes its books in a variety of electronic formats. Some content that appears in print may not be available in electronic formats. For more information about Wiley products, visit our web site at www.wiley.com.

Library of Congress Cataloging-in-Publication Data has been applied for:

Print ISBN: 9781394425228
ePub ISBN: 9781394425235
ePDF ISBN: 9781394425242

Cover Design: Paul McCarthy
Cover Images: © Lynnebeclu/Getty Images, © Sebastian Kaulitki/Science Photo Library/Getty Images
Author Photo: Courtesy of the Author

SKY10153553_041526

This book is dedicated to the memory of my parents, Rosario Vento and Concetta Giuffre Vento, for the sacrifices and commitments they made throughout their lives to provide their children, grandchildren, and now great-grandchildren, with the opportunity to live the "TRUE" American Dream.
Mamma and Papa, I love you, miss you, and think about you every single day!

***ChatGPT-5** was used to*
analyze drafts for clarity, consistency, and coherence.
This AI-assisted review complemented
human expert review across editorial, legal, and AI expert teams. All AI
feedback was evaluated and selectively incorporated based on
human judgment.

Contents

Foreword

It's been a privilege knowing and working with John Vento during the four decades our firms have been associated with each other. We're two sides of the same coin—John and his team provide tax-focused financial advice and wealth management services to his clients, and as John's financial services partner, we provide John with the tools, technology, resources, and specialists to support his firm in service of his clients.

John is among the very best at embodying our shared mantra: "*It's not how much you make; it's how much you keep.*"

And while that statement sounds simple, its calculus has never been more complicated than today with increasingly complex tax laws and sweeping tax reforms. You don't need to look far for proof, for example, President Trump's "One Big Beautiful Bill Act," a document of nearly 900 pages, that can impact every financial plan, including those already established.

In *The Generational Wealth Code: A Tax-smart Roadmap to Financial Independence,* John Vento looks at the "One Big Beautiful Bill Act" and provides insights and strategies that can help not only those just starting their financial journey but also veteran investors.

The impact of taxes, both new and long-standing, is bound to the heart of this book—tax-focused financial planning and wealth management—because every investment decision is a tax decision. And as John explains in his book, everything as it relates to a financial plan should be viewed through the lens of tax.

John approaches his clients' financial welfare holistically, being mindful of taxes that can impact a client's financial plan if not planned for properly. After all, taxes are one of the greatest expenses of our lives.

Do you want to avoid unnecessarily overpaying taxes? Do you want to keep more of what you've earned so you can pursue your financial dreams as powerfully as possible? If yes, then you'll find help in the following pages. You'll learn at a high level how embracing tax and financial planning helps put you on a path to reach your goals.

As you'll read in the following pages, achieving your financial goals involves much more than "saving and investing." There are so many small nuances that can have huge impacts on whether you can live the life you want today and in retirement.

In short, it's not just about accumulating assets—you need to consider how ignoring taxes can significantly erode your nest egg. Looking through the lens of tax together, you and a tax-intelligent financial advisor can agree on a plan that pays close attention to asset classes and the types of accounts in which those assets are held, so you're as tax-efficient as possible.

This is why John's book and his tax-focused approach are so key, because most people think about accumulating, but not decumulating; in other words, when it comes time to draw on those investments to replace income during retirement. Were those assets managed in a tax-optimized way? Was there a focus on proper asset location within taxable, tax-deferred, and nontaxable accounts?

The approach sounds logical if not simple! But far too few financial advisors consider these tax-impacting nuances. John committed to tax-focused financial planning decades ago, and the efficiencies and higher returns that can come from a tax-optimized approach to wealth management—what the financial industry calls "Tax Alpha"—has made a meaningful impact for countless clients.

Beyond making sound financial sense, one could argue that helping people accumulate assets and showing them how to tax-efficiently invest in their future is morally right.

After all, financial advisors like John help guide clients so they understand how to protect their loved ones by providing the security they require and setting realistic goals to help them pursue their future financial needs.

We all encounter life's twists and turns—marriage, buying a house, career or job changes, having a family, caring for aging parents—and everyone has their own view of what financial independence means.

In addition to tax-focused financial planning, John guides you through many of these facets, explaining insurance for you and your property, what it takes to plan for your child's college, and planning for your retirement.

Let this book serve as your initial guide, because the information here can help you understand what you'll need for your financial journey.

As you navigate your path, find an advisor who fits with you—and to keep more of what you make, find a financial advisor who believes in marrying tax and financial planning, so you can vigorously pursue the financial future of your dreams.

Andy Watts
President of Avantax

Preface

Living the American Dream

My first clients were quintessential examples of successful American Dreamers. They came to the United States from Italy after World War II with nothing, and they created a wonderful life for themselves and their children by working hard, living modestly, and saving. I confess I learned more from their example than from any college course or studies to gain my many licenses. As you might guess, these clients were my parents.

Rosario Vento, my father, was born in the small town of Messina, Sicily, in 1923. My mother, Concetta Giuffre Vento, was born in 1921 and came from an even smaller village nearby called Sant'Agata. They lived through the Great Depression (which was as bad in Europe as it was in the United States), survived World War II by seeking shelter in the hills of Sicily, and were married shortly after the war's end. It was clear that opportunities in Sicily and throughout Italy were limited because of the devastation of war, so they made the difficult decision to place their hopes and dreams on a new life in America.

Because they could not afford to pay for two tickets, my dad initially came to America alone. After a year, he was able to afford to rent a small but comfortable apartment in Bensonhurst, Brooklyn, a four-story walk-up, and had saved enough money to purchase a one-way ticket to the United States for my mother. She joined him, and they began the great journey of their life together, eager to work hard and reap the rewards of living the American Dream.

Neither one had more than an eighth-grade education, nor did either one speak English very well. After arriving in the United States, my father worked as a barber, and my mother as a seamstress in a sweatshop. They had three children in quick succession and then, after a gap of eight years, one more (me). Together, they earned a modest income, but they always managed to live within their means and save what they could. They never owned a car; instead, they got around the city by walking or using public transportation. They rarely went out to dinner; instead, my mother always prepared fresh, homemade meals. Before they spent a dime, they always asked, "Is this necessary?" If the item was in fact a necessity, they would then ask: "Is there a less-expensive alternative?"

This was my parents' attitude toward money throughout their lifetime, in both good and bad times. During the early years of their life in Brooklyn, they saved enough for a down payment on a house and obtained a mortgage, which they paid off over 30 years. They put all four of their children through college; one became a teacher, one a medical doctor, one a social worker, and one a certified public accountant and CERTIFIED FINANCIAL PLANNER® (again, me).

After I graduated from college, I began helping my parents manage their finances, although, as mentioned, they taught me much more about money than I was ever able to teach them. Each year, I prepared a Statement of Financial Position and a Statement of Cash Flow for them, an exercise that, for me, was not only a pleasure, but also a powerful reconfirmation of the values they had taught me. They always lived well within their means, were careful savers, and were usually able to add funds to their investable assets. Over the years, I was able to assist them in developing a well-diversified investment portfolio.

Ultimately, the year my mother turned 75, they achieved a financial milestone that they had never thought possible. I was sitting at their kitchen table, sipping the espresso that my mother always prepared for me whenever I came to visit. On this day, I was there to talk to them about their finances. To my great joy, I was able to look my mother straight in the eyes, and say: "Congratulations, you and Papa are millionaires!" The combined value of their home, their invested assets, and their cash totaled just over a million dollars and, of course, they had no debt.

Words cannot do justice to the expressions on their faces and the tears of joy in their eyes. At that moment, my parents knew that they had accomplished one of their most cherished goals, financial independence. For them, the American Dream was not just a dream anymore; it was now their reality.

My mother passed away in 2006 and my father in 2011. They left this earth knowing that they had lived comfortably and responsibly. They had been able to raise, care for, and educate their children, and they never became a burden to us. In fact, upon their passing, they were able to leave their children with a solid financial legacy that could be measured both in dollars and by their example. That is why this book is dedicated to them.

Now, as my children build their own careers and families, I've come to realize that true financial success isn't measured only by what you earn or save, but by the generational wealth you create: your values, your wisdom, and the foundation you leave behind for your loved ones to build upon.

This book is part of that legacy. For the first time, I've had the privilege of writing alongside my children, each of them professionals with their own insights and experiences. Together, we bring a shared commitment to helping others achieve what my parents achieved and what I've worked toward my entire life: lasting financial security and the opportunity to pass it on.

My hope is that the guidance in these pages will help you not only achieve financial independence for yourself but also create something that lasts, something your family can benefit from long after you are gone. That is the true power of this book. That is the real American Dream.

John J. Vento

Acknowledgments

I want to thank everyone who helped to make this book possible.

First, I would like to thank Andy Watts for recognizing the value this book could have in increasing financial literacy throughout the country. The support from many of Cetera's subject matter experts has truly taken this book to a whole new level. I am truly grateful to Clint Brookshire, Jerry Patterson, Gene Goldman, Barry Holt, and Carol Ventura (retired) for the value they added by sharing their wealth of knowledge. I give my sincere thanks to Craig Johnson for coordinating this effort and to Ladan Massir, along with her team, for their creative ideas.

I want to thank Christina Pasaturo for her contribution and expertise in estate and elder care planning. I also want to thank John Manning for his valuable insights on qualifying for a mortgage and managing debt. The advice and guidance these experts provided raised the bar in these areas.

Many thanks to my entire staff for their support and assistance. I especially want to acknowledge Ashley Arcamone for being the glue that kept the office together and functioning. She not only jumped in and helped many of our staff with their work overflow but also acted as one of the final proofreaders for this book. I also can't thank Melissa Perez enough for managing this project, proofreading the transcript, and adding her insight, all while still being a full-time dedicated mother to her son, Luke. She proved herself as a tremendous asset to the creation of this book.

When I wrote my first book, *Financial Independence: Getting to Point X*, my three children, John, Christine, and Nicole, were teenagers. Even then, they were by my side every step of the way, helping me bring my thoughts and words to life. That experience opened their eyes to the world of business and finance. Little did I know it would also plant the seeds for what has now become a shared professional journey. Today, I am proud to say that all three of my children are not only successful professionals in their own right, but also coauthors of this book.

John Jr., a CPA and CFP®, is a partner in Vento Tax & Wealth Management Group, where he leads our tax and accounting division and serves as our lead expert on tax law and tax-smart strategies. His contributions to Chapter 2, "Understanding Taxes," Chapter 8, "Planning for Retirement," and the tax-smart strategies throughout the book, brought tremendous value.

Nicole, a CPA and CFP®, joined our wealth management team as a financial advisor in 2024 after years of experience with two of the largest banking and investment firms in the country. Her work elevated every chapter, particularly Chapter 4, "Managing Debt," Chapter 5, "Insuring Your Health and Life," Chapter 7, "Paying for College," and Chapter 9, "Managing Your Investments." Her years of experience as a trader and advisor to ultra-high-net-worth clients brought an extraordinary level of insight, especially to the investments chapter, where her deep understanding of markets and strategy truly shines through.

Christine, also a CPA, serves as a senior vice president at a privately owned, nationally recognized commercial real estate firm. Her work on Chapter 11, "Investing in Real Estate" added a critical dimension to this book. With years of experience in both financial services and real estate investing, her perspective was not only relevant, but invaluable.

They have all contributed countless hours, including many late nights and weekends, not just as editors or contributors, but as true coauthors. This book now reflects our collective experience, perspectives, and commitment to helping others achieve financial independence and generational wealth. The word "proud" does not begin to describe how I feel. Watching my children choose to follow in my footsteps, and now walk beside me in this work, has been one of the greatest joys of my life.

Speaking of my greatest joys, my son and his wife, Mateamarie, have blessed me with a beautiful granddaughter, Sofia Jo, who turned two just as we were putting the finishing touches on this book. My daughter, Christine, and my son-in-law, Justin, recently welcomed their first child, my grandson, Zachary, born on July 7, 2025, just three days after the One Big Beautiful Bill Act was signed into law. I can only hope that one day, one or more of my grandchildren will join my children in continuing this incredible journey.

Last, but most certainly not least, to Doreen, thank you for sharing your life with me for over 40 years, and for the last 36 as my wife. You have been an incredible mother to our children, shaping their lives with love, strength, and balance. You've shown me, our children, and now our grandchildren what truly matters in life. As my mother always said, "Without family, there is nothing."

Happiness is being married to your best friend and soulmate. Thank you for being the most important person in my life, my greatest supporter, and for standing by me, especially in moments when I probably didn't make it easy.

John J. Vento

Introduction: *The Generational Wealth Code: A Tax-smart Roadmap to Financial Independence*

Getting to *point X.* Every kid over the age of five knows this expression. It can refer to many things, but the strongest image for most of us is an ancient, moldy pirate map showing precisely where a long-lost treasure is buried. This book was written to help you discover your own "buried treasure." Of course, this is not a child's game. It is a guide to the necessary knowledge (with a special focus on tax-smart strategies) to help you accumulate the wealth you need to lead the life you desire.

I have been a certified public accountant (CPA) for over four decades and a CERTIFIED FINANCIAL PLANNER® (CFP®) for more than two decades. I started my career working for KPMG (one of the Big Four CPA firms) and then established my own practice in 1985. I have worked one-on-one with literally thousands of individuals, assisting them in their pursuit of a secure financial future. I have helped these clients pursue their financial goals, and this has given them and me tremendous pleasure. However, I have also seen individuals who, for a variety of reasons, have struggled to achieve financial independence, and the consequences can be deeply troubling.

With this book, my hope is to help individuals and their families at every stage of their financial journey. That includes those who are still working toward financial independence, as well as those who have already achieved it and want to build on that foundation by creating and maintaining generational wealth.

Whether you are a dual-income couple managing a mortgage, college tuition, and aging parents, or a high-income earner focused on long-term planning and wealth preservation, the goal remains the same: to build lasting financial strength. By combining financial planning with tax-smart strategies, this book may help readers increase their personal wealth and pursue their financial independence, a position I refer to as *point X*.

But *point X* is not the final destination; in fact, it's just the beginning of creating and maintaining generational wealth. This book provides the code to help you unlock that next level of financial success, not just for you but for your family for many generations to come.

While *point X* is about achieving enough wealth to live without relying on a paycheck, generational wealth is about building, protecting, and passing on your wealth in a way that creates lasting security, opportunity, and purpose for future generations. It means aligning your financial decisions today with the legacy you hope to leave behind. A legacy that includes not just assets, but a foundation your family can continue to build upon.

Reaching generational wealth requires more than saving and investing wisely. It demands long-term strategies that integrate family planning, education, estate preservation, and a commitment to financial literacy across generations. You've already taken the first step by picking up this book; the rest of the journey starts here.

Financial Literacy and Why We Wrote This Book

Before I explain how to achieve financial independence, I want to share why I wrote the original books on this subject and how that journey has evolved into this new book, coauthored with my three children. I will also explain why it's critically important for every reader to share a copy of this book with their own family members.

Financial literacy has always been important, but in recent years it has become a national conversation. With each passing decade, new challenges, economic shifts, and legislative changes have made it clear that individuals need practical, reliable guidance to take control of their financial future.

Financial literacy means having a firm understanding of fundamental financial concepts and strategies, and the ability to manage money responsibly in order to ensure financial security. Financial literacy is essential to ensure the financial stability of individuals and their families, as well as the overall economic health of society as a whole.

The worldwide financial crisis of 2008 made it clear that our nation needed to improve the financial literacy of our citizens.

That moment revealed just how unprepared many individuals and families were for sound financial management and lasting security. It took me five years to write and publish my first book, *Financial Independence: Getting to Point X.* A second edition followed in 2018, prompted by the sweeping changes of the Tax Cuts and Jobs Act of 2017, which reshaped the financial and tax planning landscape on a massive scale.

Today, the need for practical, reliable guidance is greater than ever, especially with the growing acceptance of socialism with the younger generation. Americans face a new landscape of rules, risks, and opportunities. This book was written in direct response to this transformation.

But more than that, it was written to reflect a bigger shift in thinking. It is no longer enough to reach financial independence for yourself. Once you have achieved financial independence, the next step is creating generational wealth. This means creating long-term, sustainable wealth that your family can build on, preserve, and pass down for generations to come.

Building on the foundation laid in *Financial Independence: Getting to Point X*, this book introduces new material that reflects the evolving financial world. It includes an in-depth look at the One Big Beautiful Bill Act (OBBBA) legislation and what it means for you, along with an entirely new chapter on one of the most powerful generational wealth-building opportunities available today: investing in real estate.

What makes this work especially relevant is the team behind it. This book was coauthored by four financial professionals, each with a distinct perspective shaped by their own stage of life and area of expertise. Together, we bring a multigenerational approach to wealth building and financial planning that speaks to the needs of a wide and diverse audience. Our goal is to provide actionable guidance that helps you and your family create a legacy of wealth, stability, and opportunity.

The Move from Capitalism to Socialism in the United States

Even with the right tools and intentions, families today are facing a financial environment filled with growing challenges and dangerous misconceptions. Stagnant wages, crushing student loan debt, rising housing costs, and record levels of consumer debt have made it harder than ever for families to get ahead. Add to that the recent surge in inflation and persistent economic uncertainty, and it becomes clear why financial stability feels out of reach for so many Americans.

Somehow over the last several decades, I believe since the end of World War II, many people in our society have come to believe incorrect notions about money. These financial myths include many incorrect ideas:

- “Owning your own home is everyone’s right.”
- “The real estate market will always rise.”
- “You can live ‘large’ on credit and never pay any consequences.”
- “If you need to work, you can always find a job.”

These myths represent a distorted view of the American Dream. They were already unraveling long before the crash of 2008, but the years since have made clear just how dangerous they can be. The lessons in frugality learned by the earlier generations, people who lived through the Great Depression of the 1930s and World War II, have been lost. Too many Americans remain unprepared for the financial realities of life.

At the same time, we are witnessing an undeniable shift in public sentiment, with socialism gaining traction in ways not seen since the American Socialist Movement between 1900 and World War I.

Voices like Bernie Sanders, Alexandria Ocasio-Cortez, and members of the progressive “Squad” are leading a movement that emphasizes government control, redistribution of wealth, and increased entitlement programs.

On November 4, 2025, Zohran Mamdani, a 34-year-old self-described democratic socialist and state assemblyman, was elected mayor of New York City. His victory is heralded as a significant shift in urban politics, one that embraces an explicitly socialist agenda in the heart of one of the world’s most iconic capitalist cities.

While some praise his ideals of economic equity, critics warn his anti-capitalist bent risks undermining the very market dynamics that have fueled America’s prosperity. Historical examples of socialism’s failure from the Soviet Union’s economic collapse to Venezuela’s humanitarian crisis serve as cautionary tales that government control of goods and services often stifles growth, innovation, and individual freedom.

While these ideas may sound appealing to some, I firmly believe that capitalism is the reason America has become the most prosperous and opportunity-filled nation in history. It is the system that rewards hard work, innovation, and personal responsibility, the very principles at the heart of financial independence.

This book comes at a moment when its lessons are needed most. We all must relearn some essential financial truths, become financially responsible, and prepare for the financial realities of life. In other words, we must become *financially literate.* We must learn all we can about our money so that we can make the most informed financial decisions in all facets of our lives.

Millennials were the generation most significantly affected by the financial crisis of 2008, but that was only the beginning. In their formative working years, they lived through not only the Great Recession but also a long period of stagnant wages, historic levels of student loan debt, skyrocketing housing costs, and now the crushing impact of inflation. Just as many were beginning to regain their footing, the COVID-19 pandemic brought layoffs, uncertainty, and economic disruption that once again hit younger workers especially hard. For many, the dream of homeownership feels out of reach, and even renting an apartment has become a financial stretch. As a result, more young adults have moved back in with their parents than at any point in modern history, with the exception of the temporary spike during the COVID-19 pandemic.

Gen Z, now entering adulthood, has faced many of the same challenges. They watched their parents and older siblings struggle during the Great Recession, only to step into an economy still weighed down by high housing costs, student debt, and limited job opportunities. Inflation has further eroded their purchasing power, making it harder to build savings or plan for the future.

The promises made to these younger generations, that hard work and a college degree would lead to financial security, have often proven untrue. Saddled with debt and disillusioned by limited economic opportunities, many millennials and Gen Z have grown skeptical of capitalism. This disillusionment has given rise to growing interest in socialist ideas among younger Americans.

A March 2025 survey conducted by the Cato Institute and YouGov found that 62% of Americans aged 18–29 view socialism favorably, with 34% of that group also expressing positive views of communism. Many even said they would consider supporting openly socialist candidates.

I find these results alarming, as they reflect a troubling shift in the direction our country is heading. One that, in my view, runs counter to the very principles that built the nation's strength and prosperity.

By contrast, older generations continue to show much stronger support for capitalism. The divide between baby boomers, Gen X, millennials, and today's younger generations could not be more pronounced.

I remain hopeful that the significant improvements in the US economy over the past several years will help shift attitudes away from skepticism toward capitalism. With unemployment steadily declining, economic growth on the rise, and renewed prospects for prosperity, I believe this generation can rediscover faith in the true American Dream, that this country is the land of opportunity, not the land of entitlements.

At the same time, the baby boomer generation must acknowledge that the financial mistakes of their generation played a big role in fostering the very socialist mindset now embraced by many younger Americans. Changing this perception of what it means to be an American may take decades, but I am optimistic that the shift will come sooner rather than later.

While millennials and Gen Z have faced tremendous challenges, I believe their struggles will ultimately strengthen them. They are learning first-hand the dangers of debt, the risks of living beyond their means, and the importance of building financial security. These lessons, though difficult, may give them the discipline and resilience needed to create a more stable financial future for themselves and their families. That gives me optimism not only for their future, but for the future of America as a whole.

For this reason, this book and the guidance it provides will be essential in teaching all generations of Americans that there is hope in achieving their own financial independence. The first step we must take as a society is to educate ourselves and our families in becoming financially literate. This book will unlock the code to achieving financial independence and will also lay the foundation to creating and maintaining generational wealth.

Point X: Our Fundamental Financial Goal

Point X is literally and fundamentally the point at which we can stop working for our money and our money starts working for us. It is the spot at which our savings and investments alone generate enough income to support our chosen lifestyle and allow us to continue to live that lifestyle without having to work for a paycheck. It is the place where we have achieved true financial independence.

For most of us, getting to *point X* is our most fundamental financial goal. It is the position we hope to achieve so that we can retire. Even if we do not wish to retire from productive and enjoyable work, we all still yearn to arrive at *point X*, often sooner rather than later, to feel financially secure and financially free.

What that number may be in terms of dollars is different for each of us. Some people can manage rich full lives on a modest income and seem to be able to find their *point X* with ease and clarity. Others have multimillion-dollar annual incomes yet still find themselves living way beyond their means and view getting to *point X* as an arduous and perhaps an impossible journey. How you determine your personal *point X* depends on several variables:

- Understanding your present standard of living
- Projecting how you want to live after you retire (or after you stop receiving a paycheck)
- Figuring out how many years of saving it will take for you to reach *point X*
- Figuring out how many years of financial independence you hope to enjoy after you reach *point X*

Determining your personal *point X* also involves some mathematical calculations:

- The rate of return you hope to achieve on your investments
- The effects of inflation and taxes on your investments before and after you retire

Although this process of defining *point X* may look like grad-school calculus right now, I promise you it is really not all that difficult, and my purpose in writing this book is to explain this process in the simplest way possible.

The Next Level of Financial Independence: *The Generational Wealth Code*

The *Generational Wealth Code* represents the set of guiding principles and disciplined financial behaviors that, when practiced consistently, transform income and assets into enduring, multigenerational wealth. It is the roadmap to mastering the 12 critical areas of comprehensive wealth management from living within one's means and optimizing tax-smart strategies to harnessing the power of compounding and building lasting value through investing. Rooted in the pursuit of financial independence, the *Generational Wealth Code* aligns daily financial decisions with long-term purpose, ensuring that wealth is not only created but also sustained, protected, and passed on as a legacy of knowledge and opportunity for future generations.

Generational wealth is the next step beyond reaching your own *point X*. Once you have achieved financial independence for yourself, the natural question becomes: What now? For many, the answer lies in using that independence not just to enjoy life, but to create long-term financial stability for the people you care about most, your children, grandchildren, and generations beyond.

Generational wealth is not about accumulating wealth for its own sake. It is about building a financial foundation that can support your family for decades, or even centuries. It means having the resources and the plan in place so that your children are not starting from scratch. It means ensuring that the values, habits, and strategies that helped you reach financial independence can be passed on and sustained over time.

Creating generational wealth does not happen by accident. It requires intentional planning and discipline. It also requires a mindset shift. Instead of asking only what you need to do to retire or live comfortably, you begin by asking what steps you can take to help future generations do the same. This might include the following:

- Teaching financial literacy to your children and grandchildren
- Implementing tax-smart strategies
- Investing in assets that can retain value across generations
- Structuring your estate plan to minimize taxes and preserve assets
- Building a family legacy plan that reflects your values as well as your goals

Reaching generational wealth also involves protecting what you have built. That includes thinking carefully about risk, taxation, and long-term sustainability. It may involve complex tools and codes, but the underlying goal is simple: to leave your family better off, not just for the next few years, but for the next century.

Generational wealth is about legacy, but it is also about responsibility. Financial independence gives you the freedom to make choices. Generational financial independence gives your loved ones the same freedom. This book will help you move beyond *point X* by showing you how to create a generational wealth code, your tax-smart roadmap to financial independence for you and your family for many generations to come.

The 12 Critical Areas of Comprehensive Wealth Management

No matter how you define your particular *point X*, whether it is an annual income of $100,000 or an estate of $500 million, you need to understand and effectively deal with the 12 critical areas of comprehensive wealth management:

1. Committing to living within your means and conscientiously saving for the future
2. Understanding taxes and how to effectively minimize your tax obligation
3. Defining your standard of living, including your net worth and your current cash flow
4. Managing debt
5. Insuring yourself and your family in case of extreme illness or death
6. Protecting your property
7. Planning for the education of yourself and your children
8. Planning for retirement
9. Investing intelligently and tax-efficiently
10. Preserving your estate
11. Investing in real estate
12. Taking advantage of the time value of money

Throughout our lives, we are in a perpetual state of change, financially and otherwise. Our needs and wants are constantly altering along with our income and our standard of living. What may seem like a financial priority at the age of 18 (buying a car; paying for college) is probably quite different by the age of 30 (purchasing a first home or planning for the birth of a child).

At 60, we may be considering retirement while simultaneously paying for a child's college education or an elderly parent's care. At 70 or beyond, we may be focused on estate planning, reducing tax exposure, and ensuring that our assets are passed on efficiently and responsibly to the next generation. What makes these financial issues even more challenging is that our economy is also in a constant state of flux.

Throughout our lives, we will encounter many questions and problems relating to money, but every one of them will fall, in some way, under one or more of these 12 critical areas of comprehensive wealth management. It is important that you understand them and work within them productively, so that you may become financially literate. Depending on how you prepare and handle each of these wealth management areas will determine how successful you will be on your path to financial independence.

Moreover, these issues are interrelated, and how you deal with one very often will influence how you treat others. For example, if you fail to manage debt properly, you will find it difficult to save for a home of your own, your child's education, or your retirement. Or, if you neglect to properly insure yourself against sickness or premature death, your spouse and family could be wiped out financially.

Woven into the critical areas of wealth management is a common variable. Throughout this book, we provide tax-smart strategies that will focus on minimizing this most significant expenditure, that is, *taxes.*

Our Biggest Expense

Have you ever gotten to the end of the week, the month, or the year, and asked yourself, "*Where did all my money go?*" Many, maybe most, people are baffled by this question and do not understand how, even if they are earning a respectable salary, their entire salary could be used up, particularly when they were not especially extravagant. They find themselves with little or no savings, or even worse, in additional debt.

What do you consider to be your biggest expense? Most people think it is their mortgage or their rent. Others who have children in college feel sure that it is those endless educational expenses. Still others who may have serious health issues may believe it is their perpetual doctor, hospital, and prescription bills.

Well, I promise you, it is none of the above. It is taxes! Yes, that is where most of your money has gone and continues to go: taxes, taxes, and even more taxes.

For 2025, the maximum federal income tax rate is 37%. On top of that, the combined Social Security rate is 15.3% (half paid by the employer and half paid by the employee). Employers also must pay additional payroll taxes under the Federal Unemployment Tax Act (FUTA) and State Unemployment Tax Act (SUTA). Depending on where you live, you may also be paying well over 10% of your paycheck on state and local taxes; for example, New York City residents pay a combined state and city income tax, which can be as high as 14.78%.

If payroll taxes were not enough, we also pay income and capital gains taxes on our other earnings, such as income from investments. We pay sales tax on many items we purchase, and we pay numerous excise taxes and other special taxes on many items we frequently do not even think about, such as alcohol, tobacco, and fuel. We pay certain licensing fees, registration fees, parking meters, tolls, tickets, and summonses, all of which are forms of taxation. We also pay real estate taxes, school taxes, water and sewer taxes, mortgage recording taxes, and transfer taxes on property. If you choose to give large gifts to a friend or family member, you may be subject to a gift tax. I would be remiss if I didn't mention tariffs, which are built into the price we pay for many goods imported into the United States. Clearly the government will tax you to death; in fact, ironically it already taxes you for dying, a little something called estate tax.

If you take a close look at how much you pay for various taxes, chances are this number would be more than 50% of your overall expenditures. Keep in mind that some of these taxes are hidden but nevertheless included in your cost of living.

So, what would be the single most important expenditure for you to focus on in order to keep more of what you make and dramatically increase your savings? The answer, of course, is taxes, taxes, and more taxes.

But the fact is, most people completely overlook the importance of minimizing their taxes in order to help maximize their wealth accumulation. You must implement a tax-smart strategy for each of the twelve critical areas of comprehensive wealth management discussed throughout this book.

An article from *Accounting Today* defined tax alpha as

> the value that is added to a client's financial plan by optimizing sound tax strategies. If 'alpha' is the return generated by an advisor's skill in picking and managing investments, then 'tax alpha' protects that return and generates a boost by making sure that taxes don't eat away more of a client's wealth than absolutely necessary.

Traditionally, the term tax alpha has referred only to boosting investment returns by using tax-smart investing strategies. What sets this book apart is that it broadens the concept, applying tax alpha to the entire financial planning process. We will show you how to transform the Internal Revenue Code into the Generational Wealth Code.

Within these pages, we outline hundreds of tax-smart strategies across these critical areas of comprehensive wealth management. Providing practical tools that will help you build wealth faster and significantly improve your chances of achieving financial independence and then maintaining generational wealth for you and your loved ones.

Take a Financial Planning Checkup

Before we begin to discuss specific strategies, you should evaluate your financial situation by completing this *Comprehensive Wealth Management Questionnaire*. This questionnaire will help you start thinking about the financial issues you have under control and others that may need attention.

Comprehensive Wealth Management Questionnaire

The following 20 questions are designed to assist you identify your financial strengths and weaknesses, clarify your goals, and create a tax-smart roadmap to financial independence for you and your family for generations to come.

1. Do you save 10% or more of your gross income (pay yourself first) before determining your standard of living? If you answered *no*, read Chapter 1, "Committing to Living within Your Means."
2. Do you have easily accessible funds to cover at least three to six months of your living expenses in case of an emergency? If you answered *no*, read Chapter 1, "Committing to Living within Your Means."

3. Do you know if you are taking advantage of every tax deduction and tax credit available to you? If you answered *no*, read Chapter 2, "Understanding Taxes," and pay particular attention to the tax-smart strategies at the end of each chapter.
4. Do you know the value of your financial net worth? If you answered *no*, read Chapter 3, "Determining Your Financial Position."
5. Do you have a clear understanding of your cash inflows and outflows? If you answered *no*, read Chapter 3, "Determining Your Financial Position."
6. Do you maintain a zero balance on your credit cards and maintain no other high-interest rate loans? If you answered *no*, read Chapter 4, "Managing Debt."
7. Do you know whether you have the most favorable terms on your home or investment property mortgage(s)? If you answered *no*, read Chapter 4, "Managing Debt."
8. Do you (or your parents) have a plan for paying for a nursing home or long-term home health care costs? If you answered *no*, read Chapter 5, "Insuring Your Health and Life."
9. Do you have long-term disability insurance to help pay your expenses if you or your spouse were unable to earn an income? If you answered *no*, read Chapter 5, "Insuring Your Health and Life."
10. Will your family receive sufficient funds from your life insurance policies upon your death or the death of your spouse to ensure your family's continued support and lifestyle? If you answered *no*, read Chapter 5, "Insuring Your Health and Life."
11. Do you carry a minimum of $1,000,000 in personal liability insurance? If you answered *no*, read Chapter 6, "Protecting Your Property with Insurance."
12. Are your assets that you cannot afford to replace properly covered by insurance (e.g., car, home, fine jewelry, art)? If you answered *no*, read Chapter 6, "Protecting Your Property with Insurance."
13. Do you have sufficient funds set aside to pay for your children (or grandchildren) to attend college? If you answered *no*, read Chapter 7, "Paying for College."
14. Do you know if you will be financially ready to retire or become financially independent at your desired age? If you answered *no*, read Chapter 8, "Planning for Retirement."
15. If you are changing jobs or retiring, are you confident that you understand your financial options and are making the right choices? If you answered *no*, read Chapter 8, "Planning for Retirement."
16. Do you fully understand the different investment choices (stocks, bonds, hybrid securities, mutual funds, exchange traded funds, alternatives, etc.) available to you? If you answered *no*, read Chapter 9, "Managing Your Investments."

(*continued*)

(*continued*)

17. Do you (and your spouse) have a will in place? Has it been reviewed by an attorney within the past five years, and was it drafted in your current state of residence? If you answered *no*, read Chapter 10, "Preserving Your Estate."
18. Do you (and your spouse) have a health care proxy, living will, power of attorney, and the appropriate trusts in place? If you answered *no*, read Chapter 10, "Preserving Your Estate."
19. Do you fully understand the advantages and best strategies for investing in real estate? If you answered *no*, read Chapter 11, "Investing in Real Estate."
20. Do you truly understand the power of compounding and the secret to accumulating wealth? If you answered *no*, read Chapter 12, "The Time Value of Money."

How to Use This Questionnaire

To answer many of these questions, you will need to gather certain documents including copies of your will, health care proxy, insurance policies, banking, and brokerage statements. After you have answered these questions accurately and completely, you will quickly be able to identify the critical areas of comprehensive wealth management you need to focus on.

Many of these areas should be addressed no matter what your age or situation. For example, even if you are single and still in your twenties, you should have sufficient health insurance, be saving for the proverbial rainy day, and be planning financially for retirement, if only by participating fully in your employer's retirement plan. Also, you may need a will, a health care proxy, and power of attorney. If you are married, have children, and own a home and other valuable property, additional issues will become increasingly important, like sufficient life insurance, long-term disability insurance, and property insurance. As you get into your late thirties and beyond, you will be increasingly more concerned with paying for your children's education, possibly caring for aging parents, and (again) saving for retirement.

All these subjects are addressed in detail in this book.

The Power of This Book

Becoming financially independent is not something that happens by chance; it requires focus, discipline, determination, sacrifice, and a lot of hard work. If you are serious about achieving financial independence and are willing to make the commitment to do what it takes, then this book will provide you with the necessary tools to pursue your financial goals. In short, it will guide you toward reaching your own personal financial independence and the generational wealth legacy you can leave to your loved ones.

Using financial planning strategies, the 12 critical areas of comprehensive wealth management, and many real-life (though anonymous) client stories, we show how to navigate through the most critical factors that affect you and your family's financial life. Most importantly, we explain how to employ the most current tax-smart strategies in order to save thousands, and perhaps tens of thousands of dollars every year. By doing so, you will not only minimize your biggest expense, but you will also maximize the money you can put into your pocket (or your investment portfolio), helping you reach financial independence and position your family for long-term financial success.

Thus, this book is a complete resource for anyone determined to build wealth and financial security in today's no-guarantee financial environment. Authoritative, comprehensive, and up to date, this book is an essential financial guide for individuals and their families who are not only working to achieve financial independence but also striving to build a lasting legacy for generations to come.

CHAPTER 1

Committing to Living Within Your Means

There is no dignity quite so impressive, and no independence quite so important, as living within your means.

—*Calvin Coolidge, Thirtieth President of the United States*

We all want to live the American Dream. Beginning with the earliest European settlers, Americans have sought the height of success and prosperity for themselves and their children, and we have believed firmly that we could achieve it, no matter our race, religion, nationality, or gender. All it took was hard work and discipline.

The American Dream Becomes the American Nightmare

Our country was founded on the conviction that it was the land of opportunity and prosperity. That was the definition of the American Dream. In the early years of our country's existence, infinite real estate was available for the taking, a great boon for a basically agrarian society. If you wanted more land, all you had to do was pack up your wagon, travel farther west, and claim it. If you were willing to work hard, you could earn an honest living, rear and educate your children, and save for your family's future. These principles stood firm for almost two centuries.

Nevertheless, perhaps because of the decades of affluence that followed World War II, this land of "equal opportunity" turned into the land of "expected entitlements." People came to believe that living beyond their means, usually on credit, was acceptable, and "living large" became the norm. Younger people no longer thought they needed to save for a down payment on a house, a new car, or a luxurious vacation. They could just pay with a credit card or take out a loan. Even professional financial institutions fed into this false sense of affluence, giving credit cards, large home mortgages, and home-equity loans to people they knew full well could never pay them off. This distorted definition of the American Dream significantly contributed to the financial crisis of 2008 and turned this dream into a nightmare for many people.

The COVID-19 pandemic, recent spikes in inflation, and growing household debt have shown once again how easy it is to lose financial ground without strong saving habits. Although the road to recovery was a long and painful one since 2008, many people have since dug themselves out of this hole by following the very principles outlined in this chapter and book.

If my parents were able to come to a foreign land with only an eighth-grade education, barely able to speak the language, and end up as millionaires, certainly anyone blessed with the education and opportunities available to most Americans today can become financially independent. Anyone can get to *point X*, the point at which you can support yourself and your family financially with your *investments*, not a salary. All it takes is knowledge of good financial practices and the discipline to carry them out.

Living Within Your Means: The Essential Step

The single most important step you must take to become financially independent is to commit to living within your means. This sounds obvious; this sounds easy. But in reality, it is not!

Amazingly, many people do not understand what "living within your means" actually implies! The definition of "living within your means" is living on *less than* your take-home salary and any other resources you receive, such as income from an annuity or a trust. Living within your means does *not* mean existing from paycheck to paycheck. Living within your means does *not* mean living on credit or on loans. Living within your means does *not* mean turning to parents or friends to pay the tab when you cannot quite meet the rent or need to buy a new computer. It means not only figuring out how to pay for your needs and wants, but also budgeting your income so that you still have a little money left over.

Paying Yourself First

In addition to living within your means, if you are ever going to become financially independent, you must also *save* money. (You will ultimately need to invest this money productively, but that is covered in Chapter 9, "Managing Your Investments.") This exercise is called *paying yourself first*. Therefore, "living within your means" includes not only such necessities as shelter, food, utilities, and clothing, but also payment into your personal savings. Ideally, that payment should be 10% or more of your gross pay. You may think that this is impossible, but once you get started, you will realize how easy it can be. And, of course, if you can afford more, by all means put those funds in savings or invested assets.

The following is an example of how this could work and how this will help you achieve financial independence. If you are earning $52,000 a year, that is $1,000 a week in gross income, and you are probably bringing home about $700 of that after taxes. If you *pay yourself first* by funding your 401(k) plan with 10% of your gross income, that is $100 per week (or $5,200 a year), which may earn a rate of return with compounding over the time invested.

If you start saving that at age 21 and retire at age 65, you will have saved $228,800 over those 44 years. Also, that $100 you save affects your take-home pay by only $70 (assuming a 30% tax rate), so you will be taxed on $900 instead of $1,000 per week, which means you will bring home $630 instead of $700 per week. Yes, that is $70 less money you must spend on your needs and wants, but you get the full benefit of $100 saved.

Assuming you can earn 7% per year on your 401(k) investments over the 44-year period, you may be able to accumulate $1,383,829 by the age of 65. Saving now is a small price to pay for financial independence in the future. There is no easier way to achieve financial independence. By the way, this does not even factor in employer-matching dollars, which can significantly increase your savings.

Paying yourself first must be as much a necessity as the roof over your head, the food on your table, and the clothes on your back. It is not a luxury; it is not something you will start doing next week or next month or next year, but it is an essential expense that you must pay *now*.

Know the Difference Between What You Need *and What You* Want

If you asked most people to define the necessities (or essentials) of life, they would probably say shelter, food, and clothing. There is another essential to add to that list: saving money on a regular basis or paying yourself first. However, defining what is essential and not essential in terms of shelter, food, clothing, and savings requires some additional attention:

- Shelter should not be the biggest house in the best neighborhood decorated with the most expensive furniture (not essential); instead, shelter means a house or apartment that gives comfort and safety to your family, which you can pay for and maintain with the money you have available (essential).
- Providing food for yourself and your family does not mean eating out every night at the fanciest restaurants or even ordering in from the local pizzeria or Chinese restaurant (not essential), but it means preparing healthy meals from foods paid for within a food budget you have established (essential).
- Clothing does not mean buying the latest $200 jeans or other overpriced designer apparel (not essential), but it means planning for your family's clothing needs based on a well-thought-out budget (essential).
- In terms of saving money, you need not try to sock away 25% of your salary, especially if money is tight (not essential); you simply need to get in the habit of saving 10% or more of your gross pay (essential).

In other words, you need to begin to discriminate between the nonessentials and the essentials, your wants and your needs.

In working with the finances of thousands of people over the past 40 years, there is one common trait in everyone who ultimately achieves financial independence: they experience anxiety every time they are faced with the decision to make a purchase that is not essential. Whether it is an expensive cup of coffee or an expensive car (or even a not-so-expensive car), if they buy it, they experience anxiety and guilt. In other words, for these people, the pain of purchasing a nonessential item exceeds the pleasure.

Usually, when faced with such a decision, instead of acting impulsively, they ask themselves if the purchase is necessary. "*Do I need a new suit for my first day at a new job?*"

If the answer is no, they are comfortable with the decision. "*I can wear my old suit; I will have it dry-cleaned and pressed, and no one will know that I have had it for three years.*"

If the answer is yes, "*My old suit is looking a little worn and having a new suit will help me to feel confident on my first day on the job,*" they always look for a less expensive alternative. "*Can I find an equally good suit at another store or on sale? Will a less expensive suit look just as good and make me feel just as self-confident?*"

The fact is, most Americans view this essential versus nonessential concept in completely the opposite way. Many people believe it is imperative to keep up with the Joneses, to quote that old-fashioned expression, which implies a perceived necessity to appear as affluent as our friends, neighbors, and professional colleagues. Other expressions such as "shop till you drop" and "retail therapy" are now commonplace in our world and are considered acceptable, amusing, and even cool. Shopping till you drop is thought by many people to be as beneficial to one's health as an afternoon of bicycling in a park; retail therapy is firmly believed to be a form of entertainment and even an antidote to anxiety and stress.

We are supposed to feel good about racking up thousands of dollars on our credit cards, and many people actually do get immense pleasure from excessive shopping (at least until the bills arrive). As for putting money into the bank instead of splurging on a new big-screen TV, forget it. This behavior has nothing to do with providing the essentials of life; it has to do with satisfying our wants, not our needs. And, of course, more often than not, it has everything to do with living beyond our means.

Discerning the difference between essentials and nonessentials, wants and needs, is imperative if you are going to live within your means, save sufficient money, and ultimately become financially independent. You may need to train yourself to associate anxiety and guilt instead of pleasure with making those exciting but nonessential purchases. You may need to frequently remind yourself and members of your family that short-term gratification from buying nonessentials is not nearly as important or satisfying as achieving the long-term goal of financial security. When the pain you associate with sacrificing your financial future is greater than the immediate gratification of providing yourself and your family with nonessential items, you have mastered the skills necessary to become financially independent.

Daily Financial Affirmation

Securing my own and my family's financial future is my number one priority.

I live within my means.
I always *pay myself first.*
I say *no* to nonessential purchases.

****

After you have written down this Daily Financial Affirmation, say it out loud. Then post copies of it around your house in places where you (and other members of your family) will see it repeatedly throughout the day, in the center of your refrigerator door, on your bathroom mirror, and on your bedside table. Post another in your workplace, such as next to your telephone or on your computer screen saver. Place a copy in your wallet or purse. Consciously read your Daily Financial Affirmation first thing in the morning and last thing at night. During the day, if you experience a moment of weakness and are about to spend money on a nonessential expenditure, read your Daily Financial Affirmation out loud once again.

A Simple Savings Plan

A traditional savings account is the first place you should consider putting the money you are paying yourself. Having enough cash on hand to see you through an illness, injury, job loss, or other financial emergency can help you avoid taking on debt or tapping into your retirement assets. It is just a smart move.

How much you save will depend on your needs, responsibilities, and comfort level. My rule of thumb suggests that you should have enough cash in savings to cover at least three months of expenses for couples with both partners earning an income, and you should have enough cash in savings to cover six months of expenses if you are single or married with only one spouse earning an income. If you fear that your job is in jeopardy or think it will take you longer than six months to get back on your feet financially should you lose your job, you should try to have even more in savings. Also, if you are saving for anything other than the proverbial rainy day, such as for a house, wedding, new car, or special trip, count these funds as extra.

Given that interest rates on cash instruments such as savings accounts and certificates of deposit (CDs) may not always keep up with inflation, you may still lose some purchasing power over time. However, do not let this alarm you too much. Saving in this way is still an essential part of becoming financially independent. Also, these savings come with Federal Deposit Insurance Corporation (FDIC) insurance of up to $250,000 per depositor, so your money is safe.

What Is the FDIC?

It is important to understand the added safety and reduced risk of saving your money with the protection of the FDIC. For some people, having the peace of mind of knowing their money is guaranteed to be returned to them is priceless. Traditional types of bank accounts, such as checking accounts, savings accounts, and CDs, are insured by the FDIC.

Banks also may offer what is called a *money market deposit account*, which earns interest at a rate set by the bank and usually limits the customer to a certain number of transactions within a stated period. All these types of accounts generally are insured by the FDIC up to the legal limit of $250,000 per depositor, per institution, and sometimes even more for special kinds of accounts or ownership categories. For more information on deposit insurance, visit the FDIC website at www.fdic.gov.

Many banking and brokerage institutions also offer consumers a broad array of investment products such as mutual funds, annuities, life insurance policies, stocks, and bonds. Unlike traditional checking or savings accounts, however, these nondeposit investment products are *not* insured by the FDIC. Many people are under the false impression that if they purchase one of these products through their bank, they will be protected by the FDIC. This clearly is not the case, and you must always understand the risks associated with putting your money into non-FDIC-insured accounts.

Saving for Special Situations

There is an old saying: "*All work and no play makes Jack a dull boy.*" We could adjust that adage slightly and say, "*All saving and no splurging makes Jack a dull boy.*" But perhaps it is the word *splurge* that needs the adjustment.

Achieving ultimate financial independence means you can stop working for your money, and your money can start working for you. But for most of us throughout our lives, other expensive essentials (and nonessentials) will undoubtedly present themselves, and these will require special savings. These might include major purchases, such as buying a first home, paying for your own or a child's lavish wedding, celebrating a daughter's "sweet 16" birthday party or your parents' 50th wedding anniversary, or finally taking a lifelong dream vacation, such as going on a safari to Africa or a trip to the Far East.

When planning for these special events and purchases, you need to view them as requiring additional savings beyond your cash security savings, and they should be added as line items to your budget. You might even consider opening separate savings accounts to help you budget for these special situations and earmark these funds for that special purpose. Nevertheless, you should never sacrifice your primary long-term goal of achieving financial independence in order to meet these other shorter-term desires.

Easier Said Than Done

Granted, a world of difference exists between knowing what to do and *actually* doing it. We know that to become financially independent, we must spend less than we make and save more from our salaries or *pay ourselves first.* But now comes the hard part: We must actually do it! The prospect can be overwhelming, both emotionally and financially.

We live in a society of instant gratification; we want more, and we want it now, whether it is a daily $7 cappuccino from the local coffee house, frequent delivery app orders, a $700 pair of shoes, a $70,000 car, or a $700,000 house. These examples may be exaggerations, but many of us feel bad about ourselves if we seem to be faring less financially well than our friends and colleagues. We feel a need to maintain a high standard of living, even if that standard of living is based on borrowed money and is measured in such superficialities as expensive coffees and prestigious labels. Also, as discussed, many of us have learned to experience excessive spending as pleasurable, not painful. These emotional factors attached to living within our means can be troublesome and difficult to overcome. But, like dieting, it is essential to your health that you become aware of these feelings and correct them.

For many people, the reality is that they have already dug themselves into a huge financial pit, and getting out of it is going to be time consuming and painful. They may need to pay off thousands of dollars of credit card debt (see Chapter 4, "Managing Debt") or enormous student loans (see Chapter 7, "Paying for College"), before they feel that they can begin to seriously save. This is daunting, to be sure, but not hopeless.

Stop the Insanity

Insanity is often defined as "*doing the same thing over and over again and expecting a different result.*" If you have been living beyond your means and not saving, and wondering why you never have any money, now is the time to stop the insanity! Stop splurging on small nonessentials and start saving for the big essentials, the greatest being your own and your family's financial security. You must commit to living within your means, discriminate between nonessential wants and essential needs, and save for your future. It is your treasure, and ultimately, it is your *point X*.

An Action Plan for Committing to Living Within Your Means

1. **Make a serious commitment to live within your means.** Discuss this commitment with your spouse and children and urge them to commit as well.
2. **Pay yourself first.** Include saving money in your budget just as you do any other essential living expense.
3. **Open a savings account. Save 10% or more of your gross pay.** Ask your bank to automatically move the designated amount from your checking account to your savings account.
4. **Make sure you know the difference between what you need and what you want.** You need to begin to discriminate between the nonessentials and the essentials, your wants and your needs.
5. **Keep sufficient cash available** to cover three to six months of your basic living expenses, depending on your needs.
6. **Place the "Financial Affirmation" in key places** around your house where you and members of your family will refer to it frequently.
7. **If you are saving money for a special purpose, add that amount to your budget** as an additional line item and consider opening a separate account for that purpose.
8. **Complete the Comprehensive Wealth Management Questionnaire** (see "Introduction") to assist you in establishing your financial priorities and goals.
9. **Buy a copy of this book for your entire family.** Ask them to read it and have them make a commitment to live within their means.
10. **After making this commitment, have your entire family walk the walk and talk the talk of the values shared in this chapter.**
11. **Share the generational wealth code of living within your means with your entire family so that your financial legacy can endure for generations to come.**

CHAPTER 2

Understanding Taxes

The hardest thing in the world to understand is the income tax.
—*Albert Einstein, Father of Modern Physics*

Taxes are the price we pay to live in our society. Our federal and state income taxes pay for everything from roads, public schools, public libraries, and hospitals to national parks, dams, the US military services, and the salaries of all the people who work for the US government, including the president of the United States. Our taxes also pay for Social Security, Medicare, and other social services. Although we want, need, and appreciate these services, many of us fear that a tremendous amount of money is wasted in the management of government and we are paying for it.

The fact is, the average American family still pays a significant portion of its income in federal, state, and local income taxes, including property taxes, excise taxes, tariffs, sales taxes, and other hidden taxes on items like cigarettes, liquor, and certain luxuries. This means that the average person works all day Monday and most of Tuesday for the government, and then they work the rest of the week for their own benefit. Just another reason to hate going to work on Mondays! In other words, for just about everyone, taxes are our biggest personal expense, by far.

To reach *financial independence*, it is imperative that you understand the basics of our tax system. You must practice careful and creative tax preparation and planning so that your personal tax burden does not deplete your income unnecessarily and your wealth can accumulate quickly and securely. Tax laws are incredibly complicated, and there is no reason for you to read or understand the virtually infinite ins and outs of the often arcane US Tax Code. Most people need help from professional tax advisors to benefit from tax-smart strategies; however, you should have enough basic knowledge about taxes and the tax system to ask the right questions and find the appropriate help to suit your own unique financial and tax needs. That is what this chapter provides: an understanding of the basics you need to know to be financially literate.

A Brief History of the US Tax System

This chapter begins with a brief history of taxes in the United States so that you can be prepared for what is to come. One of the earliest lessons we learned in school was that history tends to repeat itself, and nowhere is this more evident than in the evolution of tax policy.

The subject of taxes has been a significant part of American history since long before the American Colonies became the United States of America. Every school child remembers the story of the Boston Tea Party of 1773, when the citizens of Boston dressed as Native Americans and dumped tea into Boston Harbor to protest Britain's unfair taxation on tea throughout the colonies. This rebellious act played a strong role in the start of America's Revolutionary War.

Actually, taxes had already been a part of the American Colonial government since almost the moment the first colonists arrived. In addition to taxes imposed by Britain, each individual colony imposed local taxes on themselves. The first property taxes were imposed on colonists as early as 1634, less than 15 years after the Pilgrims landed at Plymouth Rock. Other forms of taxation, such as poll taxes, excise duties, and licensing fees, were also common during the colonial era.

However, in the early years of the new nation, taxes were imposed by the individual states, not the federal government. The Articles of Confederation, the predecessor to the US Constitution, were drafted in 1777 and ratified by all 13 states between 1778 and 1781 for their mutual benefit. Article VIII of this document provided that all taxes for the common treasury be allocated to each of the states based on the estimated value of land, buildings, and improvements under the laws and authority of each state. However, the national government had no power to enforce tax collection, leaving it dependent on voluntary compliance by the states.

The Articles of Confederation were replaced by the US Constitution, which created a national government, commencing in 1789. Article I, Section 2 apportioned to the states' direct taxation and the number of representatives in the House of Representatives based on the populations of the states as defined by that section. Except for tariffs on imports, virtually all power for taxation rested with state and local governments, and until the mid-nineteenth century, many of the states relied on property taxes as a major source of revenue. Although the Constitution gave Congress the power to levy taxes, federal direct taxation remained relatively limited in the early years of the republic.

Income Taxes and the Sixteenth Amendment of 1913

After the American Revolution, tax on personal income was imposed by some state governments, but only in a limited way. The first federal income tax was adopted as part of the Revenue Act of 1861 to help finance the Civil War, but it was allowed to lapse after the war ended. However, by the late nineteenth century, the increasing importance of intangible property, such as corporate stock, caused the states to shift to other forms of taxation. In 1913, the Sixteenth Amendment to the Constitution, which permitted the federal government to directly levy an income tax on individuals and corporations, was ratified.

The Sixteenth Amendment defined income as "all income from whatever source derived." In 1939, the law was organized as the US Code, or the Internal Revenue Code, and included taxes on income, estates, gifts, excise, and certain other items. Over the years, particularly in 1954 and 1986, the Code was revised and expanded, but its foundation has remained largely unchanged for nearly a century.

Federal income tax rates have fluctuated wildly since they were established in 1913. In 1913, the proponents of the federal tax assured citizens that the federal tax on income would be small. The opponents of the income tax urged that, at least, there should be a provision to the Sixteenth Amendment capping the tax rate at no more than 10%. However, in 1918, when the government wanted money to fight World War I, the federal income tax rate was increased to an astonishing 77% for those in the highest income bracket.

Significant income tax cuts have been made over the years, usually based on the belief that tax cuts would spur economic growth. One such series of cuts was made during the 1920s; unfortunately, the last such cut in that series, made in 1928, was followed by the stock market crash in 1929 and the Great Depression. Taxes were raised again in the latter part of the Depression and reached new heights of 94% during World War II, again in an effort to pay for a very popular war. Income tax rates were reduced significantly during the Johnson (1960s), Nixon (early 1970s), and Reagan (1980s) presidencies, and again between 2001 and 2008 during George W. Bush's presidency. Although Obama raised rates again during his presidency, President Donald Trump reduced rates across the board through his sweeping 2018 tax reform, the Tax Cuts and Jobs Act (TCJA) of 2017.

Many of these provisions were initially set to expire after 2025, but those changes have now been made permanent under the One Big Beautiful Bill Act (OBBBA), signed into law on July 4, 2025. This act solidified this lower-rate structure for the foreseeable future. Exhibit 2.1 illustrates the dramatic changes in income tax rates since 1913.

Exhibit 2.1 Highest Marginal US Income Tax Rates, 1913–2025

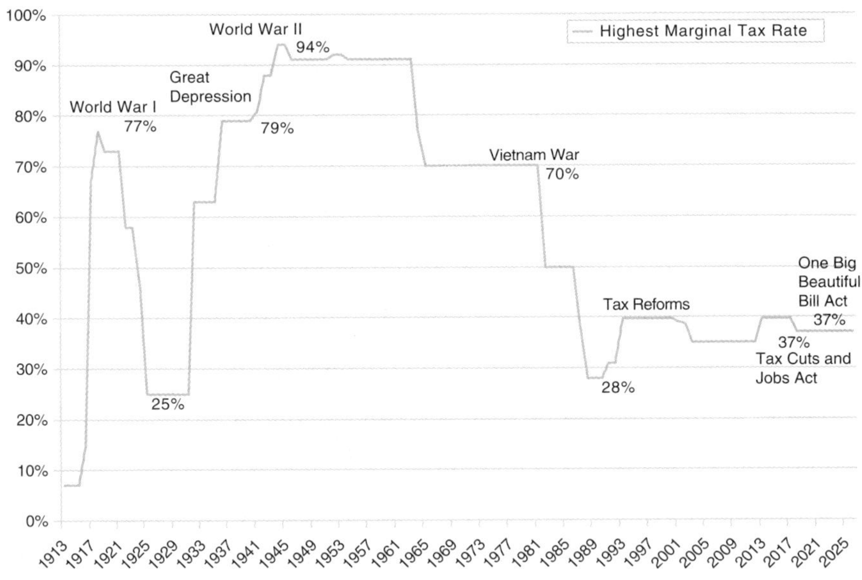

Source: Internal Revenue Service (IRS), "SOI Tax Stats Table 23: US Individual Income Tax: Personal Exemptions and Lowest and Highest Bracket Tax Rates, 1913–2023," and IRS Form 1040 Instructions (Tax Rate Schedules), 2018–2025.

The Emergence of State and Local Income Taxes

Although states have taxed individuals since even before the formation of the US Constitution, most of these were taxes on property. Today, many states and some localities continue to rely heavily on property taxes as well as on retail sales taxes. By the 1920s, many states had adopted taxes on income for both individuals and corporations, similar in definition and structure to the taxes imposed by the federal government. Currently, most states impose income taxes. However, nine states, including Florida, Texas, and Tennessee, do not tax wage income at all. The remaining states generally tax residents on all of their income, including income earned in other states as well as income earned by nonresidents in some state.

For example, many people who earn income in New York City live in the nearby states of New Jersey, Connecticut, and even Pennsylvania. As a result, they are taxed by New York State for the income they earn there, and then typically get a tax credit in their resident state.

Where Are We Now with Regard to Taxes?

For the past several years, federal income tax rates have ranged from 10% at the low end to 37% at the high end. (Refer back to Exhibit 2.1, which shows the highest marginal income tax rates from 1913 through 2025.) As a result of President Trump's comprehensive 2017 tax reform, the TCJA, income tax rates decreased across the board for nearly all income levels. In 2025, the OBBBA then made those seven individual income tax brackets (10%, 12%, 22%, 24%, 32%, 35%, and 37%) permanent, preventing the scheduled increase to the top rate back to 39.6% in 2026.

Although the hope is that the nation will enjoy a continued downward trend in tax rates, legislation can clearly change dramatically with a new administration or national crisis. Therefore, it is very important that you take into consideration the possibility of any future tax increases when implementing tax-saving strategies. Minimizing your largest expenditure (taxes) is critically important to your wealth accumulation plan and to your ability to become financially independent. See "Appendix C" for some basic concepts and definitions of various types of taxes.

Organizing and Retaining Your Records

Tax records should be carefully kept on a year-round basis, not tossed into a drawer or shoebox and pieced together just before your annual tax appointment. Without tax records, you can lose valuable deductions by forgetting to include them on your tax return, or you may have unsubstantiated items disallowed if you are audited.

Generally, tax returns can be audited for up to three years after filing; however, the IRS may audit for up to six years if it identifies a substantial understatement of income, typically more than 25% of gross income. The three- and six-year limits start with the filing of a tax return; if no return is filed, the time limit never starts to run. In other words, if you have failed to file a return, you can be audited and taxed at any time.

Which Records Are Important?

The following are some of the records that you will need to retain for tax purposes:

- Records of income received
- Tax-deductible expense items
- Home improvements, sales, and refinances (particularly for homes with capital gain potential exceeding $250,000 for single filers or $500,000 for married couples filing jointly)
- Investment purchases and sales information
- Documentation for inherited property
- Medical expenses
- Charitable contributions (keep receipts or written acknowledgments; additional documentation is required for donations of over $250)
- Interest and taxes paid
- Records on nondeductible IRA contributions

How Long Should Records Be Kept?

Just how long you should keep records is partly a matter of judgment and a combination of state and federal statutes of limitations. Because federal tax returns can be audited for up to three years after filing (six years, if underreported income exceeds 25% of gross income), it is a good idea to keep most records for six years after the return filing date. There is no time limit if a return was never filed or is found to be fraudulent.

Some records are worth keeping permanently, partly because of long-term needs and partly because they take up very little room. Consider permanently retaining a copy of each year's tax return. Contracts, real estate buy and sell records, and records of property improvements should be retained for at least seven years after the property is sold.

If you are in business, your record requirements are more extensive.

As many businesses and individuals turn to paperless filing systems, it has become much easier to retain records for longer periods. The IRS accepts digital records, so thanks to technology, it now makes sense to keep your tax documents permanently in an electronic form. Going paperless can reduce the clutter, benefit the environment, and make files more accessible. Just keep an external backup drive or secure cloud storage to protect you from losing your important data.

Tax-preparation Services

After reading Appendix C, it should be undoubtedly clear to you that calculating and paying your income taxes is a complicated process, and the annually changing laws and codes affecting taxes make the job even more difficult. Bear in mind that you are legally responsible for the accuracy of your tax returns whether you prepare them yourself or hire someone else. You have several choices.

Tax Planning and Preparation Software

In general, two kinds of tax-related software are available: tax planning and tax preparation.

1. Planning programs help you to look into different strategies for managing taxes.
2. Preparation programs, such as H&R Block at Home or TurboTax® software packages, guide you through the preparation process.

If your taxes are relatively simple, these programs can save you time and money. However, if you have experienced major life changes (marriage, divorce, a significant inheritance), invest in the stock market, or are self-employed, you should probably secure the help of a tax professional.

Hiring a Tax Preparer

Most taxpayers conclude that preparing their own taxes is simply too difficult and time-consuming, and they turn to private professionals for help. A professional tax preparer helps you prepare the most accurate tax return and protects you from liability. A good tax preparer should also provide *advice* on tax strategy and help manage more complex tax problems. In fact, if your tax preparer is not saving you many times the cost of their fee in tax-saving strategies, it may be time to look for another tax advisor.

Tax advisors come in several forms, with varying credentials and degrees of competence. The four most common are tax preparers (nonlicensed), enrolled agents (EAs), certified public accountants (CPAs), and tax attorneys, described in the following paragraphs. Appendix A offers a more in-depth overview of various professionals who can help you with your wealth management goals. You can also visit IRS.gov for more information on each of these designations.

1. **Nonlicensed National and Local Tax Services:** These preparers can be found in companies such as H&R Block and independent local firms. They must now register with the IRS and pass tests to prove that they have the minimum acceptable competence to prepare tax returns. These services are best if you have straightforward, simple tax returns.
2. **Enrolled Agents:** EAs are required to pass an extensive examination on various topics of taxation and must meet minimum continuing education requirements annually. They are also licensed and authorized to represent you before the IRS, should you be audited.
3. **Certified Public Accountants:** CPAs are highly trained and have passed complex and extensive examinations in the areas of accounting, taxation, auditing, and business law in order to be licensed. They must obtain advanced degrees that include rigorous courses in both accounting and taxation. They must also meet a minimum work experience requirement before they can be granted a license. CPAs are required to meet minimum continuing education requirements on an annual basis and are authorized to represent you before the IRS, should the need arise. They also must adhere to a fiduciary standard to their clients.

4. **Tax Attorneys:** These are lawyers who specialize in tax planning and are most appropriate for those who have a complex tax situation that could result in legal problems, such as the sale of a business or a messy divorce.

Frankly, if you are committed to becoming financially independent, it is strongly recommended to secure the services of a professional tax advisor, who is appropriate for your income and tax needs. In addition, schedule at least one additional meeting during the year, preferably before or after tax season, to discuss all of your tax planning and financial needs and goals.

Accumulating Wealth Through Tax Planning

As mentioned, our single largest expenditure is our tax obligation. When you factor in federal, state, and local income taxes and then Social Security and Medicare taxes, at current tax rates, for the average taxpayer more than 35% of our paychecks go toward taxes. Then, when you consider sales tax, cigarette tax, fuel tax, and other excise tax, property tax, estate and gift tax, this number can easily exceed 50% of your income.

So, if our single largest expense is taxes, then tax planning can be the most significant step you can take toward saving money and accumulating generational wealth. The government requires you to pay no more than the amount of taxes you are legally obligated to pay, but believe it or not, the majority of taxpayers pay much more simply because they do not spend the time to understand more about tax planning. You should consider the tax consequences when making any major financial decision, whether it is buying a house or taking out a loan for your child's college education.

Tax Avoidance *Is Not Tax Evasion!*

The term *tax evasion* has a scary connotation. Most of us know that tax evasion (not paying our taxes by illegal means, such as underreporting income or overstating deductions) is illegal. People have been known to spend time in jail for tax evasion. Tax evasion is illegal, pure and simple.

Tax avoidance, however, is perfectly legal. Tax avoidance is the legal utilization of the tax code to one's own advantage; in other words, you can reduce the amount of tax you pay by means that are within the law.

What Is Tax Planning?

Tax planning is just another way of saying *legal tax avoidance.* It is a way to maximize the amount of money you keep by minimizing the amount of taxes you pay. Tax planning means educating yourself and your family on the many ways to avoid overpaying your taxes. By focusing on tax avoidance techniques, you will be able to minimize your taxes and maximize your generational wealth accumulation. More than any other method, it is one of the most effective strategies to save money and accumulate wealth without sacrificing your lifestyle.

Specifically, tax planning involves taking every tax deduction, tax credit, and tax deferral method allowed in the tax code and using it to your advantage. You must make tax planning part of your everyday life and always ask yourself, "*Is this the most tax-smart way to handle this financial situation?*"

How Do I Learn About Tax Planning?

If you're feeling overwhelmed at this point, you're not alone. Many people find tax planning complicated at first, especially when reading advice from professionals who work in this area every day. Each of the authors of this book is a CPA with deep experience in tax strategy and financial planning, so these concepts may seem second nature to us. If you are like most people, your knowledge of taxes is probably limited. You bring your receipts to your tax accountant every year (if that), and hope for the best.

However, becoming knowledgeable about taxes is not that difficult. Once you begin to see how much money you can save by taking advantage of various tax credits and other tax-related opportunities, you will become very motivated. Actually, you have already taken your first big step in your educational process by reading this chapter.

Your next step should be to read the remaining chapters of this book based on your answers to the comprehensive wealth management questionnaire (see "Introduction"). Then encourage your entire family to do the same. This will assist you in setting financial goals with a tax-smart roadmap to financial independence for you and your family for generations to come.

Beyond this book, speak to your employer's human resource department about any and all employee tax-related benefits available to you, and make sure you take advantage of them. Finally, communicate with your tax accountant and financial advisor. You need to do this more than once a year at tax time, when he or she is busiest. Instead, set up a meeting during the summer months, when most tax advisors have the time to really focus on your needs and think creatively on your behalf.

Each chapter in this book concludes with a summary of tax-smart strategies as they relate to the critical wealth management area covered in that chapter. We believe that these sections will be the most valuable to you in your wealth-accumulation process. Read them carefully and discuss them with your tax advisor to ensure that you are not paying a penny more in taxes than the law requires.

Tax Benefits

You can help reduce the amount of tax you owe by taking advantage of any number of tax benefits available to you. The goal of tax planning is to choose which tax benefits make the most sense for you and then implement them.

These tax benefits are how Congress rewards you for making certain types of financial decisions. For example, you may be able to reduce your total taxable income (and therefore your progressive tax rate) if you contribute money to a retirement account, such as a 401(k) or IRA plan. This is Congress's way of encouraging you to save for your retirement.

The income tax system is voluntary. You are free to arrange your financial affairs in such a way as to take advantage of any tax benefits. *Voluntary* does not mean that the tax laws do not apply; you must pay your taxes. However, *voluntary* does mean you can choose to pay less tax by managing your finances in a manner that minimizes your tax liability.

Before you focus on your particular concerns, you need to get an accurate picture of your true net worth, figure out where your money is coming from (and going to) at this very moment, establish your financial goals, and begin to budget for the future. Chapter 3, "Determining Your Financial Position," shows you how to do this. After all, you cannot get to *point X* if you do not know precisely where your starting point is before you begin your financial journey.

The One Big Beautiful Bill Act of 2025

On July 4, 2025, President Donald Trump signed the One Big Beautiful Bill Act (OBBBA) into law. This legislation builds upon and expands the Tax Cuts and Jobs Act (TCJA) of 2017, removing sunset provisions and introducing new tax benefits for individuals and business owners alike. As one of the most comprehensive overhauls of the tax code in modern history, the OBBBA makes permanent many of the reforms that had previously been set to expire and adds new provisions that offer meaningful opportunities for tax savings and financial planning.

This book reflects the latest tax law changes under the OBBBA, and many of the new provisions are included in the "Tax-smart Strategies" section at the end of each chapter. Unless otherwise noted, the following provisions are effective beginning in the 2025 tax year and apply to both individuals and business owners.

The following are highlights of the most significant changes that may impact your tax-smart journey on the roadmap to financial independence and generational wealth. For more detailed guidance on these strategies, refer to the "Tax-smart Strategies" section in the relevant wealth management chapters to follow.

- Made permanent the individual income tax brackets introduced under the TCJA, maintaining rates at 10%, 12%, 22%, 24%, 32%, 35%, and 37%
- Permanently increased the standard deduction to $15,750 for single filers, $23,625 for heads of household, and $31,500 for married filing jointly (MFJ)
- Temporarily increased the state and local tax (SALT) deduction cap to $40,000 from 2025 through 2029, with phaseouts for higher-income taxpayers
- Created a new senior deduction of $6,000 for individuals aged 65 or older, available from 2025 through 2028 with income limits
- Introduced a deduction of up to $25,000 for qualified tip income from 2025 through 2028, subject to income phaseouts
- Allowed a deduction of up to $12,500 for qualified overtime compensation (or $25,000 for joint returns), effective 2025 through 2028 and subject to phaseouts
- Expanded the estate and gift tax exemption to $15 million per individual ($30 million per couple) beginning in 2026
- Allows an above-the-line deduction of up to $10,000 of qualified passenger vehicle loan interest on US-assembled vehicles for 2025 through 2028, subject to income phaseouts
- Created Trump Accounts for minors under age 18, with annual contribution limits of $5,000 and a $1,000 one-time government contribution for children born between 2025 and 2028

- Increased the Child Tax Credit to $2,200 per qualifying child and made permanent the $500 nonrefundable credit for other dependents
- Increased the maximum Child and Dependent Care Credit rate to 50%, with phaseouts based on adjusted gross income
- Raised the dependent care assistance program exclusion limit from $5,000 to $7,500
- Allowed partial refundability (up to $5,000) of the adoption tax credit
- Made the TCJA's increased Alternative Minimum Tax (AMT) exemption permanent, while reducing the phaseout threshold and increasing the phaseout rate
- Made permanent the mortgage interest deduction limit on home acquisition debt at $750,000
- Clarified that casualty loss deductions now include some state-declared disasters
- Made permanent the repeal of the Pease limitation on itemized deductions and replaced it with a new reduction formula tied to income over the 37% tax bracket starting in 2026
- Capped the deduction for gambling losses at 90% of the losses, limited to the amount of gambling winnings
- Created a new credit of $1,700 ($3,400 MFJ) for contributions to scholarship organizations, and excluded K–12 scholarships from income
- Increased qualified 529 plan usage for elementary and secondary education from $10,000 to $20,000 per student annually, as well as expanded usage for credentialing programs
- Allowed a charitable deduction of up to $1,000 for nonitemizers ($2,000 if filing jointly) starting in 2026
- Restored the Form 1099-K reporting threshold to $20,000 and 200 transactions, easing the burden on small sellers and gig workers

For business owners, the OBBBA includes several major provisions that may impact planning and strategy:

- Preserved full deductibility of state pass-through entity taxes (PTET) under the PTET workaround
- Permanently extended 100% bonus depreciation for qualified property placed in service on or after January 19, 2025

- Increased Section 179 expensing limits to $2.5 million, with phaseouts beginning at $4 million
- Made the 20% Qualified Business Income (QBI) deduction permanent and added a $400 minimum deduction for those with at least $1,000 in QBI
- Made Opportunity Zones permanent, though narrowed the definition of eligible low-income communities starting in 2027
- Phased out many clean energy tax incentives over the coming years
- Raised the 1099 reporting threshold to $2,000 annually for payments to individuals engaged in trade or business activities

With so many changes, it is strongly recommended that you work closely with a qualified tax advisor to evaluate how this new legislation impacts your specific situation. The OBBBA introduces significant opportunities for reducing tax liability, optimizing savings strategies, and accelerating your journey to financial independence. Use this book as a guide and be sure to revisit each chapter's tax-smart strategies to take full advantage of these new rules.

Tax-smart Strategies for Wealth Accumulation

Here are several tax facts and strategies that will address your wealth accumulation goals in a powerful and sustainable way. This will be part of your tax-smart roadmap to financial independence. This is how you can transform the tax code into part of your generational wealth code.

- Maximize your tax deductions.
- Take full advantage of every tax credit.
- If possible, shift income and deductions to the tax year that will result in lower taxes.
- If possible, shift income among family members to take full advantage of lower tax brackets.
- Defer the payment of taxes to future years by using tax-deferred accounts.
- Maximize your tax-free sources of income.
- With greater certainty surrounding long-term tax rates after the passage of the OBBBA, effective multiyear tax planning becomes possible.
- Seniors should keep an eye on their income to remain under the senior deduction threshold, potentially eliminating tax on a portion of their Social Security income.

- Taxpayers should consider paying their real estate tax bill before the end of the year as well as their fourth quarter state and local estimated tax bill to take advantage of the higher $40,000 SALT limitation.
- Meet with your employer's human resources department to ensure that you are taking advantage of all tax-free fringe benefits available to you and the appropriate reporting of income. This includes the newly created qualified tip income deduction and the overtime deduction.
- Taxpayers with dependent care costs should work with their HR department to ensure they are taking advantage of the maximum tax-deductible benefits available.
- Taxpayers with either casualty losses or gambling losses should carefully monitor and report these related costs for maximum tax deductibility.
- Taxpayers in the 37% tax bracket should consider shifting itemized deductions into 2025 before the new limitations come into place.
- Nonitemizers should consider frontloading donations in 2025 and leaving at least $2,000 for 2026 to maximize their deductions in both years.
- Taxpayers who are looking to support education funding should carefully monitor and report qualified scholarship-granting donations to take advantage of the tax credit available.
- Speak with your tax and financial advisor quarterly, or at least twice a year, not just at tax time.
- Update Form W-4 to adjust your tax withholdings through your employer, to ensure you are not dramatically overpaying or underpaying your taxes based on the most recent tax law changes. Although most people like a big tax refund at the end of the year, this simply means you are giving the government an interest-free loan. Adjusting your exemptions is one of the simplest ways to improve your cash flow.
- Refer to this book and other tax references periodically to keep you on track with your finances and to ensure you are using relevant and current tax-smart strategies.

An Action Plan for Wealth Accumulation

1. **Carefully read through this chapter and Appendix C.** By doing so, you will have begun to acquaint yourself with the basics of the US tax system and the process of taxation. Remember, this is your biggest expense, and you need to become aware of tax-smart strategies that can reduce it.
2. **Begin to take control of your own taxes.** Create files and save appropriate paperwork in an organized and comprehensive way. Remember saving secure electronic copies is acceptable to the IRS and will save you space,

(continued)

(continued)

time, and money. Check and update these files throughout the year and then go through them again when you are preparing to meet with your tax advisor.

3. **Hire a professional tax preparer,** find a highly qualified tax advisor who best suits your needs. (Appendix A describes the differences between various professionals.)
4. **Consult with your tax advisor throughout the year, not just when it is time to prepare your tax return,** so you can identify tax-smart planning strategies and implement them before the end of the year.
5. **Familiarize yourself with *Tax-smart Strategies*** at the end of each chapter so that you can discuss them with your tax advisor and incorporate them into your financial life.
6. **Make tax planning part of your life.** Always ask yourself, "*Is this the most tax-effective way to handle this financial situation?*" By far, this is the most efficient way to save money and accumulate wealth, without sacrificing your current lifestyle.
7. **Read the remaining chapters of this book based on your answers to the Comprehensive Wealth Management Questionnaire** (see "Introduction").
8. **Encourage your entire family to do the same.** This will assist your family members in setting their own individual financial goals with a tax-smart roadmap of their own to financial independence for generations to come.
9. **Read the summary of the One Big Beautiful Bill Act of 2025** in this chapter to see what new tax-smart money-saving opportunities are waiting for you and your family.
10. **Use the tax-smart roadmap to financial independence to transform the tax code into part of your generational wealth code.**

CHAPTER 3

Determining Your Financial Position

A budget is telling your money where to go instead of wondering where it went.

—Dave Ramsey, American Businessman, Author, and Radio Host

Now that you have taken an extremely important step of committing yourself to living within your means and you understand that taxes are a significant expenditure in your life, it is time to determine what your financial situation currently looks like. This does not mean simply knowing your annual salary or identifying how much you take home in every paycheck. Although that is certainly part of it; to truly live within your means, you must have a clear and accurate understanding of your financial assets, liabilities, and net worth by preparing a *statement of financial position.*

You also need to know, and to track on a regular basis, where all your personal funds come from and where they are going. This is your *statement of cash flow.* Finally, after carefully evaluating your current financial position, you must determine your financial goals, whether for the next 5 years, 10 years, or throughout your retirement years. Only then can you realistically budget for the future and, of course, achieve financial independence.

Calculating Your Financial Net Worth

You cannot *achieve financial independence* unless you know your starting point. To determine that, you need to figure out precisely how much you are worth financially. This process involves preparing an essential document: a personal statement of financial position.

To help guide you in its preparation, we have put together a sample statement of financial position, shown in Exhibit 3.1, based on the financial lives of a hypothetical couple, Glenn and Holly Mitchell. Much of the discussion in this chapter references Exhibit 3.1, so you can use it to follow along. (We have many clients who are similar to Glenn and Holly, but the Mitchells are purely fictional.) To help you prepare your own personal statement of financial position, we've included fillable forms that you can utilize and gain access to by visiting our website, www.ventotaxandwealth.com, selecting "Getting to Point X" and scrolling down to "Fillable Forms."

Case Study: How One Couple Was Able to Accelerate Their Journey to Financial Independence and Position Themselves to Create Generational Wealth

Glenn and Holly Mitchell are a hardworking American couple in their early forties. They have been married for 14 years and have two children, a boy and a girl, ages 12 and 9. They live in a fast-growing suburb of Austin, Texas.

Glenn is a dentist who worked for several years as an associate at a local Dental Service Organization (DSO) before opening his own practice nearly a decade ago. Three years after launching the business, he purchased the commercial building where his practice is located. He purchased this building for $650,000 and still owes $435,000 on the mortgage. The current estimated fair market value is $770,000, since real estate values have been increasing over the past several years. At the time, Glenn realized that purchasing the building, getting the benefit of the phantom deduction called depreciation, and paying rent to himself is a better strategy than just paying rent to a landlord. (See Chapter 11, "Investing in Real Estate," for more on the benefits of property ownership.) Glenn collects the rent from his dental practice, which is paid to his limited liability company (LLC) real estate holding company, and in turn, uses this money to pay the building's mortgage and other direct property expenses.

Exhibit 3.1 Glenn and Holly Mitchell, Statement of Financial Position

Glenn and Holly Mitchell				
Statement of Financial Position as of December 31, 2024				
Assets			**Liabilities and Net Worth**	
Cash/Cash Equivalents			**Liabilities**	
Cash	$ 7,200			
Money Market	—		Current:	
Savings Account (1% interest rate)	38,300		Credit Card 1—H (at 20%)	$ 5,000
CD's	—		Credit Card 2—W (at 17%)	2,000
US Government Treasury Bills	—			
Total Cash/Cash Equivalents	$ 45,500		Current Liabilities	$ 7,000
Invested Assets at FMV				
Business Owned	$ 95,000			
Office Building (FMV, paid $650,000)	770,000		Long Term	
Investment Portfolio (100% growth stock)	58,000		Auto Loan—W (at 5.5%; 3 years remaining)	$ 22,000
Variable annuity	—		Auto Loan—H	—
IRA—H (100% growth stock)	32,000		Student Loans—H (at 7%; 10 years remaining)	35,000
IRA—W (100% money market)	41,000			
SIMPLE IRA—H (100% growth stock)	15,000		Mortgage: Office Building—20 years at 6% fixed, 13 years remaining	435,000
Solo 401(k)—W	—		Mortgage: Primary residence—30 years at 7% fixed, 20 years remaining	275,000
529 Education Savings Plan	11,000			

(*Continued*)

Exhibit 3.1 ***(Continued)***

Glenn and Holly Mitchell

Statement of Financial Position as of December 31, 2024

Assets		**Liabilities and Net Worth**	
Life Insurance—H (Cash surrender value; death benefit $300,000)	2,000		
Life Insurance—W (cash surrender Value)	—		
Total Investments	$ 1,024,000	Total Long-term Liabilities	$ 767,000
Personal Use Asset at FMV			
Primary residence (Paid $500,000)	$ 685,000	**Total Liabilities**	$ 774,000
Personal property and furniture	35,000		
Auto 1—H	22,000	**Net Worth**	$ 1,058,500
Auto 2—W	21,000		
Total Personal Use	$ 763,000		
Total Assets	$ 1,832,500	**Total Liabilities and Net Worth**	$ 1,832,500

Note to financial statements:
H = Husband
W = Wife
FMV = Stated at the current fair market value

Holly has managed to juggle caring for her family and working as a part-time interior designer since the birth of her children. Before becoming a mother, she worked as a teacher in a nearby school district. When she left her full-time position, she rolled over her 403(b) plan into an IRA. She is self-employed and earns $30,000 per year after direct operating expenses, working for friends and family in the community.

Glenn and Holly bought a three-bedroom house about 10 years ago for $500,000, which was within their budget. The house currently has a fair market value of $685,000, and the Mitchells owe $275,000 on their mortgage.

In terms of other anticipated personal expenses, they know that they need to do a better job in saving for their children's education. The public schools in their town are excellent, so private school costs for elementary and high school for the Mitchell children are not an issue. However, Glenn and Holly know that they will be sending their children to college within the next six to eight years, and they will be paying college costs for at least six years. For one of those years, they expect they will need to pay for two children's college costs at the same time. It is also likely that their children, who are good students, will want and need financial help from Glenn and Holly to go to graduate school.

Glenn and Holly do not foresee having to care for aging parents. Holly's parents have both already passed away, and Glenn's parents are financially comfortable with adequate long-term care insurance.

At this moment in their lives, Glenn and Holly are feeling financially sound. But is this accurate? A statement of financial position will provide a clear picture of their true *financial net worth*. This will begin to point out areas that may not feel problematic now but should be addressed before they become overwhelming in the future.

Measuring Net Worth

A personal statement of financial position measures your financial net worth by assigning values to all your financial assets and liabilities. Once you have identified the specific amounts of your assets and liabilities, you simply subtract the total of your liabilities from the total of your assets, and that amount is your financial net worth.

This calculation represents one of the most basic accounting equations: (A – L = NW), or *assets* minus *liabilities* equal *net worth.* Let us walk through the process.

Identifying Assets

Your first step in this process is to identify every financial asset you have. An asset is simply anything you own that has a monetary value, including cash, investments, your primary residence (if you own it), any other real estate you own, your automobiles, retirement accounts, furniture, and jewelry. Once you have identified all the assets you own, you should classify them in the following three categories: cash and cash equivalents, invested assets, and personal-use assets. These are described in the following paragraphs and referred to in the statement of financial position shown in Exhibit 3.1.

- **Cash and cash equivalents:** Include cash on-hand, bank accounts (savings and checking), money market accounts, and Treasury bills (T-bills). These accounts reflect what is called *liquid cash,* or money that is readily available for emergencies. Glenn and Holly have $45,500 in cash and cash equivalents, as can be seen on their statement of financial position.
- **Invested assets:** All assets that are reasonably expected to generate income. (These, of course, are the most important assets in achieving financial independence since these are the assets that will be working to make money for you.) Examples of invested assets include a privately owned business, an investment portfolio, retirement accounts, and fixed and variable annuities. Glenn and Holly have $1,024,000 in invested assets, which are stated at current fair market value on their statement of financial position.
- **Personal-use assets:** Assets that, in effect, measure your standard of living. Personal-use assets typically do not generate income; instead, they require you to use additional resources to maintain or replace them. This would include a primary home, a vacation home, automobiles, furniture, jewelry, and artwork. Glenn and Holly have $763,000 in personal-use assets, which are stated at their estimated fair market value on their statement of financial position.

Listing Liabilities

Liabilities include any financial obligations you may have that require you to make payments, either currently or in the future. When you list your liabilities on your personal statement of financial position, they fall into two categories:

- **Current liabilities:** Full payments that are due within one year (i.e., short-term loans or credit card balances).
- **Long-term liabilities:** Payments that can be stretched out for one year or longer (such as student loans, business loans, mortgages, and home equity loans).

When listing liabilities, be sure to include their terms as well as their current outstanding balance. Terms refer to the interest rates being paid, the number of payments to be made, and any prepayment penalties. (It will be essential to know and list these terms when evaluating your debt, which is discussed in detail in Chapter 4, "Managing Debt.")

Glenn and Holly have current liabilities of $7,000 and long-term liabilities of $767,000. Therefore, their total liabilities are $774,000. Technically the current portion of their long-term liabilities, which are the payments that they are required to make over the next 12 months, should also be listed as current liabilities. However, for ease and clarity, we have not made this distinction and have included only their credit card debt as current.

Calculating Your Financial Net Worth

Now that you have listed all your assets and liabilities, the moment of reckoning has come. When you subtract your total liabilities from your total assets, you will know your personal financial net worth.

The number that represents your financial net worth (and indeed, your entire personal statement of financial position), may well be an eye-opener for you. It will reveal your financial strengths and weaknesses. For some people, this is a positive experience, making them feel financially secure and sound. However, for many people (maybe even the vast majority), these calculations often reveal areas that need improvement and may even uncover serious financial problems. Nevertheless, identifying and facing financial realities serves as a starting point for putting your financial house in good order.

Glenn and Holly's total assets are $1,832,500. Their total liabilities are $774,000. This results in a financial net worth of $1,058,500.

Analyzing a Statement of Financial Position

In Glenn and Holly's case, their financial net worth as of December 31, 2024, is $1,058,500. At first glance, this may appear strong for a couple in their early forties. However, despite including a growing practice, an office building, and a home, their overall financial position reveals several areas of concern that could impact their ability to achieve financial independence.

If Glenn and Holly liquidated all their assets and paid off all their liabilities, they would be left with $1,058,500 in cash; this, of course, does not count any closing costs, transaction fees, taxes, etc. If they invested this amount conservatively and earned a 5% return, it would generate approximately $52,925 per year before taxes. Their current combined cash inflows are approximately $223,353 per year (as shown later in the statement of cash flow, Exhibit 3.2), which is 4.2 times what their net worth could conservatively generate. This clearly shows that they have not yet accumulated sufficient investment assets to be financially independent.

Chapter 8, "Planning for Retirement," discusses in detail how the Mitchells can close this gap so that they can achieve financial independence by the time that they are ready to retire.

Their financial statement also reveals several key weaknesses. Their net worth of $1,058,500 is modest given their age, professional standing, and long-term goals. They have only $45,500 in cash or cash equivalents, which is adequate in the short term but slightly below the recommended minimum of three months of cash inflows. For their household, that target would be approximately $56,000.

Their invested assets total $1,024,000 and include equity in Glenn's business, their office building, retirement accounts, and a taxable investment portfolio. However, the investment portfolio and retirement accounts are heavily weighted toward growth stocks. While this may support long-term growth, it exposes them to unnecessary volatility. A more diversified allocation, including bonds or other income-generating assets, would reduce risk and support a more stable long-term plan. Their retirement accounts total $88,000, which is not enough for a couple in their early forties with plans to retire in their sixties. Like many business owners and self-employed professionals, Glenn and Holly have often prioritized other financial needs and delayed consistent retirement contributions. They will need to increase their savings rate significantly in order to reach their retirement goals. (Again, for more information on this, see Chapter 8, "Planning for Retirement.")

With just $11,000 saved in their children's 529 education account, Glenn and Holly are underprepared for the rising costs of higher education. Their oldest child will be attending college in just a few years, and they can expect to be covering tuition for both children during one overlapping year. They will need to make ongoing contributions and explore other funding options. Chapter 7, "Paying for College," offers guidance on building an education funding strategy.

In terms of life insurance, Glenn has $300,000 in permanent coverage with a cash surrender value of $2,000, while Holly does not currently have a policy. Given their family obligations and dependence on both incomes, Holly would not be able to maintain their current standard of living in the event of Glenn's death. They should secure additional coverage for both spouses to protect their financial plan. Securing term insurance would provide them with significantly more life insurance at a fraction of the cost, and given their multitude of financial needs and limited resources, this may be a more appropriate choice for them. Chapter 5, "Insuring Your Health and Life," provides a more detailed discussion of appropriate life insurance planning.

Glenn's office building has a mortgage of $435,000, which is substantially less than the building's current fair market value of $770,000. Fortunately, they may be able to refinance this loan and lower their monthly payments. Although commercial lending standards are generally more restrictive than residential, and refinancing may require full income verification and property appraisal, the equity they have built gives them a solid foundation. If they can refinance this loan over a new 20-year term, they should be able to reduce their monthly payment significantly. Doing so would allow Glenn to redirect funds toward his retirement plan, the business's operating reserves, and their family's long-term savings goals.

Glenn and Holly are also in a strong position to refinance the mortgage on their primary residence. They currently owe $275,000 on a 30-year fixed mortgage at a rate of 7%, with 20 years remaining. Their monthly principal and interest payment on this loan is approximately $2,132.

If they refinance the existing loan, along with an additional $70,000 of home equity, into a new 30-year fixed mortgage at an estimated interest rate of 6%, their total new mortgage would be $345,000. The monthly payment on this new loan would be approximately $2,068. This would lower their monthly mortgage payment by about $64, resulting in annual cash flow savings of $768.

The $70,000 in excess funds they would be able to extract could be used to immediately eliminate high-interest, nondeductible debt. Glenn and Holly currently carry $7,000 in credit card balances, with interest rates of 17% and 20%. This will save them $1,340 in minimum payments per year. They also have a $22,000 auto loan at 5.5% with three years remaining that's costing them $7,972 per year; this amount will also be eliminated. Lastly, Glenn has a $35,000 student loan at 7%, with 10 years remaining, which costs them $4,877 per year, this payment will also be eliminated. If they use the excess funds from refinancing to pay off their credit card, auto and student loan debt, they will eliminate the monthly minimum payments of $1,182 in payments, which comes to a cash flow improvement of $14,189.

Altogether, refinancing would reduce their total monthly obligations by approximately $1,246. This includes the $64 saved on the mortgage payment and the $1,182 in payments eliminated by paying off the credit card, auto, and student loan debt. The impact on their monthly cash flow would be significant, freeing up funds they could redirect into retirement contributions, 529 education savings, and they just added the $6,000 to their emergency funds, giving them over the three-month minimum we look for as a safety blanket.

To keep the example simple, we, of course, are not factoring in any out-of-pocket refinancing costs. Although we are extending the number of years remaining for their payments, they're getting an opportunity to fund and save for their other financial goals.

It is also important to understand the tax implications of this refinance. Under current IRS rules, only interest on acquisition indebtedness is tax-deductible. This means that the $275,000 portion of their new mortgage, which replaces the original home loan, remains fully deductible. However, the $70,000 used to pay off credit cards and the auto and student loan does not qualify for the mortgage interest deduction, as it is considered home equity indebtedness. These rules were made permanent by the One Big Beautiful Bill Act (OBBBA), which extended the Tax Cuts and

Jobs Act (TCJA) suspension of the home equity interest deduction indefinitely.

Some financial advisors caution against using secured home equity to pay off unsecured consumer debt. That concern is valid, especially for households at risk of overspending or, even worse, filing for bankruptcy. However, in Glenn and Holly's case, using the refinance to consolidate high-interest debt and spreading it out over more years is a practical and effective way to improve their financial health. As long as they avoid rebuilding credit card debt, this strategy allows them to reduce interest costs, strengthen cash flow, and redirect funds toward long-term goals like retirement and education.

An Important First Step

Analyzing your statement of financial position is an important first step in developing financial goals and implementing prudent financial strategies to help you *achieve financial independence*. The figure that represents your current financial net worth is perhaps the most significant number in your quest to financial independence. You should calculate this number at least once a year to track your progress.

Personally, I analyze and update my own statement of financial position at the end of each year. This process helps me set realistic and meaningful financial goals for the year ahead, and it has become an essential part of my New Year's resolutions. I strongly encourage you to make it part of your annual routine as well.

Making Sense of Cash Flow

Building your personal financial net worth requires minimizing your liabilities and increasing your assets, particularly your investment assets. In addition to calculating your net worth, you need to get a firm grip on where your money is coming from and, perhaps even more important, where it is going. In other words, you need to create a detailed personal statement of cash flow.

Quite simply, a statement of cash flow will show all your *cash inflows* and all your *cash outflows* (as we refer to them in the accounting profession) for a designated period, usually one year. As discussed in Chapter 1, the secret to achieving financial independence is to live within (and ideally below) your means, and to *pay yourself first* (i.e., save money). If your cash inflows exceed your cash outflows, then you will have discretionary income, which can (and should) be used to increase your savings and build your accumulated wealth.

However, if your cash outflows are greater than your cash inflows, then you are living beyond your means, are likely accumulating debt, and are severely limiting your chances of achieving financial independence. As for the statement of financial position, we have created a sample statement of cash flow (shown in Exhibit 3.2), representing the current financial life of Glenn and Holly Mitchell, and will refer to it to help you identify relevant issues in your own situation.

Before you begin preparing your own statement of cash flow, you will need to gather copies of your pay stubs, your most recent income tax return, and your bank and credit card statements for the preceding 12 months. To help you prepare your own personal statement of cash flow, we've included fillable forms that you can utilize by visiting our website, www.ventotaxandwealth.com, selecting "Getting to Point X" and scrolling down to "Fillable Forms."

Identify Your Cash Inflows (Sources of Income)

Begin your statement of cash flow by summarizing all of your sources of income. This includes your annual salary (or salaries, if you have multiple income streams or if you are preparing a cash flow statement for a couple where both spouses work). Include any freelance or self-employment income, interest or dividend income, pension, Social Security income, and any and all other sources of income you may have. Do *not* include any earnings from tax-deferred accounts such as 401(k)s, IRAs, and annuities because these funds are not available to pay for cash outflows. However, if you received *distributions* from these tax-deferred accounts, you should include them as part of your cash inflows. Finally, these figures should reflect your gross income, or before-tax income. Your taxes appear under cash outflows.

Glenn and Holly Mitchell's cash inflows include Glenn's salary of $190,000 from his dental practice and Holly's net self-employment income of $30,000 from her work as an interior designer. In addition, they receive $840 in dividends and $383 in interest income from their savings account. They also have cash inflow from Glenn's office building, where his dental practice is the tenant, of $2,130. As shown on the statement of cash flow, their cash inflows total $223,353.

Exhibit 3.2 Glenn and Holly Mitchell, Statement of Cash Flow Before and After Recommendation

	Glenn and Holly Mitchell **Statement of Cash Flow (Before Recommendations)** For the period January 1, 2024, to December 31, 2024		Glenn and Holly Mitchell **Statement of Cash Flow (After Recommendations)** For the period January 1, 2024, to December 31, 2024		**Net Cash Flow Increase**
Inflows					
Self-Employment Income—H	—		—		
Wage Income W2—H	190,000		190,000		
Self-Employment Income—W	30,000		30,000		
Wage Income W2—W	—		—		
	220,000		220,000		
Dividend Income	840		840		
Interest Income	383		1,724		
Net Rental Income ($50,400 Rental Income Less Mortgage Payment on Office Building)	2,130		13,002		
Total Inflows		**$ 223,353**		**$ 235,566**	$ 12,213
Outflows					
Invested Assets (Pay Yourself First)					
Simple Plan Contributions—H	$ 5,000		$ 5,000		
IRA Contribution—W	1,500		1,500		
Solo 401(k)—W	—		—		

(Continued)

Exhibit 3.2 (***Continued***)

	Glenn and Holly Mitchell **Statement of Cash Flow (Before Recommendations)** For the period January 1, 2024, to December 31, 2024		Glenn and Holly Mitchell **Statement of Cash Flow (After Recommendations)** For the period January 1, 2024, to December 31, 2024		**Net Cash Flow Increase**
Dividend Reinvested	840		840		
Interest Reinvested	383		1,724		
Total Outflows to Invested Assets		$ 7,723		$ 9,064	($1,341)
Housing					
Mortgage Home	$ 25,584		$ 24,816		
Rent	—		—		
Cable	1,650		1,320		
Cell Phone	1,980		1,584		
Cleaning	4,800		2,400		
Electricity	2,400		2,400		
Gardner/Snow Removal	2,000		2,000		
Insurance (Home)	2,500		1,900		
Gas	1,320		1,320		
Internet	600		600		
Maintenance and Repairs	1,200		1,200		
Phone (Land Line)	550		—		
Supplies	700		700		
Property Tax (Home)	14,728		11,782		
Water and Sewer	1,400		1,400		
Total Outflows to Housing		$ 61,412		$ 53,422	$ 7,990

Transportation					
Bus/Taxi Fare	$ 840		$ 840		
Fuel	6,550		6,550		
Insurance	2,800		2,380		
Licensing	100		100		
Maintenance	400		400		
Tolls	350		350		
Other	125		125		
Total Outflows to Transportation		$ 11,165		$ 10,745	$ 420
Family Risk Management					
Health	—		—		
Life	1,400		1,400		
Long-Term Disability	1,200		1,200		
Long-Term Care	—		—		
Other	—		—		
Total Outflows to FRM		$ 2,600		$ 2,600	0
Food					
Groceries	$ 5,500		$ 6,500		
Dining Out	10,500		5,250		
Other	600		600		
Total Outflows to Food		$ 16,600		$ 12,350	$ 4,250

(*Continued*)

Exhibit 3.2 (***Continued***)

	Glenn and Holly Mitchell **Statement of Cash Flow (Before Recommendations)** For the period January 1, 2024, to December 31, 2024		Glenn and Holly Mitchell **Statement of Cash Flow (After Recommendations)** For the period January 1, 2024, to December 31, 2024		**Net Cash Flow Increase**
Personal Care					
Clothing	$ 6,000		$ 4,000		
Dry Cleaning	850		850		
Hair/Nails	1,000		700		
Health Club	1,200		600		
Medical – Out of Pocket	5,000		3,000		
Organization Dues/Fees	350		350		
Other	—		—		
Total Outflows to Personal Care		$ 14,400		$ 9,500	$ 4,900
Entertainment					
Streaming Subscriptions	$ 550		$ 550		
Concerts	1,300		1,300		
Live Theater	600		600		
Movies	380		380		
Sporting Events	600		600		
Other	—		—		
Total Outflows to Entertainment		$ 3,430		$ 3,430	0

Loan Payments					
Credit Card 1 – H	$ 1,000		—		
Credit Card 2 – W	340		—		
Auto Loan 1 – H	7,972		—		
Auto Loan 2 – W	—		—		
Student Loan 1 – H	4,877		—		
Student Loan 2 – W	—		—		
Other Personal Loans	—		—		
Total Outflows to Loan Payments		$ 14,189		—	$ 14,189
Taxes					
Federal Income Tax	$ 38,026		$ 38,026		
Social Security Tax – H&W (Employee's Portion)	12,778		12,778		
FICA/Medicare	3,190		3,190		
State Income Tax	—		—		
Other	250		250		
Total Outflows to Taxes		$ 54,244		$ 54,244	0
Gifts and Donations					
Charity 1	$ 2,400		$ 2,400		
Charity 2	1,200		1,200		
Charity 3	500		500		
Total Outflows to Gifts and Donations		$ 4,100		$ 4,100	0

(*Continued*)

Exhibit 3.2 ***(Continued)***

	Glenn and Holly Mitchell **Statement of Cash Flow (Before Recommendations)** For the period January 1, 2024, to December 31, 2024		Glenn and Holly Mitchell **Statement of Cash Flow (After Recommendations)** For the period January 1, 2024, to December 31, 2024		**Net Cash Flow Increase**
Professional Fees and Legal Obligations					
Accounting and Legal Fees	$ 1,200		$ 1,800		
Alimony	—		—		
Payments on Lien/Judgement	—		—		
Other	—		—		
Total Outflows to Professional Fees and Legal Obligations		$ 1,200		$ 1,800	($600)
Child Care and Other Expenses					
Child Care	$ 6,000		$ 6,000		
Clothing	1,000		1,000		
Domestic Help/Babysitting	250		250		
Lunch Money	1,050		1,050		
Medical	250		250		
Organization Dues/Fees	300		300		
School Supplies	250		250		
School Tuition	—		—		
Toys/Games	600		600		
Other	200		200		
Total Outflows to Child Care and Other Expenses		$ 9,900		$ 9,900	0

Pet Care and Other Expenses					
Food	—		—		
Grooming	—		—		
Medical	—		—		
Toys	—		—		
Other	—		—		
Total Outflows to Pet Care and Other Expenses		—		—	0
Personal Expenses					
Cash Withdrawals	$ 1,500		$ 1,500		
Dues/Subscriptions	600		600		
Education	—		—		
Gifts (Birthday, Holiday, etc.)	1,200		1,200		
Vacation/Travel	3,500		3,500		
Other	500		500		
Total Outflows to Personal Expenses		$ 7,300		$ 7,300	0
Total Outflows		$ 208,263		$ 178,455	$ 29,808
Discretionary Cash Flow*		**$ 15,090**		**$ 57,111**	**$ 42,021**

Note: *cash inflows less cash outflows.

Identify Your Cash Outflows (Expenses)

Cash outflows include *essential* items such as housing, food, clothing, transportation, as well as *nonessential* items, or basically everything else you spend money on throughout the year. List each one of these basic items as a subheading (*Housing, Food, Personal Care, Entertainment,* etc.), then go through your checking account and credit card statements and summarize these payments in as much detail as possible. (Do not worry if you are not absolutely perfect; general trends will show up fairly quickly.) Some items will remain constant, such as your mortgage, your car loan payments, and your student loan payments. Others, however, may fluctuate, or jump out as excessive.

Your cash outflows should also include items that many people do not commonly consider as part of their personal or family budget. For example, in the spirit of paying yourself first, the first line items under the heading of *outflows* on your statement of cash flow should be your savings. This includes 10% or more of your gross pay, contributions to retirement accounts such as a 401(k) or IRA, and any reinvested dividend income. These funds should be considered an essential outflow of money, just as important as your rent or mortgage, electricity bill, or grocery bill.

Also, all your tax payments (even those paid through your employer) should be highlighted and included as part of your cash outflows, including all tax payments from your income such as federal income tax, FICA and Medicare, and state and city income tax. In today's environment, where tax laws continue to evolve, keeping track of total tax payments is an important part of monitoring your overall financial picture. If you are self-employed or have additional income sources, remember to account for quarterly estimated payments as well.

Separating Essentials from Nonessentials

Once you have listed your cash outflows in as much detail as possible, take some time to analyze your statement closely. Begin to identify which items are *essential,* and which are *nonessential;* which ones are *needs,* and which are *wants.* If you are married, go through your statement with your spouse. You should even show it to your older children, particularly teenagers who may be racking up significant expenses for a car, cell phone, or other expenditures.

At first glance, certain items may appear to be necessities, such as shelter, food, clothing, and transportation. However, with a closer look, these apparent necessities can sometimes resemble luxuries. For example, your home may be costing you more than you can realistically afford. You may have no trouble meeting the basic mortgage payment, but your utility bills, lawn and garden maintenance, and property taxes may be stretching your budget too thin. A thorough analysis of your cash outflows might suggest that it could be worthwhile moving to a smaller house or a less expensive neighborhood.

Transportation costs are another area where the line between necessity and luxury can blur. Is owning a $50,000 car really that important? In a household with teenagers, the need for two or even three cars may seem imperative, but are the costs becoming prohibitive? Like a house, the cost of a basic automobile may not be unaffordable, but the price of gasoline, insurance, and maintenance can put a big dent in a family budget.

With a close look at your statement of cash flow, items that are completely nonessential are sure to jump out. Costs for such indulgences as manicures, theater tickets, or expensive birthday gifts may suddenly seem not only excessive, but frivolous. Also, small cuts, when added together, can turn into big savings for you and your family.

And let us not forget the power of bargaining. Not everything sells for the asking price. Most financially successful people view bargaining as a game and do not experience any feeling of embarrassment for doing so. Personal finance experts routinely recommend reviewing your bills and negotiating for better deals whenever possible. Whether it is on a phone plan, a medical bill, or a home service contract, there is often room to save simply by asking.

Consider the following analysis of the Mitchells' statement of cash flow. It should inspire additional ideas for ways your family can cut costs.

Analyzing a Statement of Cash Flow

Analyzing Cash Inflows Before implementing our recommendations, Glenn and Holly Mitchell had total cash inflows of $223,353 as outlined earlier. To improve their financial position, we made the following recommendations. Rather than keeping their funds in a local bank savings account earning only 1%, we advised them to purchase three-month or six-month US Treasury Bills, which were yielding approximately 4.5% at the time. This change alone increased their annual interest income from $383 to $1,724, boosting their cash inflows by $1,341.

In addition to offering a significantly higher return, T-bills are 100% guaranteed by the federal government and exempt from state and city income tax. Since the Mitchells live in Texas, where there is no state income tax, they will not benefit from this particular tax advantage, but the improved interest rate still strengthened their cash position.

We also recommended refinancing the mortgage on their office building to a 20-year fixed rate, which they were able to secure at 6%. Although this extended their loan term by seven years, it reduced their monthly payment from $4,023 to $3,117. This lowered their mortgage payment by $906 per month, which comes to $10,872 annually. Therefore, the net rental income of the office building increased to $13,002 from $2,130.

As a result of these key strategies, the Mitchells' total cash inflows increased from $223,353 to $235,566 for a total increase in net cash inflows of $12,213.

Analyzing Cash Outflows Glenn and Holly Mitchell's cash outflows for the 12 months ending December 31, 2024, (before the recommended changes) are broken out in the following categories:

- Invested assets: $7,723
- Housing: $61,412
- Transportation: $11,165
- Family risk management and insurance: $2,600
- Food: $16,600
- Personal care: $14,400
- Entertainment: $3,430
- Loan payments: $14,189
- Taxes: $54,244
- Gifts and donations: $4,100
- Professional fees and legal obligations: $1,200
- Childcare and other expenses: $9,900
- Other personal expenses: $7,300

In total, the Mitchells' current cash outflows amount to $208,263, leaving them with a discretionary cash flow of $15,090. (Cash inflows of $223,353 minus cash outflows of $208,263.)

In other words, Glenn and Holly are currently spending $15,090 less per year than they are earning. This is obvious based on the total cash and cash equivalents they have on hand at the end of 2024. This confirms that the Mitchells are living within their means.

Based on the 2024 National Financial Capability Study by FINRA, 26% of Americans admit to spending more than they earn, which is up from 20% from the previous year. Furthermore, a staggering 62% of Americans report relying solely on their regular paycheck to cover living expenses with very little or no emergency cash reserves. This means that the average American is literally living paycheck to paycheck.

Although the Mitchells appear to be on the right track, the question is: Are there financial planning strategies that will improve their net cash flow and accelerate their path to financial independence and position themselves to create generational wealth? Clearly, the answer to this is yes, and we will identify the specific changes they can make.

The changes they will need to make will increase their net cash flow so that they can add to their invested assets (pay themselves first) and use the resulting surplus to reduce debt and increase long-term savings. As part of the analysis of their statement of financial position, they (working closely with their CERTIFIED FINANCIAL PLANNER®) were able to uncover multiple strategies that allowed them to reduce their cash outflows.

By consolidating personal debt, they reduced their cash outflow by $14,957 (credit card as well as car and student loan payments by $14,189 and the mortgage payment by $768). Please note, the debt consolidation effected many of the categories on this statement. Furthermore, by closely analyzing their statement of cash flow, they were able to further improve their cash flow by eliminating some nonessential expenses. Finally, they were able to find additional creative ways to save on taxes and other expenses.

We're now going to discuss how the Mitchells were able to cut their basic living costs, and we will cover this based on the same categories outlined in their statement of cash flows, but more specifically, their outflows. They utilized Appendix B to assist them in identifying ways for each of their family members to try and save $20 or more per day.

How One Family Cut Basic Costs

After the Mitchells held a family meeting (which included their two children, even though their kids are relatively young), they were able to begin to identify which of their basic expenses were absolutely essential and which were nonessential. With a little cooperation and compromise, they identified those expenses they could either minimize or eliminate. (As mentioned, these figures are listed in detail on Glenn and Holly's statement of cash flow, shown in Exhibit 3.2. It will help if you refer to it throughout this discussion.)

Invested Assets (Pay Yourself First) As mentioned earlier, the Mitchells reallocated the funds in their savings account to T-bills, since the T-bills are yielding a higher return. This increased their interest income by $1,341.

Housing In addition to reducing their mortgage cost by $768 from refinancing, they were able to make some substantial cuts in their housing category. They eliminated two of four premium cable boxes and kept their streaming services, reducing their cable cost by $330 per year. The family agreed to only use their cell phones within the family plan allowance, which saved them $396.

With regard to their house itself, Glenn and Holly discussed the possibility of downsizing, acknowledging that they lived in one of the largest homes in their neighborhood, which was truly a nonessential expense. Even though they agreed that a home this size was not a necessity, they were not willing to downsize at this time. They were emotionally tied to the home, and they felt this was the best place to raise their children. They did make a commitment that once their children were away at college, they would revisit this financial issue and make the decision about downsizing at that time.

They also agreed to cut their cleaning service from once a week to every other week, saving $2,400 per year. They reviewed their homeowner's insurance policy and increased their deductible, saving $600 per year. They did this by following the recommendations outlined in Chapter 6, "Protecting Your Property with Insurance." Because each family member already had a cell phone, they eliminated their household landline, which saved them an additional $550 per year.

Finally, they also worked with a local property tax attorney to appeal their assessed value, which successfully lowered their property taxes by $2,946 annually. With these relatively small sacrifices, all nonessentials, along with debt restructuring, their total housing cash outflows were reduced by $7,990 per year.

Transportation After taking a close look at their transportation costs, the Mitchells found that their only real opportunity for savings was their auto insurance. They contacted their insurance agent, who made them aware of discounts they would be entitled to, such as increasing their deductible and taking a defensive driving course. By taking advantage of these offers, they were able to reduce their auto insurance by 15%, or $420 per year. Therefore, their total transportation outflows were reduced by $420.

Family Risk Management After reviewing their other insurance costs (listed under "family risk management" in Exhibit 3.2), they realized they were underinsured and therefore were not able to reduce their expenditures in this area; in fact, they needed to increase them. Glenn and Holly made a commitment to meet with their life and disability insurance agent to discuss their needs and to make sure they had sufficient coverage. They followed the guidance provided in Chapter 5, "Insuring Your Health and Life," and although they have not made this change yet, they plan to next year after further analysis. For now, we'll assume they were not able to reduce this cost, but the plan is to increase their coverage and to utilize some of the excess cash flow from this analysis to help fund it next year. This category of cash outflows will remain unchanged for now.

Food Under the category of food, both Glenn and Holly were surprised to learn they were spending more than $900 per month dining out, over $10,000 per year. They agreed to reduce this to no more than twice a month and instead cook more meals at home. This simple change cut their dining out expenses in half, saving $5,250 per year. At the same time, this increased their grocery costs by $1,000 so the net savings to them was $4,250.

Personal Care Under the personal care category, the family agreed to stick to a stricter budget of no more than $4,000 per year for clothing, resulting in a savings of $2,000.

Holly agreed to reduce the number of times she goes to the salon each year by 30%, reducing her beauty service costs from $1,000 to $700, resulting in a $300 savings.

Glenn agreed to eliminate his monthly fitness club membership, since he had not been to the gym for more than two years. Although Holly kept her membership, they were able to save $600 per year.

With the help of their CPA, they also decided to establish a Health Savings Account (HSA), as their insurance plan qualifies as a high-deductible health plan. By contributing $5,000 to the HSA and using those funds for out-of-pocket medical expenses, they received a tax deduction that reduced their net medical costs by $2,000. (See Chapter 5, "Insuring Your Health and Life," for more details on health savings accounts.) These changes resulted in total personal care outflows of $4,900.

Entertainment Music and movie subscriptions, concerts, theater, and sporting events remained priorities for the family, so their entertainment costs remained unchanged. This category of cash outflows will remain unchanged.

Loan Payments As a result of their debt consolidation strategy, their personal loan payments (credit card and auto/student loan) were reduced by $14,189, which added to their discretionary cash flow.

Taxes After reading Chapter 2, "Understanding Taxes," they had a brief conversation with their CPA, who informed them that they were eligible for the child and dependent care credit on their tax return for 2024 as well as prior years. Based on their adjusted gross income, and two children under the age of 13, they were entitled to a tax credit of 20% of $6,000, or $1,200. (Please note that this credit increased under the OBBBA; refer to Chapter 2 for more details.)

For 2024, we will assume there are no tax savings in this category, but we are confident they will uncover thousands, if not tens of thousands, of dollars in tax savings each year going forward by implementing the tax-smart strategies outlined throughout this book.

In addition, because they had not previously claimed the child and dependent care credit, their CPA will be able to amend their tax returns for the past three years, which will result in total refunds of $3,600. Going forward, this deduction will add $1,200 per year to their discretionary cash flow until their children reach age 13.

Gifts and Donations Since their total charitable contributions are only $4,100 per year and represent just under 2% of their overall income, we agreed there is no room to reduce this expense. This category of cash outflows will remain unchanged for now.

Professional Fees and Legal Obligations After Glenn and Holly read through this book, they came to realize that working with a qualified CPA to do tax planning is actually a profit-center and not a cost to them. They understand that they could save many times this cost in tax savings. They agreed to meet with their tax advisor at least once a year for tax-smart planning advice. This added a $600 cost in this category.

Child Care and Other Expenses After reviewing their childcare costs, they could not identify any specific items that they could eliminate or reduce but were able to lower their overall childcare costs by $1,200 because of the childcare credit. Since this will come in the form of a tax reduction, we are not reducing this category to the outflow here, but instead it would come out as a tax savings that will increase the cash flow by $1,200 going forward.

Pet Care and Other Personal Expenses Since they do not have any pets, there were no costs to analyze in this category. With regard to their personal expenses, they agreed there was no fat to trim here, so both categories remain unchanged.

To Sum Up Our Analysis of Their Statement of Cash Flow Glenn and Holly were amazed with the results after analyzing their statement of cash flow before and after our recommendations, which would increase their discretionary cash flow from $15,090 to $57,111 going forward. This freed up an additional $42,021 in cash available to meet their long-term financial goals. This is before factoring in the tax-smart strategies that we'll be able to implement for them with this excess cash flow.

If you recall, as part of the refinancing and after paying off all of their nondeductible debt, they were able to add $6,000 to their emergency cash funds. In addition, with their free discretionary cash flow, we are projecting they should easily meet their liquid cash reserve needs of three months of living expenses.

Glenn decided to increase his Simple Plan contribution from $5,000 to the maximum of $16,500, not including the company's employer match. After reading through Chapter 8, "Planning for Retirement," Holly realized she was eligible to establish a Solo 401(k) and instead of contributing only $1,500 a year to her traditional IRA account, she would now be able to contribute $23,500 into this plan. She opted not to do the Roth deferrals since she felt it was more important to her to get the immediate tax savings up front. Talk about turbo-charging their retirement plan! This will be a game changer for them.

Since their oldest child is 12 and only five years away from attending college, and their younger child is nine and eight years away, one of their other important financial goals is to accumulate enough funds to cover four years of college for each of their children. They currently only have $11,000 saved for their children's education. They agreed to contribute $20,000 a year to their 529 plans. After reading through Chapter 7, "Paying for College," they determined this would be the amount needed to meet this goal of being fully prepared to cover their children's undergraduate studies.

In addition, they were also finally able to commit to purchasing the proper amount of life insurance (for both Glenn and Holly) and long-term disability coverage (for Glenn), which came to $5,000.

They were able to further improve their cash flow based on the following tax savings, which came from the $1,200 child tax credit, and the $7,800 ($32,500 times their 24% tax rate) tax savings from the additional funds that came from the contributions to their two retirement plans. This added another $9,000 to their discretionary cash flow.

Exhibit 3.3 will show you their projected statement of cash flow for 2025, *after* implementing the tax and financial planning strategies we outlined above.

Exhibit 3.3 Glenn and Holly Mitchell, Statement of Cash Flow (After Tax and Financial Planning Strategy Implementation)

Glenn and Holly Mitchell
Statement of Cash Flow
(After Tax and Financial Planning Strategy Implementation)
For the period January 1, 2025, to December 31, 2025

Inflows		
Self-Employment Income—H	—	
Wage Income W2—H	190,000	
Self-Employment Income—W	30,000	
Wage Income W2—W	—	
	220,000	
Dividend Income	840	
Interest Income	1,724	
Net Rental Income ($50,400 Rental Income Less Mortgage Payment on Office Building)	13,002	
Total Inflows		**$ 235,566**
Outflows		
Invested Assets (Pay Yourself First)		
Simple Plan Contributions—H	***$ 16,500*****	
IRA Contribution—W	—	
Solo 401(k)—W	***23,500*****	
529 Plan Contributions	***20,000*****	
Dividend Reinvested	840	
Interest Reinvested	1,724	
Total Outflows to Invested Assets		$ 62,564
Housing		
Mortgage Home	$ 24,816	
Rent	—	
Cable	1,320	
Cell Phone	1,584	
Cleaning	2,400	
Electricity	2,400	

(Continued)

Exhibit 3.3 (*Continued*)

Glenn and Holly Mitchell
Statement of Cash Flow
(After Tax and Financial Planning Strategy Implementation)
For the period January 1, 2025, to December 31, 2025

Gardner/Snow Removal	2,000	
Insurance (Home)	1,900	
Gas	1,320	
Internet	600	
Maintenance and Repairs	1,200	
Phone (Land Line)	—	
Supplies	700	
Property Tax (Home)	11,782	
Water and Sewer	1,400	
Total Outflows to Housing		$ 53,422
Transportation		
Bus/Taxi Fare	$ 840	
Fuel	6,550	
Insurance	2,380	
Licensing	100	
Maintenance	400	
Tolls	350	
Other	125	
Total Outflows to Transportation		$ 10,745
Family Risk Management		
Health	—	
Life	***2,600*****	
Long-Term Disability	***2,400*****	
Long-Term Care	—	
Other	—	
Total Outflows to FRM		$ 5,000
Food		
Groceries	$ 6,500	
Dining Out	5,250	
Other	600	
Total Outflows to Food		$ 12,350

Glenn and Holly Mitchell **Statement of Cash Flow** **(After Tax and Financial Planning Strategy Implementation)** For the period January 1, 2025, to December 31, 2025		
Personal Care		
Clothing	$ 4,000	
Dry Cleaning	850	
Hair/Nails	700	
Health Club	600	
Medical – Out of Pocket	3,000	
Organization Dues/Fees	350	
Other	—	
Total Outflows to Personal Care		$ 9,500
Entertainment		
Streaming Subscriptions	$ 550	
Concerts	1,300	
Live Theater	600	
Movies	380	
Sporting Events	600	
Other	—	
Total Outflows to Entertainment		$ 3,430
Loan Payments		
Credit Card 1—H	—	
Credit Card 2—W	—	
Auto Loan 1—H	—	
Auto Loan 2—W	—	
Student Loan 1—H	—	
Student Loan 2—W	—	
Other Personal Loans	—	
Total Outflows to Loan Payments		—
Taxes		
Federal Income Tax	***$ 29,026*****	
Social Security Tax—H&W (Employee's Portion)	12,778	
FICA/Medicare	3,190	
State Income Tax	—	
Other	250	
Total Outflows to Taxes		$ 45,244

(Continued)

Exhibit 3.3 (*Continued*)

Glenn and Holly Mitchell
Statement of Cash Flow
(After Tax and Financial Planning Strategy Implementation)
For the period January 1, 2025, to December 31, 2025

Gifts and Donations				
Charity 1	$	2,400		
Charity 2		1,200		
Charity 3		500		
Total Outflows to Gifts and Donations			$	4,100
Professional Fees and Legal Obligations				
Accounting and Legal Fees	$	1,800		
Alimony		—		
Payments on Lien/Judgement		—		
Other		—		
Total Outflows to Professional Fees and Legal Obligations			$	1,800
Child Care and Other Expenses				
Child Care	$	6,000		
Clothing		1,000		
Domestic Help/Babysitting		250		
Lunch Money		1,050		
Medical		250		
Organization Dues/Fees		300		
School Supplies		250		
School Tuition		—		
Toys/Games		600		
Other		200		
Total Outflows to Child Care and Other Expenses			$	9,900
Pet Care and Other Expenses				
Food		—		
Grooming		—		
Medical		—		
Toys		—		
Other		—		
Total Outflows to Pet Care and Other Expenses				—

Glenn and Holly Mitchell
Statement of Cash Flow
(After Tax and Financial Planning Strategy Implementation)
For the period January 1, 2025, to December 31, 2025

Personal Expenses				
Cash Withdrawals	$	1,500		
Dues/Subscriptions		600		
Education		—		
Gifts (Birthday, Holiday, etc.)		1,200		
Vacation/Travel		3,500		
Other		500		
Total Outflows to Personal Expenses			$	7,300
Total Outflows			$	225,355
Discretionary Cash Flow*			**$**	**10,211**

Note: *cash inflows less cash outflows.
**changes after implementing tax and financial planning strategies.

As shown in this Exhibit, and highlighted with ***bold and italicized*** numbers, they were able to increase their cash outflows bringing their total contribution to Glenn's Simple IRA to $16,500, Holly's Solo 401(k) to $23,500, and their children's 529 plan contributions to $20,000. Furthermore, they were finally able to get the appropriate life insurance and long-term disability coverage, which totaled $5,000 per year and through tax-smart saving strategies, reduced their total federal income tax to $29,026. When all was said and done, they still had $10,211 of discretionary cash flow available after implementing all these strategies.

Finally, the Mitchells made a commitment to meet with their tax advisor at least once during the year (in addition to their annual tax visit) to discuss further tax-smart saving strategies. They believed that, in addition to the items they had already identified, they could reduce their taxes even further with proper tax planning. With all these cost-cutting efforts, the Mitchell family has come a long way toward the right path to achieving financial independence and creating and maintaining generational wealth.

Little Things Mean a Lot

If you and your family work closely to identify areas in your life where you could minimize expenses, each of you could easily save $20 or more per day. Consider this: by saving $20 per day, you would be saving $140 per week, about $608 per month, and $7,300 per year. If you are 30 years old, and if you invest that savings of $7,300 annually for 35 years (until you are 65) at an assumed 8% rate of return, you will amass $1,257,914. To assist you in coming up with a few easy ways to save money, see Appendix B, "101 Ways to Save $20 or More per Day."

Establishing Your Financial Goals

By classifying your cash outflows as *essential* or *nonessential*, you begin to acknowledge and separate your *needs* from your *wants*. As a result, you start to define your true standard of living, the lifestyle you want to be living, the one you are actually living, and the one you need to be living if you want to achieve financial independence.

Defining Your Lifestyle, What Do You Consider "Wealth"?

In our society, *wealth* is often defined as earning enormous paychecks; amassing huge investment portfolios; owning cavernous houses filled with expensive furniture and state-of-the-art electronics; driving multiple, high-end automobiles that cost in the six figures; owning vacation homes and enjoying luxurious trips to ski resorts, Caribbean islands, and European capitals. Having closets bursting with designer clothing (even for infants) has become a cultural symbol of success. Even so-called "middle-class" families seem to want these things, perhaps on a slightly smaller scale, but the pursuit of material goods is the same.

Of course, none of these things are necessities, even for the truly wealthy; they are things we *desire*. But if we cannot afford them, many people go into enormous debt to buy them, causing immense stress for themselves and their families. This is a book about personal finance, so we will not discuss the social and emotional challenges often associated with great wealth. These can include workaholism, strained marriages, lack of time for children, loss of friendships, and even the diminishing of personal integrity and what we call the *soul*. What my parents considered the "American Dream," the freedom to work hard to have a secure and happy life for themselves and their children, has become warped.

The fact is that *wealth* need not mean aspiring to possess a breathtaking amount of money. For some people, wealth may mean living in a small house in a less affluent neighborhood so that they can afford to send their children to the best colleges. For others, wealth may mean giving up luxurious material goods in order to work in a less high-paying but personally rewarding career, such as teaching, social work, or the arts.

It is imperative that you define what *wealth* means to you. In other words, you need to be clear about what standard of living you aspire to and how you propose to achieve it financially. And the curious fact is, no matter what you choose, you can still achieve financial independence. As we have noted before, we have had clients who earn hundreds of thousands, even millions, of dollars, annually, yet struggle to pay their monthly bills. At the same time, we have had clients who live on modest wages yet are well on their way to achieving financial independence and leaving a financial legacy to their children. My parents are proof that this can be accomplished even for moderate to low-income earners.

Achieving Financial Independence and Building Generational Wealth

Remember, this is a book about how to achieve financial independence, the point where we can stop working for our money and our money starts working for us. For most people, financial independence means reaching a stage where they have accumulated enough assets and income to live comfortably without relying on a paycheck.

At the same time, financial independence is not the only goal, nor should it be. In addition to preparing for retirement, many of us want to buy a home, educate our children, take an annual vacation, and provide our children with special experiences such as a beautiful wedding. Some may aspire to start a business. Others may face responsibilities that involve significant financial obligations, such as supporting an aging parent or providing lifelong care for a disabled child.

The journey toward financial independence is also the foundation for something even more enduring, generational wealth. The *Generational Wealth Code* represents the set of guiding principles and disciplined financial behaviors that, when practiced consistently, transform income and assets into enduring, multigenerational wealth. It is the roadmap to mastering the 12 critical areas of comprehensive wealth management from living within one's means and optimizing tax-smart strategies to harnessing the power of compounding and building lasting value through investing. Rooted in the pursuit of financial independence, the *Generational Wealth Code* aligns daily financial decisions with long-term purpose, ensuring that wealth is not only created but also sustained, protected, and passed on as a legacy of knowledge, discipline, and opportunity for future generations.

Ultimately, your financial goals extend beyond simply reaching financial independence. As with your overall lifestyle, only you can decide what those goals are and how you want your wealth to impact the generations that follow.

Your Financial Goals: What Is Most Important to You?

Although we cannot tell you what is most important for you personally, as CPAs and CERTIFIED FINANCIAL PLANNER®, we will express our professional opinions about the value of certain financial decisions. By completing the Comprehensive Wealth Management Questionnaire in the "Introduction" section of this book, you and your family members will be able to identify their most significant financial goals and then be able to prioritize them in order of importance. Here are our thoughts and recommendations:

- **Paying yourself first (saving):** As we have said repeatedly, unless you have an extraordinarily high-paying job, expect to receive a large inheritance, or know for certain that you will win the lottery, you must save your money and pay yourself first. You need to have cash in savings for that rainy day. In my opinion, this means enough cash to cover at least three- to six-months' worth of living expenses. To reach your other financial goals, including *achieving financial independence,* you need to pay yourself first. (See Chapter 1, "Committing to Living within Your Means.")
- **Paying off your debts:** You should pay off all your bad debt, especially high-interest credit card debt, as quickly as possible, before you can begin to save seriously. If paying off your existing bad debt is one of your goals, turn to Chapter 4, "Managing Debt."
- **Saving for retirement:** If you are in your twenties or thirties, the prospect of retirement probably seems incredibly remote, especially if you are planning a wedding, buying a house, or

expecting a new baby. However, we cannot say it more strongly: if you want to become financially independent, you need to begin planning for retirement and saving for it *now.* (We discuss this in detail in Chapter 8, "Planning for Retirement" and provide proof in Chapter 12, "The Time Value of Money.")

- **Buying a home:** Most people are eager to own their own home, which is typically a good financial decision. But remember, you should consider your house as a *personal-use asset,* not as an investment asset. Aside from being certain that you can afford the mortgage and maintenance costs, you should plan to hold on to a property for at least a decade. Owning a home is a long-term proposition. (Purchasing a home is discussed further in Chapter 4, "Managing Debt.")
- **Owning your own business:** Many people dream of owning their own business. The financial ramifications of starting your own business are complex. Still, owning your own business can be an excellent road to *financial independence.* Although the financial benefits of business ownership can be significant, so are the risks and time commitment required to achieve success.
- **Educating your children:** We believe strongly that educating your children is the best way to secure their financial future. That said, not every child needs to obtain a four-year college degree. Some may possess special skills and talents that are better suited to trade school or vocational training. Do not buy into the myth that going to college guarantees a good job. We need plumbers, carpenters, electricians, and other skilled tradespeople. Many of these jobs pay much better than white-collar professions.

  These days, paying for college (and private elementary and high school, if that is your choice) is not only incredibly expensive, but is full of financial pitfalls. (See Chapter 7, "Paying for College," for a full analysis of this issue).
- **Funding unexpected situations:** Some people face unexpected or challenging life situations, such as caring for a disabled child or aging parent. These may become their most important financial priorities and require careful planning. There are several financial tools and strategies for these types of needs. (See Chapter 5, "Insuring Your Health and Life," and Chapter 10, "Preserving Your Estate" for more information).

- **Funding special purchases:** We all have dreams and most of them cost money. Whether it is a trip around the world, a ski chalet in Utah, or a state-of-the-art gourmet kitchen, these goals require planning. Unfortunately, in recent decades, many people have fallen into the habit of financing these dreams on credit. It used to be that if you wanted a new car, an expensive wedding, a trip to Paris, or a remodeled kitchen, you saved for it. Now, people frequently rely on credit cards or loans, creating large debts with high interest rates. That is a costly mistake! You need to save. (See Chapter 1, "Committing to Living Within Your Means," and Chapter 4, "Managing Debt" for more information).
- **Creating and maintaining generational wealth:** For some, creating generational wealth is not a financial priority. You may not have children or heirs to pass your assets onto, or perhaps you believe that every family member should achieve financial independence on their own. Others, however, feel a deep moral obligation to ensure that the next generation is better off than the one that came before. Whether or not this becomes one of your primary financial goals is entirely up to you. The importance of leaving a financial legacy is a highly personal decision, one that reflects your values and long-term vision. While this topic is not treated as a separate wealth management issue, it is woven throughout each chapter of this book. As you work toward achieving your own financial independence, consider how your actions today may influence your family's financial future tomorrow.

Finding Trusted Advisors

To effectively take care of all your financial needs, you will very likely need the help of several professionals, including a financial advisor, a tax advisor, a lawyer, and an insurance advisor. Please refer to Appendix A, "Selecting a Trusted Advisor," to assist you in evaluating the qualifications and the type of advisor who would be most suited to assist you. Selecting a trusted advisor to guide you to financial independence is perhaps one of the most important decisions you can make on your journey to *financial independence and create and maintain generational wealth.*

If you do not pay attention to the tax consequences of your financial position, you may end up paying significantly more in taxes than the law requires. Therefore, you must include tax planning as part of your overall wealth accumulation strategy. Using an approach that incorporates tax-smart strategies will help you preserve and grow your wealth more efficiently and maximize your financial position.

Tax-smart Strategies for Determining Your Financial Position

Here are several tax facts and strategies that will address your wealth accumulation goals in a powerful and sustainable way. This will be part of your tax-smart roadmap to financial independence. This is how you can transform the tax code into part of your generational wealth code.

This tax-smart strategies section is organized using the same format and categories found on IRS Form 1040.

Filing Status and Exemptions

- Choose the proper filing status when filing your income tax return, as it determines your standard deduction and the tax rates that will apply to your taxable income. If you qualify as *head of household*, take advantage of it. This filing status generally lowers your tax liability.
- Tax preparers are now required to exercise due diligence when verifying eligibility for head of household status, the American Opportunity Tax Credit, Earned Income Tax Credit, and Child Tax Credit. Failure to do so may result in a penalty of $500 per occurrence.
- If either of your parents qualifies as your dependent, you may claim *head of household* status even if they do not live with you, provided you pay more than half of their household expenses.
- The personal exemption, which previously allowed a deduction per taxpayer, spouse, and dependent, was eliminated under the TCJA and remains unavailable under the OBBBA. This continues to affect larger families by limiting their ability to reduce taxable income through exemptions.

Income

- Find a job for your dependent children to help fund some of their living expenses. In 2025, a dependent child can earn up to $15,750 without being subject to federal income tax, thanks to the increased standard deduction under the OBBBA.

(*continued*)

(*continued*)

- The adoption tax credit remains in place and has been adjusted for inflation. For 2025, parents may claim a nonrefundable credit of up to $17,280 for qualified adoption expenses, up to $5,000 of which may be refundable under the OBBBA. This amount may be excluded from income if provided as employer assistance, but you cannot claim both for the same expenses.
- If you qualify for the foreign bona fide residence test or the physical presence test while living abroad, you may exclude up to $130,000 of foreign earned income (employee or self-employed) from federal tax in 2025. In addition, you may exclude housing costs exceeding a base amount of $20,800, subject to caps based on location. Depending on your qualifying foreign income and foreign location, special rules and limitations apply.
- You can contribute up to $5,000 of pre-tax income to a dependent care flexible spending account (FSA) to help offset childcare expenses for 2025. You may use both the FSA and the childcare credit, although you cannot use them for the same expenses. Starting in tax year 2026, the OBBBA increases the Dependent Care FSA limit to $7,500 per household (and $3,750 for married filing separately).
- You may exclude up to $250,000 ($500,000 if married filing jointly) of gain on the sale of your primary residence if you owned and used the home for at least two years during the five-year period ending with the date of the sale. This tax-free income is by far one of the most favorable reasons for home ownership.

Adjustments to Gross Income

- While the TCJA eliminated the moving expense deduction for most taxpayers beginning in 2018, the OBBBA made this suspension permanent. The deduction is now preserved only for active-duty members of the US Armed Forces who move due to a permanent change of station. All other taxpayers remain permanently ineligible to deduct moving costs.
- The TCJA eliminated the alimony payment deduction for the payer and the inclusion as income for the payee. For any divorce or separation agreement executed after December 31, 2018, the Act provides that alimony and separation maintenance payments are not deductible by the paying spouse. It also repeals the provision that considered these payments as income by the receiving spouse. Any divorces finalized before January 1, 2019, will be grandfathered in, allowing the continued deduction for qualifying alimony and reporting of payment received as income. It is important to note that any modifications made to an existing divorce agreement will then be subject to the new rules. The OBBBA made this treatment permanent, so these rules now apply indefinitely.

- For 2025, K–12 teachers, instructors, counselors, principals, and aides may deduct up to $300 of eligible unreimbursed classroom expenses ($600 if both spouses qualify and file jointly). You must work at least 900 hours per year in a school that provides elementary or secondary education. Eligible expenses include books, supplies, equipment, software, professional development, and other classroom-related materials.

Itemized Deductions

- The standard deduction has increased under the OBBBA and IRS inflation indexing. For 2025, the standard deduction is $15,750 for individuals, $23,600 for head of household, and $31,500 for married couples filing jointly. Taxpayers age 65 or older and blind individuals receive an additional $2,000 if single or head of household, or $1,600 per spouse if married filing jointly. With these significantly higher amounts, far less taxpayers will itemize their deductions.
- Beginning in 2025, the OBBBA created a new additional standard deduction for seniors. Individuals age 65 or older may claim an extra $6,000 deduction on top of the base standard deduction and the existing aged/blind addition. Married couples filing jointly may claim up to $12,000 if both spouses qualify. This provision is designed to reduce taxable income for older Americans on social security below certain income limitations.
- Charitable contribution deductions are allowed up to 60% of your adjusted gross income (AGI) for cash gifts if you qualify to itemize. Beginning in 2026, however, the OBBBA introduces a new 0.5% AGI floor for individuals, meaning the first 0.5% of your AGI given to charity will not be deductible, and also creates a new above-the-line deduction of up to $1,000 ($2,000 if married filing jointly) for taxpayers who do not itemize.
- If you are planning to make a large charitable contribution to a qualified charitable organization, consider donating appreciated property such as stocks, bonds, mutual funds, exchange-traded funds, or real estate that you have held for more than one year. You can deduct the full fair market value of the property, and the gain will not be subject to tax. This strategy increases your deduction while avoiding capital gains taxes.
- If you will be itemizing deductions and expect to be in a higher tax bracket this year than next, consider prepaying your January mortgage payment in December. You will get the tax deduction this year, and the tax break will be greater if your tax bracket is lower next year. This strategy is especially helpful if you receive a large bonus or gain from the sale of property or investments.
- Increase your tax-free income by ensuring your employer reimburses you for business-related expenses that meet employer and IRS guidelines. These include business travel, meals, vehicle expenses, and continuing education.

(*continued*)

(*continued*)

Since 2018, unreimbursed employee business expenses are no longer deductible, so employer reimbursement under an accountable plan is essential.

- The loss of the unreimbursed employee business expenses can be remedied by speaking to your employer about setting up an accountable plan to reimburse you for these out-of-pocket work expenses. Since you are no longer allowed to take these deductions as an itemized deduction, this is a must. This will give you an opportunity to pay for these work-related expenses in pre-tax dollars.
- You can still write off personal gambling losses to the extent of winnings, provided you itemize deductions and your itemized total exceeds the standard deduction. However, under the OBBBA, beginning in 2026, gambling loss deductions will be capped at 90% of gambling winnings. This means at least 10% of gambling winnings will always remain taxable, even if your losses equal or exceed your winnings.
- Casualty and theft losses are deductible only if tied to federally declared disasters or, beginning in 2026, certain state-declared disasters (expanded by the OBBBA). Deductible losses must still be reduced by $500 per incident but are not subject to the 10% of AGI threshold when tied to a qualified disaster. Losses not meeting that criteria remain wholly nondeductible.
- As of 2018, you are no longer able to take an itemized deduction for such items as personal tax preparation fees, safety deposit boxes, and other personal investment-related expenses, as well as other miscellaneous items that were previously deductible and subject to the 2% AGI limitation.
- It is important to now *allocate costs* such as tax preparation fee to the individual schedules prepared, such as Schedule C for self-employed or Schedule E for rental properties. These costs are deductible under these schedules if they directly relate to these activities, but no longer deductible on Schedule A as a personal itemized deduction.
- You should pay all your IRA fees directly from your IRA account since you are no longer allowed an itemized deduction for these fees on your Schedule A.
- Starting January 1, 2018, high-income taxpayers benefited from the repeal of the overall limitation on itemized deductions (known as the Pease limitation). Under the OBBBA, beginning in 2026, a new phaseout applies for taxpayers in the 37% bracket: allowable itemized deductions are reduced by 2% of adjusted gross income (AGI) above the applicable threshold. This provision limits deductions for the highest earners without reinstating the prior Pease rules.
- The most controversial aspect of the TCJA regarding individual taxpayers involved the state and local tax (SALT) itemized deduction. The TCJA capped the deduction at $10,000 for all filers. Under the OBBBA, this cap is raised to $40,000, retroactively to January 1, 2025, and the cap is indexed to increase

by 1% per year through 2029. However, the SALT deduction becomes subject to a phaseout once modified AGI exceeds $500,000, effectively reducing the benefit for higher-income households.

- If you own unimproved investment or non-income-producing land, you should consider making a section 266 election under the new tax law. This election would allow you to capitalize any real estate taxes and interest to the cost of the land rather than deducting it in the current year. You can elect to capitalize one or both of these costs. If you otherwise would not be entitled to a deduction because of the new limitations, you would then be able to deduct these costs as part of your cost basis upon the sale of your property. This election must be made on an annual basis and requires a statement to be attached to your tax return.
- High-income earners who reside in high tax states have a bigger incentive to move to states that do not impose their own income tax, such as Alaska, Florida, New Hampshire, Nevada, South Dakota, Tennessee, Texas, Washington, and Wyoming. By moving to a no-income-tax state and establishing residency there, you may avoid paying state and local income tax.
- With the significant changes mentioned above, millions of taxpayers will no longer be able to benefit from itemizing their personal tax deductions. With the reduction and elimination of many previously deductible items, the standard deduction may become the better choice for most. This move toward simplification of personal tax preparation should make preparing your tax return much easier and should also dramatically reduce the odds of an IRS tax audit going forward.

Tax and Credits

- The TCJA set individual income tax rates at 10%, 12%, 22%, 24%, 32%, 35%, and 37%, giving Americans the opportunity to keep more of what they make. These brackets have now been made permanent under the OBBBA.
- The vast majority of taxpayers that were subject to the AMT tax in the past were in that position because of the required add-back in the AMT calculation for state and local income tax, sales tax, real estate taxes, and miscellaneous itemized deductions. Reduction and elimination of many of these add back items has made AMT a nonfactor for most taxpayers. The OBBBA made the higher AMT exemption permanent.
- If you finalize an adoption and pay qualified adoption expenses before the end of the year, you may qualify for the adoption credit. Under the OBBBA, this credit has been increased, made partially refundable up to $5,000, and will continue to be indexed annually for inflation.
- Under the OBBBA, you may now be able to claim a child tax credit of $2,200 for each qualifying child who is younger than age 17 at the end of the year.

(*continued*)

(*continued*)

The maximum refundable amount of this credit is $1,700. The modified AGI threshold at which these credits begin to phase out was increased substantially to $400,000 for married taxpayers filing a joint return and $200,000 for other taxpayers.

- A nonrefundable credit of $500 for qualifying dependents, who are not your qualifying children, may be available to you.
- If your children are 17 years old or older or you care for elderly relatives, you can claim a nonrefundable $500 credit.
- The Child and Dependent Care Credit is expanded under the OBBBA. Starting with tax year 2026, the maximum allowable expenses remain $3,000 for one qualifying individual and $6,000 for two or more. The credit rate has increased to a maximum of 50% for families with AGI up to $15,000, then phases down by 1% for each additional $2,000 of AGI, reaching 35% at $75,000 AGI ($150,000 for joint filers), and floors at 20% beyond that. This provides a greater tax credit for those families with lower incomes.
- If you have a qualifying dependent of any age who is disabled and lives with the taxpayer for more than half of the year, you may still qualify for the dependent care credit described above.
- The marriage penalty has been largely eliminated, except at the very highest income levels. Under pre-2018 tax rules, two single individuals each earning $80,000 would have fallen into the 25% bracket; if they had married, their combined $160,000 income would have placed them in the 28% bracket, triggering a marriage penalty. Under today's seven-bracket system (made permanent by the OBBBA), most bracket thresholds for married couples are exactly double those for single filers, so the penalty no longer applies for middle-income households. However, at the top 37% bracket, parity is not perfect: in 2025, the 37% bracket starts above $626,350 for single filers but only above $751,600 for married filing jointly, so couples with combined taxable income above that level will still face a marriage penalty.
- Under current law, the "kiddie tax" applies to a child's net unearned income. For 2025, the first $1,350 of unearned income is tax-free, the next $1,350 is taxed at the child's rate, and any amount over $2,700 is taxed at the parents' marginal rate. Earned income is taxed using the child's own tax brackets. The kiddie tax generally applies to children under age 18 and to full-time students ages 19–23 who don't provide more than half of their own support.

Payments

- Do not use the government as your banker. When cash flow is tight, it may be tempting to pay other bills before paying your required taxes, but this is a costly mistake. The IRS charges interest on unpaid balances, currently 7%

annually for 2025, compounded daily (adjusted quarterly based on federal short-term rates). In addition, a failure-to-pay penalty of 0.5% per month (up to a maximum of 25% of the unpaid tax) applies, and if you fail to file altogether, the penalty is far harsher, 5% per month, up to 25%. Combined, these charges can quickly make tax underpayments far more expensive than other forms of borrowing. The government should always be treated as the lender of last resort.

- If you discover that you have not taken advantage of tax deductions or credits that you were entitled to, you can file an amended return to claim an additional refund. Generally, the statute of limitations is three years from the date you filed your tax return. Therefore, if you uncover a recurring error, you can claim a refund for the last three years of tax returns. This is a great way to improve your cash flow, and another reason to meet with your tax advisor throughout the year.
- You may be able to qualify for the Earned Income Tax Credit if you have qualifying children and meet certain requirements. In limited cases, you may also qualify for this credit even if you do not have children. For tax year 2025, the maximum credit is $8,046 for married taxpayers filing jointly with three or more qualifying children, $7,152 for two children, $4,328 for one child, and $649 with no children. Eligibility and credit amounts are based on your income, filing status, and number of children. If you consider yourself a low-income earner, this credit is most definitely worth exploring.

An Action Plan for Determining Your Financial Position

1. **Prepare your personal statement of financial position.** To know your true financial net worth, you need to prepare this statement and update it at least once a year. You can utilize the worksheet on our website to accomplish this at www.ventotaxandwealth.com, selecting "Getting to Point X" and scrolling down to "Fillable Forms."
2. **Analyze your statement of financial position** as your first step in developing financial goals and implementing prudent financial strategies to help you achieve financial independence and create and maintain generational wealth.
3. **Prepare your personal statement of cash flow** as detailed as possible. Working together with your spouse and children, identify and eliminate as much nonessential expenditures as possible. Use the worksheet on my website to assist you.

(continued)

(continued)

4. **Analyze your statement of cash flow** as your second step in developing financial goals and implementing prudent financial strategies to help you achieve financial independence and create and maintain generational wealth. This must include analyzing your cash inflows and cash outflows to implement strategies to increase your inflows and minimize your outflows.
5. **Pay yourself first.** Use the money you save to decrease your bad debt and increase your invested assets.
6. **Establish your financial goals and define your lifestyle.** Carefully figure out what *wealth* means to you and then determine how you can financially achieve and support that lifestyle. Of course, discipline yourself and members of your family to live within your means, no matter what sort of lifestyle you choose.
7. **Set long-term goals.** Annually, set goals for where you would like to be financially one year from now, five years from now, and in your retirement years. Revisit these goals throughout the year to make sure you are on track.
8. **Work with a highly qualified tax advisor and financial planner** who best suits your needs and work with them closely throughout the year to identify additional tax and money saving opportunities. See Appendix A, "Selecting a Trusted Advisor."
9. **Familiarize yourself with current tax-smart strategies.** Discuss them with your tax advisor throughout the year and incorporate them into your personal life.
10. **Use the tax-smart roadmap to financial independence to transform the tax code into part of your generational wealth code.**

CHAPTER 4

Managing Debt

Debt is the slavery of the free.
—Publilius Syrus, Ancient Latin Writer and Former Slave

Case Study: How Two Doctors Went Bankrupt in Only a Few Years, What Not to Do

In March 2006, a young, recently married couple from Baltimore became clients at our firm. Both Ethan and Olivia Martin were physicians who had recently completed their residencies and were about to embark on their careers. Ethan was an internist, and Olivia was a gynecologist and pediatrician. At the time, both Ethan and Olivia had found positions in existing practices. Of course, they were no longer interns, but they were the low doctors on the totem pole in their respective practices and, like most young professionals, had much to learn. Nevertheless, one of their dreams was to set up a full-service family practice where they could work together, and they wished to make that happen as soon as possible.

Ethan and Olivia expressed concerns about starting their professional and married lives with a combined student loan debt of more than $600,000, which was even more significant during that time. Yes, this is a lot of money, but they were both only 30 years old, and their medical careers would provide them with the opportunities to make a well-above-average income for many years to come. With persistence, a focus on saving for larger purchases (such as launching a practice or buying a home), and by avoiding unnecessary credit card debt, their long-term outlook could have been solid.

Unfortunately, that is not the path they chose. Ethan and Olivia made just about every financial mistake imaginable, and then some. In fairness to Ethan and Olivia, they were often led astray by bankers and mortgage lenders, who in my opinion, exercised behavior that bordered on unethical.

Instead of deciding to work for four or five years with other doctors in established practices (to learn the realities of the day-to-day life of a doctor and the business of running a medical practice) and saving their money, they immediately borrowed more than $500,000 to establish a family practice of their own. The bank (which was a specialty cash flow lender) was willing to provide the funds based on Ethan and Olivia's *potential* income (future cash flow), not their financial reality, which was, quite literally, no cash, no patients, absolutely no experience managing a medical practice, and a half million dollars of student loan debt. But Ethan and Olivia were feeling flush with their success (or the idea of it), and none of the advice provided by the so-called experts from their banks hinted that they might be living in a dream world, or more to the point, in a financial nightmare.

And things got worse. While they took out their business loan, they leased two cars, a Mercedes-Benz and a BMW, which they viewed as rewards for their hard work during medical school as well as symbols of their (potential) success. The monthly payments on the car leases seemed affordable, and, again, the financing company was more than willing to put up the money for the loans.

Ethan and Olivia found a location for their new practice, and they moved ahead with leasing the space, but it needed lots of renovation to become usable as a medical office. They thought the renovation would take three or four months, so they both kept their respective positions. Still, with both working full-time and building out a medical office at the same time, they ran into several challenges.

The construction ran into additional delays and ultimately took 11 months to complete, not the four months they had originally planned, which, for one thing, adversely affected their business loan. Still, their bank said, "No problem," and instead generously offered to defer the payments on their business loan. These deferred payments were simply added to the principal of their loan. Therefore, on top of the $500,000 they borrowed to build out the office, they now owed an additional $50,000 in interest, which had accumulated over the additional 11 months. That is nearly an 11% annualized interest rate.

During the months they were waiting for their office to be ready, they also decided to look for a house to buy so they could get out of the relatively small one-bedroom apartment they were renting in downtown Baltimore. They met with a realtor who, in turn, introduced them to a mortgage broker. They soon found their dream home (five bedrooms, five baths, a beautiful yard, an in-ground pool, etc.), which was selling for "only" $1,400,000. They still had no savings for a down payment or cash for the closing costs, and the earnings from their jobs just barely covered their monthly expenses. But shockingly, the mortgage broker was able to work with a bank to provide them with some creative financing.

The bank was willing to give Ethan and Olivia 80% financing if the seller was willing to provide an inflated purchase price on their contract and then give back a seller concession for that amount. In essence, the seller agreed to artificially increase the contract price of the home so that Ethan and Olivia would qualify for a larger loan. With this type of loan, at the closing, the seller agrees to lower the price, which ultimately allows the borrower to borrow more than 80% of the purchase price. This was a very common practice before the housing collapse of 2008. The banks, the lawyers, and the government regulators were fully aware of this practice and encouraged it to promote home ownership.

(Today, any attempt to inflate the purchase price and offset it with a concession would be considered loan fraud, exposing both the buyer and seller to serious legal and financial consequences. After the 2008 crisis, regulators and lenders tightened oversight dramatically. Although seller concessions are still allowed, they must be fully disclosed and can no longer be disguised as an inflated purchase price. Lenders rely on independent appraisals, and if the appraisal does not come in to support the loan amount, the loan amount will be reduced. Fannie Mae/Freddie Macs now have stricter concession limits.)

The bank was also "nice enough" to make it an *interest-only loan* with negative amortization. This meant that Ethan and Olivia were paying only part of the monthly interest on their mortgage loan; meanwhile, the principal balance increased every month, making the monthly payment more affordable in the short-term. The mortgage broker also provided them with a *combo loan*, which allowed them to take on a home-equity loan for the remaining 20% of the purchase price.

Ethan and Olivia were overjoyed. Their particular American Dream (two successful doctors, practicing together in their own office, and living in a beautiful home) seemed to be coming true very quickly, and they did not have to come up with a cent to pay for any of it. Or so it seemed, at least for a short period. They moved into their big new house and furnished it completely, putting most of their purchases on multiple credit cards, which banks and other financial institutions were only too eager to give them.

By the time the renovation of their office was finally done, they were already having a difficult time making their monthly payments for their home mortgage, car leases, credit cards, and of course all their business loans and expenses. Also, at this time, Ethan quit his salaried position to focus full-time on building up their new practice. Olivia continued with her position because they felt it could be useful to have at least some guaranteed income coming in.

But life is full of surprises, and something unexpected happened. Not long after their office was finished and Ethan began the practice, they learned they were going to have a baby. Although they were becoming increasingly worried about their finances, and a child would certainly add to their financial burdens, they were thrilled. To complicate matters, six months into her pregnancy, Olivia had to stop working for medical reasons and remain resting at home. Then, after the birth of their beautiful and healthy baby boy, she stayed home for an additional six months to care for their new son.

Throughout this time, Ethan was not earning enough through their practice to be able to draw a salary; in fact, he began tapping into his personal credit cards for an additional $150,000 just to keep the practice and his family afloat. Not only were Ethan and Olivia sinking under their financial obligations, but in late 2008, soon after the birth of their son, the national (and international) economy spiraled into a severe recession.

People were not spending money unless it was absolutely necessary, making it very difficult for Ethan to bring new patients into his practice. Banks were no longer making loans unless they knew for certain that the loans could be paid back. As a result, Ethan and Olivia couldn't borrow from Bank *A* to make their payments to Banks *B*, *C*, or *D* and so on, a practice they had become quite good at. The credit card companies lowered their credit limits and started to demand repayment of loans that were greater than a certain limit. Real estate prices tumbled, and the house they had paid $1.4 million for only two years earlier was appraised for only $800,000, making it impossible for them to sell the house without still owing a significant debt, with no hope of ever being able to repay it.

Although Ethan began to be able to draw a small salary from the practice and Olivia went back to work full-time at her original position, their liabilities exceeded their assets by more than $2 million, and their cash outflow far exceeded their cash inflow. They had no choice but to seek bankruptcy protection against their creditors.

Today, they are finally starting to see the light at the end of the tunnel. They were forced to sell their home in a short sale; they gave up their fancy cars; and they are now finally living within their means. The bankruptcy eliminated all their credit card debt, and they were able to renegotiate the terms of their business loans, which put them in a position that will allow them to pay their monthly obligations. The damage they did to their credit took seven years to repair, and there is no telling how many years the stress has taken off their lives.

Basic Principles for Managing Debt

Ethan and Olivia's story sounds incredible, but not only is it true, it is surprisingly similar to the financial life stories of thousands of Americans who are living far beyond their means. Over the past decade, many people have experienced severe financial setbacks due to economic disruptions, from global recessions to the pandemic to periods of high inflation. While the economy has shown signs of resilience, job loss, underemployment, and rising costs have pushed many households into unsustainable debt.

However, for many others, their financial crises are the result of irresponsible behavior toward money. The fault lies with individuals, as well as financial institutions and our own government, which failed to regulate, and in fact encouraged, this type of behavior. Since 2008, both the regulators and bankers have been implementing stricter lending practices, which was a move in the right direction. Unfortunately, history tends to repeat itself, but we are hopeful that reading this chapter will prevent you and others from doing the same.

Ethan and Olivia's story could have had a much different ending if they had simply followed some basic financial principles like those outlined in the following sections.

Learn the Meaning of Financial Responsibility

Being financially responsible implies learning the basics of personal financial literacy: calculating your net worth, tracking and carefully watching your cash flow, and learning about the other financial tools required to make you secure. In Ethan and Olivia's case, they were clueless about their personal financial situation while working toward opening a medical practice, which is a business proposition that requires a tremendous amount of financial savvy. They made no efforts to teach themselves about personal and business financial practices until it was too late.

Live Within Your Means and Always Pay Yourself First

Ethan and Olivia started their life together at "less than zero" financially by a huge amount; they had student loans of more than $600,000. Had they begun working in established practices, determined how much they could earn as medical doctors, assessed their net worth, created a thoughtful and realistic cash flow, and, most of all begun saving, they could have moved toward the lifestyle that represented their American Dream on a much surer footing.

Know (and Respect) the Difference Between Your Wants *and* Needs

Ethan and Olivia *wanted* to share a successful medical practice, but they *needed* to learn more about the real life of a doctor and to begin saving for their goals. They *wanted* a lavish and beautiful home, but they *needed* a roof over their heads. They *wanted* to drive expensive automobiles and have all the other trappings that indicated success, but they *needed* a modest car (maybe two), some furniture, and some savings for unexpected surprises such as a baby. Even with their student loans, they could have bought a small house, decorated it modestly, and started saving for their joint family practice. They might even have bought a larger house where they could have both lived and worked. In any case, they did not need it all at once.

As mortgage expert, John Manning, an experienced and highly ethical mortgage broker, advises his clients when purchasing a home, "*Live like you're broke. Don't buy anything. Don't take a vacation. Don't get a new car. Nothing. Even after you close. Wait a year to see how much your house really costs. Then you can buy the things you want but not necessarily need.*"

Learn to Say No

Of course, they should have been saying *no* to many things from the beginning. This doesn't mean they needed to deprive themselves of every luxury, but to quote a useful cliché, *if something looks too good to be true, it probably is.* For example, the ease at which they were able to get both a large business loan and a home mortgage loan should have been red flags, especially because they initially felt uneasy about carrying their student loans. They should have said *no* to starting their own medical practice before they were ready. They should have said *no* to owning an enormous, expensive house when a modest one would have served them well for many years. They should have said *no* to driving two expensive cars when two more modest ones would have been sufficient. And they should have said *no* to buying all the items that resulted in their maxed-out credit cards.

Although many individuals face difficulties with debt, Ethan and Olivia's story remains one of the most extreme tales of poor debt management. Managing debt is critical if you want to achieve *financial independence. However*, as Ethan and Olivia's story illustrates, managing debt can be complicated and difficult, even for intelligent, well-intentioned people, and it can get out of hand quickly and disastrously.

To achieve financial independence, you must first fully understand the concept of debt, and then you must make sure your own personal debt is under control.

Debt Red Flags: 10 Warning Signs You're Headed Toward Trouble

1. You are approved for large loans with little to no documentation.
2. You feel pressure to buy now and figure it out later.
3. You are borrowing based on future income, not current savings or cash flow.
4. Monthly payments are manageable only because of teaser rates or interest-only terms.
5. You rely on credit cards for everyday living expenses.
6. You feel anxious or unsure before signing but go through with it anyway.
7. You make financial decisions to keep up with peers or to project success.
8. You skip savings goals in favor of lifestyle purchases.
9. You do not fully understand the terms of your loans or leases.
10. You assume future raises or promotions will fix shortfalls.

Good Debt Versus *Bad* Debt

Debt. In a funny way, the word alone conjures up dank Dickensian prisons in the backstreets of London, where families were chucked inside, starving, because they owed the local butcher, baker, and candlestick-maker.

Debtors' prisons, as these sorts of places were known, imprisoned people (together with their families) who were unable to pay their bills. Although the act of being imprisoned for nonpayment of debt was outlawed in the late nineteenth century, in today's world of relatively trouble-free bankruptcy, some financial experts believe it might not be a bad idea to bring it back. That would be extreme, but there are times when it seems far too easy for people to walk away almost scot-free from gross financial irresponsibility. As a society, we need to move away from rewarding people for bad behavior and penalizing them for good behavior.

Conversely, for many people, debt is a scary concept, although it need not be. The fact is that not all debt is *bad debt.* Some debt is not only *good* but also essential for establishing good credit, and it can be an important factor in growing wealth and helping you achieve financial independence. In any case, understanding the difference between *bad debt* and *good debt* is imperative to becoming financially literate and financially independent.

Basically, *good debt* is money that people borrow for purchases and situations that, in the long term, will help them amass wealth and ultimately achieve financial independence. Some examples of *good debt* includes student loans, business loans, certain investment asset loans, and some personal-use asset loans, such as an affordable home mortgage.

In contrast, *bad debt* is money that people borrow (usually on a credit card) for the purchase of nonessential expenditures, as well as many personal-use assets. (Recall from Chapter 3 that personal-use assets are assets that define your lifestyle, such as homes, automobiles, boats, jewelry, works of fine art, etc.) These items have value, but they require additional expense to maintain them, and, in some cases (such as with a car or boat), they depreciate over time. Another way to define *bad debt* versus *good debt* is to consider whether the item is an *essential* or *nonessential* expense; is it a *need* or is it a *want?*

For example, if you wish to become a doctor, you may *need* to take out a student loan to pay for your education, putting you in substantial debt for many years. However, ultimately, you will be able to use your education to earn an above-average living. As a result, this is *good debt.* However, if after earning your degree, you *want* to buy all the accoutrements that supposedly define success or an affluent lifestyle, like luxury cars and large houses, you can put yourself in serious financial straits, as Ethan and Olivia did. This, of course, is *bad debt.*

When you do not use debt properly, it can lead to significant financial hardship and can prevent you from ever becoming financially independent. However, when you use debt to leverage yourself in the pursuit of accumulating wealth, it can be a very powerful tool.

Credit Card Debt

The most common form of consumer debt is credit card debt. In today's world, we can use a credit card to charge anything from a toothbrush to a summer vacation in Europe. However, if we do not pay off the credit card charges when the bill arrives, the money used to buy the items purchased with the card becomes *debt.* Credit card debt is like cancer; if not properly controlled, it can destroy financial health.

Ideally, you should use credit cards only as a convenient form of payment, which is often safer than using cash. Nevertheless, you should pay any credit card charges at the end of each billing month. If you cannot afford to pay your complete credit card balance at the end of each month, whether you have used it to buy a sweater or a sofa, you are *going into debt* to pay for the item or items you have purchased. Not only that, but you are going to *pay interest* on those purchases, often quite a large interest, so the item is costing you much more than you originally thought.

Basically, when you start using your credit cards without paying them off each month, you are subtly (or perhaps not so subtly) indicating that *you cannot really afford the purchases you have made.* To put it another way, these purchases are very likely *nonessential*; they are *wants* rather than *needs.* And when you begin charging true *essentials on your credit cards,* such as food, medications, or diapers, and are unable to pay for them when the bill comes due, you may be on the brink of financial disaster.

The Insatiable Credit Card

Credit card companies sometimes offer teaser rates of 0% so that you will use their credit card and maintain a running balance for a few months. Do not fall for this; it is a trap that lures you in until you have charged more than you can pay for, and then they sock you with a double-digit interest rate after the teaser rate period ends. Likewise, some retail stores offer 10%, 15%, or even 25% discounts on purchases, if you are willing to apply for an in-store credit card. Do not be lured in unless you can pay off the purchases when the bill shows up in your mailbox. Again, it is just a way to make you feel that you can afford a host of *nonessentials.* Credit cards can eat you alive.

To understand the voracious nature of credit cards and what it can mean to your financial future, consider the following scenario. Your end-of-summer vacation week is coming up and you have no plans. You go online and find a great vacation package to Montreal for you and your spouse. This vacation will cost you $2,000, plus you have always wanted to go to Montreal. (Note the term *want.*) You book the trip, have a nice week away, and then with all the incidentals and souvenirs included, you realize that your trip cost you closer to $3,000. At the end of the month, you have a few other unexpected bills, so you do not have the cash available to pay for the trip when the bill arrives, and you leave the charges on your card.

Over the next four months, several old friends come to visit from out of town, and you decide to entertain them at a few expensive restaurants and throw in a couple of concerts and some sporting events; before you know it, you have added another $2,000 to your credit card.

Now winter is approaching, and you *need* a new winter coat. While you are out shopping, you see a few great buys on sweaters and simply cannot resist a pair of expensive boots. Suddenly, you have added another $2,000 to your credit card.

Now, it is a week before Christmas, and you realize that you have not purchased any gifts for your relatives and friends. You do not have a lot of extra cash, but, yes, you do have that credit card. There goes another $3,000.

Without really thinking about it, you have just spent $10,000 over just a few months for the purchases of any number of nonessential items, all *wants,* not *needs.* You have justified this in your own mind, since your monthly minimum payment is only $200, an amount you can comfortably cover each month.

However, let us take a closer look at this scenario. You now have a $10,000 credit card balance, the interest rate on your card is 23% (not unusual), and the minimum monthly payment is 2% of the balance, or $200. The fact is, if you pay only the minimum each month, *it will take you more than 15 years to pay off this credit card balance;* even worse, *you will end up paying more than $26,000 in interest.* In other words, over that period, *you would be paying* more than $39,000 for those nonessential items that you originally thought cost you $10,000, nearly four times more than you expected. These purchases, and undisciplined financial planning, have robbed you of the potential to save that $39,000 toward reaching your financial independence.

Every time you use a credit card to pay for a nonessential item that you cannot afford to pay for at the end of the month, you are severely jeopardizing your financial future. Money can compound quickly, or grow exponentially, almost magically, if it is saved. The power of compounding can be your best friend or your worst enemy, depending on whether you choose to be a saver or a spender. (For a detailed discussion on the power of compounding, see Chapter 12, "The Time Value of Money.") This same powerful tool has the *opposite* effect if you borrow money or maintain a large balance on your credit cards. Your debt can compound as quickly and magically as your savings. You cannot accumulate wealth if you are maintaining balances on your credit cards.

Paying Down Credit Card Debt

When evaluating a client's statement of financial position, it is often apparent that he or she is maintaining credit card balances and paying double-digit interest rates, sometimes as high as 20% or more. At the same time, the client has money sitting in bank savings accounts or invested in other assets that are earning a lower rate of return than the interest being paid on credit cards. In situations like these, it is usually wise to use the available cash to pay off the credit card debt.

Let us assume you are paying your credit card company 20% interest on a $7,000 credit card balance, and at the same time, you have $15,000 in a savings account earning 1% interest, as well as $25,000 in an aggressive mutual fund account, where you hope to earn 10% or more on average per year over the long run while taking on a greater degree of risk. If you had the following choices, which one would you choose?

1. Would you want to earn 1% on your money in your savings account (taxable as ordinary income) with FDIC insurance?
2. Would you want to possibly earn 10% (while taking on a greater deal of risk) on average over the long run through an aggressive mutual fund (taxable at capital gain rates)?
3. Would you want to save 20% interest tax-free on $7,000, guaranteed by paying off your credit card balance?

The answer is obvious: you would pick option 3, which is 20% guaranteed tax-free savings. Therefore, if you have high credit card balances, your best investment choice would be to *eliminate that debt.* One caveat: if you use your savings or investments to pay off your credit card debt, you must not turn around and run up more credit card debt as soon as your cards are clear. Sooner or later, you will run out of money, and you will find yourself in even worse financial shape.

Other Surprising Resources for Reducing Debt

If you do not want to raid your savings or money market accounts, other resources may help bring out-of-control credit card debt back in line. Here are a few suggestions.

Take Out a Home-equity Loan If you own your home and have sufficient equity, you might want to consider taking out a home-equity line of credit and using it to pay off your credit card debt. A home-equity loan can help you in several ways. First, by using the loan to pay down the credit card debt, you are trading a 20–25% interest rate (on your credit cards) for a 7.5–8% interest rate (on the home-equity loan). The other advantage to a home-equity loan is that although it spreads your payments over many years, it can help you improve your monthly cash flow.

As of 2025, the tax deductibility of the interest on a home equity loan is limited to situations where the loan proceeds are used to buy, build, or substantially improve the home that secures the loan. However, it can still be a useful tool in lowering your cost of financing and bringing down your monthly obligation.

Please be aware that credit card debt is unsecured and home-equity loans are secured against your home. In other words, debtors can put a lien against your house with a home-equity loan. For this reason, this approach is not right for everyone. If you are significantly in debt and could potentially have to file for bankruptcy at some point, switching unsecured debt for secure debt would not be the best choice.

Borrow Against Your Life Insurance If you have a whole-life insurance policy, you can borrow against it and use the money to pay your debt. However, be sure to pay it back. If you die before the loan from the policy is paid off, the outstanding balance (plus interest) will be deducted from the death benefit of the policy, meaning your beneficiaries will pay the price.

Borrow Against Your 401(k) If you have a healthy 401(k) account, you may be able to borrow up to 50% of its value or $50,000, whichever is less. The interest is lower than credit cards, plus you are borrowing from yourself, not a bank or mortgage lender.

Bear in mind that borrowing from your 401(k) can have severe drawbacks, including these:

- You will be paying back the loan and its interest with after-tax dollars.
- You must repay the loan within five years.
- If you have a qualified retirement plan loan that becomes taxable because you left your job or defaulted on the loan, current law gives you more time to roll it over tax-free into another qualified plan. Instead of the previous 60-day deadline, you now have until the due date of your federal income tax return, including extensions, for the year the loan offset is treated as a distribution. If you discover before your filing deadline that you would owe taxes and a penalty, you can still complete the rollover in time to avoid both.

This strategy is not ideal, but it's better than using a credit card.

Borrow from Family and Friends If you find yourself deep in credit card debt, consider borrowing from your parents, your siblings, your rich great-aunt or uncle, or your best friend to get rid of the money-sucking interest on a high credit card balance. However, be sure to arrange to pay them back quickly, preferably with interest, not only to preserve good relationships, but to be sure that you treat this transaction as business (not a gift).

Reducing Credit Card Debt the Old-fashioned Way

What if you do not have lots of extra cash in savings, a thriving 401(k) account, equity on real estate or a life insurance policy, or a rich great-aunt, and you have run up $10,000, $15,000, $20,000, or more in credit card debt? You are probably anxious and frightened about this situation (and if you are not, you should be). But all is not lost; you can actually reduce your debt the old-fashioned way: pay it back yourself. Here are some constructive actions you can take to get yourself back on track financially if faced with off-the-charts credit card debt:

- **Stop using your credit cards:** While it is financially wise to have one or two (but not 10) active credit cards, stop using them until you pay them off. After you have paid them off, do not run up nonessential charges again. (Note: *Do not cancel* all your credit cards. Canceling your cards can have a negative effect on your credit score. When deciding which credit card to keep, always keep the one that you have had the longest. This will help you maintain an overall higher credit score. More information about credit scores is provided at the end of this chapter.)
- **Consider using a prepaid credit card or a debit card:** Visa and MasterCard offer both types of cards. *Prepaid credit cards* are prefunded reloadable cards requiring payment in advance, after which you can use the card until the payment is depleted. You can use them anywhere you can use credit cards, as well as at ATMs. *Debit cards* provide electronic access to your bank accounts, and most relay a message to the bank to withdraw funds from a designated account. You can use debit cards as you would use cash or a check.
- **Know the enemy:** Paying off credit card debt is war! You need to know yourself (and your apparent weakness for buying *nonessentials*), and you need to know and understand the details of the credit cards you have been abusing. How many cards do you have? What is the sum of all your credit card debt? What interest rates are you being charged? How quickly can you pay this down?
- **Reduce your interest rates:** Many financial institutions will lower your interest rates if your credit is good, and sometimes even if it is not so good. Contact the institution and plead your case or put higher-interest-rate balances on lower-interest-rate cards.
- **Take advantage of 0% APR offers:** Many credit card companies offer 0% introductory APR promotions, which means you may not be charged interest on qualifying purchases for a set period, often ranging from 6 to 21 months. These offers can be useful for consolidating balances or making planned purchases, but only if you are confident that you can repay the balance in full before the introductory period ends. Be

cautious not to open too many new accounts, as this can hurt your credit and tempt overspending.

- **Set a due date to repay your debt:** As with any long-term project, it helps to have a firm goal in terms of time. Depending on how much debt you have, give yourself a date when you want to finish paying off your debt. Recheck your date each month, and make sure you are making significant progress.
- **Give yourself a break:** Paying off credit card debt is admirable and rewarding, but it is like dieting, it takes strength and discipline, and you occasionally need to have a treat. This does not mean you should charge a trip to Paris on your newly cleared credit card. In fact, avoid anything having to do with credit cards. But perhaps, using cash, buy yourself a new outfit or enjoy dinner at your favorite restaurant. In other words, spend a little money, just do not put it on a credit card.

Auto Loans

Buying a car is usually the first major purchase any of us make. However, unless you are a 17-year-old who has saved up tips to buy a third-hand jalopy, or unless you have significant disposable cash, you are most likely going to need an auto loan to purchase a new car. Most people do not buy cars frequently. In fact, the average length of car ownership in the United States is 79 months or 6.6 years.[1] Many families have multiple vehicles, sometimes one for each member of the household. In today's market of high car prices, purchasing a vehicle can be nearly as complex as buying a home. This is true even without considering luxury vehicles like a Porsche. Buying a car is a very significant addition to your personal debt and potentially a real speed bump on your road to financial independence.

Like any major purchase, you need to research the automobile market thoroughly before deciding which car and financing structure best suit your needs. You must decide if you want to buy a used (pre-owned) car or a new car, which you will own once the loan is paid in full. Alternatively, you might consider leasing, which requires you to return the vehicle at the end of the lease term, similar to renting rather than owning.

---

[1]Perry, Z. (2025, April 21). *Car Ownership Trends: How Many Cars Do People Own?* ShunAuto. Retrieved from https://shunauto.com/article/what-is-the-average-car-ownership

For many people, the price of a car they can afford really depends on the amount of a monthly loan payment they can add to their budget. A good guideline is to allocate no more than 15% of your monthly take-home pay toward your car loan payment.

Another option to consider is whether leasing or purchasing an automobile makes the most sense for your situation. Although leasing has become a very popular way to obtain a new or used car, it may not be as attractive as some people think. If you are willing to own a car for five or more years, in general, purchasing would be much less costly in the long run than leasing would be. At the end of your loan term, you will have a car that you will own outright and have equity in it. You can use the *Should I Buy or Lease an Auto?* calculator, available at www.ventotaxandwealth.com under the Resources > Calculators & Tools section to determine if financing or leasing would be the best option for you.

A recent tax law change under the One Big Beautiful Bill Act (OBBBA) may impact your decision since it created a limited auto loan interest deduction. For tax years 2025 through 2028, interest on loans for new US-assembled vehicles used for personal purposes can be deducted above the line, up to $10,000 per year. The deduction is subject to income phaseouts (starting at $100,000 AGI for single filers and $200,000 for joint filers) and applies only if the vehicle meets final assembly requirements, as specified by the IRS.

In addition to the auto loan or the cost of the lease, you need to consider the fact that maintaining your car can be expensive. Moreover, your car comes with a host of other necessary costs: insurance, annual license plate fees, and, of course, the cost of gasoline.

Given their high cost both to purchase and maintain, automobiles can be among the most treacherous purchases we make, not only financially but also psychologically. For many people, automobiles symbolize relative status. Are you a Porsche or a Nissan type? There is nothing wrong with wanting to own a Porsche, unless you take out a loan for one when all you can really afford is the Nissan.

Most of us consider a car to be a necessity, an essential expense, a *need* rather than a *want*. However, among the many decisions involved in buying a car, some entail giving in to very expensive *wants* (a new Porsche) rather than more economical *needs* (a used Nissan). If you live within a city, public transportation would be a much more economical alternative, even if you occasionally must use a taxi or Uber.

Student Loans

Whenever you make an investment in yourself and your future that may provide you with a better life and higher income, then the money you borrow to achieve that goal should be considered *good debt.* Therefore, if you need to take out a loan (or loans) to attend college or pursue an advanced degree or professional license, you should feel comfortable that you are incurring *good debt.* With that said, be careful not to buy into the misnomer that everyone needs to go to college. Also keep in mind that, if you don't maintain good grades, you may never get that high-paying job you were counting on, which can quickly turn this *good* debt into *bad* debt. This will be discussed further in Chapter 7, "Paying for College."

If you have low-interest-rate student loans, you need not be in any rush to pay them off. Nevertheless, make sure you make every payment on time so that you can improve your credit score. (More information on credit scores is provided at the end of this chapter.) Also, student loans may allow a useful tax deduction. You may be able to deduct up to $2,500 of student loan interest paid from your taxable income if you qualify under the income threshold.

For 2025, the maximum $2,500 of student loan interest may be deductible if the taxpayer's modified adjusted gross income is below $85,000 for single and head of household taxpayers and below $170,000 for married taxpayers filing jointly. The amount of the student loan interest that is deductible is phased out with higher modified adjusted gross income (MAGI), until there is no deduction for singles and heads of households with $100,000 MAGI and married filing jointly taxpayers with $200,000 MAGI.

Although student-loan interest is considered consumer debt, if you use it wisely, your return on investment could far exceed your cost of interest. In other words, it is *good debt.*

Home Mortgage Loans

On a national, and perhaps international, level, we are still dealing with the long-term effects of one of the most serious financial debacles since the Great Depression of the 1930s. A large part of the problem had to do with a serious (some might say almost criminal) mishandling of home mortgage loans.

For several years leading up to the 2008 meltdown, banks were lending money for the purchase of homes, sometimes without even verifying a person's income (with loans called *no-income-verification loans*) or ability to repay the mortgage. If the bank determined that someone could not afford the mortgage payment, the bank would simply adjust the terms and provide an interest-only loan, an adjustable-rate loan, a balloon payment loan, or some other form of creative financing so that you could purchase a little piece (and sometimes quite a large piece) of the "American Dream."

But, of course, as we know, it ultimately all came crashing down. It has taken decades for many people to recover from the aftermath, and many more still have not recovered. Everyone was to blame, the federal government (regulators), the banks (lenders), and even the consumers (borrowers). We all should have known better. Bankers were drinking and driving, consumers went along for the ride, and the government continued to pour the wine, until they crashed the economy into the Great Recession of 2008.

It is hard to believe that it has already been more than 15 years since the financial crisis. Although many of these aggressive lending programs and practices have been eliminated, there are still programs out there sponsored by the federal government, such as the Federal Housing Administration (FHA) and state-sponsored programs, such as the State of New York Mortgage Agency (SONYMA). These programs allow as little as 3% down payment with credit scores of 580 or higher on a home purchase. Let's hope that history does not repeat itself here.

Owning a Home: Not Necessarily Good *Debt*

The notion of owning a home has long been a significant facet of the American Dream. Since the economic boom in the years following World War II, Americans came to believe that possessing a home of their own was almost a right. They certainly thought owning a house made sound financial sense, mostly because, for several decades, the value of a home escalated, sometimes very quickly.

One of the valuable lessons learned during the Great Recession of 2008 is that the value of homes can in fact go down, sometimes substantially. Buying a home and expecting its price to go up in the short-term is not a sure thing. The purchase of a home may be a good decision (and taking out a home mortgage can be considered *good debt*), but only if you can meet certain criteria.

Before you begin picking out your dream home in your favorite neighborhood, you need to figure out precisely how much house you can afford. Use the *How Much Home Can I Afford?* calculator, available at www.ventotaxandwealth.com under the Resources > Calculators & Tools section to help calculate this.

For example, if your current income is $100,000 from all sources, your monthly auto payment is $400, your minimum monthly credit card payment is $300, and your monthly student loan payment is $400, how much of a home can you afford? Before we can answer this, we also must make further assumptions that you will be taking a 30-year mortgage, can obtain a 7% interest rate, and have $100,000 available for a down payment. Based on these facts and the guidelines we have set for home affordability, you can afford to purchase a home for $328,468 with a $228,468 mortgage. Your monthly payment on this mortgage would be $1,520. This is without the real estate tax and insurance, which sometimes is added to your monthly mortgage payment when paid directly by the bank.

Moreover, before purchasing a home, it is generally advisable to have saved 20% of the total purchase price of the home as a down payment, as well as all closing costs. Finally, before you buy, you should compare the costs of renting versus the costs of purchasing. If you cannot afford the monthly payments and costs of maintaining a home, you may need to rent rather than buy or scale down your *wants*.

Also, given the high costs of acquiring (and ultimately selling) a house, you must be committed to living in this home for at least 10 years for it to begin to potentially increase in value. In addition, you should tally the everyday costs of home maintenance: property taxes, homeowner's insurance, heating, electricity, gas, and so forth. Finally, you also need to consider the cost of ongoing home maintenance: painting, major repairs, etc. And note, we have not mentioned those wonderful cosmetic accoutrements (also known as *nonessential wants*), the new furniture, the beautiful decorations, the renovated family room in the basement, the gorgeous deck, and the in-ground pool.

A house should meet your basic living standards (*needs*) and should not be based on your ego (*wants*). Still, a house can increase in value if you hang on to it for many years and maintain it well. It can also help you financially in other ways.

Why a Mortgage Is Still Good Debt

The reason a home mortgage is usually considered *good debt* is that, from the moment you buy the house, it offers certain financial reliefs and leverage. For starters, your home mortgage interest may be tax-deductible.

The deduction applies to mortgage debt up to $750,000 for loans taken out after December 15, 2017, and up to $1 million for older mortgages. This applies to combined debt on a primary and secondary residence. Interest on home-equity loans or HELOCs is only deductible if the funds were used to buy, build, or substantially improve the property securing the loan.

If you are in the 40% tax bracket (federal and state combined) and paying 6% interest on your mortgage, your after-tax financing cost might effectively be around 3.6% once the tax savings are factored in.

Real estate taxes remain deductible, and under the OBBBA for 2025, the state and local tax (SALT) cap has increased from $10,000 to $40,000 for individuals earning under $500,000 (phasing out for incomes up to $600,000). This expanded cap may allow more homeowners to itemize deductions.

After building equity by paying your mortgage over time, that equity can be leveraged for financial needs or investments. Unlike rent, which provides no tax benefits or investment value, mortgage payments help build ownership over time. This is when a mortgage clearly becomes *good* debt.

Defying the Old Adage: Why Rent When You Can Own?

In recent years, renting has emerged as a financially prudent and lifestyle-aligned choice for many Americans, particularly when compared to the escalating costs and responsibilities of homeownership. The traditional notion that "renting is just throwing money away" is being reevaluated as home prices and mortgage rates reach unprecedented highs post the pandemic.

Renting can often be a more sensible choice than buying a home, especially in today's market, where rising home prices and mortgage rates are making homeownership increasingly difficult. With home prices in the United States reaching all-time highs, and mortgage rates around 7%, making monthly payments can be significantly higher than the cost of renting. This financial strain is compounded by the limited housing inventory caused by the "lock-in effect," where homeowners with favorable mortgage rates are hesitant to sell, further driving up prices. Additionally, owning a home comes with unpredictable expenses, including maintenance costs and repairs, which can add up quickly. Homeowners also face ongoing costs such as property taxes, insurance premiums, and general upkeep. These costs can be difficult to manage, particularly when unexpected repairs arise, leading many homeowners to delay essential maintenance.

Demographic trends show that more people are opting to rent rather than buy, a shift that has been particularly noticeable in suburban areas and is driven by high home prices and mortgage rates. As a result, many individuals, including older adults and affluent millennials, are choosing the flexibility of renting over the long-term financial commitment of homeownership. Institutional investors are also taking note, investing heavily in build-to-rent communities to meet the increasing demand for rental properties. This trend reflects a broader cultural shift toward renting, as it offers greater financial flexibility and stability without the responsibilities and risks associated with homeownership.

In addition to these financial considerations, renting can be a more prudent choice for those considering a move to a new area, such as during retirement. Renting before buying allows individuals to explore a new location without committing to the substantial costs associated with purchasing a home. It's important to rent first to ensure that you truly want to settle in the area, especially since buying a home involves significant upfront costs, like closing fees and potential renovation expenses. As a rule of thumb, you should not purchase a home unless you are certain that you will want to live there for at least 10 years, as buying too early in a new location can result in expensive mistakes. Renting provides the flexibility to live in a new area for an extended period before making such a major financial commitment, giving you time to fully assess whether it's the right place to call home.

As the housing market continues to be affected by high prices, rising mortgage rates, and unexpected maintenance costs, renting is increasingly seen not as a fallback but as a strategic choice for many individuals. Renting offers financial advantages, greater flexibility, and the ability to avoid the burdens of homeownership. Renters can also benefit from investing the money they would otherwise use for a down payment, closing costs, and maintenance. Ultimately, renting makes sense when financial flexibility or the ability to explore new areas is a priority, while buying may be the right choice for those who plan to stay in one location for at least 10 years and are ready to take on the responsibilities, both financial and nonfinancial, of homeownership.

Refinancing a Home Mortgage

Over the last few years, refinancing has become far less common. During the pandemic, ultra-low interest rates sparked a surge in refinance activity, allowing millions of Americans to lower their monthly payments and improve their cash flow. But as mortgage rates climbed, doubling from their historic lows, refinancing has slowed dramatically. As of 2025, with average 30-year fixed mortgage rates hovering around 6.7%, many homeowners are choosing to hold onto the rates they locked in years ago.

Still, the basic purpose of refinancing remains unchanged. The goal is to lower the cost of borrowing, reduce your monthly expenses, and free up cash that can be used to help you move closer to your ultimate goal of financial independence.

To determine whether it makes sense to refinance your mortgage, you need to perform a breakeven analysis. Quite simply, you must determine the number of months it will take you to recover the costs of refinancing from the interest cost you will be saving.

If you plan on living in your home past your breakeven period, then generally refinancing may be the right decision for you. Many bankers and mortgage brokers determine the breakeven period by taking the total cost of refinancing divided by the monthly reduction in your mortgage payment.

Mortgage refinancing is a complex and potentially expensive process in which you pay off one or more existing debts with a new home loan. Therefore, before you refinance, you need to know what your upfront closing costs will be, what your current and new interest rates will be, and several other details. Closing costs to refinance your mortgage can include loan origination fees, appraisal fees, attorney fees, mortgage recording tax, and so forth. In some cases, these costs could be as high as 2–5% of your loan amount.

However, if the figures work, every month after your breakeven point would result in a savings to you. In some cases, you may actually be able to reduce the number of years on your loan without increasing your monthly payment. There are numerous possibilities and what-if scenarios you need to consider when refinancing. To determine if you should refinance your mortgage, you can use the *Can I Refinance My Mortgage?* calculator, available at www.ventotaxandwealth.com under the Resources > Calculators & Tools section.

To clarify how to determine your cashflow breakeven point, consider the following example. Let us assume that you owe $300,000 on your current mortgage, you are paying 7.5% per year, and you have 20 years remaining on this loan. Let us also assume you can refinance this loan and obtain a new mortgage at 6.5% with the same 20-year term. If the bank and other fees associated with refinancing this loan come to $6,000, how many months will it take for you to recover your upfront closing costs and then ultimately have true savings because of refinancing? Please note in this example, we are not going to include the closing costs in the new loan amount.

Using the earlier financial calculator and inputting all the facts in this example, we have determined a breakeven number of months to be 34. Therefore, if you plan on staying in your home for more than 34 months, refinancing may be a wise financial choice for you. Your monthly payment would be reduced from $2,417 to $2,237, putting an extra $180 each month into your free cash flow. You can ultimately save $43,200 in payments throughout the 20-year life of this loan.

You should go through a similar example with your own set of facts to determine your breakeven point in terms of months.

Refinancing was extremely favorable during the pandemic with ultra-low rates, when reportedly one-third of all outstanding mortgage debt was refinanced. However, this has become far less appealing as rates have now doubled to the high 6% range. With most mortgaged homeowners locked into much lower rates, refinance activity has stalled and dropped dramatically from its peak. Until rates fall substantially, well below current levels, refinancing will likely remain limited.

In some cases, we must look beyond what the breakeven point is and assess whether it makes sense to refinance, and extend the terms of the loans, to free up immediate cashflow to meet other short- and long-term financial goals and needs. As was the case in the example in Chapter 3, although the Mitchells did not substantially lower their mortgage rate, their cashflow was improved dramatically by extending the term. The increase in cashflow that resulted allowed them to fund their child's education, save significantly more for retirement, eliminate high-interest credit card debt, and allowed them to have a clear path to achieving financial independence.

Get Professional Advice

For most people, buying a home is the single most significant purchase they will make throughout their lifetime. Do not rely on your gut instincts or your emotional *wants*. Do hard research into the financial aspects of making this significant purchase. Before making a final decision about the purchase of a house, consult with an independent party, such as your tax and financial advisor.

Business and Investment Loans

The best investment you can make is in yourself. For some people, this means furthering their education (see Chapter 7, "Paying for College"); for others, it means going into business for themselves; and for some, it may mean both.

Going into business for yourself could be one of the most rewarding decisions you could make, but it could also be one of the costliest mistakes of your life. You should never jump into a business venture without first determining the likelihood of its success and your reasonably expected rate of return on your time and investment. Starting your own business could be one of the quickest roads to financial independence. Sadly, for many, it could also be the quickest road to financial ruin. If you do not study this carefully and fully comprehend the risks, then this potential *good debt* could easily become a *bad debt.*

If you believe you have a great business plan that has a high probability of success and profit, can reasonably be expected to exceed your cost of financing, and has an acceptable return on investment, then this may be considered *good debt.* Every time you evaluate a business opportunity or investment, you must do your best to determine not only your hard and soft costs, but also your opportunity costs for entering this business venture. *Opportunity costs* represent what you would have been able to earn with that money if you had invested it elsewhere.

Although the best investment you can make is an investment in yourself, do not take out any business loan without researching it carefully. Consult with others who have gone into similar businesses, study appropriate literature, and discuss the financial details with your tax and financial advisor. The same applies to investment loans.

Understanding Credit

What is *credit*? Credit is the act of borrowing money with the agreement to pay it back at some future date. In fact, credit sounds suspiciously like *debt,* which includes all the subjects we have just covered (auto loans, student loans, home mortgages, business loans, and, curiously enough, *credit* cards). Indeed, the process of establishing good credit involves precisely these sorts of common loans.

As with debt, there is good credit and bad credit. If you have *good credit,* it means you pay what you owe on time; *bad credit* means you have a history of not paying your bills on time and letting debts (again, very often credit card debt) build up, usually with high, speedily compounding interest rates. *Good credit* paves the way to achieving financial independence and creating and maintaining generational wealth; *bad credit* is almost always a serious roadblock to reaching financial independence.

A Word About "No Credit"

You may also have *no credit.* This means that you have never borrowed money from a commercial lender (such as taking out a credit card), and you have no payment history.

Note that many boarding school and college students away from home for the first time have no credit in their own names, but credit card companies and retail shops are quick to try to lure students into "establishing credit." This can be a good thing so long as the students pay their bills. However, it can be a tragic situation if a student takes out a host of credit cards, runs up huge balances, and then either leaves his or her parents to pay them off or is not responsible. Before they even venture out into the workplace, they could end up with huge debts and very likely a shaky credit history.

Actually, some people prefer to maintain a no-credit history, or what is known as a *nontraditional credit history.* If this is your choice, be sure to pay your bills (rent, telephone, utilities, medical) in a timely way and save all your receipts for up to three years. Then, if you want to apply for a loan of any kind (such as an auto loan or a home mortgage), you can use your receipts to prove your good credit.

Establishing and Maintaining Good Credit

The trick to establishing and maintaining good credit is pretty basic. At the most fundamental level, you need to do the following:

- Open a checking account.
- Apply for a low-interest credit card.
- Pay off your credit card balance every month.
- Always pay your bills on time, never missing a payment.

Beyond these fundamentals, you may also go after the bigger-ticket items like an auto loan or a home mortgage. How you handle these loans will affect your *good credit,* but conversely, the state of your credit will affect whether you qualify for these loans in the first place.

Establishing and maintaining good credit also involves living within your means financially and even paying yourself first. Toward that end, you need to establish a budget for all your expenses, and then, of course, stick to it. (If necessary, reread Chapter 1, "Committing to Living Within Your Means" and Chapter 3, "Determining Your Financial Position.")

Only when you understand your financial realities (and not your dream lifestyle) can you create a budget that is appropriate for your financial situation and that you can maintain effectively. This involves being realistic about your spending habits and knowing where you are spending most of your money. Save your receipts and study your bills each month.

It also means saving up for expensive items, new furniture, vacations, a down payment on a house, and not putting these items on your credit card, unless, of course, you can pay them off at the end of the month. Staying on budget will help you maintain *good* credit, build financial independence, and lay the foundation for creating generational wealth for your family.

Your Credit Report and Your Credit Score

Your credit report is like your school report card, and your credit score is the grades you have that represent how financially responsible or irresponsible you have been. Understanding how to get your credit report as well as what it takes to improve your credit score is an important part of achieving and maintaining financial independence throughout your lifetime.

What Is a Credit Report?

Anybody who has ever used a credit card or made a loan payment has a credit report: it is a formal statement that sums up, among other things, all your "credit" behavior, such as timely payments, missed payments, and the number of credit cards you have. Your credit report determines whether you are in sound financial shape.

These reports are made to (and through) three major credit reporting agencies that maintain information on your credit history:

1. **Equifax Credit Information Services**
   P.O. Box 740241
   Atlanta, GA 30374
   1-866-349-5191
   www.equifax.com
2. **Experian (formerly TRW)**
   P.O. Box 4500
   Allen, TX 75013
   1-888-397-3742
   www.experian.com
3. **TransUnion**
   P.O. Box 1000
   Chester, PA 19016
   1-800-888-4213
   www.transunion.com

Lenders, employers, landlords, and other service providers buy your credit information in the form of a credit report to help them decide whether to approve your application for a loan, credit card, job, or housing, or to offer you a product or service at a particular rate.

What Is Included in Credit Reports?

Your credit reports from Equifax, Experian, and TransUnion include the following information:

- **Personal information:** Compiled from credit applications you have filled out in the past, this information normally includes your name, current and recent addresses, Social Security number, date of birth, and your employment history.
- **Credit history:** The bulk of your credit report consists of details about credit accounts that were opened in your name or that list you as an authorized user (such as a spouse's credit card). Account details, which are supplied by creditors with which you have an account, include the date the account was opened, the credit limit or amount of the loan,

the payment terms, the balance, and a history that shows whether you have paid the account on time. Closed or inactive accounts stay on your report for 7–10 years from the date of their last activity, depending on the manner in which you paid them.

- **Credit report inquiries:** Credit reporting agencies record an inquiry whenever your credit report is shown to another party, such as a lender, service provider, landlord, or insurer. Inquiries remain on your credit report for up to two years.
- **Public records:** Matters of public record obtained from government sources such as courts of law, including liens, bankruptcies, and overdue child support, may appear on your credit report. Most public record information stays on your credit report for several years.

What Is Not *Included in Your Three Credit Reports?*

None of the credit reports from Equifax, Experian, and TransUnion include information about your checking or savings accounts, bankruptcies that are more than 10 years old, charged-off or debts placed for collection that are more than seven years old, gender, ethnicity, religion, political affiliation, medical history, or criminal records. Also, your credit score (discussed in the next section) is generated by information on your credit report, but it is not part of the report itself.

Checking Your Credit Report

You should check your credit report on a regular basis, at least once a year, and ideally two or three times a year, because the reports and your credit scores are constantly in flux. The three major credit reporting bureaus, Experian, TransUnion, and Equifax, are required by law to give you a free copy of your credit report each year on request. Call 1-877-322-8228 or go to www.annualcreditreport.com to order your free credit reports.

You should take a close look at these reports to ensure that they are accurate and complete. If you identify errors or accounts that you do not recognize, you should report this to the credit bureaus immediately. These problems could jeopardize your credit score and may also be an alert to possible identity theft (discussed in the next section of this chapter).

What Is a Credit Score?

Your credit score, called a *FICO* score (named for the Fair Isaac Corporation), is a mathematical model designed to predict credit risk, based on data contained within your credit report. In effect, your credit score summarizes your credit information. Lenders typically review your credit report and credit score to determine whether to extend credit (i.e., whether to lend you money) and on what terms. A higher score usually means you pose a lower risk to the lender, who will, in turn, be more likely to offer you favorable interest rates.

Several factors can affect your credit score, including these:

- **The number of loans you are carrying:** These include a home mortgage, auto loans, student loans, retail store credit cards, and bank credit cards.
- **Types of credit used:** Creditors prefer a variety of loans, mortgages, auto loans, store credit, and so forth.
- **Payment history:** The credit score considers whether you have repaid your loans in a timely manner and consistently.
- **The length of your credit history:** The longer your credit history, the higher your score.
- **Public records:** Have you filed for bankruptcy? Have reports been made for lack of alimony payments or child-care payments? If so, these factors will affect your credit score adversely.
- **New accounts:** Have you added new accounts to your debt, and if so, how many? Try to maintain no more than three or four credit cards because more than this can lower your FICO score, which would make you appear to be a higher credit risk to a lender.
- **Inquiries into your credit file:** Have lenders requested copies of your credit information? Fair Isaac's research shows that opening several credit accounts in a short period can be an indication of greater credit risk to the lender.

As the information contained in your credit report files change over time, so might any new scores based on your data. Your credit score from a month ago may have changed if there has been any recent activity on your credit file.

Your credit score is by far the most important factor that creditors look at to determine whether you are a credit risk. Credit scores range from 300 to 850, with the higher value representing lower credit risk. (In other words, the higher your score, the easier it should be for you to obtain credit.)

The median score ranges from 690 to 720. A poor credit score (below 600) can cost you the ability to access additional credit, insurance, utility services such as telephone and electricity, a rental unit, and even a job. Conversely, an excellent credit score (720 or above) will increase your chances of loan approval, as well as attractive interest rates and terms. This, of course, will indicate that you are headed in the right direction to becoming financially independent.

How to Improve Your Credit Score

If you would like or need to improve your credit score, here are a few good suggestions:

- **Watch your credit utilization:** Make sure your revolving credit balances (including all credit cards) remain under 30% of your available credit limit, ideally below 10% for the best impact on your credit score.
- **Use credit accounts regularly but conservatively:** Pay them off completely each month, as soon as the bill arrives.
- **Pay all of your bills on time:** The sooner the better. Even one late payment can negatively affect your credit score.
- **Reduce the amount you owe:** Pay off your credit cards and other loans as quickly as possible. (See the section on paying down credit card debt earlier in this chapter.)
- **Maintain credit cards that you have held for long periods:** If you have accounts at retail stores or credit cards that you have had for years, keep them open. Use them conservatively and pay off balances at the end of each month. Creditors like to see that you have sustained long-term credit.
- **Get rid of your newest credit cards:** Cancel any cards you have applied for within the last six months, unless you have moved high-interest balances to cards with lower-interest balances. Do not apply for new credit cards until the balances on old cards are clear.
- **Avoid applying for new loans:** Creditors like to see that you can handle different types of loans, including auto loans, home mortgages, and student loans. However, do not take on more debt simply to improve your credit score. This is seen as a negative.

- **Check your credit reports regularly:** You are permitted one free credit report each year; however, ideally, it is better to check them more frequently.
- **Fix disputes quickly:** Do not let disputes go beyond 30 days or into collection.

Preventing Identity Theft

So, you followed all the rules, paid all your bills on time, and maintained a terrific FICO score. Now you must also be prepared to take the necessary steps to protect it. Identity theft has become a widespread problem throughout the country. Identity theft occurs when someone steals your (financial) identity: in other words, they borrow money in your name, take out credit cards, open bank accounts, file tax returns using your name, or simply sign your name to a letter.

To commit identity theft, perpetrators often need only your personal information: your name, address, Social Security number, date of birth, and perhaps your mother's maiden name. If they obtain your credit card, driver's license, or birth certificate, you become very vulnerable. These criminals steal millions of identities each year by rummaging through trash, posing as government or financial representatives, updating change-of-address forms, or copying your credit card for purchases. Today, one of the top avenues for theft is cybercrime, by hacking online services, corporations, or government systems. Perhaps the most notable example was the 2017 Equifax data breach, which exposed the personal data of tens of millions of US consumers.

Do not become a victim. Always be cautious with your personal information. To guard against identity theft, consider these 12 proactive steps:

1. Check your credit report today and on an annual basis.
2. If you believe you are being electronically hacked, you should immediately shut down your computer and unplug all your devices.
3. Buy a good shredder and keep it handy so you can use it before discarding any sensitive personal documents.
4. File a police report if any of your personal financial information has been lost or stolen.
5. Immediately close any bank or brokerage accounts that have been accessed without your knowledge.

6. If you think you have been a victim of identity theft, put your credit report on fraud alert with all three credit bureaus. Consider paid identity protection services (e.g., LifeLock) that offer credit monitoring, alerts, recovery support, and possibly reimbursement. Your bank or financial institution may cover the cost of these services if you were a victim due to their data breach.
7. Never print or write your telephone number, driver's license number, or Social Security number on your personal or business checks.
8. Do not sign the back of your credit card and definitely do not leave it blank. Instead write in "Photo ID Required."
9. Always keep your PINs and passwords in a safe and secure location.
10. Do not put your credit card number or vendor account numbers on your checks when making payments.
11. Make a photocopy of everything in your wallet today and lock it up in a safe or some other secure place. If your wallet is lost or stolen, you will have all the relevant information such as account numbers and phone numbers to make the necessary calls to cancel them.
12. Report any identity theft to the Federal Trade Commission. You can also complete and submit IRS Form 14039, Identity Theft Affidavit, especially if you believe your tax return was involved, and someone tried to claim a refund on your behalf.

The Rising Risk of AI-driven Identity Theft

In recent years, identity theft has grown far more sophisticated, and dangerous, due to the emergence of artificial intelligence (AI). Criminals are now using AI tools to impersonate individuals and commit fraud, making scams more convincing.

Voice cloning, deepfake videos, and synthetic identity creation have made it alarmingly easy for scammers to mimic voices, forge documents, and bypass security measures. With only a few seconds of audio, AI can replicate someone's voice well enough to fool family members, coworkers, or even financial institutions. These scams often begin with phishing or social engineering and escalate quickly, targeting victims through phone calls, emails, or fraudulent websites.

Recent reports confirm this troubling trend. In 2024 alone, consumers lost more than $12.5 billion to identity fraud, a 25% increase from the previous year. According to Entrust, deepfake attacks occurred roughly once every five minutes in 2024, and digital document forgeries surged by 244%. Organized criminal groups are using these technologies to commit account takeovers, tax fraud, and other forms of financial identity theft.

Given the rise of AI-driven fraud, it is more important than ever to verify who you are speaking with. Be cautious with personal data, especially over the phone or online, and remain vigilant even if a voice or message sounds familiar. Always confirm identities using a secondary method before sharing sensitive information.

Taking extra steps to protect yourself, such as using multifactor authentication, biometric authentication with anti-spoofing technology, enrolling in identity protection services, and regularly reviewing your credit report, can help prevent becoming a victim of these increasingly sophisticated scams. Beyond these conventional measures, consider implementing unique security practices to add an extra layer of protection. One innovative approach is to use code phrases or custom answers for secure communication with trusted contacts. For instance, instead of answering routine questions like "What did you have for lunch?" with an expected response, you can reply with a pre-agreed, unusual answer (i.e., "velvet cactus") to ensure that only the person you're communicating with knows the correct response.

Analyzing Your Debt

The essential starting point to debt management is analyzing your debt. To do this, take another look at your statement of financial position, which you should have prepared after reading through Chapter 3 and going through the example in Exhibit 3.1. Your personal statement of financial position is a snapshot of your current financial standing.

As discussed in Chapter 3, *debt* refers to all of your financial liabilities, or all the financial obligations you must pay currently (within one year) and in the future (one year or longer). Gather all the supporting documentation for your liabilities and verify their terms. These terms include outstanding balances, monthly payments, interest rates, number of payments remaining, and any prepayment penalties.

Identify the debt that you have incurred to finance your lifestyle and focus on reducing and eliminating that type of debt going forward. If your consumer debt balances are high, you will need to implement a debt management program. A properly structured debt management program helps you identify which debt to eliminate first, along with the necessary steps to make your monthly payments easier to handle. Your number one priority should be to retire the debt with the highest interest rate while still making all of your required monthly payments.

If there are less expensive alternatives, such as swapping high-interest credit cards for low-interest credit cards, you should take advantage of these lower rates. Many consumers have successfully shopped around for lower rate credit cards and then used this as a means of negotiating with their current credit card companies for a more attractive rate. Never assume that the interest rate you are paying is the lowest rate available to you. Negotiate, negotiate, and then negotiate again. It will make a difference in the long run. You should also consider consolidating your consumer debt, as long as you can lower your overall interest rate.

As part of your debt analysis, you will also need to evaluate your existing mortgage and apply the principles discussed above under mortgage refinancing. If you go through the breakeven analysis and come up with a favorable breakeven point, take advantage of the lower rate. You should carefully consider the pros and cons of using your home as collateral to refinance and consolidate unsecured consumer debt, such as credit cards and car loans.

If you are facing financial difficulties, your unsecured consumer creditors are generally unlikely to take your property for nonpayment. Very often, you can renegotiate these loans and perhaps obtain forgiveness of debt. If you have a very weak balance sheet where your liabilities exceed your assets, then debt forgiveness may be a viable option to consider before bankruptcy.

Conversely, if you have a very strong balance sheet and your assets significantly exceed your liabilities, you may want to consider consolidating your high-interest consumer debt into your mortgage refinancing. You will not only be able to lower your cost of interest, but you may still be able to write off the interest to the extent that it is part of your home acquisition indebtedness. Please remember that any excess amount borrowed over this amount may not be tax-deductible. This strategy is best reserved for those with a solid net worth and a low likelihood of defaulting on their loans.

Once again, you cannot move forward effectively and efficiently on the road to financial independence until you clean up the liabilities section of your statement of financial position, your debts. Minimizing your liabilities and reducing your costs of financing will allow you to accumulate invested assets much faster.

If you do not pay attention to tax consequences while managing debt, you may be paying significantly more in taxes than the law requires. Therefore, you must include tax planning as part of your overall debt management and generational wealth strategy. Using a financial planning approach that takes advantage of tax-smart strategies will help maximize your ability to build wealth while reducing debt.

Tax-smart Strategies for Managing Debt

Here are several tax facts and strategies that will address your wealth accumulation goals in a powerful and sustainable way. This will be part of your tax-smart roadmap to financial independence. This is how you can transform the tax code into part of your generational wealth code.

- Beginning with tax year 2025 and continuing through 2029, the OBBBA allows taxpayers to deduct up to $10,000 of interest on qualified auto loans, limited to personal-use vehicles that meet requirements set by the IRS. The deduction phases out for taxpayers with modified AGI above $100,000 (single) and $200,000 (married filing jointly), providing a time-limited incentive for financing US-assembled vehicles. If your income falls below these thresholds, you should consider financing domestic assembled vehicles for maximum tax deductibility.
- The mortgage interest deduction on the combination of your primary residence and second home can only be taken on acquisition indebtedness of up to $750,000 for mortgages taken out after December 15, 2017. Earlier mortgages remain grandfathered at the previously higher limit of $1 million.
- Acquisition indebtedness refers to debt incurred to acquire, construct, or substantially improve a qualified residence and must be secured by that residence. Refinanced acquisition debt remains deductible only up to the amount of the original acquisition debt.
- Interest on home-equity loans or lines of credit is deductible only if the funds were used to buy, build, or substantially improve the home; otherwise, it is not deductible.
- If any interest paid on loans is in excess of the acquisition indebtedness described in the previous points, it is generally not tax-deductible and treated as personal interest. If you can show (have an audit trail) that this excess was used as a business or investment loan, it may then be deductible under a separate set of rules.
- The tracing principle allows you to deduct interest paid from borrowed money on your personal residence for business or investment purposes by making a 10-T election. This will allow you to trace the borrowing to the activity it relates

(*continued*)

(*continued*)

to and deduct the interest against that activity. *This election must be attached to your tax return in the year of borrowing and then applies thereafter.*

- If you pay points to a bank as prepaid interest, they are deductible over the term of the loan, unless they are paid on the purchase or improvement of your principal residence. In this case, they would be deductible in the year you pay them.
- Investment interest paid to buy or carry investments is deductible up to the amount of net investment income. If you do not have investment income, you may not deduct investment interest paid. The investment interest paid in excess of net investment income may be carried forward and deducted in future years when you have net investment income. You may not deduct interest paid on loans used to buy or carry tax-exempt securities.
- If you have a qualified retirement plan loan that becomes taxable because you left your job or defaulted on the loan, current law gives you more time to roll it over tax-free into another qualified plan. Instead of the previous 60-day deadline, you now have until the due date of your federal income tax return, including extensions, for the year the loan offset is treated as a distribution. If you discover before your filing deadline that you would owe taxes and a penalty, you can still complete the rollover in time to avoid both.
- If you incur a nonbusiness bad debt, you can deduct it as a short-term capital loss. For example, if you make a personal loan to a family member or friend, you expect to get repaid, and you are not normally in the business of making loans, you may be able to take this as a loss on your income tax return. You will have to prove that this was a bona fide loan, and it should be put in writing along with its terms.
- Normally if a debt is cancelled or forgiven, it must be included in your gross income for tax purposes. If, however, you were insolvent immediately before the cancellation, or it occurred as part of a Title 11 bankruptcy case, it would generally not be taxable to the extent of your insolvency.
- Student loan interest may be deductible (above the line deduction) up to $2,500 from your taxable income, if you qualify under the income threshold. The maximum $2,500 of student loan interest may be deductible if the taxpayer's modified adjusted gross income is below $85,000 for single and head of household taxpayers and below $170,000 for married taxpayers filing jointly. The amount of the student loan interest that is deductible is phased out with higher MAGI, until there is no deduction for singles and heads of households with $100,000 MAGI and married filing jointly taxpayers with $200,000 MAGI.
- Under current law, student loan debt discharged, whether due to death, total and permanent disability, income-driven repayment forgiveness, Public Service Loan Forgiveness, or other qualifying program, is tax-free at the federal level through December 31, 2025, pursuant to the American Rescue Plan Act. After that date, unless new legislation is enacted, forgiveness may again be taxable.

An Action Plan for Managing Debt

1. **Understand the basic principles of managing debt** by being crystal clear about the difference between *bad debt* and *good debt*.
2. **If you have a large balance on your credit card(s), make every effort to pay it off** as quickly as possible and to maintain a zero balance.
3. **If you have significantly high-interest credit card debt, consider using cash from savings or investments to pay off the balance.** Or consider other ways to get rid of high-interest credit card debt, such as borrowing from your life insurance or 401(k). With that said, be sure you understand any potential implications of borrowing from these other sources. After you have paid off your credit cards, *do NOT run up the balance on your cards again!*
4. **If you have an outstanding auto loan or lease, check it carefully.** Are the fees and costs you are currently paying in line with your budget? Could you scale back on automobile costs? If you are paying for more than one automobile, could you eliminate one or more family cars?
5. **If you have a student loan, make every payment on time** to maintain good credit. Check to see if you qualify to deduct student loan interest as an adjustment to income.
6. **If you are considering buying a home, calculate carefully how much you can realistically afford.** Do not forget that you should pay at least 20% of the purchase price as a down payment, plus closing costs, from your available funds. Consult a financial expert to help you make this decision.
7. **Avoid taking out a business loan for a fledgling business** until you have researched your business idea thoroughly. Discuss new business plans in detail with your tax advisor or a financial planner.
8. **Order your credit report and implement the necessary steps to improve your score.** Request a copy of your credit report from each of the three credit-reporting agencies at least once a year. (By law, you are entitled to one free copy from each agency each year.) If your credit score is under 720, take steps to raise it. You should always work on improving it.
9. **Take the necessary steps to avoid identity theft.** If you fear you are the victim of identity theft, report it immediately to the three credit-reporting agencies and the Social Security Fraud Administration.
10. **Stay alert and take proactive measures to prevent identity theft through AI.** Scammers are now using deepfake videos, synthetic voices, and fake identities to impersonate individuals, hack accounts, and commit financial fraud. Always verify the identity of anyone requesting sensitive information, even if they sound familiar.
11. **Analyze your debt.** The essential starting point to debt management is analyzing your debt. To do this, take another look at your statement

(continued)

(continued)

of financial position and focus on the make-up of all your short- and long-term liabilities. Take steps to eliminate your bad debt and where possible, improve your existing terms on these loans.

12. **Work with a tax-advisor and CERTIFIED FINANCIAL PLANNER®** that can provide you with the tax-smart advice covered in this chapter. Please refer to Appendix A, "Selecting a Trusted Advisor."
13. **Work with a financial planner** that will provide you with the necessary advice and guidance that includes the 12 critical areas of comprehensive wealth management covered throughout this book.
14. **Use the tax-smart roadmap to financial independence to transform the tax code into part of your generational wealth code**.

CHAPTER 5

Insuring Your Health and Life

If we are wise, let us prepare for the worst.
—George Washington, First President of the United States

Even a sound, carefully planned investment strategy can fall apart if you have not prepared properly for unforeseen problems concerning your health and life. If you or a member of your family is hit with a prolonged illness, a severe injury, a disability, or death (especially of the primary wage earner), the planning and investing you have so carefully developed can quickly disintegrate.

The premiums you pay for health and life insurance provide you with the peace of mind that comes with knowing your assets and family will be protected if and when the unexpected happens.

Having the right kind of health and life insurance at the appropriate stages of life is as important as the insurance itself. The type and extent of insurance you need will change throughout your lifetime. The family health and life risk management issues that are important to a young couple are usually dramatically different from those that are important to an older couple in their retirement years. For example, a young couple may need health insurance to cover prenatal care or life insurance to replace the income lost if one of the spouses should die before the children are grown. In contrast, an older retired couple may have little need for life insurance but may want to protect themselves against the high cost of long-term care. They therefore need to consider investing in long-term care insurance.

The major health and life risk management issues are the following:

- Health (or medical) insurance
- Disability insurance
- Long-term care insurance
- Life insurance

Each of these issues is discussed in this chapter. Your particular situation will determine what type of insurance you need, what kind of policy or policies will work best for you, and the amount of coverage you should carry.

Choosing a Health Insurance Plan

Health insurance is imperative, no matter what your circumstance, young or old, single or married, childless or raising a family. Without proper health insurance, a serious illness or accident experienced by you or any member of your family can bankrupt you and rob you of all your savings. Given the high cost of health care these days, it can happen very fast.

Nevertheless, even with government-mandated health care, as of the end of 2024, the Centers for Disease Control and Prevention estimates that nearly 27.2 million Americans are not covered by health insurance, and that includes 3.7 million children. This is an appalling and frightening statistic. While the Affordable Care Act (ACA) expanded health insurance coverage to millions of previously uninsured Americans, it did so at a significant financial burden to middle-class families through higher premiums and suppressed wage growth. Under the One Big Beautiful Bill Act (OBBBA), many of these coverage expansions are being rolled back to ease that burden. This will reduce costs for taxpayers and employers but will also result in millions losing access to government-subsidized health insurance.

We often meet people who tell us that they do not have health insurance coverage. Very often, these are younger people who do not think they need coverage, individuals who have not been able to maintain a long-term job, and very often self-employed individuals who are struggling to pay their bills. Usually, their reason is that they simply cannot afford to pay the high premiums. Our response to this way of thinking is that you cannot afford to be *without* health insurance coverage.

All it takes is one major illness or accident, and you can be completely wiped out financially. A prolonged visit to the hospital for a week or two could easily cost you several hundred thousand dollars. Adding this type of unexpected debt to your finances can hold you back and may even prevent you from ever becoming financially independent. If you are truly not able to pay for health insurance, you will want to find out if you are eligible for Medicaid or some other government-sponsored health insurance program. If you cannot be covered under Medicaid, then you have no choice but to purchase some other form of health insurance, even if the policy covers only catastrophic illness or accident. Health insurance is not a choice; it is a necessity that you simply cannot do without. Life is about choices, so eliminate some of your wants and replace them with this vital need.

If you have never purchased insurance, it may be helpful to define some of the following terms before we get into the types of policies that may be available to you. These terms may also be useful for understanding the remaining sections in this chapter, as well as Chapter 6, "Protecting Your Property with Insurance."

- A *premium* is the amount you would be periodically obligated to pay the insurance company to maintain your coverage under the plan. Some or all of your premium could also be paid by your employer, union, or plan sponsor.
- A *deductible* is the amount you need to pay for your insured expenses before the insurance company will start to pay. Some basic and preventive services are covered before you meet your deductible, depending on your plan.
- A *copayment* ("copay") is a fixed dollar amount you must pay out of pocket each time medical service is received. Copayments vary by your plan and the type of care you are receiving.
- *Coinsurance* is the percentage you pay of your insured expenses, usually after you reach your deductible. The insurance company will cover the remaining cost.

When deciding which type of insurance is appropriate for you, you will need to do a fair amount of research and some important thinking about your personal health and financial situation and needs.

First, you need to understand the various types of policies available to you. Consider the following questions:

- Are you covered through some sort of group plan through your job or union? Or must you buy your own insurance?
- If you are covered by a group plan, is it sufficient for your needs? Can you afford to pay the deductible and copayments, and is there a maximum limit on the coverage?
- Does it cover any specific situation or condition you or a member of your family may have? Verify that the policy does not exclude certain medical conditions or treatments, especially if you have a family history with these situations.
- Are the doctors you use and trust available under the plan?
- Is the plan flexible, allowing you to use out-of-network caregivers?
- What sort of ongoing health care needs do you anticipate, such as a future pregnancy or care for a chronic health problem, such as asthma, diabetes, arthritis, or high blood pressure?
- How much can you afford to pay in premiums? You can determine this after analyzing your statement of cash flow and eliminating some of your unnecessary wants and replacing them with this basic need.
- How high a deductible can you afford? The higher your deductible, the lower your premium will be, so in general, if you can self-insure up to the amount of the deductible, then this would be a wise choice. This works best if you are in overall good health and are less likely to need the insurance unless a major medical situation occurs.
- If you choose a high-deductible plan, is it qualified for a Health Savings Account (HSA)? Are you eligible to make contributions? Using an HSA is a terrific way to help subsidize the cost of your health insurance and save you money. By doing so, you will not only get an upfront tax deduction, but the distributions from the account to cover your health costs would be tax-free. See the "Health Savings Accounts" section of this chapter for more information on eligibility.

For decades, most Americans got their health insurance through their employers, and this is still the case. These insurers are usually private companies (Cigna®, Aetna®, UnitedHealthcare®, and others) and corporations, unions, or other organizations can negotiate good rates for their employees and members because they are bringing so much business to the insurance company. Usually with these plans, the employer pays a portion of the cost of the plan, and the employee pays a portion, often in pre-tax dollars.

Despite employer contributions, employees continue to bear a significant portion of health care costs. Most employees are still responsible for paying an average of 25% of family plan premiums, according to the KFF 2024 Employer Health Benefits Survey. Additionally, data from the Commonwealth Fund show that for many families, the combined cost of premium contributions and deductibles now consumes more than 10% of household income. This burden is amplified by the fact that wage growth has not kept pace with the continued rise in health care expenses. Given these challenges, it is essential to carefully consider premium costs and total out-of-pocket exposure when selecting a health insurance plan.

Indemnity Plans (Fee-for-service)

Indemnity plans, or *fee-for-service* plans, were long the traditional form of health insurance, and although less common today, some employers still offer them as part of their benefits package. With fee-for-service plans, the insurer either pays the service provider (the doctor) or you (the patient) directly, usually after you have already covered the full cost of the service.

Most plans require you to pay an annual deductible, after which the insurance company pays a set percentage of what it determines to be a reasonable and customary rate for the service in your area. You are responsible for the remainder if your provider charges more than that standard rate.

These plans offer the greatest flexibility in choosing doctors and specialists since they typically do not require referrals or limit you to a specific network. However, they also tend to come with higher out-of-pocket costs, less preventive care coverage, and more paperwork.

Managed-care Health Plans

For the past 30 years or so, because of the high costs of both medical care and insurance, many employers have chosen to opt for *managed-care plans*. With this type of plan, the subscriber (or user) contracts with and makes monthly payments directly to the organization that provides the health care service. In some cases, an insurance company is not involved; however, most major insurers offer both indemnity and managed-care plans.

With a managed-care plan, the insured pays a fee or copayment for office visits and medications, and most basic medical services and preventive care services are fully covered. To keep costs down, managed-care insurers closely manage the delivery and pricing of medical care. For example, they may restrict access to a specific list of doctors; require patients to get a referral from a primary care physician in order to see a specialist (such as a heart surgeon or a dermatologist); and require that the specialist also accept the insurance company's fee schedule.

The four principal types of managed-care plans are HMOs, PPOs, EPOs, and POSs.

Health Maintenance Organizations (HMOs) An HMO is a collection of hospitals, physicians, and other health care providers who have joined to provide health care services to its members. The following are the most popular types of HMOs:

- **Group HMOs:** Provide a group of doctors who provide health care in a central facility (usually a hospital).
- **Independent practice associations (IPAs):** The more popular type, doctors practice from their own offices as well as from community hospitals that are affiliated with the IPA.

Basic HMOs tend to be the least expensive form of health insurance. Copayments, when they are required at all, are usually small, and preventive care services are almost always completely covered. In exchange, patients must see only approved doctors and need to get permission from a primary care physician before seeing a specialist or getting any care outside the HMO. IPAs may offer slightly more flexibility in provider choice.

Preferred Provider Organizations (PPOs) A PPO is a plan that shares characteristics of both an IPA and a traditional fee-for-service plan. The insurance company or provider group contracts with physicians and hospitals that agree to accept a negotiated fee for services provided for the insured. In addition (unlike a conventional HMO), a PPO also provides coverage for services not provided by the PPO network, so you can go to other doctors and hospitals at your own discretion, although you will be required to pay a higher fee. Also, PPOs allow you to see other doctors and specialists without prior approval.

Exclusive Provider Organizations (EPOs) Like an HMO, the insurance company contracts with various medical providers to offer services to members of the EPO at reduced costs, as it reimburses EPO members only when providers associated with the insurance company are used, except in case of emergencies. This plan is a good option if you want to see a specialist within your network without needing a referral from a primary care physician.

Point-of-service (POS) Plans This plan encourages you to use network providers but allows you to choose others outside of the plan, usually at a higher copayment or deductible and with a doctor's referral for specialists. This is called a point-of-service plan because you decide (at the point-of-service) whether to use it more like an HMO (within the HMO network) or PPO (outside the HMO network).

Catastrophic Plans

Indemnity and managed-care plans cover most types of health care costs, but for some people, the cost of these health plans is just too high. If you are on a really tight budget, you might consider purchasing a catastrophic plan, which is a prepaid hospital and medical expense plan that only covers you for major medical and hospital expenses if you become seriously ill or injured.

With a *catastrophic health insurance* plan, you are taking the chance that you will stay reasonably healthy and be able to pay for your basic preventive health services out of pocket. At the same time, however, you are protecting yourself from financial ruin if you should need substantial care or hospitalization.

Premiums are lower on this type of coverage because you pay out of pocket for your common medical expenses, such as checkups and minor emergencies, and you will be charged a relatively high deductible if you require hospitalization. These plans are generally limited to individuals under 30 years old or those who qualify for hardship or affordability exemption under the ACA.

Look for a policy that is guaranteed renewable, complies with current rules prohibiting lifetime dollar limits on essential health benefits, and if it includes nonessential services like adult dental or vision, clarify whether those benefits have renewal restrictions or coverage caps. After meeting the high deductible, ensure the plan covers 100% of essential services, as required by law, and understand any separate cost-sharing or limits that may apply to nonessential add-ons.

Medicare

Medicare is the US government's health insurance program. Administered under the Social Security Administration, it is funded from a portion of Social Security and self-employment taxes, as well as premiums paid by beneficiaries. It primarily provides medical insurance to citizens over age 65. It also covers Americans younger than age 65 who are collecting Social Security disability benefits for at least 24 months and people of any age with end-stage renal disease (ESRD) or permanent kidney failure requiring dialysis or a kidney transplant.

You are automatically eligible for Medicare when you turn 65, although you must apply one to three months before your 65th birthday; if you apply later, your coverage can be delayed. If you have applied, coverage begins on the first day of the month in which you turn 65. For more information, visit www.medicare.gov or call 1-800-MEDICARE (1-800-633-4227).

Medicare covers three basic health care components: hospital insurance, supplementary medical care, and prescriptions, as well as an optional plan run by private insurance companies. Medicare provides very limited coverage for only certain kinds of long-term care needs (discussed further in this chapter under the section on long-term care). Medicare Part A and B are also called *Original Medicare.*

Medicare Part A Medicare Part A covers hospital care, rehabilitation facilities, nursing home care, hospice care, and home health services. These services are generally only covered for a set period and only when medically necessary.

Medicare Part A is free to anyone who has paid Medicare taxes for more than a decade (or is married to someone who has). If you are not eligible for premium-free Medicare Part A, you can still choose to buy it for a monthly premium, usually together with Medicare Part B.

As of 2025 Medicare Part A requires a $1,676 deductible for the benefit period. Also, for over 60 days of hospitalization in any benefit period, a daily coinsurance from $419 to $838 per day can apply.

Medicare Part B Medicare Part B covers medically necessary and preventative outpatient services, such as clinical research, ambulance services, durable medical equipment, mental health services, second opinion before surgery, and certain outpatient prescription drugs.

Unlike Part A, which is usually free, Part B charges a monthly premium that is usually deducted from your Social Security check. The standard Part B premium is $185 as of 2025, but can be as high as $629, depending on annual income. There is also a small deductible ($257 in 2025), followed by a 20% copay on Medicare-approved services. Many people buy a Medicare supplemental insurance policy as well to help cover these out-of-pocket costs.

When you sign up for Medicare Part A, you will be asked if you want to be covered under Medicare Part B. You need not sign up for Part B if you are covered through insurance from your workplace or your spouse's current job; however, unless you or your spouse is actively employed and insured, you need Part B. If you fail to sign up right away (either when you turn 65 or when you stop working and are no longer covered by a private health insurance company) you may be charged an additional 10% of your premium for every year you could have signed up but did not.

Medicare Part C Medicare Part C (also known as *Medicare Advantage or MA*) offers health plan options run by Medicare-approved *private insurance companies*, including HMOs and PPOs. These plans allow recipients to receive Medicare benefits and services covered under Part A and Part B, most cover Part D (prescription drugs), and some even offer additional benefits for an additional cost. When choosing a Medicare Advantage plan, be cautious not to be lured with low to zero copays until you are certain that all your physicians are in the plan and all your prescriptions are covered.

It is extremely important to understand that when you enroll in a Medicare Advantage plan, you are leaving Original Medicare. While your benefits are still funded by Medicare, your coverage is now administered entirely by a private insurer, not the federal government. This distinction is often misunderstood, but it has significant implications for how your care is accessed and managed in retirement.

Medicare Part D Medicare Part D covers the costs of both brand-name and generic prescription drugs at participating pharmacies. All Medicare recipients are eligible for this coverage, and like Parts B and C, it is a voluntary program.

Medicare Part D also incurs a monthly premium that varies from plan to plan. The Part D coverage may also be subject to an income-related monthly adjustment amount (IRMAA), a surcharge premium based on your prior period income, which ranges from $14 to $86 for 2025.

This coverage has an annual deductible of approximately up to $590 in 2025. Once again, it is important to compare plans to be sure that your prescriptions are covered without requiring high copays.

You may have to pay a late enrollment penalty if you go without Medicare recognized drug coverage for any continuous period of 63 days or more after your initial enrollment period is over. Recognized coverage includes a Medicare prescription drug plan, a Medicare Advantage Plan, another Medicare health plan that offers Medicare prescription drug coverage, or another creditable prescription drug coverage. Because of this, it is important to get drug coverage as soon as you are eligible, if you believe you will want or need drug coverage in the future. It may be a good idea to buy the most basic and inexpensive plan as a placeholder. If you go more than 63 days without coverage after you are eligible, a penalty premium will be tacked on to your Part D premium *every month.* That penalty is 1% of the national base beneficiary premium ($37 in 2025 for a penalty of $0.37 per month) multiplied by the number of full months you did not have coverage. That can add up very quickly.

Medigap Medigap (also called *Medicare Supplement Insurance*) is a private health insurance policy designed to fill in the gaps that exist in fundamental Medicare coverage, including copayments, coinsurance, and deductibles. If you have Medicare as well as a Medigap policy, Medicare will pay its share of the Medicare-approved amounts, and then the Medigap policy will pay its share.

A Medigap policy is different than a Medicare Advantage Plan because Advantage Plans replace your original Medicare A and B plans and may offer additional benefits, whereas a Medigap policy only supplements basic Medicare benefits. You cannot carry both a Medigap policy and a Medicare Advantage Plan.

There are many different types of Medigap policies that are regulated under various federal and state laws and that vary in quality and cost. For additional information you should visit www.medicare.gov or call 1-800-MEDICARE (1-800-633-4227).

Medicaid

Medicaid is a combined federal and state program that helps with the medical costs of more than 70 million Americans in qualified categories with limited income (generally between 100% and 138% of the federal poverty level with some states at higher levels depending on the eligible category). For example, in 2025 for a family of four, the 100% federal poverty line was $32,150. In addition to being financially needy, other conditions may apply. You should check your state's Medicaid eligibility rules for more information.

Since its inception in 1965, Medicaid originally provided medical insurance to persons getting cash assistance from the government. Following the ACA, most states expanded eligibility to adults aged 19–64 with incomes up to 138% of the federal poverty level. This substantially increased enrollment, which puts a tremendous strain on a system that was already on the brink of insolvency.

In 2018, the Trump administration released guidance allowing states to pilot imposing certain work requirements on those who are receiving Medicaid based on poverty alone. The OBBBA has expanded these hurdles. Starting in 2027, able-bodied adults (19–64) must meet 80 hours per month of work, volunteer, or education. States must now verify eligibility at least twice a year, and copays, premiums, asset limits, and immigrant waiting periods may also apply.

Most of the costs of Medicaid coverage are paid by the states and federal government. Under current regulations, states have the option to charge limited premiums, enrollment fees, copayments, coinsurance, and deductibles. Depending on your state, Medicaid covers a variety of benefits, such as doctor visits, emergency care, hospital care, vaccinations, prescription drugs, vision, hearing, long-term care, and preventive care. For more information, visit www.medicaid.gov.

Children's Health Insurance Program (CHIP)

CHIP provides low-cost health insurance coverage for children (up to age 19) in families who earn too much to qualify for Medicaid but can't afford private health insurance. Some states extend CHIP coverage beyond age 19 in special cases, but most follow the standard age limit.

Depending on your state, CHIP covers comprehensive services such as routine check-ups, immunizations, hospital care, dental care, and lab and X-ray services for children. Children receive free preventive care, but states may charge low fees or premiums, usually capped at 5% of family income, for other services. Each state sets its own rules for CHIP; to find out more, visit www.medicaid.gov.

COBRA (Consolidated Omnibus Budget Reconciliation Act of 1985)

COBRA requires employers with 20 or more employees to give you the opportunity to continue your health insurance under the company's insured group for up to 18 months, at your *own* expense. You are eligible for COBRA after one of the following qualifying events:

- You leave your job voluntarily (or begin working part-time) or involuntarily.
- Your spouse, who was the primary insured member of your family, dies.
- You are getting divorced from a spouse who is the primary insured member.

The employee retains all benefits (except for disability income coverage) and pays the employer premiums, which may include an additional administrative fee of up to 2%, bringing the total cost to no more than 102% of the company's cost. COBRA coverage can be extended for up to 36 months under certain extenuating circumstances, such as death of the employee, divorce or legal separation, or when a dependent child "ages out" of the plan (typically at age 26). If you become eligible for Medicare, but your spouse isn't yet eligible for Medicare, your spouse can extend his or her COBRA coverage for up to 36 months or until he or she becomes eligible for Medicare, whichever happens first.

Workers' Compensation Insurance

Workers' compensation insurance is designed to compensate workers who are injured on the job or who become ill through work-related causes and are therefore unable to draw a salary. Each state regulates its own workers' compensation insurance program, and details vary from state to state; however, normal benefits include medical and rehab expenses, disability income, and lump-sum payments for death and certain severe injuries. In most states, this is a mandatory benefit that must be provided by employers, although specific coverage thresholds and exceptions may apply.

The Patient Protection and Affordable Care Act

On March 23, 2010, President Barack Obama signed the Patient Protection and Affordable Care Act of 2010, the central piece of legislation that overhauled the American health care system. A week later, on March 30, 2010, he also signed the Health care and Education Reconciliation Act of 2010, a shorter piece of legislation that amended several provisions in the initial Patient Protection Act. Taken together, these two pieces of legislation, nicknamed "Obamacare," provided for massive health care reform and include an estimated $437 billion in new taxes and fees. The expanded health care coverage provided by the legislation was expected to drastically reduce the number of uninsured Americans. The legislation also included several extra pieces that are only imaginatively related to health care. In July 2012, the Supreme Court generally upheld the constitutionality of the controversial 2010 health care law.

Here are some of the provisions (which include many non-health-related issues) in the health care reform laws that have gone into effect and include 2025 amounts when applicable:

- **Insurance for older children:** Children can remain on their parents' health insurance policies through age 26.
- **Insurance for pre-existing conditions:** Insurance companies cannot deny coverage because of a pre-existing condition. This went into effect January 1, 2014.
- **Adoption credits:** The credit for adoption expenses is increased to $17,280 per child, partially refundable up to $5,000, starting in 2025 under OBBBA. This credit is adjusted annually for inflation and has been permanently extended.
- **Small business tax credits for providing health care:** Small businesses (as well as tax-exempt organizations) with up to 25 full-time equivalent employees may qualify for a tax credit for the cost of purchasing health insurance for their employees through the Small Business Health Options Program (SHOP) marketplace. In general, eligibility for the credit is based partially on the number of full-time equivalent employees and

on the average annual wages per employee. To qualify for the credit, the employer must pay at least 50% of the cost of health coverage at the single rate. For 2014 and beyond, the maximum credit increased to 50% of premiums paid by businesses and 35% of premiums paid by tax-exempt organizations. The maximum credit goes to those employers who employ 10 or fewer full-time equivalent employees and who pay annual average wages of no more than $33,300 adjusted for inflation. The credit gradually phases out for firms with average wages between $33,300 and $66,600 (adjusted annually for inflation), and between 10 and 25 full-time equivalent workers. The credit is available for two consecutive years.

- **Medicare drug coverage:** For those covered under Medicare Part D, the law previously provided a 65% discount on brand-name drugs and a 56% discount for generic drugs. You were considered to be in the so-called donut hole if your plan had paid up to a certain amount for covered drugs, but you had not yet spent up to the yearly limit out of pocket. During this gap in coverage, you would be forced to pay your drug expenses out of pocket until reaching the limit that initiates coverage again. As of 2020, the amount you pay for generic drugs has decreased to a consistent 25% copay, effectively eliminating the donut hole.
- **Health insurance reporting requirement:** Starting in 2012, most employers must report the value of each employee's health insurance coverage on the employee's annual Form W-2. Under transitional rules and pending further guidance from the Internal Revenue Service, only employers filing 250 or more W-2 forms are required to report this coverage.
- **Medical savings accounts:** Unless prescribed by a medical professional, over-the-counter (OTC) medications were no longer able to be paid for with funds from a health savings account (HSA), flexible spending account (FSA), or health reimbursement account (HRA). As of 2025, new legislation allows you to use these accounts to purchase most OTC medications without a prescription.
- **Additional tax on nonqualified savings account distributions:** The additional tax on nonqualified distributions from HSAs increased from 10% to 20%. For nonqualified distributions from an Archer medical savings account (MSA), the additional

tax increased from 15% to 20%. An exception to these penalties applies to nonqualified distributions after disability, death, or attaining age 65.

- **Drug industry fee:** While the ACA initially imposed a fee on prescription drug manufacturers (totaling roughly $3 billion in annual revenue), that fee has since been repealed or suspended. As of 2025, there is no such fee being assessed.
- **FSA limits:** In 2025, the amount that can be contributed to a health FSA was limited to $3,300 per year, indexed annually for inflation.
- **Medical expense deduction:** For tax years 2017 and beyond, every taxpayer, regardless of age, is subject to the 7.5% income threshold for deducting unreimbursed medical expenses.
- **Executive pay limit:** Starting in 2018, the compensation deduction for certain health insurance companies is limited to $1,000,000 per year for high-level executives.
- **Additional Medicare tax on earned income:** Employees are subject to 1.45% Medicare tax withholding on their earnings. Self-employed individuals are subject to 2.9% Medicare tax on their self-employment earnings. An additional 0.9% Medicare tax is imposed on earned income amounts above $250,000 for married couples filing joint returns, $125,000 for married taxpayers filing separately, and $200,000 for other types of individual taxpayers. The income threshold levels remain fixed and will not be indexed for inflation.
- **Net investment income tax:** A 3.8% Medicare tax is imposed on net investment income (interest, dividends, royalties, rental income, capital gains, etc.) on the lesser of net investment income or modified adjusted gross income (MAGI) above the threshold amount. The threshold amounts for US citizens and resident individuals are $250,000 for married taxpayers filing jointly, $125,000 for married taxpayers filing separately, and $200,000 for single and head of household taxpayers.

The Health Care Mandate and Other Issues

Starting in 2014, the so-called *mandate*, which was the heart of the health care act, went into effect. This mandate required that all Americans carry some form of health care insurance. Individuals who were not covered by Medicare, Medicaid, or other government health insurance were originally required to maintain health insurance coverage or pay a penalty. Penalties were calculated using a percentage of the taxpayer's income or a flat dollar amount. Subsidies and tax credits became available to help lower-income taxpayers pay for coverage.

In addition, other factors have gradually gone into effect, including the following:

- **Health insurance exchanges:** Health insurance exchanges were established by many states to enable people to comparison shop for coverage. In other states, federally facilitated exchanges may be used for the same purpose.
- **Required coverage by large employers:** Large employers and big businesses (with 50 or more full-time equivalent employees) must provide coverage for employees or face penalties.
- **Tax credits for small businesses:** Tax credits are at a maximum of 50% of premiums paid by qualifying small businesses that provide coverage for their workers. The credit available to nonprofit employees is as much as 35%.
- **Health industry fee:** This annual fee, previously assessed on the health insurance industry and amounting to $15.52 billion in 2020, was collected for the final time that year. It was permanently repealed starting in 2021.
- **Tax on "Cadillac plans":** The ACA had originally planned for a 40% excise tax on high-cost insurance plans, but this has been indefinitely delayed and remains unimplemented as of 2025.

With the Tax Cuts and Jobs Act of 2017, the federal individual mandate penalty was reduced to $0 effective January 1, 2019. The mandate itself remains in law, but it is no longer enforced at the federal level. Several states, including California, Massachusetts, New Jersey, and the District of Columbia, have enacted their own mandates with state-level penalties.

In response to the COVID-19 pandemic, the American Rescue Plan Act (ARPA), enacted in 2021, significantly expanded premium tax credits by increasing financial assistance and removing the income cap, making subsidies accessible to a broader population. These enhancements were subsequently extended through 2025 by the Inflation Reduction Act.

However, the OBBBA, passed in 2025, provides for these enhanced pandemic-era subsidies to expire at the end of that year. The expiration of these provisions may result in substantially higher premiums and reduced affordability, particularly for those who had gained coverage through expanded eligibility and deeper subsidy support.

Since the federal mandate penalty was eliminated in 2019, ACA exchanges have remained open, and the original subsidies established under the law continue to provide support for lower-income individuals. However, with the scheduled expiration of enhanced subsidies under the OBBBA, there is growing concern that premiums will rise, and coverage will become less affordable, particularly for those who benefited most from expanded eligibility and increased financial assistance.

The original influx of individuals with pre-existing conditions increased the overall cost of coverage. If premiums do rise, more healthy individuals who do not receive subsidies may opt to leave the market. This shift could lead to a smaller, less healthy risk pool and drive premiums even higher. While the foundational structure of the ACA remains in place, changes introduced through policies like the OBBBA demonstrate the ongoing evolution in the US health care system. Additional reforms are likely to continue to emerge.

Health Savings Accounts

Created in 2003, *health savings accounts* (HSAs) are tax-free savings accounts, funded by employees, employers, or both, to spend on routine medical costs. Usually, HSAs are for individuals who are covered by high-deductible health plans (HDHPs) and have no other health coverage. HSAs can provide excellent tax benefits, so it is strongly recommended that you determine whether you can qualify.

Not all high-deductible health plans are HSA-eligible, so before choosing one, you should look for the special HSA designation on the name or details of the plan. An HDHP is generally eligible for an HSA if it has a higher deductible than the average individual health insurance plan and no insurance coverage payments until the plan deductible is met. Each year, the Internal Revenue Service determines the minimum and maximum deductibles for individual or family medical coverage for all qualifying plans.

Even if you have an HSA-qualified policy, there are limitations on whether you are actually allowed to contribute to your health savings account in a given year. You must have no other health coverage, although certain types of ancillary coverage are acceptable (accidents, disability, dental, vision, or long-term care). You also may not contribute if you are covered by Medicare or if you were claimed as a dependent on someone else's tax return that year.

If you can contribute, there are limits on how much you can fund per year. For 2025, individuals can contribute up to $4,300 for self-only coverage and $8,550 for family coverage. If you are 55 or older, you can make an additional catch-up contribution of $1,000 each. Annual contribution limits may be affected by the number of months you had a qualifying high-deductible health plan in a given year. The deadline for funding HSAs is the same as IRAs accounts and is normally April 15th of the following year. So, the good news is, even if the year has passed, you can still make a prior-year tax-deductible contribution. You get the best of both worlds, since contributions are tax-deductible, and distributions for medical expenses are tax-free.

An Archer MSA (medical savings account) is similar to a HSA in that participants must be covered by a qualifying HDHP. This can be offered by a small employer (generally less than 50 employees).

Long-term Care Insurance

If you or someone in your family develops a prolonged physical illness, a disability, or a cognitive impairment, it is likely there will be a need for some form of long-term care. Many different care providers help people with chronic conditions overcome limitations that are keeping them from being independent. Long-term care is similar to traditional medical care, except that it relates to prolonged medical care treatment. Long-term care assists individuals by providing them with the best quality of life possible under the circumstances, but it typically does not improve or correct medical conditions. Long-term care services may include assistance with the following:

- Activities of daily living
- Home health care
- Respite care
- Hospice care
- Adult day care
- Care in a nursing home
- Care in an assisted-living facility

It is extremely important to note that these types of long-term medical care are *not* covered under health insurance policies, nor are they typically covered under Medicare. Coverage is generally limited to Medicaid, but only after the individual has met strict income and asset requirements.

Don't Be a Victim of Long-term Care Costs

Anthony and Paul were two clients I had known for more than 20 years. They were twin brothers who lived next door to each other in a modest neighborhood in Brooklyn, New York. Although they were twins, their personalities were polar opposites. Anthony was a hard-working, conservative guy who always *paid himself first*, paid his bills on time, and of course, had an excellent credit score. By the time he retired, he had managed to accumulate $1.8 million in investable assets and was able to retire at age 65 without changing the lifestyle he and his wife were accustomed to. They had two grown children, three grandchildren, and were settling into a comfortable retirement life.

In contrast, Anthony's twin brother, Paul, always had difficulty maintaining a job. He lived his life in the proverbial fast lane, regardless of the consequences. He never saved any money; worse, he continuously accumulated debt throughout his life. By the time he turned 65, he owed more in liabilities than he had in assets; in other words, he was broke. He had no choice but to continue working until his age and physical condition made it impossible.

Eventually, Paul was no longer able to care for himself. Fortunately, Anthony and his wife happily found him the care he needed in a nursing home on Staten Island. Because Paul was living off only a small Social Security retirement check, he was able to qualify for Medicaid. He received care in this nursing home, and it did not cost him or his family a dime. The nursing home took over Paul's monthly Social Security check, and Medicaid took care of the rest.

Six months after Paul entered the nursing home, Anthony suffered a major stroke. Although he survived the initial stroke, he was unable to walk, feed himself, or dress himself without the help of his wife. His condition got worse, and it became impossible for his wife to continue caring for him on her own. As difficult as the decision was, his wife and children decided that Anthony would need the help only a nursing home could provide.

Anthony's family was able to get him into the same excellent nursing home as his brother Paul; in fact, they became roommates, and in a funny twist of fate, ended up living out the rest of their lives together. However, their respective financial fates could not have been more different.

As mentioned, because Paul had no assets, Medicaid paid for his nursing home care. However, Anthony, who had always lived responsibly and worked to accumulate assets that could one day provide generational wealth and security for his family, was therefore ineligible for Medicaid. As a result, his family needed to pay for the nursing home costs out of pocket, and the bill came to more than $140,000 per year. They thought they had no choice but to pay because there was no other way to care for Anthony. He lived for another 11 years, which almost completely wiped out the assets that he had worked so hard to accumulate.

Unfortunately, sometimes the Medicaid system rewards bad behavior and penalizes good behavior, and this is a classic example. Anthony's nursing home care used up his entire life savings. His wife and children were denied the fruits of his labor and the benefits of the sacrifices he made for them throughout his life. Meanwhile Paul, who lived at the same nursing home as Anthony and received exactly the same care, did not have to pay a dime. This, in my opinion, is a very sad ending to what should have been a financial success story.

Perhaps one of the most important things to plan for once you become financially independent is how to protect the assets you have accumulated. Clearly, if you do not protect your financial independence once you have achieved it, it is almost as irresponsible as never taking the steps to achieve it in the first place. This is where meeting with a financial planner and elder care attorney is critical.

Anthony could have taken the necessary steps early on to protect his family and the assets they were able to accumulate throughout their lifetime. This is one family health risk you cannot afford to take. *You must take preventive action to ensure that your life-long hard work and assets are protected in case a catastrophic long-term illness occurs.* There are numerous strategies you can employ to protect your assets; however, *obtaining an adequate long-term care insurance policy* is probably the easiest way you can accomplish this.

There are numerous other planning options available that fall under the umbrella of Medicaid planning, which include Medicaid trusts, retaining a life estate, and outright property transfers. The rules and regulations in this area are quite complex and differ from state to state. Therefore, my advice to every family is to seek out the proper help and guidance of a qualified elder care planning attorney. This planning must take place years in advance of developing the need for long-term care. If you or a family member requires long-term care and has not already implemented a plan, you should immediately meet with an elder care planning attorney to minimize the loss of your hard-earned money. Protecting your assets is essential to maintaining generational wealth for you and your family.

Please refer to Chapter 10, "Preserving Your Estate," for more guidance on this topic.

The Cost of Long-term Care

Long-term care is extremely expensive. The cost depends on the amount and type of care that you will need and where and how you get it. For example, of the 50 states, New York state has one of the highest costs for obtaining care in a long-term care facility.

According to a recent survey conducted in 2024 by Genworth Financial, the median cost of care for a private room in a New York nursing home is $186,696 per year, and the median cost to hire a home health aide is $77,792 per year. These costs not only vary state by state, but also county by county within each state. To find out the cost of the various options of long-term care treatments in your state, visit Genworth's website at www.genworth.com. Use this website to obtain a general guide of what your long-term care cost might be.

For most people, the cost of long-term care will wipe out their life savings within just a few short years. Being prepared for this type of long-term care risk is critical to maintaining your family's financial independence.

You can pay for long-term care in a variety of ways. These include using your and your family's personal resources, obtaining long-term care insurance, and receiving some assistance from Medicaid (if you qualify).

As described earlier in this chapter, Medicaid is the government-funded program that pays nursing home care only for individuals who have low income and little or no assets. To get Medicaid help, you must meet federal and state guidelines for income and assets. Many people start paying for nursing home care out of their own funds and "spend down" their assets until they are eligible for Medicaid. Medicaid may then pay part or all of their nursing home costs. You may have to use up most of your assets on your health care before Medicaid will help. Basically, you need to be broke because this is a form of public assistance.

State laws differ regarding how much money and assets you can keep to still be eligible for Medicaid. (Some assets, such as your home, may not count when deciding if you are eligible for Medicaid.) However, federal law requires your state to recover from your estate the cost of the Medicaid-paid benefits you receive. Contact your state Medicaid office or state department of social services to learn more about the rules in your state.

This is only the most general information. There are many other rules about what you can and cannot keep, but the bottom line is that if you are single or a widow(er), you must give up almost everything you have worked so hard to accumulate in order to qualify for Medicaid coverage in a nursing home. Whether you are married or unmarried, you should get legal advice regarding the options available to protect your assets. This is a very hot topic, and the law is in a constant state of flux.

Rules for married people vary from state to state. For example, in community-property states, all of your income from any source (no matter which spouse the checks are made out to) is considered to be divided equally between both of you. In any other state, only checks that are made out to you count toward your Medicaid eligibility.

In most states, if the cost of a nursing home is higher than your income, you will qualify for the Medicaid nursing home funds. An elder-care attorney is best suited to help you figure this out because each state has different formulas to determine your eligibility. Your elder-care specialist can help you estimate the amount that your stay-at-home spouse would be able to keep, or even have the amount increased according to his or her needs.

After qualifying on the income test, you also need to pass an asset eligibility test. Your home, car, and personal property are generally protected for your healthy spouse. Married couples can also keep some money in investments or cash. You may have to give up most of your other assets to qualify for Medicaid. Studies show that half of the people who ended up on Medicaid were not poor when they entered the nursing home. They had to "spend down" their assets until nothing was left before Medicaid took over.

While your spouse is living in the house, the state will not try to take it. Once your spouse dies, however, and the estate is left to your beneficiaries, the state could try to make a claim against the home by placing a Medicaid lien against it. Some 30 states actually have "filial responsibility laws," which allow care providers to come after the children of care recipients for the cost of their parents' care. They are not often enforced but do indeed exist.

Paying for Long-term Care with Insurance

Long-term care insurance is another way you may pay for long-term care. This type of insurance can pay for some or all of your long-term care.

The Health Insurance Portability and Accountability Act of 1996 (HIPAA) is a federal law that gives some federal income tax advantages to people who buy certain long-term care insurance policies. These policies are called *tax-qualified long-term care insurance contracts,* or simply *qualified contracts.* Numerous states also provide for special tax breaks for long-term care premiums. These include tax deductions and tax credits that help you pay part of the cost of your premiums. If you are paying premiums for long-term care insurance, be sure to let your tax preparer know, and ask your tax preparer to find out what special tax deduction or credits may be available in your state.

For 2025, qualified long-term care insurance contract premiums can be deducted as medical expenses with limitations based on age ($480 if you are up to age 40, $900 if you are age 41–50, $1,800 if you are age 51–60, $4,810 if you are age 61–70, and $6,020 if you are over age 70).

Should You Buy Long-term Care Insurance?

Whether you should buy a long-term care insurance policy depends on your age, health status, overall retirement goals, income, and assets. For example, if your only source of income is a Social Security benefit or Supplemental Security Income (SSI) and you have a minimal net worth, you probably should not buy long-term care insurance because you may not be able to afford the premium and you may qualify for Medicaid.

Conversely, if you have a large amount of assets but do not want to use them to pay for long-term care, you may want to buy a long-term care insurance policy. Many people buy a policy because they want to stay independent of government aid or the help of family. They do not want to burden anyone with having to care for them.

Consider buying long-term care insurance if the following apply:

- You have significant assets and income.
- You want to protect some of your assets and income.
- You can pay premiums, including possible premium increases, without financial difficulty.
- You want to stay independent of the support of others.
- You want to have the flexibility of choosing care in the setting you prefer or one in which you will be most comfortable.

Private insurance companies sell long-term care insurance policies. You can buy an individual policy from an agent or through the mail. You can also buy coverage under a group policy through an employer or through membership in an association. The federal government and several state governments offer long-term care insurance coverage to their employees, retirees, and their families. This program is voluntary, and premiums are paid by participants. You can also add a long-term care benefit rider through certain life insurance policies. Some hybrid annuity products also offer long-term care benefits, although these may differ in tax treatment and qualification standards from traditional policies.

The following paragraphs describe some of the specific terms used in a long-term care policy that will determine your eligibility under the plan. When comparing policies, be sure to compare how each of the policies defines these terms.

Activities of Daily Living The inability to cope with activities of daily living (ADLs) is the most common way insurance companies decide that you are eligible for benefits. The ADLs most companies use are *bathing, continence, dressing, eating, toileting, and transferring.* Typically, a policy pays benefits when you cannot do a certain number of the ADLs, such as two of the six or three of the six.

Elimination Period With many policies, your benefits will not start the first day you go to a nursing home or start using home care. Most policies have an *elimination period* (sometimes called a *deductible* or a *waiting period*). That means benefits can start 0, 20, 30, 60, 90, or 100 days after you start using long-term care or become disabled. The number of days you must wait for benefits to start depends on the elimination period you pick when you buy your policy. You might be able to choose a policy with a zero-day elimination period but expect it to cost significantly more.

Inflation Protection Protecting against inflation can be one of the most important additions you can make to a long-term care insurance policy, although it will increase the premium you pay. If your benefits do not increase over time, years from now, you may find that they have not kept up with the rising cost of long-term care. The younger you are when you buy a policy, the more important it is for you to think about adding inflation protection; otherwise, you will be only partially covered when the need arises. Most insurers now offer compound inflation protection as a standard option for buyers under age 75.

Underwriting Companies that sell long-term care insurance medically *underwrite* their coverage. They look at your health and family history before they decide to issue a policy. You may be able to buy coverage through an employer or another type of group without any health underwriting or with more relaxed underwriting.

Guaranteed Renewable Insurance In most states, long-term care insurance policies sold today must be *guaranteed renewable*, which means that an insurance company cannot cancel or fail to renew coverage because of a change in a person's health or age. As long as premiums are paid and benefits have not been exhausted, coverage will continue. However, it does *not* mean that it guarantees you a chance to renew at the same premium; your premium may increase over time. You should consult with an insurance agent or broker who specializes in long-term care insurance and would be able to secure a policy that will meet your specific needs.

Partnership Policies Many states offer *partnership* long-term care policies. By buying a policy that meets the guidelines of your state's partnership program, you receive asset protection from Medicaid spend down. This means that if you ever exhaust the benefits of your policy, you will not have to spend down all of your assets to qualify for Medicaid. The asset protection amount can differ by state. Some states offer asset protection up to the amount of the total benefit you purchased, and some offer total asset protection. Not all states honor partnership policies from other states. This is important to know if you plan to retire to a different state than where you currently reside.

Hybrid Policies A growing trend in the long-term care insurance market is the use of hybrid policies, which combine life insurance with long-term care benefits. These policies appeal to many individuals because they often come with guaranteed premiums, meaning the cost of coverage remains fixed as long as you continue to make payments on time. This predictability makes them especially attractive for long-term planning.

However, hybrid policies may not offer all the same benefits as traditional long-term care insurance. In many cases, they do not qualify for partnership program protection or provide the same potential tax advantages available under standalone long-term care policies. Despite these trade-offs, hybrid policies have grown in popularity and now make up a significant share of new long-term care insurance sales.

As Jerry Patterson, head of Advanced Wealth Solutions at Cetera Financial Group, explains:

> Mitigating the financial risks related to a long-term care event is not just about protecting yourself. In many ways, you are purchasing long-term care insurance to protect the people closest to you, your future caregivers. Many people underestimate the impact of an uninsured long-term care event on the family members and other loved ones that will be coordinating your care.
>
> Many people believe that long-term care insurance is a "use it or lose it" value proposition. With respect to traditional, stand-alone coverage, this might be true. However, with some of the more contemporary coverage options, such as hybrid insurance policies, these solutions may provide family members, or other loved ones, valuable insurance proceeds in the event you do not need the policy to cover a long-term care event.

Do not let your long-term care needs wipe out your family's financial independence!

Disability Insurance

If you became disabled and couldn't work, would you have enough savings to cover your living expenses until you were able to work again? For most people, the answer to this question is unfortunately no, which means that they would not be adequately prepared.

A *disability* is generally defined as a limitation of your physical or mental ability to work resulting from sickness or injury. It may be *partial,* in which case you are unable to perform certain job tasks and functions, or *total,* in which case you are unable to work at all.

According to the Council for Disability Awareness (CDA), more than one in four people entering the workforce today will become disabled before retiring, and approximately one in seven people can expect to be disabled for five years or more before retirement. A major misconception about disability is that it is typically caused by an accident or an injury. Many people think because they don't have a hazardous job or participate in hazardous activities, that they do not need disability coverage. However, the CDA reports that accidents and injuries only cause about 10% of disability claims. The remaining 90% of claims are the result of a major illness. These are startling statistics and make it clear that short- and long-term disability coverage is a necessity, especially if you are the primary wage earner in your family and your income is needed to cover your living expenses.

Most employers are required by law to provide some form of workers' compensation and short-term disability coverage for their employees. The extent of coverage under these employer-provided short-term disability plans is very limited and short in duration. Short-term disability insurance replaces part of your income while you are injured or ill for any reason for a short period. Workers' compensation only protects you if you are injured while performing your job at work. It is important to understand that very few employers provide *long-term* disability coverage, so this responsibility usually rests on your shoulders.

Depending on the state you live in and the policy you have through your employer, your benefits may be insufficient to meet your basic living expenses. Whether or not an employer is required to provide short-term disability will also vary based on your state of employment.

Using New York state as an example: employers must provide short-term disability coverage for employees who experience a non-work-related illness or injury. Statutory benefits are currently capped at $170 per week, or 50% of wages up to that amount, for a maximum duration of 26 weeks. Legislation has passed the New York State Senate that would raise this cap to approximately $1,170 per week or 67% of wages, phased in gradually beginning in 2027. However, this legislation has not yet been enacted into law. If you are unable to meet your living expenses on this limited benefit amount for six months, you need to consider supplemental long-term disability coverage to protect your financial independence.

Beyond weekly state benefits, it is useful to understand broader disability risk trends. In the United States, nearly 70 million adults, representing approximately 28.7% of the population, report having at least one functional disability. These include difficulties with mobility, hearing, cognition, independent living, and self-care. Among working-age adults between the ages of 16 and 64, the employment-to-population ratio for individuals with disabilities is approximately 38%. In contrast, the ratio for those without disabilities is about 75%. The unemployment rate for disabled workers stands at roughly 8.6%, compared with 4.1% for nondisabled workers. These statistics illustrate how a disability can quickly lead to financial instability if proper insurance coverage is not in place.

Social Security Disability Benefits

The disability qualification under Social Security is different from the general definition and most insurance companies' definition. Social Security pays only for *total disability*. No benefits are payable for *partial* disability or for short-term disability.

Disability under Social Security is based on your inability to work. You are considered disabled under Social Security rules only if you meet all the following requirements:

- You cannot do work that you were able to do before.
- The Social Security Administration (SSA) decides that you cannot adjust to other types of work because of your medical condition.
- Your disability has lasted or is expected to last for at least one year or to result in death.

The SSA uses a much stricter definition than private insurers when determining your eligibility for benefits. Under its program, the rules assume that working families have access to other resources to provide support during periods of short-term disabilities, including cash reserves from savings, workers' compensation, and short-term disability insurance. In addition, even for those who meet the stringent qualifications, the SSA imposes a mandatory five-month waiting period before SSDI benefit payments can begin. This waiting period starts from the established onset date and ensures applicants must be disabled for at least five full months before receiving any benefits.

To be eligible for Social Security disability benefits, you need to pass two tests. The first test is a "recent work" test based on the age when you become disabled. For example, if you are under 24 at that time, you need to have worked 1.5 years out of the 3 years ending with the calendar quarter you are disabled. If you are over 30, you need to have worked at least 5 out of the 10 years ending with the quarter you are disabled.

The second work-related test is called the "duration of work" test. This test measures the amount of work you have performed over your lifetime. Generally, if you are under the age of 42 and pass the recent work test, you are likely to pass the duration of work test. However, once you turn 42, you must add one quarter of work per year in order to pass the duration of work test. For example, a 46-year-old beneficiary must have worked for 6 years since turning 21 in order to pass the duration of work test, and a 50-year-old beneficiary must have worked for 7 years. The beneficiary must have earned at least 5 of those years within 10 years of becoming disabled.

The SSA calculates time spent working based on a quarter system, and that measurement is based on the amount of money an individual makes during a calendar year. In 2025, you earn one credit for each $1,810 of wages or self-employment income. Once you earn $7,240, you have earned four credits for the year.

It is entirely possible to be deemed disabled by a commercial insurance company and not by the SSA because insurance companies set their own eligibility requirements. To receive benefits, the SSA requires that you be disabled from doing almost any sort of work, whereas commercial companies may require only that you be disabled from doing your own particular type of work or profession.

The SSA's benefits for retirement, disability, survivors, or dependents were initially intended to be a safety net that could be used to replace *some* of your lost income. You cannot rely on Social Security disability alone, and this is why it is so important that you obtain a long-term disability policy through an insurance company.

Long-term Disability Insurance

If you become seriously ill or injured, long-term disability insurance can substitute a portion of your salary after a certain period. Being able to replace the salary you were earning before you became disabled and unable to work is a necessity for most people. If you do not have the proper insurance coverage, a long-term disability could potentially wipe you out financially and prevent you from ever becoming financially independent. You need to consider whether you and your family could survive comfortably without your salary. If the answer is no, then you must seek out the proper coverage immediately. This is one family health risk management solution you should not do without; it is clearly a need and not a want.

Ideally, you want to secure coverage that would pay you the typical maximum benefit of 60% of your income after an event that leaves you unable to work at your current job. It should cover you in the case of an illness or an accident.

Your policy should cover what is known as *own-occupation,* not *any occupation.* This is the option that clearly separates what is available on the market through insurance companies from what the SSA provides. If you become disabled and can no longer perform your current occupation, regardless of what other kinds of work you might be able to do, the insurance company will pay you this disability benefit. A policy that covers *any occupation* would pay you only if you could not perform any job at all.

Long-term disability insurance should be *guaranteed, noncancelable,* and *renewable.* If it is not, your insurance company can cancel your policy. By including these options, the only reason your policy can be canceled is if you stop paying your premiums. With these options, your insurance company cannot increase your premium or change any of your policy's provisions, even if your health changes in a way that increases your risk of disability.

Your policy should include *residual benefits,* which means it will guarantee a certain percentage of your former job's income in comparison to your new job's income. It should also include cost-of-living adjustments (COLAs) via a rider that can be included in your policy, typically for an extra cost. This rider allows you to increase your coverage periodically so that you can factor in inflation to future benefits without having an additional physical examination.

The elimination period, which is the amount of time after your injury or the onset of your illness when you receive no benefits, varies from policy to policy. Ideally, a 60-day elimination period is preferable, but you can select a policy with a 90-day elimination period to reduce the cost of your premiums. We would recommend the 90-day period only if you can afford to live without a paycheck for 90 days. This is also why we recommended in Chapter 1 that you have three to six months' worth of liquid cash available in case of an emergency. In essence, you are self-insuring against the possibility of a short-term disability by maintaining this cash reserve. If you do not have this emergency cash available, work toward establishing an emergency fund for yourself and your family.

Life Insurance

Life insurance was originally designed to protect people while they were relatively young, in case the family wage earner died prematurely. Later on in life, once the children had grown and the couple's retirement nest egg had already been established, there was no longer a need for life insurance, and the policy would be cancelled. For many people, this is actually the way their life insurance should be handled today. It is my opinion that most people should not be using life insurance as a savings strategy. If you're single and have no dependents, there is usually no need for you to have life insurance.

There are four basic questions to ask yourself when determining your life insurance needs:

1. Do I really need it?
2. What dollar amount do I need?
3. How many years will I need it?
4. What type of life insurance policy would best meet my needs?

Examine your statement of cash flow (described in Chapter 3, "Determining Your Financial Position"). Now imagine what your family's statement of cash flow would look like in the event that one or both wage earners were no longer alive and that income was no longer available. Could the remaining family income cover the financial obligations and dreams you have set for the future, such as paying for your children's education? If your survivors have enough money to maintain their standard of living, then you do not need life insurance. On the other hand, if there is a shortfall, you will need to make this up by securing the proper type and amount of life insurance.

Quite frankly, life insurance should really be called *after-death expense insurance.* After all, the policy cannot bring you back to life; it can only serve as a means to replace the income you would have earned if you had lived. As a general rule, many life insurance advisors recommend having at least 10 times your annual salary as a death benefit, to allow your family the ability to generate income with these funds that will partially replace the lost earnings when you are no longer around. How much life insurance you really need will depend on several factors, including these:

- What your current income is
- What percentage of this income your family will need when you are gone
- How many years your family will need this income to continue
- What inflation rate you expect during this period
- What rate of return you expect your family will earn on the death benefit over this period
- What lump-sum payments your family will need to make when you die

To help you determine what may be the right amount of life insurance for you and your family, consider the following example: let us assume you currently earn $120,000 per year before taxes and that your family would need $90,000 per year to maintain their current standard of living after your death. Let us also assume that you will need this income stream for 20 years. You assume that your family can expect to earn a 7% rate of return on this money. We will also assume you have sufficient assets set aside to cover your funeral costs, and to keep the example simple, we will not factor in any inflation. To factor in all of these other variables, we encourage you to use a financial calculator, such as the one we describe later.

This hypothetical situation can be analyzed by also saying how much money you will need at a particular point of time to ensure a $90,000-per-year income stream over a 20-year period while these funds are earning a 7% rate of return. This is a present-value-annuity factor, and you can use Exhibit 12.5 in Chapter 12, "The Time Value of Money," to assist you with this calculation.

In step 1, enter 7% and in step 2, enter 20 years. Then determine the proper present-value-annuity factor by looking at row 20 years and column 7% for a factor of 10.59401. In step 4 of this exhibit, insert $90,000 in annual cash receipts your family would need to receive. Then, multiply the $90,000 by the present-value-annuity factor of 10.59401.

Therefore, you would need approximately $953,461. We recommend rounding this off to $1,000,000, as this is really a rough estimate of your life insurance needs to replace the lost income from your unexpected death.

There are numerous ways to estimate the amount of life insurance your family would need and numerous other factors that may need to be taken into consideration. A financial calculator can assist you with analyzing these factors and your needs. For example, you can use the *Assess Your Life Insurance Needs* calculator, available at www.ventotaxandwealth.com under the Resources > Calculators & Tools section, which can assist you in going through several "what-if" scenarios. This online calculator will provide you with a reasonable estimate of the proper amount of life insurance to meet your needs.

Securing the right life insurance will provide you and your family with a tremendous amount of security, and if you choose term insurance (described next), we think you will be surprised by how affordable a large policy can be.

Term Life Insurance

We strongly believe that *term life insurance* is the best type of life insurance for the vast majority of people, and it literally costs a fraction of the price compared with permanent insurance. Term life insurance is an efficient way to protect your family, providing the highest coverage at the most affordable price.

One of your goals should be to make sure that you will have enough income from your retirement plans to support yourself and your loved ones after you are gone. Once you have enough to live on, there may be no need for life insurance. With that said, you should never cancel or attempt to change a policy without checking with your doctor and having a thorough physical, as medical issues may encourage you to keep insurance that you otherwise would not have needed. By the time you are financially independent and ready to retire, your need to have life insurance and pay the premiums may be gone.

Term life insurance protects you for a certain number of years (typically 1–20), and once the *term* of the policy is over, you can usually renew the policy and begin another term without providing evidence of your insurability, although this often comes at a higher cost. If you die during the term of the policy, the insurance company pays out the death benefit to your beneficiaries. The older you get, the more expensive term insurance becomes because it is more likely that the company will have to pay out the death benefit. By the time you are in your seventies, the premiums for term life insurance will be very high, but if you have planned properly, you should no longer need it. Depending on your particular situation and individual needs, you may want to select a level, annual guaranteed-renewable, decreasing, or increasing term life insurance policy.

As Jerry Patterson points out, "Understanding the fine print of conversion options on a term insurance policy is important. Once you're locked in, you are locked in for the term and you usually don't consider conversion until many years later when you are older and going in a different direction. If you need the insurance, it would require another medical underwriting process."

With a *level term policy*, your premiums remain the same for the term you have chosen, usually 5, 10, 15, or 20 years.

You can also buy *annual guaranteed-renewable term insurance*, where the premiums increase to reflect your new age at the end of each year that you renew the policy.

Decreasing term insurance reduces the amount of your death benefit over time. This is typically used if you want the peace of mind in knowing that, in the event of the breadwinner's death, your mortgage can be paid in full. It is sometimes referred to as *mortgage insurance*, but it is really a term life insurance policy. This kind of policy starts with a specific death benefit that decreases each year until your policy expires, which typically goes hand in hand with the payoff of your mortgage.

There is also *increasing term life insurance*, which provides a death benefit that rises steadily as the term continues. This may be an option if it meets your needs.

When selecting the number of years of coverage under your term policy, it must be long enough to protect your family financially after your death and the loss of your earned income.

Permanent Life Insurance

If you decide that you don't want term life insurance and that permanent life insurance will better meet your specific needs, there are three major types you can purchase: *whole, universal,* and *variable life insurance.* With whole and universal life policies, the insurance company will invest your cash value and give you a declared interest rate. In contrast, variable life policies give you mutual-fund type investment options for your cash value, and you have numerous investment options to choose from.

One of the major advantages of these policies is that the money you invest in a cash value life insurance policy will grow on a tax-deferred basis, similar to a fixed or variable annuity.

Whole Life Insurance A cash value policy, also known as a *whole life policy*, is a permanent policy in which you are guaranteed coverage for life. Your premiums are priced accordingly because the insurance companies know that they will eventually have to pay out the death benefits (unless you let the policy lapse by not paying your premiums). These policies have a cash value, which means that the insurance company takes your annual premium, deducts some administrative fees and a profit margin plus the cost of death protection, and puts the rest into a savings account called your *cash value*. So, you are actually buying term life insurance that will not expire, with a savings plan as an add-on. Whole life insurance is generally just a costly way to maintain a tax-deferred and in some cases tax-free, savings account.

Universal Life Insurance This is a variation of whole life insurance, except that the return on the investment portion of your insurance premiums is not guaranteed and grows at a variable rate. As with whole life insurance, the insurance company makes many of the investment decisions.

Because whole life insurance policies and universal life insurance policies have cash values, if you decide not to keep your policy, or if you suddenly need money while you are alive, you can cash out. However, if your goal in buying life insurance is to put money aside, there are far better ways to save.

Variable Life Insurance Variable life insurance is a product that has evolved significantly over the past several years. Our experience has been that this type of policy only fits a small number of clients. While it can certainly benefit the right client, you must use caution when dealing with a product that has as many moving parts as a variable life insurance policy. Make sure that you fully understand the costs and benefit features before using any of these products.

Comparing Term Life Insurance and Permanent Life Insurance In most cases, the most effective strategy is purchasing a term life insurance policy that will cover you until you are financially prepared to retire. If you do not opt into a more expensive permanent policy (whether whole, universal, or variable life), you can use the money that you save to accumulate wealth, which can be used while you are alive in retirement. If you also use these savings to fund a qualified employer-provided retirement plan or an individual retirement account (IRA), you will be able to save in pre-tax dollars. This will make a significant difference in the time it takes for you to achieve financial independence. (This is covered in more detail in Chapter 8, "Planning for Retirement.")

Second-to-die Life Insurance Policy

This type of policy is also referred to as a *survivorship life policy*: it insures two people (usually spouses), and it does not pay until both insured people have died. Such a policy is normally worth considering if you are going to leave a very large estate that will incur substantial estate taxes. The most common type of second-to-die policy is universal life, which is permanent insurance. You can also purchase 10-, 20-, or 30-year *convertible* second-to-die term life insurance, which is much more affordable. Keep in mind that the primary purpose for this type of insurance is for estate planning; therefore, you do not want to outlive the term of your policy. Ultimately, a permanent second-to-die life insurance policy will be needed for this purpose.

If you convert a term policy to a permanent policy, you will end up paying more than if you bought a no-frills permanent policy upfront. This strategy is less expensive upfront but can be significantly more expensive once you exercise your option to convert. It is only less expensive if you end up not needing to convert. If you take this route, you must buy a policy that does not limit your conversion options. Many carriers only allow you to convert to their more expensive products, potentially compounding the greater expense of conversion. They do this because most people who choose to convert do so because of unexpected health problems.

Federal tax law allows you to leave an unlimited amount of money tax-free to your spouse. When your spouse dies, federal taxes will be due on both your estates, and they usually must be paid within nine months of the death of the second spouse. A second-to-die life insurance policy could theoretically be used to cover the payment of these estate taxes.

If you have a substantial net worth and believe your estate will be subject to significant estate taxes, a permanent life insurance policy may then be the right choice for you. Although most people only need term insurance, high-net-worth individuals can take advantage of the significant tax savings a permanent insurance policy can offer. When combining a permanent life insurance policy with an irrevocable life insurance trust (ILIT), you can significantly preserve your family's financial legacy. This is one of the most effective tax-smart estate planning strategies that allows you to protect and maintain your legacy of generational wealth. (Estate planning with life insurance is covered in more detail in Chapter 10, "Preserving Your Estate.")

As you can see, having the right type of life insurance at different stages in your life is an essential part of any high-quality financial plan. Making the right choices will accelerate your progress toward achieving financial independence. You must always remember to distinguish between what you *need* and what you *want.* Life insurance is perhaps the most unselfish *need* in your life because you will not personally benefit from it; it is a need you fulfill for the benefit of your loved ones.

Buying Insurance Policies

Make sure you have done your research before purchasing insurance. Compare policies and companies to be certain you are getting what you really need at the best possible price available. (For detailed advice on comparison shopping as it relates to insurance, see Chapter 6, "Protecting Your Property with Insurance.")

If you do not pay attention to the tax consequences of insuring your health and life, you may be paying significantly more in taxes than the law requires. Therefore, you must include tax planning as part of your overall insurance and generational wealth strategy. Using a financial planning approach that takes advantage of tax-smart strategies will help maximize your wealth through proper risk management.

Tax-smart Strategies for Insuring Your Health and Life

Here are several tax facts and strategies that will address your wealth accumulation goals in a powerful and sustainable way. This will be part of your tax-smart roadmap to financial independence. This is how you can transform the tax code into part of your generational wealth code.

- Take full advantage of medical insurance premiums paid by your employer on your behalf. This is considered a tax-free fringe benefit. These medical insurance premiums are 100% deductible by your employer and tax-free to you. All payments made by the medical insurance company to cover your medical expenses are also tax-free payments made for your benefit.
- Under the Tax Cuts and Jobs Act, there are opportunities to deduct medical costs for you and your family. Your deduction is limited to the amount that exceeds 7.5% of your adjusted gross income (AGI). This is why having medical

(continued)

(*continued*)

insurance through your employer, and an HSA is so important; it allows you to pay for these costs in pre-tax dollars.

- The threshold for the medical expense itemized deduction permanently remains at 7.5% of AGI. For example, if your AGI is $80,000, you can deduct unreimbursed medical expenses over $6,000, assuming you otherwise qualify for itemized deductions.
- If your health insurance is an HSA-qualified high-deductible plan, you should establish a health savings account and fully fund tax-deductible contributions to cover future medical expenses. In 2025, individuals can contribute up to $4,300 for self-only coverage and $8,550 for family coverage. If you are age 55 or older, you can make an additional $1,000 catch-up contribution. Beginning January 1, 2026, Bronze and Catastrophic ACA marketplace plans will become HSA-eligible, expanding access to more taxpayers.
- Insurance premium costs for qualified long-term care insurance policies may be deductible, depending on your age and AGI limitations. For 2025, the maximum deductible premiums are: $480 if you are up to age 40; $900 (ages 41–50); $1,800 (51–60); $4,810 (61–70); and $6,020 (over age 70).
- Benefits paid under a qualified long-term care insurance policy, which are reimbursements of qualified expenses, are treated as tax-free. However, for indemnity or per diem policies, the exclusion is capped at $420 per day in 2025; amounts above that may be taxable.
- Workers' compensation payments for job-related injuries or illnesses are tax-free.
- Dividends on life insurance policies are generally treated as a refund of your premiums and are not taxed until they exceed the total premiums paid.
- You can exchange certain insurance policies on a tax-free basis (these are called tax-free exchanges under Code Section 1035) if they meet certain requirements. Generally, you can exchange a life insurance policy for another life insurance policy, endowment policy, or an annuity contract. You can also exchange an endowment policy for another endowment policy or annuity contract, and you can exchange annuity contracts for another annuity contract with identical annuitants. See your insurance advisor for more details.
- Life insurance proceeds you receive upon the death of the insured are generally income-tax-free to the beneficiary. If not properly structured, however, the insurance proceeds may be subject to estate taxes (the 40% rate may apply), and the beneficiary may actually receive the reduced amount. This reduction may be eliminated by setting up an ILIT. (For more details, see Chapter 10, "Preserving Your Estate.")
- If you are terminally ill, you may be eligible for a tax-free accelerated death benefit withdrawal from your life insurance policy. If the policy lacks an accelerated benefit clause, it may be sold to a viatical settlement company without paying tax on proceeds.

An Action Plan for Insuring Your Health and Life

1. **If your employer offers health insurance, make sure you understand all facets of the plan.** If details of the plan are not crystal clear to you, make an appointment with your human resources representative, and make sure it is explained to you.
2. **If your employer offers health insurance benefits, make sure your plan adequately covers your health care needs** (and your family's). If it does not, buy supplemental insurance or another policy altogether.
3. **If you are approaching age 65, become familiar with current Medicare laws.** Apply for Medicare at least one month before you turn 65, so you will be covered on the first day of the month of your birthday. Although you are automatically covered under Medicare Part A once you apply, clarify whether you want to be covered under Medicare Part B or Medicare Part D. You cannot contribute to an HSA once you are enrolled in any part of Medicare.
4. **Check to see if your employer offers long-term disability insurance** as an employee benefit because group rates are substantially lower than individual rates.
5. **If you must buy your own long-term disability insurance** (which is usually expensive), consider buying a small policy now with a rider to add more later.
6. **When considering a long-term disability insurance policy, look for ways to cut down on the price of premiums,** such as to age 65 (not lifetime), longer elimination periods, prepayment, or excluding chronic medical conditions that require treatment but will not cause permanent disability.
7. **Consider buying long-term care insurance,** especially if you are older than age 50 (or have parents who may require your help) or you have substantial assets to protect. Be aware that premiums are age-based and rise significantly each year you delay.
8. **Carefully analyze your needs for buying life insurance.**
9. **Understand the pros and cons of the basic types of life insurance** (term life, whole life, universal life, and variable life insurance).
10. **Consider securing the help of an insurance broker or advisor,** especially if you feel unsure of your insurance choices and decisions.
11. **Always secure new insurance coverage before you drop an old policy.** Never leave yourself without proper coverage.
12. **Work with a tax-advisor and CERTIFIED FINANCIAL PLANNER®** who can provide you with the tax-smart advice covered in this chapter. Please refer to Appendix A, "Selecting a Trusted Advisor."
13. **Work with a financial planner** that will provide you with the necessary advice and guidance that includes the 12 critical areas of comprehensive wealth management covered throughout this book.
14. **Use the tax-smart roadmap to financial independence to transform the tax code into part of your generational wealth code.**

CHAPTER 6

Protecting Your Property with Insurance

The personal right to acquire property, which is a natural right, gives to property, when acquired, a right to protection, as a social right.

—James Madison, Fourth President of the United States

Insuring your home, its contents, and your automobile is not only a necessity, but in some situations, a legal requirement. This chapter explains how to analyze your property insurance needs and make sure you are sufficiently covered. Protecting your property by implementing the proper risk management strategies is critical to achieving financial independence while also helping to preserve the assets you've built for the next generation. The type and extent of insurance you need will change throughout your lifetime, as will the types of assets and the extent of wealth you have accumulated.

The three major personal property risk management issues include the following:

1. Homeowners insurance
2. Automobile insurance
3. Umbrella liability insurance

Your particular situation will determine what type of insurance you need, what kind of policy will work best, and how much coverage you should have. You should consult with your property liability insurance agent or broker to fully evaluate your needs so that you can determine proper coverage to meet those needs. It is critically important to remember that you should always secure your new insurance coverage before you cancel your old policy. You never want to leave yourself unprotected without proper coverage between policies.

Insurance helps protect you and your family from the unexpected. The premiums you pay will provide you with the peace of mind of knowing that your assets and family will be financially protected if accidents or disasters occur.

This chapter begins with a client story that underscores the importance of securing the necessary property and liability insurance. This is the most tragic story in this book, but it is necessary to help you understand just how vital this topic is.

Case Study: How a Lack of Insurance Wiped Out One Woman's Life Savings

One of my clients is a medical doctor who devoted her entire life to helping children with cancer. She is one of the most caring and loving people I know. She became a doctor to care for and nurture children in need, which became her life's work. At the age of 50, she felt something was missing in her life. She had never been married and had no children of her own. She made the bold and courageous decision to adopt a child. I refer to her as Dr. Bigheart.

Dr. Bigheart started the long, emotional, and costly process of adopting a child. After several disappointments, she finally found a three-year-old child named Tania, who was living in an orphanage in Russia. The child was a beautiful, blond-haired, blue-eyed little girl. She was very thin, wore old clothing, and was teary-eyed, but she still managed to smile when she first saw Dr. Bigheart, who also had tears of joy in her eyes, because she knew she had found her daughter.

She spoke with the social worker responsible for Tania, who told her it would be at least six months before the adoption process would be completed and approved. That same day, she noticed that little Tania was very attached to a two-year-old boy named Joshua and discovered that this was Tania's brother. By the next day, Dr. Bigheart decided there was no way she could separate the siblings and leave Joshua behind. So, she completed the paperwork to adopt both children at the same time.

As expected, the process took just over six months to complete, and she made six separate trips to Russia during this time, each time hoping to return with the children. Finally, that day came and she got on the plane from Moscow with both children in her arms. To this day, she describes this as the single most important day of her life.

She watched her children grow and went through the usual joys and challenges of parenting. She finally felt that her life was complete. Through her work as a children's cancer doctor and with her new family, she felt a true sense of purpose and meaning.

On Tania's 17th birthday, her mother surprised her with a brand-new car. Tania had gotten her driver's license and was a good driver. Six months later, Tania got into an argument with her boyfriend, and he broke up with her. She was very upset and drove off, speeding down the road in her car. She spun out of control and killed a man who was getting out of his car. Her car then crashed and rolled over, killing Tania instantly.

When Dr. Bigheart got the news of the accident, she rushed to the hospital. When the emergency room doctor told her that Tania did not survive, Dr. Bigheart collapsed to the ground and could not stop crying. She was overcome with grief, could not catch her breath, and needed to be admitted to the hospital. She had just lived every parent's worst nightmare: the death of a child. The wake was heartbreaking; Joshua had lost his sister, and Dr. Bigheart had lost her daughter. The emotions she was feeling could not be described in words, but only through the expression in her face and eyes.

A month after her daughter's death, she was sued by the family of the innocent man who was struck and killed in the accident. The lawsuit was for wrongful death and the pain and suffering of his family, in the amount of $5 million. At this point, Dr. Bigheart came to me for advice, and I asked her to bring in her auto and other personal liability insurance policies. Just when it seemed like her life could not get worse, I had to tell her that she did not have enough coverage. She had a basic auto liability policy that only provided $300,000 in personal liability coverage. When I asked about her personal umbrella liability insurance, she said she had never bothered to get that type of policy.

As I feared, after her auto insurance company reviewed the claim, it refused to cover the full amount because the claim exceeded the policy limits. The insurance company informed Dr. Bigheart that it would pay the full $300,000 from the policy limits, but it would not cover the legal defense costs. Dr. Bigheart was forced to retain a lawyer at her own expense to defend this case seeking $5 million.

Along with the grief and depression that came with the loss of her daughter, she now had to deal with the fear that her life savings would be wiped out as a result of this lawsuit. The lawsuit dragged on for two years until it was eventually settled. She paid more than $80,000 in legal fees and made a final settlement to the victim's family of $800,000 of which the insurance company covered only $300,000. At the age of 67, she was forced to pay this $580,000 from her investment savings. She later said that the money was not even the hardest part of the trial. Having to relive what happened that day over and over again was truly unbearable. Dr. Bigheart is now in her mid-seventies and is still working part time. She could not fully retire because a big part of her retirement savings was wiped out.

I cannot overemphasize the importance of having the appropriate property and liability coverage. Speak to your property and liability agent or insurance broker today. If you do not have the appropriate umbrella liability coverage, you must get it immediately. Property risk management is one of the keys to achieving financial independence and creating and maintaining generational wealth.

The rest of this chapter describes what you need to know about the three major property risk management issues that are critical to protecting your property through insurance.

Homeowners Insurance

Homeowners insurance needs to cover the cost of rebuilding or repairing your home in the event of damage from a fire, storm, burglary, or other type of catastrophe. Standard policies typically cover the house (the structure) and its contents (furniture, clothing, and other personal belongings). Coverage for contents usually ranges from 50% to 70% of the amount for which you insure the structure. For example, if you have $400,000 in insurance coverage on the structure of your home, you will have between $200,000 and $280,000 of coverage for your personal belongings, in addition to the coverage for the structure itself.

Homeowners' policies also include liability coverage for damage or injuries incurred inside or outside your house.

Property Coverage

An actual *cash-value policy* will compensate you for the cost of your belongings minus their devaluation (used value), whereas a *replacement-cost policy* means that the insurance company must compensate you for the actual cost of replacing the lost or damaged items.

For example, if you have a fire in one room of your house and all the furniture in that room is destroyed, and you have a cash-value policy, your insurance company will ask how much you originally paid for that furniture. If you spent $5,000 and you owned that furniture for 10 years, the insurance company may decide that its *current* value is only $2,000 because you used it for 10 years. That is the amount the insurance company will pay you: $2,000.

In contrast, if you have a *replacement-cost policy*, the insurance company is likely to compensate you with at least $5,000 and probably even more, given that prices and inflation have increased and the cost of a new bedroom set may now be closer to $10,000 today. So, which would you want to receive: $2,000 or $10,000?

Of course, you need to consider that the premiums for a replacement-cost policy will be higher than for a cash-value policy, but the difference may be a small price to pay for the additional peace of mind you will have in knowing that you will be fully compensated if something catastrophic happened in your home. You should always opt for a replacement-cost policy for both your home and its contents because it will provide you with a reimbursement sufficient to replace your loss.

As Jerry Patterson, head of Advanced Wealth Solutions at Cetera Financial Group, explains:

> One of the most critical and commonly misunderstood elements of homeowners insurance is the distinction between cash value and replacement cost. Many people choose the lowest premium, assuming that if their property is damaged or destroyed, their insurance will automatically cover the cost to restore or replace it as good as new. That is not always the case. This difference can determine whether you recover fully from a loss or suffer a serious financial setback.

If your home is damaged and uninhabitable, your insurer may also compensate you for the costs of maintaining a temporary residence (renting a hotel room or another home) while repairs are made. Given the increasing risk of severe weather, you should review whether flood or earthquake coverage makes sense for your situation.

The majority of homeowners policies are written under the HO-3 contract form. These form numbers are standardized throughout the insurance industry, so if you purchase HO-3 insurance, you will get the identical coverage regardless of your insurance provider. The HO-3 contract form provides the following coverage:

- **Broad coverage for your dwelling:** Damage to your dwelling from most causes is covered unless specifically excluded.
- **Coverage for your personal property against "named perils" only:** Your personal property is covered only for the perils specified in the contract. For example, if you do not live in an earthquake-prone area, but you are still concerned about fire, theft, flooding, and hail damage, you may elect to get a named perils policy and only declare coverage against fire, theft, flooding, and hail, while leaving the earthquake coverage off the policy.
- **Limited coverage for stolen jewelry:** Coverage is usually limited to $1,500–2,500, depending on your state of resident and policy. Most policies do not cover jewelry that is lost or misplaced. Installing a basic monitored burglar alarm will often pay for itself through a discount on your homeowner's insurance.

Flood Insurance It is worth noting that flood insurance is one of the most misunderstood areas of property coverage. Standard homeowner's policies do not cover flood damage, so a separate policy is required. Many people assume they are not at risk, yet flooding can occur almost anywhere.

Adding to the confusion, FEMA frequently updates flood maps and risk zones, which means a property that was once considered low risk may later be reclassified as high risk. These changes can affect both insurance costs and property values.

Flood policies are typically available through the National Flood Insurance Program (NFIP) or private insurers and usually cover both the structure and contents, subject to certain limits and exclusions. Given the increasing severity of storms and other extreme weather events, flood insurance should be viewed as an essential part of a comprehensive property risk management plan.

Endorsements Provide Additional Coverage If you would like to increase the amount of your coverage for valuable items, endorsements may provide the additional coverage you desire. You can increase your limits for items such as jewelry, furs, gold, silverware, or firearms.

Some endorsements also cover modern risks such as identity theft expenses or losses related to cybercrime. This type of protection can help pay for the cost of restoring your identity or recovering from fraud or a breach involving your home's connected devices. As more households use smart technology, this added coverage can be a simple way to strengthen your overall protection plan.

Choosing the Right Deductible and Filing Claims Homeowners insurance is meant for major disasters (as mentioned at the beginning of this section), not for filing small claims, such as a broken window caused by your neighbor's son playing hardball in his yard. You may be tempted to file small claims to get back the money you contributed to premiums, but today's insurers track your claims history more closely than ever.

Even one small claim can sometimes affect your premiums or your eligibility for renewal and can stay on your record for five to seven years. Filing multiple claims can cause your insurance company to raise your premiums or even cancel your homeowner's insurance policy altogether.

It is best to have a policy with a high deductible so that you have no reason to file lower-cost claims. The higher the deductible, the lower your premium; in essence, you are self-insuring for any damage up to the amount of the deductible. The standard deductible is typically $1,000. We recommend increasing this amount to $2,000, $5,000, or even more if you feel you can cover this cost on your own. Because you will not be filing small claims anyway, why not save the premium dollars? You can then use this savings to cover these deductibles in the event a situation occurs.

Other Considerations As Jerry Patterson explains:

> Insurance requirements can also depend on how a property is purchased. When you buy a home with a mortgage, the lender will usually require minimum levels of insurance coverage to protect its interest in the property. Cash buyers, however, face no such requirements and that lack of oversight can create hidden risks.

For example, someone who buys a lake cottage in a flood plain for cash may not be required to carry flood insurance. Years later, when the property is sold, a new buyer using a mortgage may be required by their lender to obtain flood insurance, which can significantly reduce the property's market value. This is why it is essential for cash buyers to take a proactive approach to risk management and consider insurance needs just as carefully as if a lender were involved.

Liability Coverage

Liability coverage is intended to protect your assets if you are sued by someone who is injured or whose property is damaged because of your negligence. For example, you may be diligent about keeping your house clean and safe at all times, and when it snows, you are always the first one out the door with a snow shovel and rock salt to keep the sidewalk safe for others. But suppose an unexpected blizzard hits your hometown during Thanksgiving week, while you are visiting your family out of town. While you are away, you obviously cannot care for your property and ensure the safety of others by shoveling and properly cleaning the walkway. If an elderly woman trips and falls crossing your property, breaking her leg and hip, she may require major surgery and hospitalization. Without the proper liability insurance, you could be held liable for her injuries, which could cost you hundreds of thousands of dollars.

You must also have liability insurance and medical protection coverage for your visitors. For example, if your children decide to have a sleepover in your home and one of their friends falls and breaks an arm, you may need this coverage to help pay for the child's medical expenses if you are sued by the child's parents.

You should consider increased limits if you have "attractive nuisance" features on your property, such as swimming pools, hot tubs, or pets that could cause harm.

What Liability Insurance Covers and What It Does Not Cover Most homeowners' insurance covers the following:

- **Accidental injuries to visitors that take place on your property, such as slips and falls:** If that person sues you, your insurance usually provides protection against judgments where you are

found negligent and offers medical payments to others who are injured on your property.
- **Injuries to people caused by you, your household members, or your pets, even when you are away from home**.

On the other hand, your homeowner's insurance generally does *not* cover the following:

- **Deliberate actions that result in a claim or loss:** These are typically not covered by any standard insurance *policy*. For example, if your neighbor parks in your driveway and you decide to "teach him a lesson" by hitting him with a baseball bat, intentional acts of violence such as this would not be covered.
- **Known hazards and neglected risks:** Failure to take reasonable precautions to repair, correct, or fix a situation that could result in injury or loss is typically not covered by insurance. Always keep your property in good condition and address potential hazards immediately. For example, if you have a defective sidewalk that is uneven and clearly a hazard, and you choose to ignore it, your insurance company may deny coverage for a resulting injury to a third party.
- **Liability related to business activities run from your home:** A standard homeowner's policy generally does not cover injuries or damages connected to operating a business from your residence. For example, if a client slips and falls while visiting your home office, you could be personally responsible for any medical bills or lawsuits.
- **Liability related to rental activities:** If you rent part or all of your property to tenants, injuries or damages related to the rental use often require separate landlord insurance. For example, if a tenant's guest slips on an icy walkway and sues you, your standard homeowner's policy may not cover the claim.

For most people, their home is their castle and one of their most significant personal use assets. Having proper homeowner's insurance is an important step to keep you on track to achieving financial independence and creating and maintaining generational wealth. Without proper insurance, one of your major assets can be lost and impossible to replace. Furthermore, if you are sued for injuries sustained by others because of your negligence, you could be wiped out financially.

Automobile Insurance

Auto insurance is required by law, and the state you live in will determine the type and amount of coverage required. An auto insurance policy is made up of seven different primary coverage types, each with its own premium. The cost for each type will vary based on numerous factors, such as where you live, the type of car you drive, your driving record (including any past accidents or tickets), and even your credit history. The only way to find out what your cost of coverage will be is to ask for a personalized price quote. When pricing auto insurance, it always pays to shop around, and you should always obtain a minimum of two price quotes from two separate insurance companies.

1. **Bodily injury liability:** Provides protection if you injure or kill someone while operating your car. It also provides for legal defense if another party in the accident files a lawsuit against you. To protect your personal assets, you should have sufficient coverage to guard against a lawsuit after a serious accident. Bodily injury liability covers injury to people, not damage to your own vehicle. Generally, you want the same amount of coverage for all your vehicles.
2. **Medical payments, no-fault, or personal injury protection coverage (PIP):** Typically pays for the medical expenses of the injured driver and passengers in your car, regardless of who was at fault for the accident. A no-fault auto insurance system means drivers in that state file claims with their own insurer for injuries, regardless of fault.
3. **Uninsured motorist coverage:** Pays for injuries caused by an uninsured driver or, in some states, a hit-and-run driver, in a crash that is not your fault. Some states also offer uninsured motorist coverage for damage to your vehicle. Even if you live in a no-fault state, it is very important to have this coverage; you might be surprised by how many uninsured motorists are on the road. According to recent data from the Insurance Research Council, about 12–13% of US motorists (or about one out of eight) are driving without insurance and operating their vehicles illegally.
4. **Comprehensive physical damage coverage:** Pays for losses if your car is stolen or damaged by events such as floods, fires, or

animals. It does not cover collision. One strategy for keeping your insurance premium lower is to select a high deductible. Self-insuring against minor losses is wise if you have sufficient cash reserves to cover these costs when the need arises.

5. **Collision coverage:** Pays for damage to your car when your car hits, or is hit by, another vehicle or other objects. A rule of thumb is that your car value should be at least 10 times the cost of your annual collision premium. If it is not, consider dropping or reducing collision and physical damage coverage and self-insuring instead if you have the reserves to cover the cost of repairs or replacement.
6. **Property damage liability:** Protects you in the event your car damages someone else's property. It also provides legal defense coverage if a lawsuit is filed against you. For example, if you are backing out of your driveway and accidentally step on the accelerator instead of the brake, causing you to crash into your neighbor's living room, the property damage liability coverage will help pay for the repairs.
7. **Rental reimbursement coverage:** Pays for the cost of a rental vehicle when the insured person's vehicle cannot be used because of losses covered under comprehensive or collision coverage.

The insurance industry uses shorthand to describe how much coverage each policy provides. For example, a common minimum recommendation for auto liability coverage is at least *250/500/100*, which means you have

- $250,000 in bodily injury coverage per person,
- $500,000 in bodily injury coverage per accident, and
- $100,000 in property damage liability.

Most states use a no-fault auto insurance system; other states use a third-party system to settle claims where the driver at fault is financially responsible, and claims are typically made against that driver's liability insurance. Some no-fault states now have updated rules that allow drivers to choose higher PIP thresholds or optional tort coverage, which allows drivers to step outside the no-fault system and sue an at-fault driver (or be sued themselves) for certain damages that would otherwise be restricted. Be sure to review your state's current requirements and discuss with your insurance agent whether choosing a different PIP limit or tort option makes sense for your situation.

To determine whether your state is a no-fault auto insurance state, contact your auto insurance carrier or visit the Insurance Information Institute website at www.iii.org. This website was established to improve public understanding of insurance, what it does, and how it works. You can also check your state's department of insurance website for up-to-date local rules.

Even with no-fault insurance, you may still need liability coverage because if you cause an accident and the damage exceeds a certain threshold, the injured party can sue you for the difference. Without sufficient liability coverage, the shortfall would have to come out of your own pocket. In the case study discussed earlier in this chapter, the necessity of having sufficient liability coverage was underscored by the tragic real-life story of Dr. Bigheart.

If your child is going to drive, they must have insurance. Insurance companies know that young drivers are risky drivers, so they will charge you high rates to protect against this added risk. The only way to determine what the added cost of insurance will be once your young driver gets a license is to ask your insurance provider for a price quote. Knowing the answer to this question early may help you decide whether to delay your child's license until they are older.

If your teenagers are determined to get their license now, you can still save money by not purchasing another car. If you do purchase a car for your teenage driver, then you should also consider buying your child a used car because it is more sensible to have your child drive the oldest and least expensive car you own. This helps keep your cost of insurance lower than it would be otherwise. Of course, if you have an older car, make sure it is still safe to drive; your family's safety is always more important than saving some money.

Make sure you are aware of all discounts available from your insurance carrier. Good grade discounts for younger drivers can motivate your child to keep grades up. Low mileage discounts are great for those who do not drive frequently, and drivers' education discounts may be available to both young drivers and adults. Many insurers now offer discounts for using telematics devices or apps that monitor safe driving habits, though we would caution this could wind up working against you if you do not drive carefully. This can be a great way to earn savings if you drive responsibly.

An insurance company determines your premium based on certain statistics and facts about you and other drivers. These factors are based on your age, your gender, where you live, the type of car you drive, your driving record, your credit score (where allowed), etc. Although some of these factors are out of our control, the ones that you can control should be carefully analyzed before purchasing a car.

For example, the cost of insuring a red Corvette is much higher than insuring a white Dodge minivan. Selecting an eight-cylinder vehicle will generally cost you more than a six-cylinder vehicle because more power usually means more risk. When analyzing which car to purchase for yourself and family members, ask your insurance company for a price quote on each separate vehicle. This simple step can help you make a wiser and more affordable choice.

The basic rule from Chapter 1, "Committing to Living Within Your Means," holds true when purchasing auto insurance or a new automobile. Always ask yourself, is the purchase of this vehicle a need or a want? If it is a need, is there a less expensive alternative? And always remember to shop around and compare to get the very best price possible.

Umbrella Liability Insurance

Homeowners, auto, and boat insurance policies provide a limited amount of liability protection, but these policies may not offer enough coverage to protect your assets in the event of a major lawsuit. A serious lawsuit can cost you significant dollars in legal defense costs and settlement payments, far beyond what you might reasonably cover from your savings. Umbrella liability insurance policies provide you with a secondary layer of insurance protection that is above and beyond the normal coverage limits of your other policies. Umbrella insurance protects you only after your homeowners, auto, or boat insurance policy has paid or is expected to pay its maximum benefit.

For example, in the tragic story of Dr. Bigheart, her insurance company raised the white flag and surrendered. The lawsuit brought by the family of the man her daughter killed was seeking $5 million, yet Dr. Bigheart's auto insurance policy limit for liability was only $300,000. Because Dr. Bigheart did not have an umbrella liability insurance policy, she had no other resources to turn to for help.

Umbrella liability insurance is like having a secondary parachute to protect you in case your first parachute (standard policy) fails. It can offer coverage above and beyond your standard policies, often extending into the millions, if you are sued because of an accident or injury. The amount and type of coverage offered through an umbrella liability policy vary based on the policy and insurance provider. Be sure to review exactly what the policy you purchase does and does not cover.

Your total combined insurance policies for homeowners, auto, boat, and umbrella must cover at least an amount equal to or greater than your personal net worth. A personal liability umbrella policy is something that no one who owns a car and a home should do without. We recommend buying a policy that will fully protect you. Personal liability umbrella coverage typically ranges from $1 million to $5 million, although some households with higher net worth or greater risk may choose $10 million or more. The cost of that insurance is relatively low. You can expect to pay about $150–300 per year for $1 million in coverage, and each additional million typically costs about $50–75 per year.

Most insurance companies will require you to have a certain level of coverage (as described next) on your other policies before you can purchase umbrella coverage. Therefore, very often you will need to upgrade the coverage under your home, car, and boat insurance policy. Most personal umbrella policies will require you to maintain at least the following amount of coverage under your other policies to be eligible for this additional coverage.

- **Auto Insurance Policy:** $250,000 per person and $500,000 per accident for bodily injury, and $100,000 for property damage.
- **Homeowners Insurance Policy:** $300,000 liability limit.
- **Boat insurance Policy (if applicable):**
  - $100,000 liability for boats under 26 feet long and under 50 horsepower.
  - $300,000 liability for boats 26 feet and longer, or 50 horsepower and up; some carriers require this amount for any boat with an engine.

The following sections describe some of the coverage you can typically find under a personal umbrella insurance policy. It is important to review and compare these policies carefully so you can determine exactly what is and is not included.

Bodily Injury Liability

This covers the cost of damages to another person's body. For example, the cost of medical bills as well as liability claims resulting from the following:

- Injuries to other parties due to a severe auto accident where you were at fault
- Injuries to a guest in your home
- Injuries to your child's friend who falls and breaks a leg while playing in your yard
- Injuries caused to others by your dog

Property Damage Liability

This covers the cost of damage or loss to another person's physical property. For example, the cost associated with claims resulting from the following:

- Damages to someone's vehicle as a result of an auto accident where you were at fault
- Damages to public or private property accidentally caused by your family members
- Damages incurred when your dog destroys a neighbor's furniture or yard

Rental Property Insurance

If you own rental property, you can protect yourself against liability that you, as the landlord, may be subject to. For example, the cost of liability claims from the following:

- Someone who slips on ice in front of your rental property
- Someone who has been bitten by your tenant's dog

Umbrella extended coverage may also be provided in the event you are sued for the following:

- Slander, which is injurious spoken statements
- Libel, which is injurious written statements
- Malicious prosecution
- False arrest or imprisonment
- Various other personal liability situations

One of our clients experienced this firsthand when their teenage son posted false and hurtful statements about another student on social media. The family of the other student filed a defamation lawsuit, claiming that the comments caused emotional distress and damaged their child's reputation. The lawsuit sought $250,000 in damages. When my client came to us for advice, we asked to see their homeowners and umbrella policies. Thankfully, they had a $1 million umbrella liability policy in place, which helped pay for more than $40,000 in legal defense fees and covered the final settlement of $200,000. Without that added protection, they could have been forced to use their hard-earned savings to pay the entire cost of the lawsuit out of pocket.

One of the most overlooked reasons to purchase umbrella insurance is because you have children. Just think back to the tragic story of Dr. Bigheart and her daughter as well as the story about a client's teenage son. As a parent, you are legally responsible for your minor child's actions, which could cause serious financial hardships if they are found responsible for an accident, injury, or loss of life. The age of majority is the age at which a minor becomes an adult in the eyes of the law of your state of resident. This age is 18 in most states, but a few states extend the age of majority to 19 or 21.

Millions of Americans are now at or near retirement age and are working to protect what they have built. Many have followed the principles in this book and reached financial independence, but as Dr. Bigheart's story shows, a single lawsuit can erase an entire lifetime of savings. This can put not only your financial independence, but also your family's future and any plans to build generational wealth at risk.

As mentioned, the premiums for an umbrella insurance policy typically range from only $150–300 a year for $1 million in coverage, and about $50–75 a year for every additional million dollars in coverage thereafter. That is a small price to pay for the added peace of mind this protection provides.

Buying Insurance Policies

Before you purchase insurance, make sure you have done the proper research. Always shop around and compare policies to ensure you are getting what you really need at the best possible price. When doing your comparison shopping, be certain you are comparing the detailed coverage and limitations that may apply. Are these policies providing the same level of coverage? Are the deductibles the same for each policy? Does one policy exclude certain items while the other one includes them? It is easy to obtain a less expensive policy by purchasing one that provides you with more limited coverage. Do not compare based on price alone, because the cheapest policy may not be the best policy to meet your needs. You must find out exactly what the policy will specifically cover and what is excluded from the coverage. Make sure you know exactly what is required for you to qualify for the benefits.

Finally, reevaluate your needs each year and ensure that your policies still meet your requirements. As Jerry Patterson explains,

> The process should not be a once and done. Many people stick with their property insurance company for many years, often due to loyalty discounts or the complexity they fear exists in shopping around. You should review your coverage on a regular basis over a lifetime. Your level of risk, ability to self-fund that risk, and/or your need to insure against that risk is greatly affected by your life stage and your progress in building wealth and financial security.
>
> From your first day of adulthood, to married life, to kids, and then to, and through, retirement, it is really important to make sure that you have the right insurance strategy in place. You should review your coverage throughout your lifetime, especially as you move from life stage to life stage. For example, the moment you become an empty nester is probably a really good time to review your coverage across the board.

Generally, you always want to compare policies from two or more insurance companies. You may want to consider increasing your deductible, which will generally lower your premiums. Many insurance companies offer you a reduced premium if you are able and willing to pay on an annual basis instead of monthly or quarterly. You should also ask about multiple policy discounts if you are purchasing several policies through the same insurance company (e.g., your auto, home, and umbrella policies).

When shopping for a new policy, consider asking friends and family about their claims experience with the carriers you are considering.

A less expensive policy may not be such a great deal if the provider is difficult to work with or is slow to pay claims. Online reviews and customer satisfaction surveys can also help you evaluate an insurer's reputation for services and claims handling.

When choosing an insurance company, you want to make sure it is financially sound and will be around to pay your claim when the time comes. All insurance companies are not created equally, and very often, you may be quoted a lower price from a company that is not as financially sound as the others you are comparing it to. The four major rating services for insurance companies can assist you in determining a company's financial strength: check with these rating agencies before entering into an insurance contract:

1. AM Best (www.ambest.com)
2. Moody's (www.moodys.com)
3. Standard & Poor's (www.standardandpoors.com)
4. Duff & Phelps (www.duffandphelps.com)

Before you buy an insurance policy from any company, please be sure the company carries at least a rating of "AA" or better from Moody's, Standard & Poor's, or Duff & Phelps; if you are evaluating an insurance company through AM Best, look for a rating of "A–" or better.

Before you decide on any insurance policy, use this checklist to make sure you choose the right coverage, at the right cost, from a company you can trust.

STEP	WHAT TO DO	WHAT TO LOOK FOR
Shop Around	Get quotes from at least two or more reputable companies.	Compare similar types of coverage for each policy.
Compare Coverage	Read the full policy details.	Make sure coverage amounts, limits, and protections match your needs.
Check Deductibles	Note the deductible amount for each option.	Understand how a higher deductible can lower your premium.
Look for Exclusions	Check for any special conditions or limitations.	Watch for risks that may not be covered by one policy but are covered by another.
Ask About Discounts	Inquire about multipolicy or safe-home discounts.	Bundling home, auto, and umbrella policies can save money.

STEP	WHAT TO DO	WHAT TO LOOK FOR
Consider Payment Options	Find out how premiums can be paid.	Some companies offer a discount if you pay annually instead of monthly.
Review Company Reputation	Ask people you trust and read reviews.	Choose a company known for good customer service and timely claims payments.
Check Financial Strength	Verify ratings with trusted agencies.	Look for A– or better with AM Best, or AA or better with Moody's, S&P, or Duff & Phelps.
Reevaluate Annually	Review your coverage each year.	Update your policies after major life events like buying a home or having children.
Include Tax Planning	Talk to your advisor about taxes.	Coordinate your insurance with tax-smart strategies to protect your savings.
Check the Claims Process	Ask how claims are filed and settled.	Look for quick response times, 24/7 claim support, and clear steps to resolve issues.

As Jerry Patterson explains,

> Insurance companies are always on the move. Whether it's adverse weather trends or a change in strategy, insurance companies are constantly reassessing their strategies and pricing. In some cases, that means that costs could go up and coverage could go down. In others, it could mean an opportunity for you to lower your cost and/or improve your coverage by considering a switch to another insurer.

Throughout your journey to financial independence, you never know what unexpected property risk issues may arise. There are major family risk management issues that concern all of us. Obtaining the proper homeowners, auto, boat, and personal umbrella liability coverage can provide you with the peace of mind of knowing that you and your property will be protected. Being unprepared for the unexpected can rob you and your family of your pursuit of financial independence and generational wealth.

If you do not pay attention to the tax consequences of protecting your property with insurance, you may be paying significantly more in taxes than the law requires. This is why you must include tax planning as part of your overall insurance and generational wealth strategy. Using a financial planning approach that takes advantage of tax-smart strategies will help maximize your asset protection goals.

Tax-smart Strategies for Protecting Your Property with Insurance

Here are several tax facts and strategies that will address your wealth accumulation goals in a powerful and sustainable way. This will be part of your tax-smart roadmap to financial independence. This is how you can transform the tax code into part of your generational wealth code.

- Generally, the cost of personal homeowners, automobile, boat, and umbrella liability insurance is not tax-deductible. Insurance reimbursements to the extent of your loss are generally not taxable. If you receive an insurance reimbursement that exceeds your adjusted basis (what you originally paid for the property plus the cost of any improvements), this excess results in a gain you must report as income unless you acquire replacement property and elect to defer the gain. Work with your tax advisor if you expect a large insurance payout to determine if a replacement election applies to you.
- If you own a rental property, you can generally deduct most of the expenses associated with maintaining and managing the property, as well as the cost of property insurance, which includes premiums for fire, hazard, and liability.
- Casualty and theft losses attributable to personal use property may be partly tax-deductible. Under current law, these deductions remain significantly limited. Taxpayers may only take a deduction for casualty losses if the loss is attributable to a presidentially declared disaster and now certain state-declared disasters under the One Big Beautiful Bill Act.
- For example, if a major hurricane damaged your home and your property is located within a presidentially declared disaster zone, you may qualify for this deduction. This deduction would be claimed on Schedule A of your tax return but would only apply after the limitations set by the Internal Revenue Code. After the casualty or theft loss amount is determined (less insurance reimbursement), any applicable dollar floor will reduce the deductible loss.
- Casualty losses resulting from *presidentially declared disasters, as well as certain state-declared disasters*, may be deducted in the prior tax year by filing an amended return. This allows you to access needed funds sooner. If you experience this type of loss, compare the benefit of deducting it for the prior year with the benefit of claiming it in the current year and choose the option that provides the largest tax savings. This strategy has helped many taxpayers recover more quickly from major events like hurricanes or wildfires.

- Having the proper insurance coverage on your property will provide you with a tax-free reimbursement of your loss. In most cases, insurance payouts for damage or replacement are not taxable when they simply restore what you lost.
- Insurance reimbursements for the cost of added living expenses attributable to damage to your home do not reduce a casualty loss. The payments from the insurance company for these excess living costs are generally not taxable and are treated separately from the payments for property damage.
- As a matter of law, compensatory damages for physical injury or sickness are tax-free. For example, if you are injured in a car accident and you sue the other driver and are awarded $100,000 for pain and suffering, you do not have to pay taxes on this settlement payment. In contrast, damages for nonphysical personal injuries are taxable, such as from discrimination, back pay, wrongful dismissal, or injury to your reputation. So, if you sue a former employer for wrongful dismissal and the court awards you $1,000,000, you will have to pay income taxes on that amount.

An Action Plan for Protecting Your Property with Insurance

1. **Consult with your property liability insurance agent or broker** to fully evaluate your homeowner's insurance needs and determine the proper coverage to meet those needs.
2. **Make sure your homeowners insurance includes both liability insurance and medical protection coverage** for your guests. This protects you in case someone is injured on your property and brings a lawsuit against you.
3. **When buying homeowner's insurance, choose a replacement-cost policy** instead of an actual cash value policy. This will provide you with a reimbursement sufficient to replace your loss in the event of fire or other damage covered in your policy.
4. **Remember that auto liability coverage is required in all states,** and anyone who owns a home and has significant assets should strongly consider buying a minimum of 250/500/100 in coverage: $250,000 for bodily injury per person, $500,000 for bodily injury per accident, and $100,000 for property damage liability. Collision and comprehensive coverage are both optional but often recommended if you want to protect the value of your vehicle.
5. **Make sure your children and other members of your household are insured under your auto insurance policy.** (Check with your auto insurance

(continued)

(continued)

company since these rules vary by state.) Also, keep in mind that you can probably lower your insurance premiums if your children drive an older car rather than a brand-new, expensive model.

6. **Consider buying a personal umbrella liability insurance policy,** which provides a secondary layer of insurance protection that is above the normal coverage limits of your other property insurance policies. You can expect to pay $150–300 per year, which can protect you up to $1 million if you are sued.
7. **When choosing an insurance company, check with the major insurance rating services** to determine the quality of the company. Look for insurers with a solid "AA" or better rating from Moody's, Standard & Poor's, or Duff & Phelps or an "A–" or better rating from AM Best. You want to be sure that your insurer will be in business and financially sound if something happens and you need the protection offered by that company.
8. **Always secure new insurance coverage before you cancel your old policy.** You never want to leave yourself unprotected without proper coverage between policies.
9. **Work with a tax-advisor and CERTIFIED FINANCIAL PLANNER®** that can provide you with the tax-smart advice covered in this chapter. Please refer to Appendix A, "Selecting a Trusted Advisor."
10. **Work with a financial planner** that will provide you with the necessary advice and guidance that includes the 12 critical areas of comprehensive wealth management covered throughout this book.
11. **Use the tax-smart roadmap to financial independence to transform the tax code into part of your generational wealth code.**

CHAPTER 7

Paying for College

An investment in knowledge always pays the best interest.
—Benjamin Franklin, Founding Father of the United States

Most parents struggle with the difficult decisions they need to make while juggling competing financial priorities. Throughout this book, many financial goals that typically arise over the course of a lifetime are explored. These goals include building a cash reserve, minimizing debt, paying for health and life insurance, protecting property, and saving for retirement. Each time we focus on one of our goals, our limited resources require us to make sacrifices with the other goals. Therefore, parents need to make very important decisions when it comes to how to pay for education. The guidance in this chapter will help you make an informed decision and prepare you to meet this challenge.

Helping families reach their financial goals and supporting children in the pursuit of their dreams is among the most rewarding aspects of comprehensive financial planning. There is no greater satisfaction than seeing these goals become reality through careful planning and disciplined execution.

Is College the Best Choice for You and Your Child?

Before planning on how best to pay for college, you first need to decide if college is in fact the best choice. Earning a four-year undergraduate degree will not guarantee a well-paying job, or any job for that matter. In fact, many college graduates are taking jobs that they could have actually gotten right out of high school. The main difference with many of these college graduates is that they, or their family, had to lay out $100,000 to $300,000, and they may now be in debt with student loans that can take decades to pay off. So, it may be necessary to consider whether the college path makes sense before investing in this expensive journey.

A college degree is now somehow considered a *necessity* when in fact, in many cases, it is just something else that you, as a parent or your child, may *want*. Colleges and universities across the country and abroad have terrific recruiting and marketing departments that promise you and your children the world. In reality, they should not be making any promise at all, since there are no guarantees that your child will graduate. Even if your child manages to graduate with straight A's, this does not mean that all of their dreams will come true. Universities often make extremely misleading claims that your child will get a top-paying job and that it is impossible to get ahead without a college education. These statements are clearly not going to be the case for every person who attends college.

Some of the most brilliant and successful individuals are college dropouts. Many left higher education because they felt unchallenged, and they instead chose to pursue their passion. The following is an eye-opening list of just a few entrepreneurs who dropped out of college and went on to become billionaires:

- Michael Dell (Dell founder) dropped out at the age of 19
- Steve Jobs (Apple founder) dropped out at the age of 19
- Bill Gates (Microsoft founder) dropped out at age 20
- Mark Zuckerberg (Meta founder) dropped out at age 20[1]

You are probably thinking that these men are all protégée geniuses and your child may not be. However, many of the most successful people we have worked with, including those who own their own small business, have never attended college. In fact, some of them even dropped out of high school. What they all shared was passion, drive, and being relentless in the pursuit of their business enterprise. Perhaps, instead of investing $100,000 or $200,000 and four or more years in a college education, it may be best to invest some time and money in a small business.

[1] Abigail Hess, "10 Ultra-Successful Millionaire and Billionaire College Dropouts," CNBC.com, May 10, 2017.

So now you may be thinking that my children may not be passionate enough or have the skillset necessary to be an entrepreneur and start their own business. If that is the case, then they should consider pursuing some of the very high-paying jobs available to high school graduates. Some blue-collar jobs are equally important to our society. Without the butchers, bakers, plumbers, carpenters, electricians, and civil servants, our economy and society could not survive.

An article published on March 20, 2025, *by Business Insider* identified the highest-paying jobs that don't require a bachelor's degree. From that list, the top five careers that don't require a college education have been identified, each with the potential to earn $100,000 or more annually.

1. Commercial pilots—median annual pay: $122,670
2. Nuclear power reactor operators—median annual pay: $122,610
3. Power distributors and dispatchers—median annual pay: $107,240
4. Elevator and escalator installers and repairers—median annual pay: $106,580
5. First-line supervisors of police and detectives—median annual pay: $105,980

Not every young adult will go down the same path to achieving financial independence. For many of them, they need to fall down, pick themselves up, and perhaps even redefine themselves before they can reach their true full potential. I (John Sr.) am going to share my own personal story about how, as a young adult, I did just that.

As you know, my parents emigrated here from Italy after World War II with only an eighth-grade education and barely spoke English. My parents had an extremely strong work ethic and always encouraged their children to work hard and get a solid education. It is fair to say that I did not always do what my parents had asked of me.

By the time I was 16 years old, I had already worked as a newspaper delivery boy, an apprentice butcher, and a grocery store clerk. All I was concerned with was making money, hanging out with my friends, and having enough cash to pay for the gas in my seven-year-old 1972 Cadillac Coup de Ville. The things I was interested in at this age definitely did not include college. Although I considered myself to be smart, I had absolutely no interest in reading books and studying for exams at that point in my life. In fact, I dropped out of high school and took on a full-time job working as a truck driver earning $100 a day, which at the time felt like a small fortune.

My parents, as well as my siblings, were not very happy with my decision and continued to encourage me to go back to school. Although I considered being a truck driver a very respectable job, I eventually came to realize that this was not the type of work I wanted to do for the rest of my life.

With the continued encouragement and persistence of my sister Rose, I took the General Educational Development (GED) exam and earned my high school equivalency diploma by the time I was 19. I enrolled in a two-year associate program at Kingsborough Community College in Brooklyn. This is where I turned my life around and was given the opportunity for a second chance. I took this strong work ethic that was instilled in me by my parents and put it into my college studies. I transformed myself into a straight A student and, to this day, have not stopped studying and furthering my education. You can read the "About the Authors" section of this book to find out a little bit more about my accomplishments since then.

Not everyone will go down the same path in their pursuit of financial independence. No matter what path your children take, you should never give up hope or stop encouraging them to be the best that they can be. Taking a two-year break between high school and college was the right choice for me. Had I gone straight to college from high school, I might not have had the same level of enthusiasm and passion for my studies and may have never gone into business for myself by starting my own practice. My story is not a roadmap for others to follow step-by-step, but it is a reminder that success comes in many forms, and everyone must find their own path.

No one knows your son or daughter better than you, so you need to be honest with yourself and listen to what your children have to say. If you think college isn't the right choice for them and do not want to burden yourself or your children with the cost and time spent, then you have no need to read the rest of this chapter. If you still believe pursuing a college degree is the right choice for your child, please read on.

The Cost of College and What You Can Expect to Pay

If you are like most parents, one of your biggest concerns is *how to pay for your children's education when the time comes to send them off to college.* Some parents hope their children will receive academic or athletic scholarships or grants. But for most, the reality is that they will have to pay most of the cost of college from their savings, or even worse, they may have to go into debt.

The cost of college has soared over the past few decades, and while the rate of increase has slowed in recent years, it remains a significant financial burden for many families. According to the College Board, from 2015 to 2025, tuition and fees at private four-year colleges rose at an average rate of 4% per year *above* the general rate of inflation. This is following a 25% total increase between 2005 and 2015. While it's somewhat encouraging that the pace of growth has moderated, it's important to note these figures are already inflation-adjusted. This means even after accounting for the average rise in prices overall, the true cost of college has still gone up.

In today's post-COVID inflationary environment, tuition increases haven't outpaced inflation as dramatically as before, but that's largely because overall inflation is now so much higher. For the 2024–2025 academic year, the College Board reports average tuition and fees of $43,350 at private four-year institutions and $11,610 at public ones. That translates to a staggering $173,400 for a four-year private education and $46,440 for public. When you factor in room and board, the total climbs to a mind-blowing $234,400 for private colleges and $99,680 for public, making the cost of a college education even more daunting.

Exhibit 7.1 shows how four-year college costs have increased and are projected to increase through 2044 (which is when parents of babies born in 2026 will be sending those kids to college). These projections are based on the average rate of inflation for college, beyond the general inflation rate, over the last three decades. As you can see, college costs are projected to rise at an alarming rate that far exceeds the rate of inflation, so if you are a parent, you need to find ways to save for your child's education that will have a reasonable chance of keeping pace with these increasing costs.

To have a fighting chance to succeed with this financial goal, you need to avoid the financial mistakes that are made by many parents. The key to accomplishing this is to have a good understanding of the key components of paying for a college education. These components usually include some combination of personal savings, Section 529 plans, Coverdell education plans, savings bonds, Trump Accounts, financial aid (such as federal grants, loans, and scholarships), and education tax credits. Each of these components will

Exhibit 7.1 Annual Four-year College Costs and Projected Through 2044 (in 2024 Dollars)

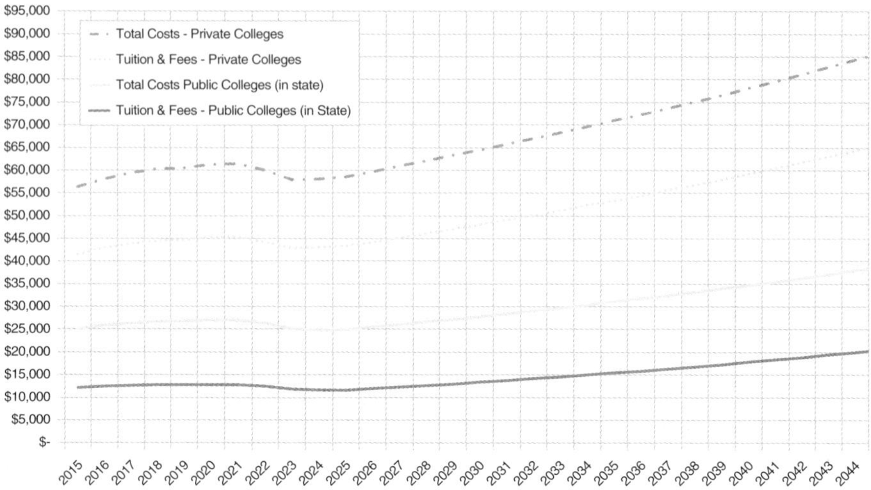

Source: Trends in College Pricing and Student Aid 2024, New York: College Boar.

be discussed in this chapter following a real-life client example. For clarity and relevance, the example applies tax laws in effect as of 2025 rather than those in place during the original time frame of the story, to reflect the current tax landscape more accurately.

Case Study: How *Not* Saving for Your Child's Education Can Ruin Your and Your Child's Finances

A young couple named Tyler and Sarah visited our office to have their income tax return prepared. During the interview, they were asked whether they had any dependents to claim on their tax return. They both looked at each other, smiled, and at the same time said, "We have a dependent on the way." Sarah was four months pregnant. We congratulated them and advised that they begin saving immediately for their child's college education. They both laughed at the suggestion, thinking it was a joke. We told them that it is never too early to start saving for a child's education and encouraged them to establish a Section 529 plan before the end of the year.

They both lived and worked in New York City and qualified to contribute to a New York State 529 Educational Savings Program. New York State allowed them both a $5,000 deduction against their New York State taxable income, which would have given them the added advantage of a $10,000 New York State and City tax deduction. This would translate into at least $1,200 in state and city income tax savings (based on a 12% tax rate). Therefore, they could have set aside $10,000 for their child's education, which would have only cost them $8,800 after the tax savings. This is like getting a $1,200 scholarship each year you contribute, even while the child is still in diapers.

We explained to them that the entire distribution, including the gain they earn from this 529 plan over the next 18 years or longer, would be distributed *tax-free* if they used it to pay for qualified education expenses. This is one of the few tax-smart strategies that qualify for a tax break when the contribution is made and still results in tax-free income when distributed as required.

However, although they appreciated the advice, they felt it was too early to start saving. They said they needed the money to pay for their child's new bedroom set, clothing, and other items. In summary, they said they could not afford to do it this year, but they would start next year.

Sarah was a schoolteacher and earned a modest salary, but she had great benefits with a lot of vacation time. Tyler was an electronics salesman, and his salary was based mostly on commissions from his sales. His income varied widely from year to year, and he did not have much in terms of employee benefits from this job.

Every year during tax season, we reminded them of the advantages of planning and preparing for their child's college education costs. But every year, they always had an excuse for why they were not able to set the money aside, even though they were losing out on the many tax benefits available. They had to set their priorities based on what was most important to them at that time. They always chose to satisfy their *immediate wants* and not set aside money for their *future needs*. Every year that Tyler earned a nice bonus, this money went toward things like vacations, new cars, furniture, remodeling their home, and a new built-in pool in the backyard. They always justified their spending with the pleasure of immediate gratification they experienced.

The days, the months, and the years went by, and then it was time for Tyler Jr. to start looking at colleges. Tyler Jr. had just turned 16, started studying for his SAT exam, and was very excited about starting his junior year of high school. Tyler Jr. was interested in medicine and told his parents he wanted to become a doctor. Sarah and Tyler were very excited and had never seen their son more motivated and eager for school. The three of them spent the afternoon doing research into what colleges would be best to attend to prepare him to become a doctor. When they saw what the average cost was, they were in shock: $40,000 to $60,000 per year seemed to be the price range for a private college, and $10,000 to $25,000 a year for a public in-state college. Although this troubled Sarah and Tyler, they did not want to let Tyler Jr. know they were concerned.

For the next two years, Tyler Jr. hit the books and brought his grade average from 3.2 to 3.7. He studied long and hard for the SAT exam and was able to score a 1,300. He applied to a dozen schools that he believed had a reasonable chance of accepting him. Some were private, and some were public. He was also committed to going away to school and did not want to apply to any local colleges. From November through April, Tyler Jr. rushed to the mailbox after school each day to see if he had received any college acceptance letters.

Of the 12 schools he applied to, he was rejected from six, accepted to four, and wait-listed at two. Of all the schools he visited, he fell in love with Quinnipiac University in Connecticut, but this was one of the two schools at which he was wait-listed. He and his parents visited the schools and did further research on the six college choices that were still a possibility for him. Two of the schools were public. One was in New Jersey, and the tuition with room and board would have been about $25,000. The other was a New York State school (SUNY) that would have cost about $7,000 per year.

Although both schools would have provided Tyler Jr. with a top-rate education, he and his parents were not completely satisfied. They felt more comfortable with a private education with small class sizes, a beautiful campus, and comfortable dorms. The other two private schools he was accepted to would have cost $40,000, and he had been awarded a $15,000 merit scholarship; still, this would have cost approximately $25,000 per year.

It was April 28 and there were only two days left before the big decision needed to be made. It was on this date that the letter came from Quinnipiac that notified Tyler Jr. he had moved from the wait-list to the acceptance list. Tyler Jr. was extremely excited, and he could not wait to tell his parents the great news. The only problem was that this school cost more than $50,000 per year, and there was no mention of a scholarship in the letter.

His parents were overjoyed when they saw how excited their son was. When Tyler Jr. said, "*I am going to Quinnipiac: this was always my first choice,*" his parents showed their excitement and acceptance, but they were thinking, *how in the world are we going to pay for this?*

Later that evening, Sarah and Tyler were lying in bed, discussing their concern about how they were going to pay for this. Tyler realized their son would qualify for little or no financial aid because their combined income was just over $150,000. Sarah looked at their savings and realized that they did not even have enough money available to cover the first semester. They both agreed that they should have listened to our advice 18 years ago, before Tyler Jr. was even born. But now it was too late, and they had to make a difficult choice: *Do we take away our son's first-choice college and send him to a public college, which will cost a fraction of the price?* Of course, they made the decision to give Tyler Jr. what he wanted and not what they could afford.

Sarah said she would be able to obtain a $50,000 loan from her 401(k) plan at work. Tyler agreed that this would get them through the first year; they would figure out a plan for the second year later.

By the time the second year came, they had to max out their credit cards to get the money needed to pay that year's tuition. They were having a very difficult time paying their bills and making the minimum payments on their credit cards, as well as the 401(k) loan. They did not want Tyler Jr. to take out any student loans of his own, and they did not apply for any government-based student loan programs. They were confused about how these loans worked, so they simply chose to ignore any of the options available.

When they looked over their finances, they realized that their main asset was their home and that they had more than $250,000 in equity just sitting there, which they could access. They immediately applied for a home equity loan and were approved for $150,000. They used these funds to get through the next two years of college and to catch up with some other bills on which they had fallen behind. To make matters worse, during Tyler Jr.'s fourth year of college, Sarah had a nervous breakdown and made the decision that she could not go back to her full-time job.

Sarah was notified by her personnel department that she was required to pay back the $50,000 401(k) loan by her federal income tax return due date, including any extensions, for the year the separation of employment occurred, or it would be deemed an early distribution. They simply had no funds available and nowhere else they could borrow from. When tax time came, they owed $15,000 in taxes plus an additional $5,000 early withdrawal penalty to the IRS for a total of $20,000.

Tyler Jr. graduated from college, but he could not go to medical school because his grades were not high enough for him to even consider applying. After six months of interviewing, he was able to get an entry-level job working in the administrative department of a local hospital.

In the meantime, the electronics industry and Tyler's employer were struggling, as was his ability to generate sales. Because of this, he did not get his usual bonus for two years due to the lower sales volume. Tyler and Sarah were in a financial mess, and they knew they needed to do something drastic to straighten out their finances and minimize the stress in their lives. So, they made the difficult but necessary decision to sell their house. They were able to sell their home, eliminate all their debt, and still have about $25,000 in cash left over.

They moved into a small rental apartment and were able to significantly minimize their monthly expenses. They were able to live off Tyler's salary and Sarah's new part-time job.

This story could have had a much happier ending if they had simply started a college savings plan early on and consulted with a financial planner before making so many other mistakes in the process. They made almost every financial mistake possible throughout Tyler Jr.'s first 22 years of life. To be financially responsible and achieve and maintain financial independence, you need to *forgo your short-term wants* and *plan for your family's long-term needs.*

Do not make the same mistakes these parents made. Start planning for your child's education as soon as possible. Be open to your children about financial decisions and what consequences these decisions will have on the family's future. Your family's financial situation is not a topic that needs to be kept private; instead, it should be shared and understood by all of your family members. Understanding the difference between your family's needs and your family's wants involves the participation of you, your spouse, and your children. Making the right choices and fully understanding the consequences of these actions is a must.

Taking advantage of college savings programs will help you get there more easily. Understanding how scholarships, government grants, and student loans can help is essential. Taking advantage of all the special tax breaks and credits that may help subsidize the cost of college is a must. This chapter will provide you with what it takes to get not only your children, but also you and your spouse through the burden and stress of paying for a college education.

Conducting a "Needs Analysis" for Your Children's College Education

The starting point for planning to pay for education is performing an education "needs analysis." Before creating an educational funding plan, you must first determine your estimated needs. For each of your children that you expect will be attending college, you will need to estimate his or her total cost for higher education. This estimate should include their tuition, fees, books, supplies, equipment, tutoring, transportation, and possible extracurricular activities. If you believe your child will be going away to school, you will also need to estimate the added room and board, meal plans, and travel costs. Once you have estimated what this cost may be per year in today's dollars, you will need to adjust this for the expected education inflation rate and determine this for each year they will be attending college.

If you are like most parents, saving for your child's education is a major financial concern. Given the fact that the current cost of a four-year college education could be well into the six figures for certain colleges and universities, this will most likely cost you a lot more than you have anticipated. We recommend using the *Saving for College* calculator, available at www.ventotaxandwealth.com under the Resources > Calculators & Tools section.

For the purpose of this example, you want to click on "How much should I be saving for college?" and you will need to answer the following questions.

- What is the current age of your child?
- What age do you expect your child to start college?
- How many years do you expect your child will be attending college?
- What is the current annual cost for attending the college of your child's choice?
- What is the expected rate of inflation for annual college costs?
- How much money do you currently have saved and earmarked for this purpose?
- What is your expected before-tax return on your investments during this time frame?
- What is your marginal tax bracket?
- What is your expected annual percentage increase in income?

After inputting your own personal information into the college funding calculator, you will be able to determine how much money you will need to save each month (or the lump sum you need now) to cover the total cost of your child's future college education needs.

Let us walk through an example together, answering each of the questions above as follows:

- What is the current age of your child? (five years old)
- What age do you expect your child to start college? (18 years old)
- How many years do you expect your child will be attending college? (four years)
- What is the current annual cost for attending the college of your child's choice? ($25,000)
- What is the expected rate of inflation for annual college costs? (4%)
- How much money do you currently have saved and earmarked for this purpose? ($18,000)
- What is your expected before-tax return on your investments during this time frame? (10%)
- What is your marginal tax bracket? (24%)
- What is your expected annual percentage increase in income? (0%)

After you input all the information, click calculate to get the following results:

- The amount you will need to meet your college goals is *$176,767.*
- To meet this goal, you will need to either invest a lump sum now of $43,097 or you will need to save and invest $356 per month.

That is only for *one* child. Fortunately, the sooner you start to save, the more manageable this financial goal becomes. For most people, this calculation becomes a reality check and a rude awakening. Unfortunately, most parents are not prepared when this day comes, and they put their children and themselves into debt (as Sarah and Tyler did, in the case study at the beginning of this chapter). This does not have to be the case for you and your family. If you apply the powerful education planning strategies discussed in this chapter, you can and will be prepared.

By taking full advantage of the tax savings offered through Section 529 "qualified tuition plans," Coverdell Education Savings Accounts, and savings bonds, you can accumulate the money you will need much faster and possibly on a tax-free basis. Understanding all the government grants and loans available and how to qualify for them may go a long way in reducing your costs. If you encourage your children to do well in high school, they may qualify for merit scholarships and other awards. Lastly, if you qualify, you may be eligible for special tax breaks and credits in the years that your children are attending college and you are paying for their college costs.

Therefore, you can use numerous strategies to make this process much more affordable. You should seriously consider state and city colleges and universities that provide a top-rated education at much more affordable prices. A college education is extremely valuable, but you must fully weigh the benefits and compare them to the cost. As we have said throughout this book, you must always be able to distinguish between your *needs* and your *wants*. Since a college education can be considered a *need* for many people, you must then ask yourself if there is a less-costly college-selection alternative. Appropriately planning how to pay for your child's education is one of the keys to achieving and maintaining financial independence.

Strategies for Saving Money for College

Here are four of the most used strategies for saving money for a college education, plus one more that can also be used for this purpose:

1. Section 529 educational savings programs
2. Uniform Gifts/Transfers to Minors Act (UGMA/UTMA) accounts
3. Coverdell Education Savings Accounts
4. US savings bonds.
5. Trump Accounts (with the passage of the One Big Beautiful Bill Act [OBBBA], effective July 4, 2026)

Each has distinct advantages as well as some drawbacks. Understanding how each of these education savings techniques works will go a long way toward helping you decide which approach (or combination of approaches) would work best for your individual circumstances. Exhibit 7.2 provides a detailed comparison of these

Exhibit 7.2 Comparison of Education Savings: Tax-deferred, Tax-exempt, and Taxable Plans

Attribute	Section 529 Plans	UGMA / UTMA	Coverdell Education Savings Accounts	US Savings Bonds	Trump Accounts
Federal taxation of account earnings	Tax-deferred growth; distributions for qualified education expenses are tax-exempt.	Taxable each year (unearned income taxed to the child, possibly subject to "kiddie-tax" rules).	Earnings grow tax-deferred; distributions used for qualified education expenses are tax-free.	Interest is taxable at federal level unless doing a qualified series EE or I bond and meeting education exclusion rules.	Earnings grow tax-deferred; withdrawals follow traditional IRA rules (ordinary income tax when withdrawn, with potential penalties if early).
Income limits	None for contributions at the federal tax level; states may have different rules.	None for establishment / contributions.	Phase-out for modified AGI: $95,000 to $110,000 for single/head-of-household filers; $190,000 to $220,000 for married filing jointly.	None for buying savings bonds; but for excluding interest from taxable income, there is a phase-out of income (education exclusion) based on MAGI.	None for establishment/ contributions.
Control of assets	The account owner (usually the donor/ plan owner) controls the account; can change beneficiary, etc.	Custodian controls the assets until the beneficiary reaches age of majority (state law governs age).	The responsible individual (parent, guardian, etc.) controls the account; must use it for benefit of the named beneficiary; after age 30 (or earlier if required by state/federal rules) the balance must be distributed unless the beneficiary is special needs.	Owner of the bond retains control; redemption decisions made by owner.	The child is owner; until age 18 contributions/ control is under rules defined by parents/ custodian; withdrawals prohibited before age 18. After age 18, is treated like traditional IRA.

Ability to change beneficiary	Can be changed to a qualified family member of the current beneficiary without adverse tax consequences.	No (beneficiary fixed, custodial account. No change to named beneficiary except perhaps via trust or legal restructure).	Yes. Can be changed to a family member of the current beneficiary, subject to rules.	Yes. The bond owner may change the beneficiary designation.	No. Cannot change beneficiary.
Penalty for nonqualified withdrawals	Subject to federal (and possibly state) income tax on earnings plus a 10% penalty on earnings portion.	No penalty: just taxation of income when distributed (earnings and gains).	Same as 529; income tax on earnings + 10% penalty for nonqualified withdrawals of earnings.	Interest is taxed at the federal level if not used under qualifying conditions.	Withdrawals prohibited before age 18; after 18, standard IRA early-withdrawal penalty (10%) applies unless exception met, with ordinary income tax on distributions.
Gift tax treatment (2025 amounts)	Contributions up to \$95,000 (\$190,000 for married couples) qualify under the five-year election of gift tax exclusion (super funding) for 529 plans.	Qualified for the annual gift tax exclusion. (\$19,000 per donor in 2025).	Qualified as part of the annual gift tax exclusion. (\$19,000 per donor in 2025). Maximum contribution limit per year is \$2,000.	Bonds are purchased with after-tax dollars; purchasing or gifting bonds may be subject to gift tax rules if in excess of annual exclusion; interest exclusion for education has phase-out by income.	Contributions are subject to annual gift tax limits; the \$1,000 government seed and \$2,500 employer contribution are exempt from donor gift tax calculations. Maximum contribution limit per year is \$5,000 before December 31 of the year your child turns 17.

five options, based on 2025 tax rules, followed by a detailed discussion of each of these strategies, plus a few more you might consider.

As you evaluate various college savings options, you should consider the control and tax advantages you have with each type of plan, as described in Exhibit 7.2. Furthermore, you need to factor in the impact, if any, on financial aid eligibility, which will be discussed later in this chapter.

Section 529 Plans (Qualified Tuition Programs)

IRS Code Section 529 was created in 1996 with the passage of the Small Business Job Protection Act. This was the birth of *qualified tuition programs (QTPs),* commonly referred to as *529 plans,* which were specifically designed to help people save and ultimately pay for college education on a federal tax-free basis. Investment assets held within a 529 plan account accumulate on a tax-deferred basis. Contributions are made with after-tax dollars at the federal level. Withdrawals of principal and accumulated earnings are free from federal income tax, if you use them for qualified education expenses at any eligible postsecondary educational or vocational institution in the United States. Some states also allow you a tax-deductible contribution for state income tax purposes, if you establish your 529 plan in that state's sponsored program.

Qualified expenses generally include the following:

- Tuition
- Room and board
- Books and supplies
- Special needs services relating to enrollment at a qualified institution

Two types of 529 plans are available:

1. **529 prepaid tuition plans:** Typically allow you to purchase units or credits at a participating college or university, which can then be applied toward future tuition payments. In some situations, they can be used to cover the cost of room and board. The majority of these plans are sponsored by individual states and have residency requirements. Investments in prepaid tuition plans are sometimes guaranteed by the sponsoring state government.

2. **529 college savings plans:** Generally, allow you to establish an account for a beneficiary for the purpose of paying the beneficiary's qualified educational costs. As the account holder, you generally have several investment choices for your contributions in the 529 savings plan, which typically include stock and bond mutual funds as well as money market funds. Some also offer age-based portfolios.

You can usually use the distributions from 529 savings plans at any US college or university and, as of January 1, 2018, was expanded to include private kindergarten through high school with certain limitations as detailed later in this section. Your beneficiary has the flexibility of choosing any college or university he or she gets accepted to, in any state. It is important to note that the investments in these 529 savings plans are not guaranteed by state governments.

The OBBBA expanded the definition of qualified K–12 expenses under 529 plans and increased the cap for such expenses from $10,000 to $20,000. In addition to tuition, families can now use funds for books, curriculum materials, tutoring, test fees, educational therapy, and certain online resources, beginning in 2026. The bill also extended eligible expenses to include professional certifications and additional workforce training programs.

If you are using a 529 plan to pay for K–12 or credential-based education, it is important to check with your individual state to confirm whether these distributions will also be treated as tax-free at the state level. While the federal government now allows tax-free withdrawals for a broader range of education expenses, not all states have adopted the same rules.

For example, New York State still does not conform to the federal law on this issue. K–12 distributions from a New York 529 plan are considered nonqualified for state tax purposes. This means that although the distributions are tax-free federally, New York State may impose income tax on the earnings and even require repayment of any previously claimed state tax deductions. Until New York changes its position to match federal law, you should avoid using a New York 529 plan for K–12 education. You can, of course, continue to use these plans to pay for higher education expenses without issue.

Even though federal law now expanded the use of 529 funds for K–12 and home education, it is recommended to use these funds for higher education purposes. The longer the funds remain in the account, the more you can take advantage of tax-deferred growth, and if used properly, distributions will be tax-free.

You can open a 529 qualified tuition program account for your children, your grandchildren, or anyone who is a US citizen or legal US resident. There are no age or family relationship limitations on 529 plan beneficiaries. In fact, you can even open an account naming yourself as the beneficiary to help with your own education expenses.

Exhibit 7.3 shows how your earnings can grow on a tax-free basis and the difference between investing $10,000 in a taxable account and a 529 plan account, with subsequent investments of $10,000 at the beginning of each year for 18 years. This example also assumes an 8% annual rate of return with a 40% marginal tax rate. This illustration demonstrates the possible value of tax-exempt earnings over time through a 529 education savings plan. As you can see, for the same amount of money invested, *you could earn almost $100,000 more* over 18 years when you invest in the tax-free 529 plan.

When it comes to financial aid, a 529 plan is counted as an asset on the Free Application for Federal Student Aid (FAFSA). This will typically be as a parent asset if parent-owned or student-owned when student is a dependent (assessed at up to approximately 5.64%) or as a student asset if student-owned and student is independent (assessed at 20%). This can reduce need-based financial aid eligibility. It is important to consider the impact of how your 529 plan

Exhibit 7.3 Growth of Savings Invested in a Tax-free 529 Plan Versus a Taxable Savings Account

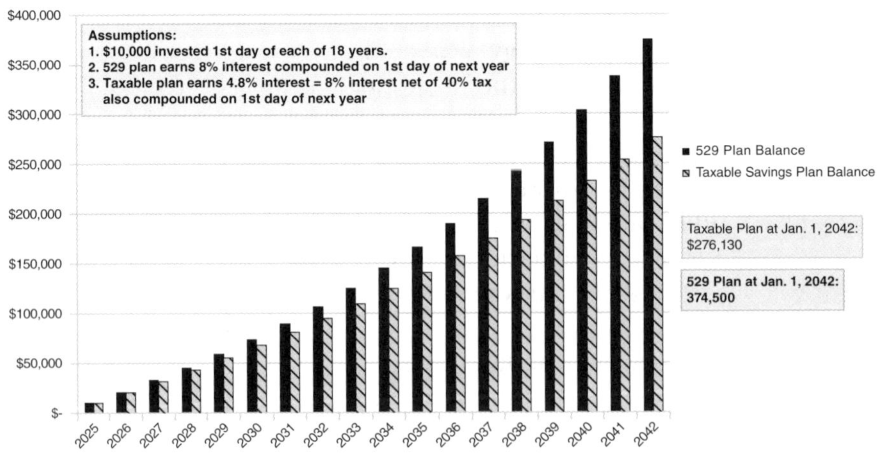

is owned if you think you will qualify for financial aid. This will be discussed in further detail later in this chapter.

With a Section 529 plan, you maintain full authority over who the beneficiary is and can even take a nonqualified distribution if desired. For example, if your firstborn decides not to attend college, you can retitle the funds to your second child or simply take a distribution that will be subject to tax and penalty. Additionally, as of 2024, you may roll over up to $35,000 in unused 529 funds into a Roth IRA in the beneficiary's name, subject to the account being open for at least 15 years and annual Roth IRA contribution limits.

A 529 plan offers a variety of noteworthy tax advantages, such as no income tax on earnings, tax-free withdrawals for qualified educational purposes, accelerated federal gifting and estate tax benefits, and, in some cases, state tax deductions. This is perhaps one of the most tax-effective strategies for saving and paying for education. There are no income limitations as to who can establish an account. High-income earners and high-net-worth individuals can take full advantage of these tax benefits.

As Barry Holt, Senior Advanced Planning Solutions Consultant at Cetera Financial Group explains:

> 529 plans offer unique flexibility and can serve as a strategic estate planning tool. By using the 5-year gift tax averaging election, individuals can front-load contributions, up to $95,000 per beneficiary ($190,000 per couple) in 2025, without immediately using lifetime gift and estate tax exemptions. This can accelerate tax-free growth and remove assets from the taxable estate.
>
> However, this strategy requires filing IRS Form 709, and if the donor dies within the 5-year period, a prorated amount may be included back in the estate. Additionally, no further gifts to that beneficiary can be made during the 5 years without gift tax implications. State contribution limits and overall liquidity needs should also be considered. For families with multiple beneficiaries, this approach can be powerful, but it works best as part of a comprehensive estate plan.

When you consider the tax benefits, the ability to maintain control, and the power of compounding, it's easy to see why we view this as our number one tax-smart education funding strategy.

Uniform Gifts to Minors Act and Uniform Transfers to Minors Act

The Uniform Gifts to Minors Act (UGMA) and Uniform Transfers to Minors Act (UTMA) accounts allow your children to invest for their college education by holding the funds in their own accounts. Any income generated from this account is subject to current "kiddie tax" rules.

These accounts provide you with a method to transfer assets out of your name and into that of a minor without having to establish a trust, which may be costly to create and maintain. Please note that these transfers are considered completed gifts and may require the donor (the person who gave the gift) to file a gift tax return if over the annual gift tax exclusion amount.

UGMA and UTMA accounts were not created specifically as savings vehicles for college, but many parents use them for this purpose because these assets typically become available to the minor when they are in the early years of college.

The accounts are managed by a custodian, usually a parent, grandparent, relative, or friend. Individuals can make an irrevocable transfer for any amount to these accounts as a gift to the minor. In the event that the custodian passes away before the child reaches majority (i.e., is considered an adult by state law, which varies from state to state between ages 18 and 21), the account may then be includable in the taxable estate of the donor (i.e., the custodian).

The key difference between UGMA and UTMA accounts is that UTMA law allows more flexibility with the type of investments that can be included in the account. The UGMA law limits the type of investments that can be held in these accounts to bank deposits, securities (stocks, bonds, mutual funds, exchange-traded funds), and insurance policies.

The main income-tax advantage to transferring these assets to a child used to be that all the income earned on these investments would be subject to tax at the child's significantly lower marginal tax rate. However, the IRS created a "kiddie tax" that significantly reduced the tax advantage of establishing these accounts. It was specifically created to close this tax loophole and to discourage this type of tax-saving strategy. This tax may apply if your child has investment income (such as interest, dividends, and capital gains).

In the past, the "kiddie tax" used the trust and estate tax rates, but under today's law (2025) a child's unearned income above a set threshold is instead taxed at the parent's marginal tax rate. Earned income is still taxed using the child's own brackets as a single filer. For many families, this approach is more favorable than the prior rules, though the impact ultimately depends on the parents' tax bracket.

The kiddie tax applies not only to children younger than age 19, but also to children who are full-time students ages 19–23 and do not have earned income exceeding half of their own support.

Another major disadvantage to these types of accounts is that all assets transferred under UGMA and UTMA laws represent an irrevocable gift (transfer). Upon reaching the age of majority under the state UGMA/UTMA laws, the child gains control of the assets and may use them in any way he or she wants. For example, if little Sofia decides to jump on the back of her boyfriend's motorcycle on her 18th birthday and head to California to start a new life, she can take the money with her because she is no longer considered a minor.

Yet another major potential disadvantage of UGMA or UTMA accounts is that they may affect the amount of financial aid your child receives. This is discussed further in the government grants and loans section of this chapter.

As a general rule, these accounts are not recommended as a method of saving for a child's education. The minimal tax savings you may achieve is usually not worth the potential pitfalls. If you want to retain control of the assets, take advantage of tax-deferred savings and qualified tax-free withdrawals, and avoid jeopardizing any potential financial aid, you should avoid these types of accounts. Instead, use one or more of the other education saving vehicles covered in this chapter.

If you do use either a UGMA or UTMA account, you should seriously consider spending down the account (instead of using your own money) for the benefit of your children for such expenses as their high school tuition, computers, and whatever else they may ask for. You will then have extra funds of your own available to fund a Section 529 plan.

Coverdell Education Savings Accounts

A Coverdell Education Savings Account (ESA, formerly known as an Education Individual Retirement Account) is a tax-advantaged educational savings account designed specifically to encourage savings to cover future education costs. These accounts can be used to pay for elementary education, secondary education, and college costs, such as tuition, books, uniforms, and other education-related expenses.

The tax treatment of a Coverdell ESA is similar to the Section 529 plan with some differences. Similar to a 529 plan, Coverdell ESAs allow your investments to grow tax-deferred, and the distributions can be tax-free for qualified education expenses at a qualified institution.

A Coverdell ESA complements a 529 plan when saving for a private elementary, high school, or college education.

The key features of a Coverdell Education Savings Account include the following:

- There are income limitations for the donor, which may affect the ability to make contributions into a Coverdell ESA. If you are a single individual, head of household, or married taxpayer filing separately, you can make the full contribution if your income is below $95,000, and then it is phased out through $110,000. A married couple filing jointly can make a full contribution if their income level is below $190,000 and then it is phased out through $220,000.
- The money held in a Coverdell ESA account is not considered part of your child's assets when applying for federal financial aid as long as your child is listed as the *beneficiary* and not as the *account owner*.
- The custodian of a Coverdell ESA account (i.e., you, the parent) can change the named beneficiary without incurring taxes or penalties, provided the new beneficiary is an eligible family member of the previous beneficiary.
- Coverdell ESAs have an annual contribution limit of $2,000 per beneficiary; therefore, the use of a Coverdell is limited.
- Coverdell ESAs allow almost any type of investment to be held, including stocks, bonds, and mutual funds.
- The funds in a Coverdell ESA must be used for qualified education expenses by the time the designated beneficiary is 30 years old. Alternatively, you can change beneficiaries to another family member younger than the age of 30 in order to avoid taxes and penalties before that time comes.
- Coverdell ESAs allow distributions on a tax-free basis for qualified elementary and secondary school expenses and college and universities.
- If distributions are taken from a Coverdell ESA and are not used for qualified education expenses, then any gain from these distributions would be subject to federal and state taxes, as well as a 10% IRS penalty on the earnings portion.

Try to fit a Coverdell ESA into your overall education savings plan. If you do not qualify to contribute to an ESA account because of the income limits, encourage other family members to do so, assuming they qualify. For example, if your child gets a summer job, the extra cash he or she earns can be invested into an ESA account (based on your child's income level). Although this education tax saving break is limited, everything you do in the aggregate will make a difference in the long run.

Savings Bonds

US savings bonds remain a low-risk investment popular for college savings. They offer modest returns, but the safety of US government backing is compelling. For example, if you purchased $1,000 in Series EE bonds or Series I bonds between May 1 and October 31, 2025, the rate would have been 2.70% and 3.98% respectively. The Series EE bonds would have earned $27, and the Series I bonds $39.80 over a one-year period, which is not a very attractive rate of return, especially when you consider the loss of purchasing power due to inflation.

Savings bonds are generally considered a safe investment because they are backed by the full faith and credit of the US government. Both the principal and earned interest is safe, which means you cannot *lose* money due to market changes, because US savings bonds are not considered marketable securities. US savings bonds are registered with the US Treasury Department; therefore, you can easily replace them if you lose them or they are stolen or destroyed.

Through a special Education Savings Bond Program, interest on certain savings bonds is tax-free when used for qualified higher education expenses. The US savings bonds that qualify for this tax-free treatment include Series EE bonds issued after December 31, 1989, and all Series I bonds.

To qualify for this tax-free treatment, you must meet the following requirements:

- The bond owner (you) must be at least 24 years old on the bond issue date (the first day of the month in which the bonds were purchased).
- Parents can purchase bonds for their children, but the bonds must be registered in the parents' name.

- The child cannot be listed as a co-owner, but the child can be listed as a beneficiary.
- You can also purchase bonds for your own education, in which case the bonds must be registered in your own name.

Currently, there is an annual purchase limit of $10,000 per Social Security number for Series EE Bonds and $10,000 for Series I Bonds. The purchase limit for Series I Bonds is not affected by purchases of Series EE Bonds; these purchase limits are independent of one another.

There are, of course, some major advantages and disadvantages to purchasing qualified Series EE and I US Savings Bonds. First, let us look at the advantages:

- You don't need to open an account with a financial institution because US savings bonds are registered and issued by the US Treasury Department. While you used to be able to buy them at most banks, savings bonds are now only available online, directly from the US Treasury, at treasurydirect.gov.
- You can buy savings bonds for as little as $25, which makes them easily affordable for most people.
- The interest on these bonds is always exempt from state and local income tax and may be fully exempt from federal income taxes when the bonds are used for qualified college expenses.

Now for the disadvantages:

- You are locking yourself into a very low rate of return, which may not keep pace with inflation over the long run. This is especially true with Series EE Bonds. This is the biggest disadvantage; therefore, you need to weigh this low return against the safety and security of knowing they are government-guaranteed obligations.
- The exemption from paying federal income taxes when you use savings bonds to pay for college expenses is more restricted than some of the other alternatives: Series EE and I Bonds are only exempt from taxation when they are used for tuition and required fees, not room, board, or books.
- There is a phase-out for excluding a US Savings Bond from taxes for qualified education purposes. For 2025, if you (as the taxpayer holding the bonds) file your taxes as single

or head of household, there is an income phase-out for adjusted gross income between $99,500 and $114,500; if you are married and filing jointly, the income phase-out for adjusted gross income is between $149,250 and $179,250. It may completely eliminate the tax advantage of using US savings bonds as a vehicle for saving for college if your income reaches these levels in the year that you need the funds. Even if you qualify in the year in which you purchase the bonds, if your income exceeds the limit in the year that you redeem them, you will not receive the federal tax benefit. Therefore, this is not a good choice for someone who expects to be in a high tax bracket.

- For financial aid purposes, savings bonds are treated as assets while they are held and as income once they are redeemed. Whether they are reported under the student or the parent depends on who is listed as the bond's owner.

Although savings bonds are a common choice for college savings, they aren't our preferred strategy, especially for high-income earners.

Trump Accounts

Trump Accounts are a new tax-deferred savings vehicle created under the OBBBA. These accounts are designed to help families invest in their children's future and may be used for a range of purposes, including college education. Since these accounts are essentially traditional IRAs, they are discussed in further detail in Chapter 8, "Planning for Retirement."

While Trump Accounts are not designed exclusively for education, they can still function as a long-term college savings tool. Because the funds grow tax-deferred and can accumulate over 18 years, they may provide a meaningful resource by the time a child reaches college age. Distributions used for qualified education expenses would be exempt from the 10% early withdrawal penalty.

Although the rules are still evolving, Trump Accounts represent an additional tool in your college planning toolkit, particularly for families who want to take advantage of long-term, tax-deferred compounding and are not solely relying on 529 plans or Coverdell accounts.

Roth Individual Retirement Accounts (IRAs)

You are probably thinking why are Roth IRAs included in this chapter as a strategy for saving money to pay for college? The simple answer to this question is that although Roth IRAs were not established as an education savings vehicle, they can serve that purpose if you use it in the right way.

Let us assume your son or daughter has been working at a part-time job and has earned $10,000 or more over the year. What would be the best use for this money? Your child might be thinking of video games or designer jeans, but that is not the correct answer, of course.

The best use for this money is to fund a Roth IRA for $7,000 and a Coverdell ESA for $2,000. The argument for doing this is even stronger if your income level does not allow *you* to contribute to these accounts on your own, but your child would qualify based on his or her level of income. We have already covered the many benefits of establishing a Coverdell ESA, so now we are going to focus on Roth IRA.

Let us also assume your child managed to save $7,000 per year from his earned income for five years in a Roth IRA and now is in his third or fourth year of college. Let us also assume that this (5 years × $7,000) $35,000 is now worth $50,000 because of some good investment choices. Your child would be able to take a distribution from this Roth account to cover the cost of undergraduate or graduate school. Assuming he took the full $50,000 in one year, only $15,000 ($50,000 less $35,000) of this amount would be subject to tax. Moreover, this income is subject to tax *at your child's low tax rate*, which could be as low as 0%, if it is structured properly (the child must provide more than 50% of his or her own support to take advantage of this lower rate).

Although the IRS levies a 10% penalty if you withdraw money from a retirement account before you are 59½ years old, one of the exceptions to this penalty is if you use that distribution to pay for qualified higher education costs. Therefore, this amount would not be subject to this penalty. However, it is important to note that while Roth IRA balances are not counted as assets on the FAFSA, any distributions, even if tax-free, are treated as income and can reduce a student's eligibility for need-based financial aid. Once again, Roth accounts were not designed to cover higher education expenses, but you can clearly use them as an additional strategy for saving for college.

Furthermore, if your child does not need the funds to cover higher education expenses, it is still a benefit for your child to have this money invested in a tax-free retirement account before he or she even graduates from college. This would give your child an amazing start and advantage to achieving and reaching his or her own financial independence. We always encourage children and their parents to start saving for retirement as soon as possible.

Government Grants and Loans

When you consider the multitude of options and opportunities available for saving and paying for college education, the subject of government grants and loans probably carries the most ambiguity. The US Department of Education's National Center for Education Statistics releases annual reports on student financial aid trends. You can download the full report at nces.ed.gov/programs/coe. These findings should give you some idea of the type and sources of financial aid that may be available.

Many students receive some form of grants and scholarships; but only about 0.1% receive enough for a "free ride," so do not expect to go to college without paying for it.

According to the 2025 Sallie Mae "How America Pays for College" report, 60% of families received scholarships, which averaged $8,004 for 2025. On average, these scholarships covered a meaningful portion of college costs and helped make college possible for those who received them.

This same report indicated that 57% of families received grants, which averaged $6,180.

The study also showed that, on average, families primarily paid for college using 48% from income and savings, 27% from grants and scholarships, and 23% from borrowing, which included both student and parent loans. The remaining 2% of college costs were covered by family or friends.

One of the most significant state-level efforts to make college more affordable has come from New York. What began in 2017 as Governor Andrew M. Cuomo's Excelsior Scholarship, the first program of its kind in the nation, is now firmly established under Governor Kathy Hochul. The program enables many New York State residents to attend an in-state university tuition-free. The scholarship currently provides tuition-free college at New York's public colleges and universities (SUNY and CUNY) for families making up to $125,000 a year.

Students must be full-time, complete 30 credits each year, and agree to live and work in New York after graduation for the same number of years they received the award.

In 2025, legislation has been introduced to expand the Excelsior Scholarship further. The proposal would raise the income cap to $135,000 for the 2025–2026 school year and $150,000 for 2026–2027. It would also make part-time students and those in approved vocational programs, such as BOCES, eligible for the benefit. The program remains a "last dollar" award, meaning it applies only after federal and state grants like Pell and TAP are used.

New York's program highlights a growing trend of states seeking to expand free access to public higher education. For more details on the Excelsior Scholarship, visit www.suny.edu. You should also check your own state's higher education website to see if similar programs are offered or under consideration.

It is also very important to understand how the federal government and institutions calculate how much aid they provide students, whether in the form of grants, federal loans, or work study. For the most part, the formula to determine the amount of need for financial aid will factor in your family's ability to pay over time. This is expressed *by the Student Aid Index (SAI).* The SAI is a number calculated by the federal government using financial and family information from your FAFSA (replaces the formerly used Expected Family Contribution calculation). If there is a gap between the cost of attendance at a school and the family's calculated SAI, a financial aid offer may be made by the school.

According to the US Department of Education, the SAI is *not* the amount of money your family will have to pay for college, nor is it the amount of federal student aid you will receive. It is a number used by the students' school to calculate how much financial aid the student is eligible to receive by law.

For a dependent student, the SAI considers the following essential factors:

- What you (the parents) currently earn
- What your child (the student) currently earns
- What the parent owns
- What the student owns directly

The studentaidrefdesk.org website further explains the SAI. The need analysis formula, which is defined in law by Congress, considers a student and family's income and asset information, as well as family size. The need analysis formula also removes the number of family members in college from consideration and allows a minimum SAI as low as −1,500. It also implements separate eligibility criteria for the federal Pell Grant program that considers a family's financial standing according to the federal poverty guidelines.

The most heavily weighed factors in evaluating eligibility for financial aid are current income received by the parent or child and then whether the parent or the child has control over financial assets. It is vital to understand the significance and importance that these key factors play in determining financial aid. You should consider these factors when you are selecting the college savings vehicles you plan to use as well as how you plan to hold ownership to these assets.

Understanding what effect your overall savings will have on your chances of receiving financial aid is critical to assessing your additional needs. There are several types of financial aid including federal, state, and institutional. Federal aid is the most widely used form of assistance available to college students. To be considered for federal aid, a student must complete the financial aid FAFSA forms.

Exhibit 7.4 provides the ranges of parental and student income and assets that are used to calculate the annual SAI for any given student. Once the SAI has been determined, a college or university's

Exhibit 7.4 Factors Used in Calculating the SAI for Financial Aid Purposes

	Parents	Students
Income	Up to 47% of Parent Adjusted Available Income (PAI) above the protected amount*	50% of Student Available Income over a protected amount of $11,510
Assets	Up to 5.64% of assets: • Bank accounts • Investments • Real estate (excluding primary residence) • 529 plans where the account owner is the parent(s) or dependent child(ren)	20% of assets held in student's name, including: • UGMA/UTMA accounts • Minor trust • Investments • Real estate (excluding primary residence) • 529 plans where the account owner is the student(s) and that student is independent

Note: *Protected income for parents is dependent upon factors such as household size.
Source: This information is based on the US Department of Education's *Federal Student Aid Language* series, Application and Verification Guide, 2025–2026: Student Aid Index and Pell Grant Eligibility Guide.

financial aid officer subtracts it from that institution's cost for attending that college or university, in order to determine the annual financial need. Exhibit 7.4 reveals that *income* is more heavily factored in the calculation than *assets*, and that *student* income and assets are factored in more heavily than the parents' income and assets. Exhibit 7.4 also highlights the impact that some of the most common college saving vehicles will have on your child's ability to qualify for financial aid.

The following assets are not considered when determining the child's financial needs:

- All retirement accounts (though distributions from these accounts are considered for income)
- Home equity in a primary residence
- Annuities
- Cash value of life insurance

Many parents believe that investing for college will hurt their children's chances of receiving financial aid. In reality, family income counts much more than assets in the formula that determines the financial aid awarded.

The information in this section provides a basic understanding of the calculations used in determining eligibility for federal student financial aid. For more detailed information regarding the financial aid process, the many different types of financial aid available, and how your particular facts and circumstances may affect the chances of qualifying, visit the following websites:

- **www.finaid.org:** One of the most comprehensive sources of information about student financial aid
- **www.ed.gov:** The website for the US Department of Education
- **www.studentaid.gov:** The website for the Department of Education's centralized site for Federal Student Aid programs, including FAFSA
- **www.collegeboard.org:** The website for the College Board, a national nonprofit membership association composed of more than 6,000 schools, colleges, universities, and other educational organizations

Government grant and loan programs are numerous. It is important for you to do your research and become thoroughly familiar with these options early when planning for your college funding needs. If you believe you may qualify for some of these programs, you can factor these funds into your college-funding plan. On the other hand, if you believe you will not be entitled to any of these programs because of your income and assets, you will clearly need to focus more on the other college savings programs described in this chapter.

Athletic Scholarships

For those proud parents who may be counting on little Zachary's football skills or Sofia's gymnastic abilities to pay their way through college, take a hard look at what your actual chances are of receiving athletic scholarships.

According to the National Collegiate Athletic Association, very few high school athletes earn athletic scholarships. In fact, only about 2% of high school athletes are awarded some form of an athletic scholarship to compete in college. For more information, you can download the NCAA Recruiting Facts Sheet from the NCAA website.

Student Loans

While grants and scholarships are the most desirable forms of aid, many families still need to rely on student loans to bridge the gap. Taking out student loans offers several key tax benefits that can help borrowers manage their financial obligations. One significant benefit is the Student Loan Interest Deduction, which allows borrowers to deduct up to $2,500 of student loan interest from their taxable income each year. This deduction applies even if you do not itemize your deductions, reducing your overall taxable income. However, it phases out depending on your modified adjusted gross income (MAGI), so eligibility may be limited. For single or head-of-household filing status, there is no deduction if your MAGI is greater than or equal to $100,000. For married filing jointly, there is no deduction if your MAGI is greater than or equal to $200,000.

For those in public service careers who have federal student loans, the Public Service Loan Forgiveness (PSLF) program offers certain loan forgiveness programs that allow for the forgiven amount to be tax-free after a certain period of minimum payments. Other repayment plans include income-driven repayment plans. The laws pertaining to loan forgiveness are constantly evolving, so students and borrowers should stay updated. These programs can significantly ease the financial burden of student loans, but eligibility criteria and specific conditions apply. The StudentAid.gov Loan Simulator is a helpful tool to compare repayment plans and determine eligibility based on income and loan balance. For personalized guidance, consulting with a financial aid office is highly recommended.

Education Tax Breaks and Credits

During the years your child is attending college, you may qualify for significant tax savings through education tax breaks and credits. Because tax credits can be a dollar-for-dollar reduction in your taxes, understanding how to use them effectively can lead to substantial financial benefits. The two major education tax credits for higher education are the American Opportunity Tax Credit and the Lifetime Learning Credit.

American Opportunity Tax Credit

To qualify for the American opportunity tax credit in 2025, your family member (student) must be taking at least one-half of the normal course load of a full-time student for the first four years of postsecondary education. This is available under the following circumstances:

- You can qualify for full credit if your tax filing status is married filing jointly with a modified adjusted gross income under $160,000.
- You can qualify for partial credit if your tax filing status is married filing jointly with a modified adjusted gross income over $160,000 but less than $180,000.
- If you are married as of the last day of the year, you must file jointly to claim this credit; married persons filing separately are not eligible.
- All other filing statuses can qualify for full credit if your adjusted gross income is under $80,000.
- All other filing statuses can qualify for *partial credit* for adjusted gross income over $80,000 but less than $90,000.
- This tax credit is available for qualified tuition and related fees incurred and paid in the first four years of postsecondary education for the taxpayer, spouse, and/or dependents.

The American opportunity tax credit is equal to 100% of the first $2,000 of qualified expenses paid in the tax year, plus 25% of the next $2,000. Therefore, the maximum tax credit allowed in any given year is $2,500 per student, if there is at least $4,000 in qualifying expenses.

It is important to note that this $2,500 credit is available for each eligible student in your household. In other words, if you qualify for this tax credit, it would be the same as receiving a $2,500 tax-free scholarship for each of your children who qualifies. In essence, the federal government is subsidizing the cost of sending your child (or other family member) to college.

Up to 40% ($1,000) of this tax credit can be refundable, even if it exceeds your tax liability for the year. *It is extremely important to note that you should not make this $4,000 payment from a 529 plan or Coverdell ESA.* This $4,000 must come from your other savings or loans, since you cannot combine this tax credit with the funds and benefits received from qualified education plans. Any amount above the $4,000 can come from one of your qualified education savings plans.

Lifetime Learning Credit

The Lifetime Learning Credit does not call for your child (or any other family member) to have a certain degree or workload requirement. This credit may be claimed for one or more courses at an eligible education institution that is either part of a postsecondary degree program or part of a nondegree program taken to acquire or improve job skills. The Lifetime Learning Credit can be claimed for an unlimited number of years. For 2025, here are the requirements:

- You can qualify for full credit if your tax filing status is married filing jointly with a modified adjusted gross income under $160,000.
- You can qualify for partial credit if your tax-filing status is married filing jointly with a modified adjusted gross income over $160,000 but less than $180,000.
- If you are married as of the last day of the year, you must file jointly to claim this credit; married persons filing separately are not eligible.
- All other filing statuses can qualify for full credit if your modified adjusted gross income is under $80,000.

- All other filing statuses can qualify for partial credit if your modified adjusted gross income is over $80,000 but less than $90,000.
- This tax credit is available for tuition and enrollment fees for undergraduate, graduate, or professional degree programs for you, your spouse, or your dependents.

The Lifetime Learning Credit provides an annual per taxpayer reimbursement for qualified tuition and related expenses per family in the amount of $2,000 per year. This means if you pay qualifying expenses for more than one eligible student, the overall credit you may claim remains $2,000, regardless of the number of children who are students in your household. This credit is based on a 20% factor on qualified expenses. Therefore, to obtain the full $2,000 credit, you must have at least $10,000 of qualified education expenses for all eligible children who are students in your family. This tax credit is nonrefundable; therefore, you will not be entitled to receive it if it exceeds your regular tax plus Alternative Minimum Tax (AMT) liability.

It is extremely important to note that you should not make this $10,000 payment from a 529 plan or Coverdell ESA. This $10,000 must come from your other savings or loans, since you cannot combine this tax credit with the funds and benefits received from qualified education savings plans. Any amount above the $10,000 can come from one of your qualified education savings plans.

If you have more than one qualifying child in college during the same year, you may have the option of using both the American Opportunity Tax Credit and the Lifetime Learning Credit in the same year; however, you cannot claim both in the same year for the same person in college.

Employee Educational Assistance Programs

Under the Employee Educational Assistance Program, an employer can reimburse an employee's tuition, enrollment fees, books, supplies, and equipment for undergraduate and graduate studies.

These working-condition fringe benefits can be excluded from the employee's income, up to $5,250 per year, including student loan repayments. Under the OBBBA, this provision becomes permanent, and the annual limit will be indexed for inflation beginning in 2026. This is a tax-free benefit to the employee (i.e., you or your spouse); at the same time, your employer receives a full business tax deduction.

It is important to note that neither the employer nor the employee can claim an education tax credit for the same expense. If the employee has expenses that exceed the $5,250 employer reimbursement, the employee will be permitted to claim the American Opportunity Tax Credit or the Lifetime Learning Credit for those expenses paid over this amount. Of course, the employee needs to meet the qualifications for these credits.

If you do not pay attention to the tax consequences when paying for college, you may be paying significantly more in taxes than the law requires. Therefore, you must include tax planning as part of your overall strategy for saving and paying for college and creating generational wealth. Using a financial planning approach that takes advantage of tax-smart strategies will help maximize your college saving goals.

Tax-smart Strategies for Paying for College

Here are several tax facts and strategies that will address your wealth accumulation goals in a powerful and sustainable way. This will be part of your tax-smart roadmap to financial independence. This is how you can transform the tax code into part of your generational wealth code.

- Establish and fund the maximum annual contribution of $2,000 per year to a Coverdell ESA for each of your children under the age of 18, if you or your child qualifies. Although there is no upfront tax deduction, all future earnings and principal will be paid out tax-free if you use it to cover private school costs from kindergarten through graduate school.
- Consider transferring appreciated property (such as stocks, bonds, and mutual funds) that you plan to sell (to cover education costs), to your children age 19 and older or children who are full-time students ages 19–23, if their earned income is more than half of the amount of their support. They can then sell this appreciated property and have the capital gain taxed at a rate as low as 0%, as long as their overall taxable income is below $48,350. They can use this money to pay for their education, and you can avoid paying federal tax on any gain.
- Keep in mind that if you buy US EE Savings Bonds or I Bonds to pay for qualified educational expenses and you defer reporting the interest, you may be eligible to exclude the accumulated interests from income when you redeem the bonds.

(*continued*)

(*continued*)

- Also keep in mind that if you receive a scholarship or fellowship as a degree candidate, these payments are tax-free to the extent that they pay for tuition, cost-related fees, books, supplies, and equipment that are required for your courses. Any amounts paid for room and board, as well as other incidentals, are taxable.
- Consider establishing a Code Section 529 savings plan. Although you do not receive any federal tax deduction for the contributions you make to these plans, the distributions are generally tax-free to the extent that you use them to pay for qualified education expenses.
- Another key feature of 529 education savings plans is that they cover more than just college expenses. Families can use up to $20,000 per year, per student to pay for private school tuition for grades K–12. There is no limit for qualified higher education expenses such as undergraduate and graduate costs.
- If your state has its own sponsored 529 educational savings plan, you may get the added benefit of a state tax deduction for any contributions you make before the end of the year. Each state has different rules, however, so be sure to check with your tax advisor.
- If utilizing a 529 plan to pay for K–12, you must check with your state to ensure that these distributions will also be tax-free at the state level. Many states that provide a state tax deduction for the contribution are currently not following the same rules as the federal government on these distributions.
- With the broadened available use of 529 plan funds, taxpayers should reconsider state tax deductibility of contributions along with tax-deferred growth and tax-free withdrawal of funds for qualified purposes.
- If you paid qualified tuition and fees for an eligible student in the first four years of college or postsecondary institution, you may qualify for the American opportunity tax credit of up to $2,500 for each eligible student. Special rules apply, and this credit starts to phase-out for married couples filing jointly with incomes over $160,000 and $80,000 for individuals filing as single, head of household, or qualifying widows and widowers, and is fully eliminated at income levels of $180,000 and $90,000 respectively.
- If you paid qualified expenses for yourself, your spouse, or your dependents who are enrolled in eligible educational institutions during the year, you may be able to claim the Lifetime Learning Credit of up to $2,000. This credit does not have a degree or workload requirement. The credit may be claimed for one or more courses that are either part of a postsecondary degree program or a part of a nondegree program to acquire or improve job skills. This credit is not limited to the first four years of postsecondary education, and there is no limit on the number of years it can be claimed. The credit is 20% of the first $10,000 paid in 2025, and the maximum credit per family is $2,000 per year. Special

rules apply, and for 2025 this credit starts to phase-out for married couples filing jointly with incomes over $160,000 and at $80,000 for individuals filing as single or head of household. The credit is fully phased out at $180,000 and $90,000, respectively.

- If you are not getting the benefit of this educational tax credit because of your high-income level and your child has his or her own tax liability against which the credit may be claimed, you can forgo claiming your child as a dependent on your tax return. This allows the education tax credit to be claimed on your child's tax return. Calculate your tax bill as well as your children's and take advantage of the method that provides your family with the greatest tax savings overall.
- If you paid interest on a qualified student loan, you may be able to claim an above-the-line deduction of up to $2,500 on your 2025 tax return. This amount is phased out in 2025 for married couples filing jointly starting at $170,000, and $85,000 for individuals filing as single or head of household. This deduction is fully phased out at $200,000 and $100,000 respectively. If you are married and filing separately, however, you may not claim this deduction, no matter what your income level.
- Leverage your employer's Educational Assistance Program to receive up to $5,250 per year in tax-free reimbursement for tuition, books, fees, supplies, and even student loan payments. This benefit becomes permanent and indexed for inflation starting in 2026 under the OBBBA. While the employer receives a full business deduction, the employee (you or your spouse) enjoys a tax-free benefit. Just be aware that the same expenses cannot be used to claim education tax credits such as the American Opportunity Tax Credit or Lifetime Learning Credit unless you use costs that exceed the $5,250 threshold.

An Action Plan for Paying for College

1. **Decide whether college is the right choice for your child** or if they are better suited to pursue their passions in setting up a business or taking a high-paying blue-collar job.
2. **Find out today what your child's college expenses might be,** even if college is still 18 years away. Do not wait until your child is in high school because, by then, it may be too late for you to save enough and you will regret not having started planning sooner.
3. **Do not spend money on what you want to buy now,** your *immediate wants,* without first setting aside money for your *future needs.* No matter what

(*continued*)

(continued)

it is you think you "want" now, furniture for your child's nursery, tennis or piano lessons for your budding prodigy, or a bigger home so your kids can each have their own bedroom, none of that is really as important as saving for your child's education. Do not make the same mistake so many parents make by not starting to save now.

4. **Conduct a needs analysis for your child's education.** Use the *Saving for College* calculator, available at www.ventotaxandwealth.com under the Resources > Calculators & Tools section, to complete a "needs analysis" for your family's education funding goals.
5. **Understand the differences among the five most used strategies to saving for college:** Section 529 educational savings programs, UGMA/UTMA accounts, the Coverdell ESAs, US savings bonds, and now Trump Accounts. Each has different tax implications, income restrictions, and factors affecting who controls the money in the account, as well as other differences, so discuss them with your tax advisor to determine which of these is best for your family's needs.
6. **Keep in mind that you have the most control and the greatest tax benefits if you save money via a 529 plan.** The example in this chapter showed a difference of almost $100,000 more if you save via a tax-exempt 529 than if you save via a taxable account. Find out how much more *you* could earn by doing a similar comparison using your specific savings plan.
7. **Understand that if you use a Uniform Gift/Transfer to Minor Act to transfer assets to your child, your child will have total control over that money** and may decide not to use it for college. Look for other ways to help your child save for college.
8. **Consider saving via a Coverdell ESA** for your child's primary or secondary education expenses if you qualify, in addition to college, if you plan to send your child or children to private schools.
9. **Recognize that although investing in US savings bonds is safe, they offer a low return,** which may make it very difficult for you to reach your child's financial needs for college expenses.
10. **Take full advantage of Trump Accounts.** Trump Accounts are a tax-deferred savings vehicle created under the OBBBA. Although these were created as retirement accounts, they can be fully utilized to pay for a college education.
11. **If your child has a part-time paying job, consider establishing a Roth IRA in your child's name.** Although this is a retirement account, your child can withdraw money from it to pay for college, and the taxable portion of the withdrawal will be taxed at your child's tax rate, which could be as low as 0%,

if structured properly. And if your child decides not to go to college or does not use the money to pay for college, he or she will have already begun saving for retirement!

12. **Learn as much as you can about what financial aid your child might qualify for,** based on your family's income and assets, as well as that of your child. See Exhibit 7.4 for 2025–2026 guidelines.
13. **Find out if you qualify for either of the two major education tax credits,** the American opportunity tax credit and the Lifetime Learning Credit. These depend on the number of courses your child is taking in college, your and your spouse's income, and your tax filing status. If you are unsure whether you qualify, talk to your tax or financial advisor.
14. **Speak with your human resources department to see if your employer offers an Educational Assistance Program.** If available, make sure to take advantage of this tax-free benefit for tuition, books, or student loan payments of up to $5,250 per year.
15. **Work with a tax-advisor and CERTIFIED FINANCIAL PLANNER®** that can provide you with the tax-smart advice covered in this chapter. Please refer to Appendix A, "Selecting a Trusted Advisor."
16. **Work with a financial planner** that will provide you with the necessary advice and guidance that includes the 12 critical areas of comprehensive wealth management covered throughout this book.
17. **Use the tax-smart roadmap to financial independence at the end of this chapter to transform the tax code into part of your generational wealth code.**

CHAPTER 8

Planning for Retirement

If you don't want to work, you have to work to earn enough money so that you won't have to work.

—Ogden Nash, American Poet

Everyone should be planning financially for retirement, regardless of their age. Many employers no longer guarantee employee pensions, so your financial needs during your retirement may rest completely on your shoulders. People reaching retirement age are facing concerns that retirees did not face 20 or 30 years ago. They must plan for their retirement funds to support them for a longer expected lifespan, and they must seriously question whether they can count on Social Security benefits when the time comes.

This chapter helps you determine your financial needs for retirement and how to properly fund them. We show you how to determine your own individual *point X*, financial independence. We also describe tax implications and other risks that might jeopardize your retirement plans, and what steps you need to take to secure the peace of mind that comes from a financially secure retirement.

Case Study: Saving Versus *Not* Saving for Retirement, The $2.2 Million Difference

When it comes to being prepared for retirement, there are generally two scenarios that most people tend to follow. One is *not having* any plan at all, and the other is *having* a well-thought-out retirement planning strategy. Unfortunately, the majority of people are in the former category and do not have any plan to achieve their retirement goals of becoming financially independent. After reading through this chapter, ask yourself whether you will follow the example set by my clients Mr. and Mrs. Poorman or Mr. and Mrs. Richman. For this example, we are using tax laws under the One Big Beautiful Bill Act (OBBBA) for 2025.

Before reviewing their specific stories, it is important to highlight four critical issues that will control and significantly affect your success or failure in reaching your retirement goals:

1. How much of your income will you save and invest each year?
2. How many years will you be setting aside money for your retirement?
3. What type of investments will you use to meet your goals?
4. Will you be disciplined and stay on track?

Consider the story of two clients, referred to here as Mr. and Mrs. Poorman. About 25 years ago, the Poormans had recently married and started their first jobs; they were about four years out of college. During the preparation of their income tax return, it was noted that they had not participated in their company's 401(k) plans and had not taken any steps in saving for retirement. The advantages of starting to save at an early age were explained to them, along with tax calculations showing their refund both with and without a $14,000 Individual Retirement Account (IRA) contribution between them. With this IRA contribution, their refund increased by $4,900. For every $1,000 they contributed to a traditional IRA, they would receive an extra $350 (35% for every $1). They were quite impressed with the tax saving incentives that would be made available by setting money aside for their retirement, either through their 401(k) or an IRA.

Although they agreed that funding a retirement plan was the smart thing to do, they said they had no money available to do so. They had just finished paying for their wedding and honeymoon, and they had no money left for savings. Although they were concerned about the future, they said they would definitely do this next year when they had some extra cash. Over the next three years, they set money aside for a down payment for their home and were not able to fund their retirement. Over the next two years, once again, they said they were unable to fund their retirement because they needed to furnish their new home. This story continued throughout their lives, with the birth of their first and then second child. Before they knew it, it was time for their two sons to go to college, and they were still not able to set money aside for their retirement.

Throughout their lives, they always had what appeared to be valid excuses for not saving for their future. They failed to understand that they must first set money aside (pay themselves first) each year and *then* determine their standard of living based on what was left over. Each year brought new events and expenses, and each year they said they would start saving "next year."

In the years that they did manage to set aside some money, they chose to keep their funds in a nonretirement account that earned little or no interest rather than investing in a well-diversified stock and bond mutual fund portfolio. Because *they* did not understand the stock and bond market, they felt it would be best for them not to get involved. They were fearful of the stock market because their parents had lost quite a bit of money in the crash of 1987. Also, even though they did not understand the basics of investing, they were not willing to work with an advisor to guide them through this process. The Poormans did not have a disciplined approach to saving for retirement and acted like they had no choice other than ignoring and avoiding the decisions that needed to be made to ensure their financial future. In fact, the Poormans had no plan to reach financial independence at any point in their lives.

Twenty-five years later, they are in their early fifties and still living paycheck to paycheck to maintain their current standard of living. In fact, they recently borrowed all the equity in their home to pay for their two sons' first two years of college at private universities.

Are you living your life in a manner similar to the Poormans? If so, you can and must change the pattern of this vicious cycle immediately. This is a matter of financial life and death, with no way to get around it unless you are willing to make the necessary changes.

At the same time the Poormans were beginning their careers, Mr. and Mrs. Richman were starting their financial journey. Their story was amazingly similar to the Poormans, but with significantly different results based on the decisions the Richmans made. The Richmans were also newly married, but they decided early on to be conservative with their spending, and they understood the importance of saving for tomorrow. They had a modest wedding and only invited their closest friends and family members. They had a week-long honeymoon and were able to get a great deal on an all-inclusive trip to the Bahamas at a discounted rate. They had no debt and more than $18,000 in combined savings when they began their careers. They also began funding their retirement accounts during their first full year of employment after college.

Even though they did not qualify for an IRA tax-deductible contribution, they both agreed that they would make an annual nondeductible IRA contribution. The Richmans clearly had a vision of what was truly important to them. When they found out the following year that they had twins on the way, they became even more disciplined and focused on their finances. Financial security for their family was now their number one priority, not the materialistic goods and services that measure a person's standard of living throughout their lifetime. They always came in and joked about the fact that they will "pay themselves first," and then determine what they can afford after they set aside their savings. They knew that what they saved and set aside was not meant to be spent on nonessential items.

They also realized the value of the tax savings the government offered them through fully funding their retirement accounts. They were able to save significantly more money because they were doing it with pre-tax dollars. This 35% tax savings (from their 401(k) contributions) meant they would have 35% more set aside each year.

The Richmans understood the power of the time value of money. They started saving from their very first paycheck and understood early on that their young age was one of their most valuable investment assets. They knew that the longer they saved, the greater their chance of achieving financial independence. They appreciated the fact that the amount of time they had to save and invest was more important than a strategy of trying to time the entry point to investing in the market. They took a dollar-cost-averaging approach to saving and investing for their future, by having a payroll deduction come out of each and every one of their paychecks to fund retirement savings.

Although the Richmans were not in the financial services industry and did not fully understand investing, they sought professional guidance and kept a large portion of their portfolio in diversified stock and bond mutual funds and exchange-traded funds (ETFs). They remained committed to a balanced approach, rebalancing annually, and holding investments through market downturns. Their strategy focused on quality investments, proper diversification, and discipline.

Today, the Richmans have more than $2.2 million in retirement savings, have paid off their home mortgage (five years early after taking advantage of falling interest rates), and have also set aside sufficient funds to get their son and daughter through four years of state college.

From early on in their relationship, even before they were married, they had a clear plan for a comfortable retirement and a strategy for achieving financial independence. If you are an able-bodied individual with a job, you can also achieve financial independence by simply paying yourself first, and then living within a budget of whatever is left over. It really is that simple. If my parents were able to do it as Italian immigrants working for modest wages and raising four children, so can you!

So, would you consider yourself like Mr. and Mrs. Poorman or Mr. and Mrs. Richman? Are you willing to do what it takes to live your life like the Richmans? If so, congratulations! You have just made your commitment to planning for a comfortable retirement and for achieving financial independence for you and your family.

Retirement Equation: Calculating Your Personal *Point X*, Financial Independence

Most people have the desire and dream to become financially independent. Wanting to achieve this goal requires planning; you cannot leave this to chance. Financial independence, or *point X*, can be defined as the point where your money starts working for you instead of you working for your money, while still maintaining your desired standard of living.

This number is different for everyone because there are many variables that need to be taken into consideration. The starting point is estimating how much income you will need in retirement and then determining whether your current savings and investment plan will be able to provide you with that desired amount. This is the centerpiece of planning for retirement, and going through the necessary calculations will show you what is required to get there.

The 12 key questions in determining your own *point X* are shown in Exhibit 8.1. Although there are many other variables to consider, these are the fundamental questions to analyze and answer when determining your retirement planning strategy.

The answers to these questions will enable you to calculate how much money you will need when you retire. The math used in this

Exhibit 8.1 Twelve Questions to Analyze Your Retirement Needs

1. What is your current age?
2. What is your current annual income?
3. What is your spouse's annual income (if applicable)?
4. What is your current total retirement savings?
5. What is your desired retirement age?
6. What is the expected number of years of retirement income needed?
7. What is the expected inflation rate?
8. What percentage of your current combined income will you need at retirement?
9. What do you expect your preretirement return on investments to be?
10. What do you expect your post-retirement return on investments to be?
11. Would you like to assume that you will be receiving Social Security benefits in retirement?
12. If you do expect to receive Social Security, what is the monthly dollar amount in today's dollars?

calculation is quite complicated because there are so many variables (including present value and future value calculations). Therefore, it is best to use an online retirement planning calculator. Keep in mind, you could use one of numerous online financial calculators, all of which may have a different variation on these questions. Always remember, these are just rough estimates based on a set of assumptions you will need to make.

You can use the *Saving for Retirement* calculator, available at www.ventotaxandwealth.com under the Resources > Calculators & Tools section. You will be able to run through an unlimited number of "what if?" scenarios to try to answer the question, "How much will I need to save for retirement?"

This exercise will give you a reality check, and you may need to alter some of your assumptions. But remember, it is best to be conservative and realistic. If the amount you need to save does not appear achievable, you will need to go back and make some adjustments in your standard of living not only now but also in retirement. Never forget the lesson of Chapter 1, "Living Within Your Means."

The High Cost of Waiting to Save for Retirement

Should I start saving now or later? That is the question. Procrastination is never the answer in life. The best time to start is always right *now*!

Almost everyone has the desire to save for retirement. But many delay this process, believing that next year it will be easier. As shown in the story about the Poormans, there will always be an excuse not to save this year. Falling into this trap can have financially devastating consequences to your financial security. Most people do not know when they should start and how much they should save each year. Quite simply, the answer is to start immediately. A general rule of thumb is putting away 10% or more of your gross annual paycheck each year.

The easy way out of making the right decision is to justify it by saying you will wait until your income level increases. Unfortunately, with every salary increase, most people simply raise their standard of living instead of their retirement savings. The longer you wait, the harder it will be to accumulate the amount you need to be financially independent. Remember one of the most valuable investment assets you have is time. The more years you save, the greater your chance of financial success.

The financial rewards of starting to save at an early age for retirement far outweigh the costly mistake of waiting and spending your money on your wants. By starting with even small amounts each month, you may be able to accumulate a great deal of retirement savings over time. By far the easiest way to do this is by contributing to your employer's retirement plan or, if that is not available, to an IRA.

Implement a retirement saving strategy that allocates a specific dollar amount or percentage (at least 10%) of your salary every pay period. Therefore, you are paying yourself first, as though saving for retirement is your number one required expense. In fact, saving for retirement is not an expense because it adds to your investable assets, but treating it as such is of utmost importance to your success.

If you are not convinced of the old saying "*time is money*," consider the following example, which compares two individuals with different approaches to the value of time as it relates to saving.

Vanessa started saving at the age of 20, setting aside $4,000 per year for 10 years, which then continued to grow for an additional 30 years. Over the 40-year period, her tax-deferred account grew at a rate of 8% per year on average, bringing the value of her account to $583,093.

Anthony delayed saving for retirement until the age of 30, when he also began to save $4,000 per year for 10 years, which then continued to grow for an additional 20 years. Over the 30-year period, his tax-deferred account grew at a rate of 8% per year, bringing the value of his account to $270,085.

Exhibit 8.2 shows the difference in how their savings grew.

Exhibit 8.2 The High Cost of Waiting to Save for Retirement

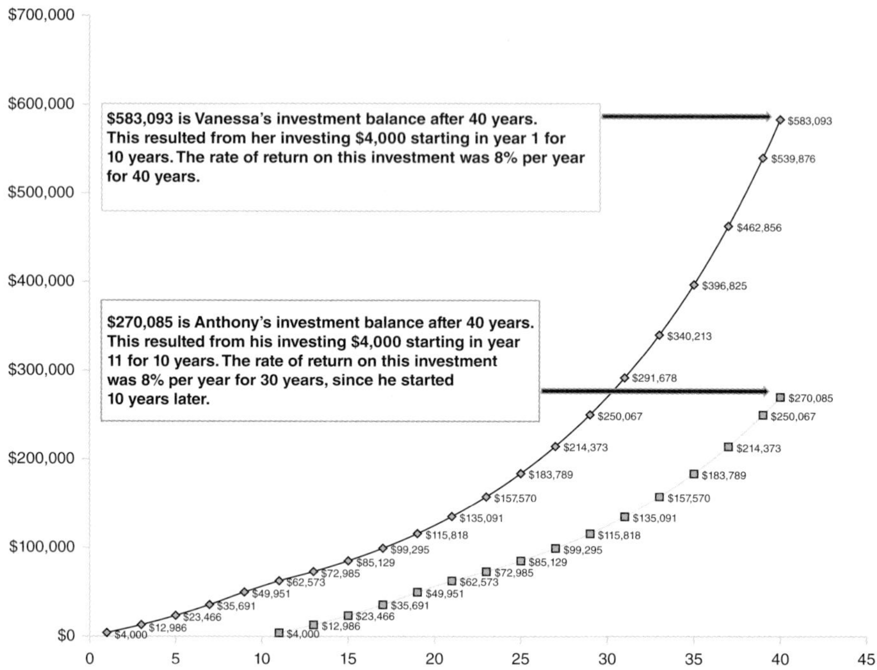

Both Vanessa and Anthony set aside $4,000 per year over a 10-year savings time span. They both managed to save $40,000, but they ended up with significantly different results when they reached the age of 65. Because Anthony started 10 years later than Vanessa, his savings were $313,008 less than Vanessa's!

This example verifies that time is money and that one of your most valuable financial assets is time. By getting off to an early start with your retirement savings program, you can take advantage of the power of compounding.

Your annual savings have the potential of earning a rate of return and so do your reinvested earnings. Look at the Rule of 72 in Exhibit 12.1 to see just how powerful compounding can be. This is the secret to financial independence: by letting your money work for you, eventually, you will no longer have to work to maintain your desired standard of living.

If you have been finding it difficult to save money on a regular basis, implement the following savings strategies that will take money directly from your paycheck on a pre-tax basis. By utilizing employer-sponsored retirement plans, you will establish a systematic strategy that will force you to pay yourself first in a tax-efficient manner, implementing a dollar-cost-averaging investment plan.

No matter what method you use, it is extremely important that you start saving now!

What You Can Expect to Receive from Social Security

Social Security benefits are viewed by many as the building blocks of our retirement planning strategy. However, advances in medicine have increased life expectancies far beyond any actuarial assumptions used when the program was originally established. These longer life spans have dramatically increased the number of people collecting Social Security benefits. At the same time fewer workers are paying into the system, placing significant strain on its finances.

On January 1, 2011, the first members of the baby boomer generation, defined as those born between 1946 and 1964, turned 65. Millions more have reached or are approaching retirement age, and Social Security remains a key source of income for them. Currently, about 10,000 Americans reach age 65 each day, a trend that is expected to continue into the 2030s. The US Census Bureau projects that by 2050 approximately 22% of the US population will be 65 or older, compared with 15% in 2015. This shift will continue to put significant pressure on both the Social Security and Medicare systems. Exhibit 8.3 demonstrates the historical and projected downward trend of covered workers to beneficiaries, as reported by the Social Security Administration (SSA). A covered worker represents someone who is employed and paying Social Security taxes into the system. A beneficiary is anyone who is receiving Social Security benefits and therefore taking money out of the system.

In 1945, when the system was first established, there were 41.9 people paying Social Security taxes for every beneficiary taking money out of the system. By 1965, that ratio had already declined to four. In 2025, there are about 2.7 workers for each beneficiary, and the Social Security Administration projects that by 2035 the number will fall to around 2.2. The cause of this is very simple to understand. Baby boomers have started to enter into their retirement age, and the population is living significantly longer than anyone could have ever anticipated. Unless there is some major change in the system, its future is going to be very uncertain.

Exhibit 8.3 Ratio of Social Security Covered Workers to Beneficiaries Over Time

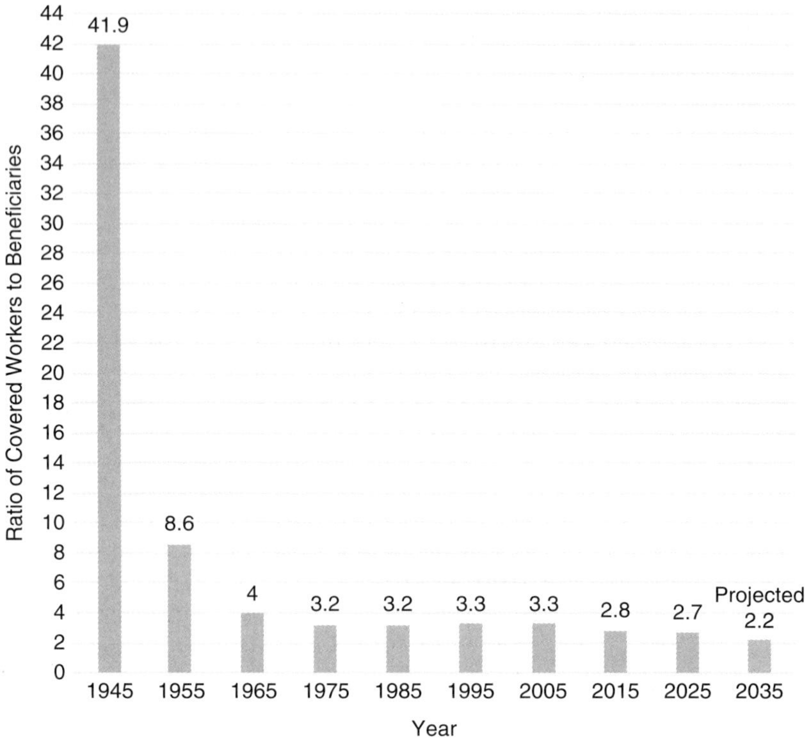

Before 2003, you could receive full Social Security retirement benefits upon reaching age 65. The eligibility age has been increasing on a graduated scale. For people born after 1937, and for anyone born in 1960 or later, full retirement age is now 67. That age is scheduled to remain in place, although many policy experts believe it will eventually rise further as part of efforts to address the program's financial challenges.

The 2025 Social Security Trustees Report confirms that program costs have exceeded noninterest income since 2010, and that this situation will persist for the foreseeable future. The Old-Age and Survivors Insurance trust fund is projected to be depleted in 2033, at which point payroll tax income will cover about 77% of scheduled benefits. When combined with the Disability Insurance trust fund, the depletion date is projected to be 2034, with about 81% of benefits payable from incoming revenues alone.

The likely outcome is that most people will probably have to wait longer to qualify for full benefits, and those benefits will replace a *smaller* percentage of preretirement income than in past generations. Higher-income earners will see an even smaller replacement rate. This is why it is critical to factor in a more limited role for Social Security when calculating the income that you will need in retirement.

It is reasonable to expect that future changes could include delaying eligibility for full benefits, reducing benefit amounts for both new and existing retirees, raising the Social Security payroll tax rate, and increasing the maximum amount of earnings subject to that tax. A combination of these adjustments may be the only way to maintain the long-term sustainability of the program and ensure continued benefit payments.

One of the first steps in developing a retirement planning strategy is estimating your Social Security benefits in retirement. The SSA no longer mails annual estimated benefit statements except in limited cases. Instead, you can access your statement online by creating a *My Social Security* account at www.ssa.gov/myaccount. Once logged in, you can view your full earnings record and use the SSA's retirement estimator, which provides a personalized estimate based on your actual Social Security earnings history. The estimator will ask for information such as the following:

- Your expected future annual earnings
- The age at which you plan to start benefits

Based on this information and your actual earnings history, the calculator will display your estimated monthly benefit under three scenarios:

1. If you retire at age 62 (the earliest date you can receive benefits)
2. If you wait until full retirement age (for most people today is between 66 and 67 depending on birth year)
3. If you continue working until age 70 before claiming retirement benefits (results in the maximum monthly amount)

For a general, nonpersonalized estimate, you can access the SSA's Quick Calculator at www.ssa.gov, search for "Benefit Calculator" and select "Quick Calculator." This tool does not use your official earnings record. Instead, it produces an estimate based on the date of birth, current annual earnings, and retirement age that you enter. Results are shown in both today's dollars and inflation-adjusted future dollars. The Quick Calculator is best used for a rough estimate and should not replace the detailed personalized figures available through your SSA account.

Qualified Retirement Plans

If the government had a program that would provide you with an interest-free loan so that you could invest that money for the long term to secure your retirement, would you take advantage of such an offer? What if this program also included a provision that if you lost some of the money through your investments, you would not have to repay that portion of the loan to the government? What if this program also allowed you to start paying back the loan gradually (also interest-free) over your life expectancy, starting at the age of 75?

Although this program sounds too good to be true, it is available to every working individual in the United States, and far too few are taking advantage of it. Quite simply, this is precisely what happens when you contribute money to a retirement account and take advantage of the tax-deferral option.

Tax deferral is a method of postponing the payment of income tax on income earned in the current year until you withdraw the funds from the tax-deferred account. The Internal Revenue Code was designed, in part, to encourage long-term saving and to help Americans achieve a secure, sustainable retirement. The Code provides many ways to take advantage of tax deferral, which can accelerate your retirement savings. There is no single better strategy for achieving financial independence, and ultimately generational wealth, than by doing it in a tax-advantaged way.

For example, IRAs and 401(k)s allow you to defer taxes on both contributions and earnings. Certain insurance products, such as fixed and variable annuities and certain life insurance contracts, also allow taxes to be deferred.

There is a significant benefit to deferring taxes as long as possible because it allows the entire principal and earnings to compound on a tax-deferred basis, which can have a dramatic effect on your retirement savings over an extended period. The benefit of this tax-deferred compounding was highlighted in Exhibit 8.2, where Vanessa accumulated $313,008 more than Anthony simply by starting 10 years earlier (even though the total amount each of them set aside was the same

$40,000). Clearly the combined effects of tax deferral with compounding are significant over long periods.

For many people, the initial tax-deferral period is during their higher-income earning years when their tax bracket is much higher. The added benefit to this is that you are deferring income during years that would require you to pay a higher tax rate and possibly picking up this income in years when you will be subject to a lower tax rate. Although there is no guarantee that you will be in a lower tax bracket in retirement (tax rates can increase in the future with new presidential administrations), tax deferral is still one of the most powerful tools available in retirement planning.

Now that you are convinced that tax-deferred compounding is the most effective way to achieve financial independence, let us look at a summary of some of the most popular plans available. Numerous options are available for funding your retirement on a tax-deferred basis, depending on your particular facts and circumstances. These options are also limited to what may be available through your employer: some plans are fully funded by your employer, some are *partially* funded by you, and some are *fully* funded by you. To clarify this even further, employer contributions come directly from your employer's funds, whereas employee contributions come from a direct reduction in your gross paycheck.

A *qualified retirement plan* is a plan that meets the requirements of the Internal Revenue Code and, as a result, is eligible to receive certain tax benefits, primarily a tax deduction to your employer and tax deferral to you. These plans must be for the exclusive benefit of employees or their beneficiaries.

There are two kinds of qualified plans: defined-benefit plans and defined-contribution plans. Keep in mind that, in most cases, withdrawals made before age 59½ are subject to a 10% penalty, unless you qualify for one of the exceptions. Withdrawals must begin no later than April 1 of the year after you turn age 73 or 75, depending on the year you were born, and are subject to income taxes in most cases.

Once you have a good understanding of the various qualified retirement plan options available, you will be in a much better position to achieve financial independence. These retirement plans are by far the most tax-efficient weapons available to you in your pursuit of accumulating wealth. Think about this for a minute. You are allowed to defer the payment of significant tax dollars, which amounts to an interest-free loan from the government. At the same time, you have the potential to earn a rate of return with these funds. You cannot afford to miss this opportunity.

The following chart summarizes the most common types of qualified retirement plans available today. While each has unique rules, benefits, and eligibility requirements, all share one powerful advantage: the ability to grow retirement savings in a tax-advantaged way. The right plan for you will depend on your employment status, income level, business structure, long-term goals, and which retirement plan type is offered through your employer.

CATEGORY	PLAN TYPE	DESCRIPTION
Defined Contribution Plans	Traditional 401(k)	Employer-sponsored plan allowing pre-tax employee salary deferral typically with an employer match, with earnings growing tax-deferred until withdrawal.
	Roth 401(k)	Employer-sponsored plan with after-tax employee salary deferral typically with an employer match and tax-free qualified withdrawals.
	Solo 401(k)	401(k) plan for business owner or business owner and spouse with no employees. Allows salary deferrals typically with an additional employer contribution.
	Safe Harbor 401(k)	Traditional 401(k) plan with mandatory employer contributions to avoid certain nondiscrimination testing.
	SIMPLE 401(k)	Simplified 401(k) plan for small businesses, with lower salary deferral limits and mandatory employer contributions.
	403(b)	Salary deferral plan for employees of public schools, nonprofits, and certain ministers.
	457(b)	Deferred compensation plan for state and local government employees and some nonprofits.
	Profit-sharing Plan	Employers make discretionary contributions.
	Money Purchase Pension Plan	Employer contributes a fixed percentage of each employee's pay annually.
	Thrift Savings Plan (TSP)	Salary deferral plan for federal employees and members of the uniformed services.
Defined Benefit Plans	Traditional Pension Plan	Employer promises a specified monthly benefit in retirement, often based on salary and years of service.
	Cash Balance Plan	Type of Defined Benefit Plan typically paired with profit sharing and Safe Harbor 401(k) provisions.

CATEGORY	PLAN TYPE	DESCRIPTION
Simplified Plans for Small Employers	SEP IRA	Simplified Employee Pension plan where employer makes tax-deductible contributions to an employee's SEP IRA account.
	SIMPLE IRA	Retirement plan allowing employee salary deferral with a mandatory employer match or nonelective contribution.
Other Specialized or Hybrid Plans	Employee Stock Ownership Plan (ESOP)	Retirement Plan that typically allows salary deferral by employees may have match or profit sharing by employer which invests primarily in employer's stock.
	Keogh Plan (HR-10 Plan)	Profit-sharing plan for self-employed individuals which are sole proprietorships or partners in a partnership. Plan may allow salary deferrals with 401(k) provisions.
	Payroll Deduction IRA	Employer either takes instructions from employees to defer salary, or the employer makes a payment to an individually owned IRA. Many state mandated retirement programs are established as Payroll Deduction Roth IRA.

The Difference Between Traditional IRAs and Roth IRAs

IRAs are available to all wage earners at any salary level as well as to nonworking spouses. You and your spouse cannot contribute more than your combined earned income to an IRA. IRAs are funded completely by the individual's contributions and not by an employer. This is why they are referred to as "individual" retirement accounts. These specially designated retirement accounts are required to be held with a bank, brokerage firm, mutual fund company, insurance company, or other financial institution. Once you set up an IRA, you have several investing options. You can choose to invest in stocks, bonds, mutual funds, ETFs, cash equivalents, real estate, and other investments. You have total control over these accounts, and you can elect a lump-sum payment or periodic withdrawals when you retire.

You can choose from two different types of IRAs, either a traditional or a Roth. These names are simply designations placed on the accounts to distinguish them from nonretirement accounts. The account type does not represent an investment itself. The decision on whether to open an IRA and which type is completely independent of how the funds will be invested once the account is established. See Chapter 9, "Managing Your Investments," for more details on investment options.

Contributions to traditional IRAs may be tax-deductible if you meet the requirements; withdrawals are taxable in the year you take them. Therefore, a traditional IRA gives you a tax deduction in the current year and a tax deferral for any earnings, but ultimately you will pay tax when you withdraw from your account.

In contrast, contributions to a Roth IRA are *not* tax-deductible, but qualified withdrawals are tax-free. Roth IRAs do not give you a tax deduction in the current year, but ultimately your qualified withdrawals, including earnings, will be paid out to you tax-free in retirement.

The real question to ask when deciding between a traditional and a Roth IRA is whether you prefer receiving the tax benefit in the current year or tax-free income in retirement.

Both a traditional IRA and Roth IRA are subject to the same contribution limits, which are $7,000 in 2025. Although you can contribute to both within the same year, this $7,000 limit applies to the maximum combined contribution. The maximum *total* annual contribution an individual can make to a traditional and Roth IRA at the same time is $7,000 (as of 2025). There is a special "catch-up" provision that allows individuals age 50 and older to save even more by allowing them to contribute an additional $1,000, for a total limit of $8,000 per year.

As Carol Ventura, former Senior IRA Solutions Manager at Cetera Financial Group, explains:

> If you are covered by a retirement plan at work, your ability to deduct Traditional IRA contributions depends on your tax filing status and your modified adjusted gross income (MAGI). If your income exceeds certain limits, your contribution may be partially deductible or not deductible at all. Even if you cannot deduct, you can still contribute up to the annual limit and report it as a non-deductible IRA contribution.

See Exhibit 8.4 for details.

Traditional IRAs

Traditional IRAs can be an excellent way to save for retirement. If you do not participate in an employer-sponsored retirement plan, or if you would like to save more money than that plan allows, then a traditional IRA could be a great choice for you. A traditional IRA is simply a tax-deferred savings account that you can establish through a financial institution.

Exhibit 8.4 IRS Tables Covering IRA Contributions

Table 1: 2025 Effect of Modified AGI on Traditional IRA Contribution *If You Are Covered by a Retirement Plan at Work*

Filing Status	**Single or Head of Household or Married Filing Separately** and did not live with spouse any time during the year	**Married Filing Jointly or Qualifying Widow(er)**	**Married Filing Separately** and lived with spouse any time during the year
MAXIMUM TRADITIONAL IRA **contribution** is the lesser of actual taxable compensation or the amount below:			
Under Age 50	$7,000	$7,000	$7,000
Age 50 or Over	$8,000	$8,000	$8,000
Maximum Modified Adjusted Gross Income for above Full TRADITIONAL IRA **deductions**:			
	$79,000	$126,000	$ZERO
The TRADITIONAL IRA contribution is phased out for higher incomes and reduced to $ZERO at the following Modified Adjusted Gross Income level of:			
	$89,000	$146,000	$10,000

Table 2: 2025 Effect of Modified AGI on Traditional IRA Contribution *If You Are Not Covered by a Retirement Plan at Work*

Filing Status	**Single, Head of Household or Qualifying Widow(er)**	**Married Filing Jointly or Separately** with a spouse who **is not** covered by a plan at work	**Married Filing Jointly** with a spouse who **is** covered by a plan at work and the other is not	**Married Filing Separately** with a spouse who **is** covered by a plan at work
MAXIMUM TRADITIONAL IRA **contribution** is the lesser of actual taxable compensation or the amount below:				
Under Age 50	$7,000	$7,000	$7,000	$7,000
Age 50 or Over	$8,000	$8,000	$8,000	$8,000
Maximum Modified Adjusted Gross Income for above TRADITIONAL IRA **deductions**:				
	No Modified AGI Limit for Full Deduction	No Modified AGI Limit for Full Deduction	$230,000	$ZERO
The Maximum TRADITIONAL IRA contribution is phased out for higher incomes and reduced to $ZERO at the following Modified Adjusted Gross Income level of:				
	No Limit	No Limit	$240,000	$10,000

(*Continued*)

Exhibit 8.4 (*Continued*)

Table 3: 2025 Effect of Modified Adjusted Gross Income on Roth IRA contributions

Filing Status	**Single, Head of Household, or Married Filing Separately** and did not live with spouse any time during the year	**Married Filing Jointly** and **Qualifying Widow(er)**	**Married Filing Separately** and lived with spouse any time during the year
MAXIMUM ROTH IRA **contribution** is the lesser of actual taxable compensation or the amount below:			
Under Age 50	$7,000	$7,000	$7,000
Age 50 or Over	$8,000	$8,000	$8,000
Maximum Modified Adjusted Gross Income for above ROTH IRA contributions:			
	$150,000	$236,000	$ZERO
The Maximum ROTH IRA contribution is phased out for higher incomes and reduced to $ZERO at the following Modified Adjusted Gross Income level of:			
	$165,000	$246,000	$10,000

One of the greatest advantages of a traditional IRA is the potential for tax-deductible contributions. If your income is below the threshold or if you and/or your spouse are not covered through an employer plan at any income level, you can qualify for a tax-deductible contribution. For example, if your marginal income tax rate is 40% and you qualify for the deduction, then a $7,000 traditional IRA contribution could save you $2,800 in income tax for that year. Would you not rather put that $2,800 aside for your own retirement than pay it in taxes to the government?

Your contributions to a traditional IRA must come from a nonretirement account in order for it to be treated as a current-year contribution, which may then be tax-deductible. You can also roll over money from a qualified employer-sponsored plan, such as a 401(k) or 403(b), after you change jobs or retire. It is important to note that these rollovers are not considered current-year contributions but are simply transfers from retirement accounts that came from prior-year contributions. Doing a tax-free rollover from one qualified plan to another will not affect your ability to make a current-year contribution to an IRA.

Not every person contributing to a traditional IRA is entitled to a tax deduction. If you *are an active participant in a qualified retirement plan through your employer* (such as a 401(k) plan), your IRA deduction may be reduced or eliminated, based on your modified adjusted gross income. If you are below the phase-out range, you will qualify for a full deduction. If you are within the range, you will qualify for a partial deduction. If you are at or above the top part of the range, you will receive no tax deduction. The following are the phase-out ranges based on your 2025 modified adjusted gross income:

- For single taxpayers covered by a workplace retirement plan, the phase-out range for income is $79,000 to $89,000.
- For married couples filing jointly, where the spouse making the IRA contribution is covered by a workplace retirement plan, the phase-out range is $126,000 to $146,000.
- For an IRA contributor who is not covered by a workplace retirement plan and is married to someone who is covered, the deduction is phased out if the couple's income is between $236,000 to $246,000.
- For a married individual filing a separate return who is covered by a workplace retirement plan, the phase-out range is not subject to an annual cost-of-living adjustment and remains at $0 to $10,000.

If you do not qualify for a tax-deductible contribution, you can always make a full *nondeductible* contribution, to the extent of earned income. This will require you to keep track of your basis in the IRA with the IRS by completing Form 8606, which must be included with your personal tax return. Once you start taking distributions, you will not be taxed on the portion of the distribution that is considered a return of your basis (nondeductible contribution). Nondeductible contributions are generally only recommended if you do not qualify for a direct Roth IRA contribution.

The money in a traditional IRA grows and compounds on a tax-deferred basis, which means you will not pay taxes until you start receiving distributions after you retire. Many retirees are in a lower tax bracket during this stage of their lives. Therefore, your tax rate and the overall amount of taxes you save when making these contributions may be much greater than the amount of taxes you will pay on the distributions in retirement. Although withdrawals are taxed as ordinary income, many states have special exclusions that may result in little or no tax paid at the state level on these distributions.

The IRS provides these significant tax advantages to encourage you to save for your retirement. However, the IRS will also penalize you if you take distributions from your retirement account before you reach age 59½ to discourage the depletion of retirement savings before retirement. In addition to paying income tax on these early withdrawals, you may also be subject to a 10% federal income tax penalty.

Exceptions to the 10% penalty in 2025 include the following withdrawals:

- Due to total and permanent disability
- For qualified higher-education expenses
- For unreimbursed medical expenses exceeding 7.5% of adjusted gross income
- For health insurance premiums while unemployed
- For a first-time home purchase (up to $10,000 lifetime limit)
- Due to certain distributions related to birth or adoption (up to $5,000)
- For qualified disaster recovery distributions (subject to special rules)

Once you reach the required beginning date, you must start taking annual required minimum distributions (RMDs) from a traditional IRA. As of 2025, the RMD age is 73 for individuals born between 1951 and 1959, and 75 for those born in 1960 or later. Those born before July 1, 1949, had an RMD age of 70½, and those born between July 1, 1949 and 1950, had an RMD age of 72. If you do not take your RMD, you may be subject to a 25% excise tax on the amount that you should have withdrawn, reduced to 10% if the missed RMD is corrected in a timely manner. RMDs are calculated based on your IRA balance as of December 31 of the prior year and the IRS Uniform Lifetime Table for your age.

Roth IRAs

Roth IRAs are another type of specially designated account that allows individuals to save money for retirement in a tax-efficient manner. You cannot deduct the contributions you make to a Roth IRA. However, qualified Roth IRA distributions are free of federal, state, and local income tax and are not included as part of your AGI once you retire. If you expect to be in a higher tax bracket in retirement, a Roth IRA could be a great choice.

An added benefit, even if you expect to be in a lower tax bracket, is that, unlike traditional IRA distributions, Roth IRA distributions are not added to your AGI. When your AGI reaches a certain level, up to 85% of your Social Security benefits can also become taxable. Many retirees who must take their RMD from their traditional IRAs are forced to pay taxes on their Social Security income; a Roth IRA could possibly avoid this additional tax.

Roth IRAs can be valuable in that you can contribute to a Roth at any age, provided you are still working and have earned income. There is no RMD requirement with Roth IRAs during the original owner's lifetime, so you will have no mandatory distributions regardless of your age. After you pass away and leave your Roth IRA to your beneficiaries, the RMD rules will apply to them under the current inherited IRA rules.

Also, you can withdraw contributions, but not the earnings on those contributions, from your Roth IRA, at any time and for any reason without paying tax, and those withdrawals are not subject to the 10% federal income tax penalty. However, the *earnings are* subject to income tax, and the IRS 10% penalty if you withdraw them before age 59 ½, unless one of the exceptions applies.

In order to make a qualified tax-free and penalty-free distribution of earnings, your account must meet the five-year holding requirement, and you must be age 59½ or older. The exceptions to this penalty are the same as under the traditional IRA.

The eligibility to contribute to a Roth IRA phases out for taxpayers with higher incomes. The rules regarding eligibility for traditional and Roth IRAs are confusing (to say the least). Therefore, we encourage you to visit the *Contributing to an IRA?* calculator, available at www.ventotaxandwealth.com under the Resources > Calculators & Tools section. This calculator will assist you in determining your eligibility to contribute to a Traditional or Roth IRA and at what maximum contribution amounts.

Every individual should take full advantage of the tax benefits available through employer-sponsored retirement plans and should fully fund their IRA accounts each year based on eligibility. There is no more efficient way to save for your retirement than to do it through a tax-advantaged account. These accounts provide an opportunity to accelerate savings over time by allowing earnings to grow without immediate taxation.

Because of the strict annual contribution limits, many higher-income individuals may not be able to save sufficient funds for retirement through conventional retirement accounts alone. Additionally, some individuals have delayed the process of saving for retirement and will not have sufficient funds set aside when the time comes.

Trump Accounts: A New Tool for Multigenerational Wealth

One of the most innovative features of the OBBBA, signed into law on July 4, 2025, is the creation of what are now known as Trump Accounts, inspired by an idea originally proposed by Michael Dell. These accounts represent a bold effort to encourage long-term investing and promote financial independence across generations. They are designed to help children begin building wealth from birth and to encourage families to think beyond their own retirement timeline.

Here is how it works. Any US citizen under the age of 18 is eligible to open a Trump Account. Children born between January 1, 2025, and December 31, 2028, are automatically eligible to receive a one-time $1,000 government-funded contribution into their account.

Parents, grandparents, other relatives, and even employers can then make additional contributions, up to a combined $5,000 per year per child. Employers may contribute up to $2,500 per child without the amount being counted as taxable income to the family, which would also be counted toward the $5,000 annual limit.

Funds inside the Trump Account must be invested in low-cost, diversified US equity index funds. These investments grow tax-deferred, and withdrawals are not permitted until the account holder reaches age 18. At that time, the account automatically converts to a traditional retirement account in the child's name, and the assets continue to grow tax-deferred under standard retirement account rules.

The long-term growth potential of these accounts is significant. With regular contributions and compounding investment returns, a child's Trump Account could grow into a six-figure or even seven-figure asset by early adulthood. According to projections by the US Treasury, a maximally funded account could reach more than $1.9 million by age 28. Even modest weekly contributions, combined with the original seed funding and long-term compounding, could result in meaningful financial security for your child.

To further highlight the power of utilizing a Trump Account with the power of compounding, refer to Chapter 12, "The Time Value of Money."

Trump Accounts could also be a useful tool for saving for college, which is discussed further in Chapter 7, "Saving for College." However, it is important to understand that these accounts are not intended to fund short-term needs. Withdrawals before age 18 are strictly prohibited, except in very limited cases involving disability. But for families committed to long-term financial planning, Trump Accounts offer a unique and tax-smart strategy to build wealth for the next generation.

This provision is still in its early stages, and regulations may evolve. But the strategy is already clear: starting early, investing consistently, and minimizing taxes can lead to extraordinary outcomes. For parents and grandparents who want to help their children or grandchildren reach financial independence, establishing and funding a Trump Account can be a powerful step. This new tool can help turn today's tax code into tomorrow's generational wealth code. Trump Accounts represent one of the most effective ways yet to build lasting, multigenerational wealth.

For official and up-to-date information on Trump Accounts visit TrumpAccounts.gov.

Fixed and Variable Annuities

By far annuities, particularly variable annuities, are some of the most controversial financial planning strategies in planning for retirement. Many financial advisors are dead set against annuities and do not believe they are appropriate for their clients. Others are strong advocates for annuities and believe they should be part of an individual's overall retirement strategy. Both sides of this argument have some merit, but the true answer lies with the needs of the individual. Annuities are not right for everyone, but depending on your specific circumstances, they may be exactly what you need. Before you consider whether annuities are appropriate for you or not, it is important to understand what they are and how they work.

An annuity is an investment product created by an insurance company that promises to provide a series of payments over time. An *annuity contract* is not a qualified retirement plan. However, it does provide tax-deferred growth similar to a qualified retirement plan. One of the biggest advantages to establishing an annuity is that there are no IRS-imposed contribution limits, which allow the opportunity to save substantially more for retirement. After fully funding your employer-provided retirement plans and IRA accounts, an annuity can be a potential option to complement your overall retirement savings strategy. This would also be a terrific way to play catch-up if you started saving money in qualified retirement accounts later in life.

One of the biggest arguments against annuities is that they have contract limitations, fees, and charges, which can include mortality expense charges, account fees, underlying investment management fees, administrative fees, and charges for various other optional benefits. The majority of annuities have backloads (surrender charges) that are assessed if the contract is surrendered before a certain period. All withdrawals of earnings are taxed as ordinary income, and the tax advantages of long-term capital gains and qualified dividends do not apply to annuity earnings. Withdrawals of the income portion of the annuity prior to age 59½ may also be subject to a 10% federal income tax penalty, unless one of the exceptions apply.

All guarantees are made by the insurance company which issues the contract and are based on its claims-paying ability. Annuities are not guaranteed by the FDIC or any other government agency.

Some annuity contracts allow you to purchase an insurance option that could pay an income for a specified period, such as your lifetime or the lifetimes of you and your spouse. The guaranteed retirement income or income-for-life option may help with your fears of outliving your money.

With both a fixed and variable annuity, you have the option of either an immediate or deferred annuity. Deciding on which is the most appropriate for you is a function of when you anticipate starting the distribution process:

- **Immediate annuity:** Typically funded with a lump-sum premium up front. Payments usually start immediately after the contract is funded and continue for the life of the contract. This type of annuity is often purchased at the beginning of retirement and is usually more suitable if you are nearing or already in retirement.
- **Deferred annuity:** Can be funded with either a lump sum or a series of contributions over time during the accumulation period. The accumulation period is the time during which premiums are paid for the purchase of an annuity. The payments

are typically deferred for a certain number of years and are based on the account value after the accumulation period. The income payment amount will depend on several factors, such as the initial investment amount, the contract's actual rate of return, the contract holder's age, and the number of years payments will be made.

Fixed Annuities

A *fixed annuity* is a contract with an insurance company that guarantees a fixed and guaranteed rate of interest on your money during the life of the contract. In essence, you give your money to an insurance company, and it promises to pay you back with a predetermined rate of interest. Fixed annuities are typically viewed as conservative investments; the biggest risk associated with them is the claims-paying ability of the insurance company making the guarantee.

In 2025, fixed annuity rates are at their highest levels in more than a decade, with multiyear guaranteed annuities (MYGAs) offering between 4% and 5%, depending on the term and the insurer. These rates are currently competitive with or higher than many certificates of deposit and other fixed-income products. However, as the Federal Reserve lowers interest rates in the future, newly issued fixed annuities will likely offer lower yields. For those seeking long-term guaranteed income, locking in a competitive rate while rates remain elevated may be worth considering.

Variable Annuities

A *variable annuity* is a long-term investment vehicle designed specifically for retirement. It is a contract, under which you, as the contract holder, agree to make a single payment or a series of payments to an insurance company in exchange for a future income. The insurer usually makes these income payments to you in retirement, and they may be structured to last for your lifetime or the lifetimes of you and your spouse (individual or joint).

During the accumulation period, you invest in a selection of investment subaccounts based on your risk tolerance, time horizons, and long-term goals. If you have purchased an annuity with income-for-life guarantees or with a guaranteed death benefit, you may be willing to take on some additional risk because of the downside protection. This allows you to participate in the growth potential of the stock market or other investment choices. The future value of the annuity and the amount of income available in retirement depend on the performance of these investments. This can provide you the opportunity for greater growth and increase your chances of outpacing inflation.

The actual account value of a variable annuity (which includes the investment principal and income) is not guaranteed. Instead, the value of your account will depend on the performance of your investment choices within the subaccounts of the variable annuity. As a result, the account value may be worth more or less than your original purchase if you ultimately choose to surrender it. The additional guarantees you may be able to purchase typically do not guarantee the actual account value, but they may guarantee an income stream for life or a death benefit.

A variable annuity may also provide the option to purchase guarantees for an additional cost. These guarantees can help protect against the downside risks of investing in the stock market through guaranteed lifetime payout options. Some contracts provide guaranteed death benefits, regardless of the actual account value. These guarantees are often what make variable annuities valuable to many individuals.

Some financial analysts believe that retirees may gain greater financial security by combining insurance products and mutual funds. Most would agree that protecting ourselves against the risk of the unknown is the prudent thing to do. Risk management is an everyday part of our lives. We have health insurance, life insurance, long-term disability insurance, long-term care insurance, auto insurance, homeowner's insurance, and other coverages to protect various aspects of life and secure our families. It is only natural to take steps to guarantee the long-term security of our retirement. With the proper riders, a variable annuity contract with an insurance company can help provide this added peace of mind. While this form of insurance may not be necessary or appropriate for everyone, in many cases, it can be an important tool used as part of your overall retirement planning strategy.

Retirement Funding: "Needs Analysis"

The starting point for planning for retirement is performing a "needs analysis." In other words, you must first estimate how much money you will need after you retire, for *the rest of your life*. You will also need to estimate the benefits you will receive from your defined-benefit retirement plan and Social Security. Then, you need to determine what investment assets you currently have that you can use during your retirement. Finally, you must identify the amount of retirement investment assets you will need to generate sufficient income to support your anticipated cost of living in retirement.

To do this, let us revisit Chapter 3, "Determining Your Financial Position," and analyze Glenn and Holly Mitchell's retirement planning needs, as an example. We have already worked through the most difficult part of this retirement planning needs analysis because we already have the Mitchell's statement of financial position (Exhibit 3.1) and their statement of cash flow after implementing tax and financial planning strategies (Exhibit 3.3).

We start by analyzing their statement of financial position and specifically focusing on their investment assets, because these are the assets that will help generate the necessary income when they retire. The total value of their investment assets as of December 31, 2024, was $1,024,000.

Then we will look at their projected 2025 statement of cash flow (after tax and financial planning strategy implementations) to determine their total cash outflow to sustain their current standard of living. The Mitchell's total cash projected cash outflow was $225,355.

To complete this analysis, we have included the Mitchell's answers to the 12 key questions and assumptions from Exhibit 8.1, shown here in Exhibit 8.5.

Exhibit 8.5 Example Answers to Analyze Your Retirement Needs

1. What is your current age? **41**
2. What is your current annual income? **$205,566**
3. What is your spouse's annual income (if applicable)? **$30,000**
4. What is your current total retirement savings? **$578,000**
5. What is your desired retirement age? **67**
6. What is the expected number of years of retirement income needed? **35**
7. What is the expected inflation rate? **3%**
8. What percentage of your current combined income will you need at retirement? **75%**
9. What do you expect your preretirement return on investments to be? **8%**
10. What do you expect your post-retirement return on investments to be? **6%**
11. Would you like to assume that you will be receiving Social Security benefits in retirement? **No**
12. If you do expect to receive Social Security, what is the monthly dollar amount in today's dollars? **N/A**

The Mitchells wanted to take the most conservative approach when completing their retirement funding needs analysis so that they can be 100% confident in their ability to retire at the desired age and to live their desired lifestyle. This will be pretty evident in the answers they gave us and that we used for this analysis.

- Glenn and Holly's current age is **41**.
- Their combined family income is $235,566 (**$205,566** from Glenn and **$30,000** from Holly), as outlined on their statement of cash flow as of December 31, 2025 (see Exhibit 3.3).
- Based on their statement of financial position (Exhibit 3.1), their total investment assets are $1,024,000. However, from this amount, we will exclude the $11,000 currently in the educational savings plan, since this will not be available during their retirement. Their total investment assets currently include a building valued at $770,000, which has a mortgage of $435,000. Therefore, this mortgage would be a reduction in their current net investment assets available to fund their retirement. That leaves them with a current net of **$578,000** in investable retirement savings assets ($1,024,000 less $11,000, less $435,000).
- Glenn and Holly's full Social Security retirement age is 67 and they will be entitled to Medicare at the age of 65. Therefore, the Mitchell's are using **67** as their expected retirement age.
- Based on Glenn's family history, he should live to age 90, giving him 23 years in retirement. Based on Holly's family history, she should live to age 95, giving her 28 years in retirement. Given that they're both in excellent health and to be confident that they won't outlive their money, we're going to assume they will live to 102. We'll therefore use **35 years** as the number of years needed for retirement income.
- Although it is impossible to accurately predict the actual rate of inflation before and during their retirement, the Mitchell's have decided to estimate a **3%** inflation rate, which is above the historical average.
- Based on the detailed needs analysis from their projected 2025 statement of cash flow, they believe they will need **75%** of that year's income in today's dollars to maintain their standard of living in retirement. They went through all their current cash outflows and adjusted them to what they can reasonably expect these numbers to be during their retirement years in today's dollars.

They also factored in additional health care costs that can be expected in their seventies, eighties, and beyond, including their portion of Medicare premiums, out-of-pocket medical and dental expenses, etc. They also factored in at least three vacations a year, since they want to enjoy their golden years traveling the world for as long as they physically can.

They reduced or eliminated certain expenses that were work related. They eliminated their mortgage payments since they will be paid in full before retirement with extra payments they plan on making within the 30-year period. They also eliminated the costs associated with their children since they expect them to be independent at that time.

- The Mitchells have also estimated that they will be earning on average **8%** per year on their investment retirement assets based on their financial ability and willingness to take risk during their preretirement years.
- The Mitchells have also estimated that they will be earning on average **6%** per year on their retirement investment based on their financial ability and willingness to take risk during their post-retirement years. In retirement, they realize they will need to be even more conservative, and they plan on increasing their allocation to bonds and dividend paying stocks.
- The Mitchells are very concerned about the financial stability of the Social Security program and are concerned that between the aging population and many Social Security experts' predictions, that the program may not be available by the time they're ready to retire. With that said, they wanted to take the most conservative approach here and did not want to include Social Security benefits in their projected needs analysis.

Clearly, they answered these questions very conservatively to be confident that they can be worry-free throughout their retirement years, even if either of them lives to 102. Ultimately, it is a personal choice on how conservative or aggressive you want to be when answering these questions for your own needs analysis.

Based on the answers to the above questions, along with the assumptions made, we are ready to determine Glenn and Holly Mitchell's *point X*, the amount of investable assets they will need to secure a comfortable retirement and maintain their current standard of living.

We utilized a retirement calculator and input all the above facts and assumptions, and we determined that, in order to achieve their inflation-adjusted income in retirement:

- The total amount needed for retirement, including amounts already saved, is **$8,050,863**, based on the current assumptions provided.
- They should save **15.3%** of their yearly income, less any employer match.

A big assumption we made in this "Retirement Needs Analysis" is that Social Security will not be around to make good on its promised benefit to the Mitchell's. If we changed that one variable and indicated to include Social Security benefits, this would significantly reduce the amount they need to save each year through their retirement age.

You can conduct a similar analysis of your own financial situation by using the *Saving for Retirement* calculator, available at www.ventotaxandwealth.com under the Resources > Calculators & Tools section. This will give you an opportunity to do numerous what-if scenarios utilizing your particular facts and circumstances.

Based on the analysis we conducted for the Mitchell's in Chapter 3, they are on a clear path to achieving financial independence.

They were saving $7,723 per year before implementing the cash flow recommendations we made. They were also able to free up an additional $42,021 after implementing the cash flow savings strategies outlined in Chapter 3 (see Exhibit 3.2).

After all our recommendations, they were in a position to, and agreed to use, their new-found excess cash flow to fund their long-term goals (see Exhibit 3.3).

- They funded Glenn's SIMPLE (Savings Incentive Match Plans for Employees) plan with an additional $11,500 (bringing him up to the maximum $16,500 for 2025) and Holly's Solo 401(k) instead of a traditional IRA with an additional $22,000 in contributions (bringing her up to the maximum $23,500 for 2025 without profit sharing).
- This will bring their total retirement savings to $40,000 ($16,500 to the SIMPLE plan, $23,500 to the Solo 401k) in combined retirement plan contributions for 2025.

- This represents 16.98% of their total cash inflows ($40,000/ $235,566) which is more than the 15.3% they need to achieve financial independence in retirement.

The Mitchells have a very clear plan to achieve financial independence, and they did this with very conservative assumptions, so if things do not go as planned, they'll have more than enough wiggle room to still accomplish their goal of reaching *point X*, financial independence. If this goes as planned, or better, they may also be able to create and maintain generational wealth for their two children and future grandchildren.

If you do not pay attention to the tax consequences when planning for retirement, you may be paying significantly more in taxes than the law requires. Therefore, you must include tax planning as part of your overall retirement planning and generational wealth strategy. Using a financial planning approach that takes advantage of tax-smart strategies will help maximize your retirement planning goals.

Tax-smart Strategies for Planning for Retirement

Here are several tax facts and strategies that will address your wealth accumulation goals in a powerful and sustainable way. This will be part of your tax-smart roadmap to financial independence. This is how you can transform the tax code into part of your generational wealth code.

- Compare the benefits of a traditional IRA to a Roth IRA and choose the one that is best for your particular situation. With a traditional IRA, you may get a current year tax deduction for your contribution and tax-deferred growth. With the Roth IRA contribution, you do not receive an upfront tax deduction, but your qualified withdrawals are completely tax-free.
- With a Roth IRA, you do not have to take the RMD during your lifetime. This may have the added benefit of keeping your AGI low enough to also avoid paying taxes on your Social Security benefits during your retirement years.
- The deadline for making a traditional or Roth IRA contribution is April 15, the due date for filing your income tax return for the prior year, even if you are filing an extension.
- Fully fund your employer-provided retirement plan before the end of the year. The deferral limit for a 401(k) is $23,500 for 2025; the deferral limit for a SIMPLE plan is $16,500 for 2025.

(*continued*)

(*continued*)

- Take advantage of the additional deferral limit "catch-up" contribution to a 401(k) of $7,500 and to a SIMPLE plan of $3,500 for each participant age 50 or older. Plus, a "super catch-up" of $11,250 for 401(k) participants aged 60 to 63, and $5,250 for SIMPLE plan participants aged 60 to 63, if your plan allows.
- Make a Roth contribution of $7,000 for 2025 per spouse ($8,000 if age 50 or older), if you qualify. In order to qualify as a married couple your AGI must be under $236,000 or you can make a partial contribution up to $246,000. In order to make a Roth contribution as a single taxpayer, your AGI must be under $150,000 or partial contribution up to $165,000. If your income exceeds these levels, establish these as traditional nondeductible IRA contributions. You can then convert these to a Roth IRA, regardless of your income level, but special rules apply.
- There is no income limitation for converting a traditional IRA to a Roth IRA. Consider converting part or all of your traditional IRAs into a Roth IRA so that all your future earnings can grow tax-free. This can be very beneficial, especially in years when you are in very low tax brackets and in years when your IRA accounts have decreased in value. Keep in mind, however, that a conversion is a taxable transfer, and you must report the conversion amount as income on your tax return in the same year.
- If you made a contribution to a retirement plan (including an IRA or Roth IRA), you may be eligible for a nonrefundable saver's credit. The income limit of the saver's credit for low- and moderate-income workers in 2025 is $79,000 for married couples filing jointly, $59,250 for head of household, and $39,500 for single. This credit can be as much as 50% of the first $2,000 of eligible retirement contributions ($4,000 if married filing jointly). This means a single filer could receive a saver's credit of $1,000 by simply making a $2,000 retirement plan contribution. Talk about great incentives to save for your retirement!
- If you are separated from your employment for any reason, such as getting laid off, quitting, or retiring, you may be entitled to a distribution from a qualified employer retirement plan, which would be fully taxable if not properly handled. You must set this up as a tax-free rollover, which allows you to make a tax-free transfer of a distribution from one qualified employer retirement plan to another qualified plan or to a traditional IRA. You should instruct your employer to directly roll over the funds either to a traditional IRA you designate or to the plan of your new employer. If you elect the distribution to be paid directly to you, you still have 60 days to complete the rollover yourself. If you do not meet these requirements, the full amount may be subject to tax and an additional 10% penalty.
- Generally, there is a 10% penalty that applies to taxable distributions made to you before age 59½ from qualified plans. You may avoid the 10% penalty if you meet one of the following exceptions: rollover, disability, separation from service if age 55 or older, medical costs, substantially equal periodic payments for at least five years, beneficiary of a deceased plan participant, IRS levy, or part of

a qualified domestic relations court order. For more details on the exceptions to the early withdrawal penalty, see IRS Form 5329 and instructions.

- In addition to the above penalty exceptions, with a traditional IRA you may avoid the 10% penalty if you use the distribution to pay for qualified higher education expenses or for qualified first-time homebuyer expenses of up to $10,000. Other exceptions now available include certain distributions for birth or adoption expenses (up to $5,000 per child), qualified disaster recovery distributions, emergency personal expense distributions (up to $1,000 per year), and distributions to domestic abuse victims (up to the lesser of $10,000 or 50% of the account balance).
- You should avoid borrowing money against your retirement plan because that can have dire consequences. For example, if you leave your employer before you pay off the loan, your employer will reduce your vested account balance by the amount of the outstanding loan and will report this loan amount as a taxable distribution in the year you separated from service. This amount may be subject to tax and the 10% penalty.
- If you have a qualified retirement plan loan that becomes taxable because you left your job or defaulted on the loan, current law gives you more time to roll it over tax-free into another qualified plan. Instead of the old 60-day deadline, you now have until the due date of your federal income tax return, including extensions, for the year the loan offset is treated as a distribution. If you discover before your filing deadline that you would owe taxes and a penalty, you can still complete the rollover in time to avoid both.
- Making elective salary deferrals to your company's retirement plan allows you to defer tax on your salary and get a tax-deferred buildup of earnings within your plan until you start making withdrawals when you retire. You should take full advantage of these plans by taking the maximum deferral allowed by your employer's plan. If you cannot manage to do the maximum, at a minimum contribute enough to receive the full employer match.
- Many employer-sponsored 401(k) plans allow employees to contribute after-tax Roth contributions. If you take advantage of a Roth 401(k), you can make significantly higher contributions than what would be available in a Roth IRA. Starting in 2023, some plans also allow employer matching contributions to be designated as Roth. Keep in mind, Roth contributions are made in after-tax dollars, so you will not receive any upfront tax savings.
- Where employer plans include a qualified Roth contribution program, conversions can be made from a pre-tax contribution 401(k) account to the Roth 401(k) account. However, you must remember that a conversion is a taxable transfer, and you must report it on your tax return for the year of the conversion.
- When rolling over retirement plan distributions, your employer must withhold 20% if the check is paid directly to you. To avoid the 20% withholding, you

(*continued*)

(*continued*)

should have your employer make a direct rollover to your new employer's qualified plan or an individual IRA.

- If you are collecting Social Security benefits, up to 85% of these benefits could be subject to federal income tax. You can avoid paying income tax on your Social Security benefits if your provisional income is $25,000 or less if you are single, or $32,000 or less if you are married and filing jointly. Planning your retirement income to include tax-free withdrawals, such as from a Roth IRA account, may allow you to keep your income under these thresholds and ultimately avoid paying tax on your Social Security benefits.
- If you are 70½ or older, you can take up to a $108,000 tax-free qualified charitable distribution to the charity or charities of your choice from an IRA. This will allow you to meet your RMD for the year without increasing your adjusted gross income. This can be used as a strategy to avoid paying taxes on Social Security benefits for lower-income taxpayers, and it can avoid the 3.8% Medicare tax on net investment income for higher-income taxpayers.
- For 2025, the maximum annual retirement distribution (benefit to be paid out in retirement years) that can be paid to a retired employee by a defined-benefit plan is $280,000 (indexed for inflation annually) with an equivalent annual contribution limit (amount to be funded by your employer into the plan in the current year) of up to $350,000 or more. The retirement plan actuary makes these calculations as the contribution amounts vary depending on the age of the plan participant.
- For 2025, an employee may make up to a $23,500 salary deferral (withholding) contribution from pre-tax dollars to a defined contribution plan such as a 401(k) or 403(b). An additional $7,500 contribution can be made if the taxpayer is 50 years old or older. The maximum combined employer and employee contribution for 2025 is $70,000 ($77,500 if age 50 or older). It should be noted that the employer's portion of contributions is not subject to Social Security or Medicare taxes.
- For 2025, an employee may make a pre-tax salary deferral up to $16,500 to their SIMPLE retirement plan. If 50 or older, the employee can make an additional $3,500 catch-up salary deferral. In a matching SIMPLE plan, the employer's contribution is the lesser of 3% of the employee's taxable compensation or actual salary deferral (there are some exceptions to this rule).
- Consider establishing Trump Account for minor child born 2025–2028 to take advantage of $1,000 government seed.
- If your child qualifies, fund Trump Accounts for $5,000 (indexed after 2027) maximum from birth through December 31 of the year your child turns 17. This would be $5,000 per year for 18 years for a maximum contribution of $90,000.
- Encourage grandparents and other family members to contribute to a child's Trump Account as part of their annual gifting strategy.
- Take advantage of employer contributions to a child's Trump Account, if in fact your employer provides this as a benefit.

An Action Plan for Planning for Retirement

1. **Conduct a retirement funding needs analysis** and **calculate your personal *point* X, financial independence.** Use the *Saving for Retirement* calculator, available at www.ventotaxandwealth.com under the Resources > Calculators & Tools section. You will be able to run through an unlimited number of "what if?" scenarios.
2. **Start saving and investing for your retirement as soon as you start working.** You may not believe it, but you *can* live on 90% of what you earn, no matter how little you think that is. So set aside at least 10% of your earnings because the earlier you start, the better off you will be. You'll have the benefit of time on your side to help that money grow. Do not continue to put off saving for your retirement until "later." Start saving *now.*
3. **Determine what you can expect to receive from Social Security in retirement.** For a general, nonpersonalized estimate, you can access the SSA's Quick Calculator at www.ssa.gov, search for "Benefit Calculator" and select "Quick Calculator."
4. **Learn the difference between various types of retirement plans.** Then find out what the maximum is that you can contribute to the plans that apply to you. If you are not sure about this, meet with a financial advisor who can review your specific financial situation and help you plan better for your future.
5. **Contribute as much as you can into your employer's 401(k) plan.** You do not have to pay income taxes on that money now because you are not receiving it currently as income. Plus, most employers still match at least some percentage of what you contribute. Getting a 3% employer match is like getting a 3% raise. If not contributing makes you ineligible for the match, that would be like turning down a raise your employer is willing to give you.
6. **Understand the difference between Traditional IRAs and Roth IRAs** and determine which would be the best choice for you. With a traditional IRA, you get an upfront tax deduction and taxable income in retirement. With a Roth IRA, you forego the upfront tax deduction but will receive tax-free income in retirement.
7. **Establish and fully fund a Trump Account each year for a child,** from birth through December 31 of the year the child turns 17. Trump Accounts are a new retirement tax-deferred savings vehicle created under the OBBBA. Not only will you be helping your child achieve financial independence, but you will also get a big head start on creating generational wealth for your family.
8. **Consider utilizing fixed or variable annuities to supplement your retirement savings.** These could be very effective tools in improving your retirement savings and income with the advantage of tax deferral and with unique guarantees you may not be able to get elsewhere.

(continued)

(continued)

9. **Do not worry about the day-to-day ups and downs of the stock market; keep in mind that you are saving for *the long haul*** for your retirement. So, if you are in your twenties, that is at least 40 years away. Even if you are in your sixties, you should realize you are investing not just until your retirement, but throughout your retirement years. So, what happened to the stock market today is not important to the money you will need and hopefully have throughout your retirement years. Just keep saving, and investing, with your long-term goals in mind.
10. **Work with a tax-advisor and CERTIFIED FINANCIAL PLANNER®** that can provide you with the tax-smart advice covered in this chapter. Please refer to Appendix A, "Selecting a Trusted Advisor."
11. **Work with a financial planner** that will provide you with the necessary advice and guidance that includes the 12 critical areas of comprehensive wealth management covered throughout this book.
12. **Use the tax-smart roadmap to financial independence at the end of this chapter to transform the tax code into part of your generational wealth code.**

CHAPTER 9

Managing Your Investments

In the 20th century, the United States endured two world wars and other traumatic and expensive military conflicts; the Depression; a dozen or so recessions and financial panics; oil shocks; a flu epidemic; and the resignation of a disgraced president. Yet the Dow rose from 66 to 11,497.

—Warren Buffett, Most Successful Investor of the Twentieth Century

This chapter provides information and guidance for dealing with investments, beginning with basic definitions of various investment vehicles: stocks, bonds, hybrid securities, mutual funds, exchange-traded funds (ETFs), and private investments. It then offers general information on the process of creating an investment portfolio that considers your financial goals, comfort levels, expectations, and the effects of inflation and taxes on these investments. It also addresses how to adjust a portfolio as your financial goals change.

The purpose of this chapter is to provide you with an understanding of investing, which normally takes people many years to learn on their own. Unfortunately, many investors learn this lesson the hard way and never recover from their financial losses. It is important that we learn from our past and do our best not to repeat the mistakes history has taught us. The rewards of proper investing have been very generous when investors have adopted an investment discipline that allows them to purchase quality investments and then allow those investments to take their course.

This may have been best said by Warren Buffett, the primary shareholder, chairman, and former CEO of Berkshire Hathaway, who is also considered by many to be the most successful investor of the twentieth century, "Put together a portfolio of companies whose aggregate earnings march upward over the years, and so also will the portfolio's market value."

The information and guidance on investments provided in this chapter are designed to help you stay the course toward financial independence and creating and maintaining generational wealth.

Analyzing Your Ability and Willingness to Take Risk

Understanding your ability to take risk is one of the most fundamental first steps you must take before implementing any investment strategy. Keep in mind that your *ability* to take risk could be different from your *willingness* to take risk, and that is why both must be analyzed.

In a practical sense, your biggest risk as an investor is the failure to achieve your goal. For example, if you know you need to achieve an 8% annual return on average over the next 10 years to retire, but you invest in fixed income paying 4% because you are afraid of market risk, you have set yourself up for failure.

That being said, you should take no more risk than is necessary to achieve your investment goal. For example, if you are closing on a house next month, the best course of action is just keeping the down payment in a high-yield savings account or, even better, a money-market fund. The downside risk of failing to close on the house far outweighs making a few extra bucks with a more aggressive investment strategy.

Besides investment goals, from an investment standpoint, when we talk about risk, we are thinking about probability and magnitude of loss, particularly in the short term.

Your *ability* to take on risk can be quantified primarily through your net worth (see Exhibit 3.1 to calculate this) and the composition of your assets and liabilities reflected on your statement of financial position. In addition to this, you must consider other factors such as your time horizon (number of years you will be invested), human capital (income from employment), and expected income from investing.

When evaluating your *ability* to take risk, you must also take into consideration what your ultimate financial goals will be and the downside risk of failure to achieve the goal. This will help you frame the minimum market risk you need to take to achieve your goal. The shorter your time horizon, the less risk you should be able to take. For example, an 18-year-old investor who has 49 years before retirement can tolerate a much greater level of risk than a 60-year-old who is only 7 years away from retirement.

With regard to *willingness* to take risk, every investor has a unique view and can only tolerate a certain amount of losses before becoming emotional, which may lead to bad investment decisions. Of course, a higher level of risk corresponds to the potential for a higher rate of return on your investments. If your investing risk tolerance was as simple as stating you want the highest rate of return in the long run, then you would simply invest in the most speculative types of investments. But it is not that simple; instead, you need to examine your own personal tolerance to risk so that the ultimate investment portfolio you choose will have staying power in both good and bad times. Staying power means that no matter how bad things appear, emotionally you will not make the bad decision to sell at market lows, sell too early, or chase investment returns. It is important to remember that it is you, the individual investor, who must have the staying power.

In a perfect world, willingness to take risk would be framed by the targeted return to achieve the desired investment goal. Unfortunately, people's willingness to take on risk at an emotional level sometimes undermines their investment discipline, as shown in the following examples of common emotional mistakes.

- **Selling at the bottom:** The best time to be in the market is at the bottom because stocks and bonds are poised to rise. This obviously results in gains as long as you, the investor, have staying power. Unfortunately, many investors bring emotions into the investment decision-making process, and emotions cost money. When the economy is booming and the stock market reaches new highs, people are more likely to invest their money because of all the positive news and emotions surrounding the market. Naturally, the opposite is true when the economy is doing poorly and the world is filled with negative news. Most investors are not willing to invest then; in fact, many sell their investments at lower prices at this time.

  If Macy's department store ran a 50% off sale on every item in the store, most people would rush to Macy's and buy everything they could. On the other hand, if Macy's increased its prices by 50% from the original price, very few people would shop in their store. However, when it comes to investing, human nature causes us to react very differently than this, and many people tend to buy high and sell low. It is a very expensive portfolio decision to miss the rebound.

- **Selling early:** When the investment has gone up, undisciplined investors sell too early to "capture most of the gain." This means they miss any additional growth, incur trading costs, and potentially have tax consequences.
- **Buying late to chase returns:** Too often, investors pile into last year's best investment strategies to chase returns. Unfortunately, this is sometimes the worst time to invest. An asset class that has had a significant run-up may be fully valued and may underperform next year. Worst case, the run-up has created a bubble, and there will be severe losses. Reference Exhibit 9.3 to see why chasing returns typically does not pay off.

Therefore, it is critically important that you select an investment model that you are willing to stay with, even in the worst of markets. The appropriate investment plan for you should be the one that provides you with the highest potential rate of return in the long run that is within your risk tolerance.

Part of determining your risk tolerance goes back to analyzing your personal behavior and how you deal with your other life issues. For example, if you typically are a nervous individual and tend to go down the straight-and-narrow path in life, then you most likely will choose a more conservative investment risk model. On the other hand, if you are fearless and like to live life in the fast lane, then you would most likely choose a more aggressive investment risk model.

Because the question of your personal risk tolerance revolves around human behavior and emotions, it is important to understand your own investment psychology. This can be thought of as the investor's psychological evaluation of his or her risk tolerance. There are many ways to measure your risk tolerance and numerous questionnaires are provided on many investment websites. Exhibit 9.1 provides a simplified questionnaire. Please take a few moments to answer these questions to determine your own investor risk tolerance profile and score.

Exhibit 9.1 Eight Questions to Assess Your Investor Risk Tolerance Profile and Score

I. How long do you plan to keep your money invested?

1. ___ Less than 2 years
2. ___ 2–4 years
3. ___ 5–7 years
4. ___ 8–10 years
5. ___ More than 10 years

II. When you begin withdrawing money from your investment account, how do you expect to take those withdrawals?

1. ___ I plan to withdraw the full amount in a lump sum.
2. ___ I'll take occasional withdrawals over a short period (up to 3 years).
3. ___ I'll make regular withdrawals for several years (up to 6 years).
4. ___ I expect to take consistent withdrawals (up to 10 years).
5. ___ I'll rely on withdrawals as a long-term or indefinite source of income (10 or more years).

III. Which statement best reflects your general attitude toward life and investing?

1. ___ "Slow and steady wins the race."
2. ___ "I prefer a cautious and consistent approach."
3. ___ "A balanced approach works best."
4. ___ "I'm willing to take calculated risks for greater reward."
5. ___ "The greater the risk, the greater the potential return."

IV. If you invested $100,000, which range of possible annual outcomes would you be most comfortable with?

1. ___ Between $98,000 and $102,000 (±2%)
2. ___ Between $95,000 and $105,000 (±5%)
3. ___ Between $90,000 and $110,000 (±10%)
4. ___ Between $85,000 and $115,000 (±15%)
5. ___ Between $80,000 and $120,000 (±20%)

V. When investing, what do you consider most important?

1. ___ Preserving my capital, even if returns are very low
2. ___ Earning steady income with minimal risk
3. ___ Achieving a balance of income and growth
4. ___ Growing my portfolio substantially over time with moderate volatility
5. ___ Maximizing long-term growth, even if it means short-term losses

VI. A year after making a $100,000 investment, the investment account value drops to $80,000 while the S&P 500 is down 20%. How would you react?

1. ___ I would sell immediately to avoid further losses.
2. ___ I would be very uncomfortable and consider reducing my investment risk.
3. ___ I would be concerned, but willing to listen to my financial advisor's recommendation.
4. ___ I would see this as a normal fluctuation and hold steady.
5. ___ I would view it as a buying opportunity and invest additional funds.

VII. Which of the following hypothetical portfolios would you feel most comfortable owning for the next year?

1. ___ Portfolio 1: Could gain up to **5%** or lose up to **2.5%**
2. ___ Portfolio 2: Could gain up to **10%** or lose up to **5%**

(Continued)

Exhibit 9.1 (*Continued*)

3. ___ Portfolio 3: Could gain up to **15%** or lose up to **10%**
4. ___ Portfolio 4: Could gain up to **20%** or lose up to **15%**
5. ___ Portfolio 5: Could gain up to **25%** or lose up to **20%**

VIII. Which statement best describes your comfort level with investment risk?

1. ___ I prefer no risk and stable returns.
2. ___ I am willing to take minimal risk for modest returns.
3. ___ I am comfortable with some fluctuations for balanced growth.
4. ___ I am willing to accept higher risk for higher potential gains.
5. ___ I seek maximum growth and can tolerate significant market swings.

Now that you have answered these eight questions, you are ready to determine your risk profile score. Simply add up the numbers next to each answer you checked off in the questionnaire. For example, if you checked off item number 3 for each question, your risk profile score would be 24. This would place you in the upper end of the Moderate (Balanced) portfolio with the objective of balanced growth and income as outlined below.

TOTAL SCORE	INVESTOR RISK TOLERANCE	OBJECTIVE
8–13	Conservative	Preservation of capital
14–19	Moderately Conservative (Income-oriented)	Income with limited growth
20–25	Moderate (Balanced)	Balanced growth and income
26–31	Moderately Aggressive (Growth-oriented)	Long-term growth with some income
32–40	Aggressive (Growth/equity)	Maximum capital appreciation

The answers to the questions in Exhibit 9.1 provide you with a numerical score that measures your tolerance to investment risk. This risk tolerance measurement is the gauge by which we determine your *willingness* (psychological) to take risk. The higher your score, the more risk you would be willing to tolerate. Understanding your risk tolerance is the second step you must take before implementing any investment strategy.

If your *ability* and *willingness* to take risk bring you to the same result, then you have accurately determined the proper investment strategy for you. Very often, the results from this analysis could vary significantly. Consequently, investors who have high *ability* to take risk may not be *willing* to take on that level of risk; conversely, the opposite is true as well. You may need to make a compromise between both results, but ultimately you must decide for yourself what level of risk makes you comfortable.

Understanding Investment Risk

Now that you have evaluated your own risk tolerance, it is important to understand exactly what the investment risks are. This will help you to be better prepared to make more informed investing decisions, put together an investment portfolio that includes various asset classes, and manage your investments. The most common risks include inflation risk, interest rate risk, default risk, market risk, economic risk, company- or industry-specific risk, political risk, and liquidity risk.

- **Inflation risk:** The threat that your investment returns will not keep pace with the rate of inflation. For example, if inflation increases each year by 3%, but your investments are only growing by 1%, you are effectively losing money. This is because the general price of goods and services is rising faster than your investment, so each year you can effectively buy less.

  In order for your portfolio to have a reasonable chance of beating inflation, it should include growth-oriented stocks, growth and income stock mutual funds, and other growth-related investment vehicles. These types of investments have historically outpaced the rate of inflation over the long term, although there is no guarantee that they will do so in the future.
- **Interest rate risk:** Typically associated with bonds and other fixed-income investment vehicles, which tend to be sensitive to changes in interest rates. When interest rates rise, the value of these investments falls. Of course, the opposite is true as well: as interest rates drop in our economy, the value of these investments increases. One way to protect against interest rate risk when you believe interest rates will be rising is to shorten the duration of your bond holdings (closer maturity dates).
- **Default risk:** Typically associated with bonds and other fixed-income investment vehicles, where credit is extended. This is the risk that a company or other issuers of debt will be unable to make the required payments on their obligations.
- **Market rate risk:** The risk of the overall market experiencing a decline. It typically drags down the value of all securities at the same time. Market rate risk is a result of the aggregate movement

in the market and may not relate specifically to your investments. Market risk can affect almost any type of investments, including stocks, bonds, commodities, real estate, and many others.

- **Economic risk:** Occurs when the overall economy experiences a downturn, such as during a recession. These economic downturns can result in a decrease in earnings and profits from the underlying companies you may be invested in. This can diminish a company's ability to pay a dividend or even the interest on its bonds. It is important to note that certain companies and industries may be more sensitive to economic changes than others. For example, companies that produce luxury items will be much more sensitive to economic downturns than companies that produce necessities.
- **Company- or industry-specific risk:** Occurs when an event affects only a specific company or industry. For example, if a company is fined by regulators for breaking the law, the financial and reputational costs could weigh down its performance, regardless of the broader market and industry trends. These types of events can have a significant effect on a company's value, as well as the confidence investors can place in its management. By far, this is the strongest argument for a well-diversified portfolio and why you should never keep all your eggs in one basket.
- **Political risk:** The chance that changes in a country's government, or its decisions, could hurt the value of an investment. This can happen when new laws are passed or political tensions cause problems for businesses. For example, when some countries raised tariffs during the recent trade disputes, it made certain products more expensive to buy and sell. This can reduce the profits of certain companies, especially those with operations abroad, which in turn can lower returns for the investors who own their shares. This fear is what caused markets to largely selloff in the early stages of the global trade dispute in the first quarter of 2025.
- **Liquidity risk:** The risk that an investment can't be quickly sold or converted into cash without significantly lowering its price. This often happens when there aren't enough buyers in the market or when market conditions are stressed, making it harder to find someone willing to pay a fair price. For example, selling shares of a large, well-known company is usually easy because there's always demand, but trying to sell a rare collectible or shares in a small private business could take much longer and may require accepting a lower price than expected.

Stocks, Bonds, Hybrid Securities, Mutual Funds, ETFs, and Private Investments

The most efficient and popular way to invest is by purchasing individual stocks, bonds, hybrid securities, mutual funds, ETFs, and private investments. Therefore, it is essential to provide you with a description of each of these investment vehicles.

Stocks

A stock represents a fractional ownership interest in a corporation. When you invest in a corporation, you become a partial owner in the company's business and can participate in the company's profits or losses. As a shareholder in a corporation, you have the benefit of limited liability protection, which minimizes your downside to no more than your investment in the company.

When the corporation makes a profit, you may be rewarded with a dividend. Furthermore, if the corporation continues to grow its revenues and profits, the value of the stock you own will likely grow as well. You can also realize these gains in the stock's value by selling your shares on the open market.

If the company does not do well, you may never see the payment of a dividend, and in fact, the value of your stock could decline. The risk and potential reward associated with investing in stocks are generally much higher than with many other investment vehicles. Therefore, you should be prepared to experience high volatility when investing in stocks.

Bonds

A bond represents a loan that you make to a corporation or government entity, which then promises to pay you back with interest over time. In essence, you act as the banker (lender), and the bond issuer is the borrower.

The bond issuer typically needs to raise money to meet other obligations or to finance certain projects. If you decide to invest in that issuer's bond, you are willing to lend your money in exchange for the promise to be paid back with a specific rate of interest. The bond investor usually will receive regular interest payments every six months. The interest payments on a bond are usually fixed and stated as a percentage of its "face" value.

It is important to understand that bonds come with interest-rate risk (described previously). As noted, the values of bonds have an inverse relationship with the direction of interest rates in our economy. The longer the time frame to maturity, the more sensitive the fluctuation in market price will be.

When you own individual bonds purchased at face value and hold them to maturity, you will receive the interest payments plus your original principal. This, of course, assumes that the bond issuer does not default on its promise and ultimately pays you back.

Not all bond issuers are created equal. The stronger their balance sheet and the higher their credit rating, the lower the risk involved. The opposite is also true. Therefore, it is logical that the higher the risk associated with purchasing the bond, the higher the rate of return that will be offered by the bond issuer. Bonds are typically considered safe investments, but keep in mind that the higher rate of return being offered is usually associated with a higher potential for default risk.

Bonds can be divided into three major categories: US Treasury bonds, municipal bonds, and corporate bonds. Each category has its own unique features, which you should take into consideration when selecting and evaluating the components of your bond holdings.

US Treasury Securities Bonds, bills, and notes issued by the US government are also known as Treasuries and typically represent the highest-quality bonds available to investors. However, in August 2011, credit-rating agency Standard & Poor's (S&P) announced that it had downgraded the US credit rating for the first time in history, sending shock waves through the credit markets. S&P stated that "political brinksmanship in the debate over the debt had made the US government's ability to manage its finances less stable, less effective, and less predictable." While S&P has maintained its "AA+" long-term and "A-1+" short-term ratings since then, the other two major credit-rating agencies have since followed suit.

Fitch downgraded the United States from AAA to AA+ in August 2023, citing a steady deterioration in governance and repeated debt-ceiling standoffs along with rising debt levels. Most recently, in May 2025, Moody's lowered its rating from Aaa to Aa1, the first such downgrade in its history, pointing to persistent large and growing fiscal deficits and ongoing political polarization. With federal debt now at record levels and deep partisan divides remaining, it appears unlikely that the United States will regain its top-tier credit status in the foreseeable future.

In spite of this, many people continue to invest in US Treasury securities, clearly for their known safety and peace of mind. While Treasury yields are currently above the inflation rate, offering investors a positive "real" return, this has not always been the case, and market conditions can change quickly. Periods when yields fall below inflation can still lead to a loss of purchasing power, meaning that even a safe and conservative investment like Treasuries is not entirely risk-free.

US government bonds are issued by the US Department of the Treasury. They are extremely liquid and traded on the secondary market. Treasury securities are backed by the full faith and credit of the US government. They are considered to have less risk than other bonds and are considered a safe haven, especially during turbulent economic times. The interest earned on Treasury bonds is exempt from state and local taxes. There are four major categories of US Treasury securities:

1. **Treasury Bills (T-bills):** Short-term bonds that mature in less than one year. They are sold at a discount from their face value and do not pay interest until their maturity.
2. **Treasury Notes (T-notes):** Earn a fixed rate of interest every six months and have maturities ranging anywhere from 1 to 10 years.
3. **Treasury Bonds (T-bonds):** Have maturities ranging from 10 to 30 years. Similar to Treasury notes, T-bonds also have a coupon payment every six months.
4. **Treasury Inflation-protected Securities (TIPS)**: Inflation-indexed bonds. The principal of TIPS is adjusted by changes in the Consumer Price Index (the standard measure for inflation within the United States). They are typically offered in maturities ranging from 5 to 30 years.

Municipal Bonds Municipal bonds are issued by state and local governments. The money raised by the issuance of these bonds is typically used to pay for public service projects, such as the construction of public schools, highways, low-income housing, sewer systems, and other municipal projects. Municipal bonds are exempt from federal, state, and local income taxes for investors who live in the jurisdiction where the bond is issued: this "triple tax-free" treatment can make them very attractive investments to high-income taxpayers. Exhibit 9.2 shows the equivalent corporate bond rates

Exhibit 9.2 Municipal Versus Corporate Bonds

In-state Municipal Bonds Rate	Corporate Bond Equivalent Rate at Marginal Federal, State, and Local Tax Rates			
	10%	20%	30%	40%
1.00%	1.11%	1.25%	1.43%	1.67%
2.00%	2.22%	2.50%	2.86%	3.33%
3.00%	3.33%	3.75%	4.29%	5.00%
4.00%	4.44%	5.00%	5.71%	6.67%
5.00%	5.56%	6.25%	7.14%	8.33%
6.00%	6.67%	7.50%	8.57%	10.00%
7.00%	7.78%	8.75%	10.00%	11.67%
8.00%	8.89%	10.00%	11.43%	13.33%
9.00%	10.00%	11.25%	12.86%	15.00%
10.00%	11.11%	12.50%	14.29%	16.67%
If $10,000 investment, the annual amount of return based on the above table				
$100	$111	$125	$143	$167
$200	$222	$250	$286	$333
$300	$333	$375	$429	$500
$400	$444	$500	$571	$667
$500	$556	$625	$714	$833
$600	$667	$750	$857	$1,000
$700	$778	$875	$1,000	$1,167
$800	$889	$1,000	$1,143	$1,333
$900	$1,000	$1,125	$1,286	$1,500
$1,000	$1,111	$1,250	$1,429	$1,667

Note: This exhibit shows the equivalent full taxable interest rate at different marginal tax rates to result in the same after-tax rate for in-state municipal bonds.

of return to municipal bonds. For example, if you have a marginal tax rate of 40%, you will have to earn 15% on a corporate bond to equal a 9% rate of return on a municipal bond.

There are two major categories of municipal bonds issued by state and local government:

1. **General obligation bonds:** Secured by the full faith and credit of the issuer and are supported by the issuer's taxing authority.
2. **Revenue bonds:** Unlike general obligation bonds, are secured by the revenues specified in the legal contract between the bond holder and bond issuer. These revenues must be used for repayment of the principal and interest on the bonds.

They are not backed by the full faith and credit or taxing authority of the municipality; instead, they are backed solely by the revenue-generating ability of the municipal project, such as a bridge toll and other user fees. Under certain circumstances revenue bonds may be subject to federal, state, or local alternative minimum tax.

Corporate Bonds These bonds are issued by corporations and other for-profit business entities, which issue bonds to raise capital for expansion and other operating needs. Corporate bonds pay a higher level of interest than government bonds because they are not backed by the government, but rather they are backed by the issuing company's ability to repay.

A business with a strong balance sheet, solid earnings, and an excellent credit rating will pay a much lower rate of interest than one that is less financially stable. It is important to understand that, when a corporation provides a higher interest rate on their bonds, all else equal, these bonds generally come with greater risk. Lastly, it is essential to note that interest earned on corporate bonds is subject to ordinary income tax rates.

Corporate bonds are broken into two categories:

1. **Investment grade bonds:** Indicate that there is a low risk of default and that the company has a strong capability to repay the debt.
2. **High yield bonds:** Have a lower credit rating because of the higher risk of default. To compensate investors for this risk, high yield bonds pay a significantly higher yield to investors (2% or more annually).

Hybrid Securities

Over the past 20 years, investing in hybrid securities that contain features of both equities and bonds has risen in popularity. Among the more notable securities which you should consider for your portfolio are the following:

- **Real Estate Investment Trusts (REIT):** An investment vehicle used to invest in real estate. REITs can own income-producing property and mortgages. What makes REITs unique is that, as long as they distribute at least 90% of their taxable income, they are not taxed at the company level. Because of this rule, REITs typically provide above-average dividends. However, since they already avoid corporate taxation, those dividends are generally taxed as ordinary income rather than at the lower qualified dividend rate. See Chapter 11, "Investing in Real Estate" for more detailed information on REITs.

- **Master Limited Partnership (MLP):** A limited partnership that is publicly traded. The MLP structure is heavily used for gas pipelines.
- **Business Development Company (BDC):** A closed-end investment company that provides loans to small and mid-sized companies.
- **Preferred Equity:** A class of ownership with a higher claim on assets and earnings than common stock. The investment allure of preferred equity is that they have dividend seniority to common stock. The dividend yield is normally higher than the company's fixed-income interest payment.
- **Convertible Debt:** A type of bond that can be converted into common stock of the company. The allure of convertible debt is that investors benefit from fixed income payments and have the ability to convert to equity if the equity appreciates.

Under current tax law, pass-through entity owners, including individuals, estates, and trusts, may be eligible for a deduction of up to 20% of their qualified domestic business income. This Section 199A deduction applies to the aggregate amount of qualified REIT dividends, qualified publicly traded partnership income, and qualified cooperative dividends for the taxable year.

Mutual Funds and ETFs

Mutual funds and ETFs are two of the most popular ways to gain exposure to individual stocks and bonds. They offer a more efficient approach to building a diversified portfolio than selecting individual securities. For most investors, mutual funds and ETFs are preferable to choosing individual stocks or bonds because the benefits of professional management and diversification often outweigh the added costs.

Technically speaking, a mutual fund is an investment security where individual investors pool their money into a professionally managed fund. Mutual funds also offer investors easy access to investing your money at all levels, whether investing a small or large amount.

When you invest in a mutual fund, you become a shareholder of that fund. As a shareholder, you will participate in the profits and losses of the mutual fund. Keep in mind that investing in mutual funds is similar to investing directly in an individual corporation, in that your liability is limited to the amount you invested.

The mutual fund itself is professionally managed by one or more investment managers, assisted by a team of investment analysts who decide what and when to buy within the framework defined in the mutual fund's prospectus. These investment decisions involve trading securities, recognizing capital gains and losses, and generating interest and dividends, all on behalf of the mutual fund and its investors. As one of the mutual fund's investors, you participate in these results in proportion to your holdings.

Like a stock, you make your money from dividends and capital appreciation of the underlying securities. However, unlike stocks, you don't control when capital gains distributions happen. The fund manager decides when to sell the underlying securities, which can trigger taxable events for investors. The price is set at the end of the day based on the *net asset value* (NAV) of the underlying securities. The NAV is set by the total value of securities owned divided by the number of mutual fund shares. You have yet another way to participate in the success or failure of your mutual fund investment by selling the shares you own.

If you sell your mutual fund shares at a price higher than you originally paid, you may realize capital gains and conversely, if you sell them for less, you may realize capital losses. As a result, mutual funds provide you with three opportunities for growth of your investments:

1. Dividends (decided by the underlying investments within the mutual fund)
2. Capital gains distributions (from the sale of investments within the fund which gets decided by the mutual fund manager)
3. Possible capital gains on the sale of your investment in the fund (decided by you or your financial advisor)

When you invest in a mutual fund, you are pooling your money with many other investors under the common control and management of an investment company. A mutual fund company is responsible for overseeing and executing your portfolio strategy.

Each mutual fund company has a list of various mutual fund investment options with varying objectives as stated in their prospectus. You can pick and choose the mutual fund type that is best aligned with your own long-term objectives.

One of the drawbacks to mutual funds is that they cannot be traded throughout the day; although the order may be placed at any time, the transaction is not executed until the fund's NAV is calculated at the end of the trading day.

Another drawback is that mutual funds aren't always tax-friendly because you can end up owing taxes even if you didn't sell any of your shares. This is because the fund's manager buys and sells investments inside the fund throughout the year. When those investments are sold for a profit, the gains must be paid out to everyone who owns the fund, and those payouts are taxable. That means you could get a tax bill because the manager made changes within the portfolio, even if you personally didn't sell anything.

A popular alternative to a mutual fund is the ETF. Like a mutual fund, an ETF holds assets such as stocks, bonds, or commodities. However, unlike a mutual fund, but similar to a stock, an ETF's value fluctuates throughout the day, and there is immediate transparency into the underlying holdings. Also like a stock, you generally only recognize capital gains when you choose to sell your shares, which can make ETFs more tax-efficient than mutual funds.

Many ETFs are based on a particular index, such as the S&P 500, the Dow Jones Industrial Average, gold index, corporate bond index, or health care index. Keep in mind that you cannot invest directly in an index. Most ETFs are not actively managed; instead, they simply hold investments that represent a particular index. This makes ETFs with passive strategies more attractive to certain investors because they typically have lower costs, and most mutual fund managers cannot consistently outperform the indexes.

As a clarification, in the investment world, an index is a passive benchmark for the asset class. It is the baseline measure for determining manager expertise. Popular indexes include the following:

- **Dow Jones Industrial Average (Dow):** A price-weighted stock market index that tracks 30 large, publicly traded US companies, often referred to as blue-chip stocks. In a price-weighted index, each company's influence is based on its stock price rather than its market capitalization.
- **S&P 500:** A stock market index that measures the performance of 500 of the largest publicly traded US companies. It is market capitalization-weighted, meaning each company's weight in the index is proportional to its total market value (share price × number of shares outstanding).
- **Russell 2000:** A popular measure of small-cap companies that consists of the smallest 2,000 companies in the Russell 3000 index and is a capitalization-weighted (market cap) index.

- **NASDAQ Composite:** A market capitalization-weighted index that tracks more than 3,000 publicly traded companies whose shares meet specific listing requirements, including minimum market value and trading volume. The index represents a broad range of industries but has a heavy concentration in technology and growth-oriented businesses.

The expectation is that good fund managers should outperform a passive index for their asset class. Otherwise, it would make more sense to invest in a low-cost ETF that replicates the index.

When selecting a mutual fund or ETF, the following are the major considerations:

- **Investment strategy:** Does it's strategy and asset class focus fit within your portfolio?
- **Investment track record:** Does it consistently beat its index?
- **Expense ratio:** All else being equal, you should choose a fund/ETF with lower costs.
- **Risk tolerance:** Do the asset class and manager approach fit your risk tolerance?

If you prefer investing in asset classes and do not put much weight on the value of active investment management, then ETFs may be better suited for you than investing in mutual funds. Conversely, if you do value the decision-making abilities of professional investment managers, then mutual funds may be the better choice for you.

Finally, it is worth touching on the major asset classes that you might want to include in your portfolio:

- **Fixed income (bond funds):** Invest primarily in bonds and other debt instruments.
- **Tax-exempt bond funds (muni bond funds):** Invest in municipal bonds (debt securities issued by a state, municipality, county, or special-purpose district).
- **Money market funds:** Earn interest while trying to maintain a net asset value of one dollar per share, typically invested in short-term securities representing high-quality, liquid debt, and monetary instruments.
- **US equities:** Are typically further divided into *large-cap funds, mid-cap funds,* and *small-cap funds.* These divisions are based on the market capitalization of the companies.

    - ***Large-cap funds, or large-market capitalization funds*** generally invest in securities of companies with a market capitalization of $10 billion or more.
    - ***Mid-cap funds, or middle-market capitalization funds*** generally invest in securities of companies with a market capitalization of $2 billion to $10 billion.
    - ***Small cap funds, or small-market capitalization funds*** generally invest in securities of companies with a market capitalization of $300 million to $2 billion.
- **International funds:** Invest in securities in nations besides the United States. This is typically further divided into *developed nations* and *emerging nations.*
    - ***Developed markets funds*** invest in securities in developed nations in terms of economy and capital markets (besides the United States).
    - ***Emerging markets funds*** invest in securities in a single developing country or a group of countries, typically in Eastern Europe, Africa, Latin America, and Asia.
- **Real asset funds:** Invest in real assets like real estate, infrastructure, and energy/Master Limited Partnerships (MLPs).

Each of these broad categories includes many subcategories, with new ones being created every year; therefore, you should always consult with your investment advisor and read the prospectuses before investing in any fund or ETF.

As with any decision in life, you must weigh the advantages and disadvantages of investing in stocks, bonds, hybrid securities, mutual funds, or ETFs. For many people, the right choice may be a combination of all of the above.

Private Investments

Over the past 20–25 years, investment firms have shifted from describing private investments (such as private equity, private real estate, and private credit) as niche or "specialty" options to presenting them as an essential part of a core investment strategy. This change accelerated after major market downturns, including the dot-com bust in the early 2000s, the 2008 financial crisis, and again in 2022, when both stocks and bonds declined at the same time.

Typically, bonds rise when stocks fall, serving as a hedge to offset losses, but in these periods, they moved in the same direction. This undermined confidence in the traditional stock-and-bond portfolio, leading private investments to be promoted as a "third pillar" intended to provide added protection.

The message often portrays private investments as a hedge that can keep a portfolio steadier during turbulent markets. On the surface, they do appear less volatile, but this is largely because they are not priced daily like publicly traded stocks and bonds. Instead, their values are updated only a few times a year, which makes short-term performance look smoother. In reality, their underlying value can fluctuate just as much as public assets; the changes simply are not reflected immediately.

Another critical consideration is liquidity. Most private investments require multiyear commitments and offer limited or no opportunities for early withdrawal. If early sales are allowed, they may come at a steep discount. While these characteristics can be acceptable for investors with long time horizons and sufficient resources, they make such investments unsuitable for others. Private investments are not inherently low-risk or easily accessible, and these factors should be carefully weighed before including them as a core holding.

Despite the risks, alternative investments can play a valuable role for the right investor. For those with longer time horizons and the ability to take on additional complexity, these strategies may provide diversification and potential return opportunities that traditional stock-and-bond portfolios cannot always offer. They can serve as a complement to your portfolio, offering exposure to different types of risks and income streams.

We will discuss a subsector of private investments, which is private real estate, in Chapter 11, "Investing in Real Estate."

Diversification, Asset Allocation, and Rebalancing

The most important tool to manage risk is *diversification*. As can be seen with Exhibit 9.3, the returns of various asset classes can fluctuate significantly from year to year. You need to have multiple asset classes within your portfolio to mitigate the financial impact if any one asset class falls short of expectations and to capture the upside when an individual asset class has a strong year.

Exhibit 9.3 Annual Returns for Eight Major Asset Classes over the Past 12 Years, from Best to Worst

2013	2014	2015	2016	2017	2018
Small Cap Stocks 38.8%	REITs 28.0%	REITs 2.8%	Small Cap Stocks 21.3%	Emerging Market Stocks 37.8%	Cash 1.8%
Large Cap Stocks 32.4%	Large Cap Stocks 13.7%	Large Cap Stocks 1.4%	High Yield Bonds 17.5%	Int'l Developed Stocks 25.6%	High Grade Bonds 0.0%
Int'l Developed Stocks 23.3%	High Grade Bonds 6.0%	High Grade Bonds 0.6%	Large Cap Stocks 12.0%	Large Cap Stocks 21.8%	High Yield Bonds −2.3%
High Yield Bonds 7.4%	Small Cap Stocks 4.9%	Cash 0.0%	Emerging Market Stocks 11.6%	Small Cap Stocks 14.7%	REITs −4.0%
REITs 2.9%	High Yield Bonds 2.5%	Int'l Developed Stocks −0.4%	REITs 8.6%	REITs 8.7%	Large Cap Stocks −4.4%
Cash 0.1%	Cash 0.0%	Small Cap Stocks −4.4%	High Grade Bonds 2.7%	High Yield Bonds 7.5%	Small Cap Stocks −11.0%
High Grade Bonds −2.0%	Emerging Market Stocks −1.8%	High Yield Bonds −4.6%	Int'l Developed Stocks 1.5%	High Grade Bonds 3.5%	Int'l Developed Stocks −13.4%
Emerging Market Stocks −2.3%	Int'l Developed Stocks −4.5%	Emerging Market Stocks −14.6%	Cash 0.3%	Cash 0.8%	Emerging Market Stocks −14.3%

2019	2020	2021	2022	2023	2024
Large Cap Stocks 31.5%	Small Cap Stocks 20.0%	REITs 41.3%	Cash 1.6%	Large Cap Stocks 26.3%	Large Cap Stocks 25.0%
REITs 28.7%	Emerging Market Stocks 18.7%	Large Cap Stocks 28.7%	High Yield Bonds −11.2%	Int'l Developed Stocks 18.9%	Small Cap Stocks 11.5%
Small Cap Stocks 25.5%	Large Cap Stocks 18.4%	Small Cap Stocks 14.8%	High Grade Bonds −13.0%	Small Cap Stocks 16.9%	High Yield Bonds 8.2%
Int'l Developed Stocks 22.7%	Int'l Developed Stocks 8.3%	Int'l Developed Stocks 11.8%	Int'l Developed Stocks −14.0%	High Yield Bonds 13.5%	Emerging Market Stocks 8.1%
Emerging Market Stocks 18.9%	High Yield Bonds 7.5%	High Yield Bonds 5.4%	Large Cap Stocks −18.1%	REITs 11.4%	Cash 5.3%
High Yield Bonds 14.4%	High Grade Bonds 6.1%	Cash 0.0%	Emerging Market Stocks −19.7%	Emerging Market Stocks 10.3%	REITs 4.9%
High Grade Bonds 8.7%	Cash 0.6%	High Grade Bonds −1.5%	Small Cap Stocks −20.4%	High Grade Bonds 5.5%	Int'l Developed Stocks 4.4%
Cash 2.2%	REITs −5.1%	Emerging Market Stocks −2.2%	REITs −24.4%	Cash 5.1%	High Grade Bonds 1.3%

Asset Class	Index	Average	Best	Worst
REITs	FTSE NAREIT All Equity Index	8.6%	41.3%	−24.4%
Emerging Market Stocks	MSCI Emerging Markets Index	4.2%	37.8%	−19.7%
International Developed Stocks	MSCI EAFE Index	7.0%	25.6%	−14.0%
Small Cap Stocks	Russell 2000 Index	11.1%	38.8%	−20.4%
Large Cap Stocks	S&P 500 Index	15.7%	32.4%	−18.1%
High Yield Bonds	BofAML High Yield Index	5.5%	17.5%	−11.2%
High Grade Bonds	Barclay's US Aggregate Bond Index	1.5%	8.7%	−13.0%
Cash	3 Month Treasury Bill Rate	1.5%	5.3%	0.0%

For example, in 2021, REITs were the top performer of all asset classes that year, and in 2022, they were the worst asset performer.

Exhibit 9.3 also illustrates the best, the worst, and the average over the past 12 years for each of the eight asset classes listed. This highlights the importance of having staying power with your portfolio. When an asset class performs very poorly one year, it could be followed by a very good year.

As Gene Goldman, CFA, chief investment officer at Cetera Financial Group explains:

> Market volatility is a normal part of investing even in bull markets. For example, since 1980, the S&P 500 has been positive in 37 of the past 45 years with an average annual total return of 13.5%. Even in this bull market, the average annual drawdown or market selloff is −14.1%. Diversification is an important way to mitigate or reduce that downside risk to make sure you are invested for the long term.[1]

Therefore, the first step to constructing a portfolio is *asset class allocation*. Asset allocation is an investment strategy that provides a systematic approach to diversification that may help you establish the most efficient blend of assets based on your particular risk tolerance and investing time horizon. Asset allocation seeks to manage investment risk by diversifying a portfolio among the major asset classes.

Each asset class has a different level of risk as well as a potential rate of return. The basic idea is that, while one asset class may be increasing in value, another may be decreasing. Therefore, asset allocation and diversification may help you ride out market fluctuations and protect your portfolio from a major loss in any one asset class.

They may also provide you with staying power and control over your emotions even after a big downturn in the market. Furthermore, it is smart to diversify within an asset class to minimize the risk of any individual security. This is one major reason to invest in mutual funds and ETFs, because they are the most efficient way to diversify within an asset class.

---

[1] Cetera Investment Management, FactSet, YCharts. The annual total return includes dividends. The annual max decline is the largest price decline in each calendar year. Return and max drawdown data based on closing prices. Data as of 12/31/2024.

However, it is important to understand that asset allocation and diversification do not guarantee against loss. They are simply strategies that may help smooth the ride to your financial independence and generational wealth goals.

It is fundamental to find a mixture of asset classes with the highest potential return within your risk profile. Exhibit 9.4 shows six sample asset allocation models that can be used as a theoretical guide to fit into your own risk tolerance level. Please understand that these are hypothetical models and do not represent actual

Exhibit 9.4 Six Sample Asset Allocation Models (1 = Most risk-adverse investor; 6 = Most aggressive investor)

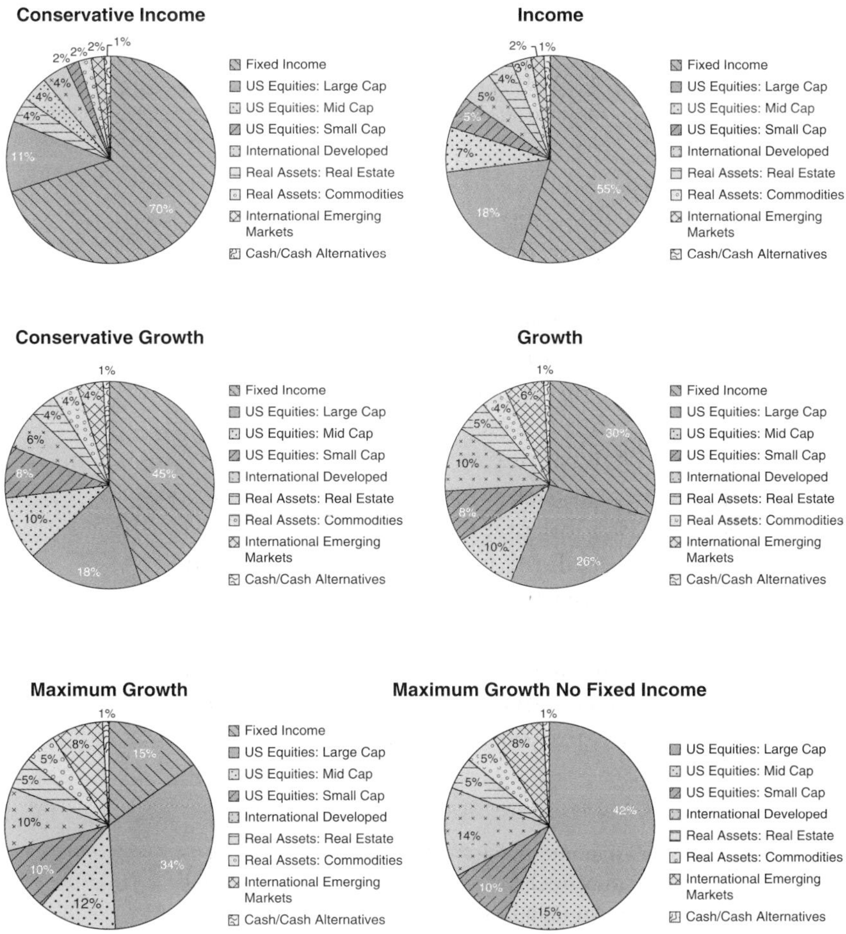

recommendations to be used. There are, of course, an unlimited number of variations to these sample models.

For our portfolio construction, we will focus on the following asset classes. For now, we will assume you are investing in a nontaxable account. If you were investing from a taxable account, you might want to switch some of your fixed income exposure to municipal bond funds.

- **Cash and Cash Equivalents:** Includes currency, coins, checking accounts, savings accounts, money market accounts, and certificates of deposit
- **Fixed Income (bond funds):** Includes US treasuries, municipal bonds, investment grade bonds, and high-yield bonds
- **US Equities:** Includes large-cap funds, mid-cap funds, and small-cap funds
- **International:** Includes developed market funds and emerging market funds
- **Real Assets:** Includes real estate and commodities

It is worth highlighting an implicit assumption in these models. Fixed income is less risky than other asset classes. In some economic and market scenarios, such as rapidly rising interest rates, this assumption is false. Additionally, it is important to remember that less risky does not mean there is not still a risk of loss. For example, in times of extreme negative swings, like 2022, virtually all assets decline except cash, although short-duration investment-grade debt suffer a less severe drop.

The second key assumption in these models is that the projected returns meet your long-term goals. If the model selected based upon your risk tolerance cannot achieve your long-term goals, either your goal must be modified, or you must accept additional risk.

The third key assumption in these models is that we have no insights into the returns of asset classes for next year. In the real world, at any given time, an asset class might be over- or undervalued relative to other assets, and we might choose to opportunistically tweak allocations.

Finally, before we dive into the models, a key component to effective portfolio management is *rebalancing*. As Exhibit 9.3 illustrates, asset class returns widely fluctuate. Rebalancing allows us to take advantage of these fluctuations. Rebalancing is the act of selling out of our "winner" asset classes and buying our "loser" asset classes to bring the portfolio back to its original allocations. Effectively, by partially selling out of our winners and buying our losers, we are shifting our investments from overvalued to undervalued asset classes. Over time, this could enhance returns. We further discuss rebalancing after these models.

We want to emphasize that these are just example hypothetical asset allocation models and could differ significantly from what we would recommend. These are just shown for educational and comparison purposes only.

Depending on your risk tolerance and time horizon, you can select anywhere from model 1 to model 6, for example:

- If you need money in the near future, you should consider a model that involves less risk, such as model 1 or 2.
- If you are saving for retirement and have 10 or more years until you will need access to these funds, you may be able to take on more risk to increase your potential for growth. In this case, models 3, 4, 5, or 6 may be more suitable.
- If your time horizon is less than a few years, you should probably not be investing at all; instead, you should keep your cash in a high-yield savings, money market accounts, or US T-bills for easy access and safety. Investing should always be viewed as a long-term commitment.

It is very important to keep in mind that there is no one approach that will fit every individual investor.

Now that you have selected your ideal asset allocation model based on your acceptable risk tolerance, it is important to monitor and maintain this allocation. Rebalancing your portfolio is one of the essential aspects of maintaining a successful investment strategy over time. Rebalancing requires you to analyze the changes in your asset allocation model periodically and make adjustments in an attempt to bring you back to your original allocation. You do this by selling and buying various investments within each asset class to maintain your established asset allocation.

Suppose the original asset allocation model you established included 1% cash, 80% stock, and 19% bonds. During a period of falling interest rates, your bond values increased to represent 24% of your portfolio, and your stock values now only represent 75%

of your overall portfolio. Rebalancing will require you to sell off part of your bond portfolio and to purchase additional stock holdings to bring you back to your original model. This also forces you to sell some of the bond holdings that have done well at a higher price and allows you to purchase stocks that have not done well at a lower price.

This is a systematic approach to buying low and selling high for at least some portion of your overall investment holdings. It is also important to note that by maintaining your asset allocation, you will keep your risk tolerance level within your comfort zone.

To further highlight how the rebalancing would work, refer to Exhibit 9.5. Here, we start with an example bond-only investment model, conservative bond income, with 15% allocated to fixed high-yield bonds, 35% allocated to fixed-income investment-grade bonds, and 50% to fixed-income short-term and money-market. After year 1, the initial asset allocation percentages have changed because of the performance of each asset class.

To rebalance and return your model to its original allocation, you would be required to purchase $1,875 of fixed-income short-term bond mutual funds and money market, and you would have to sell $788 of fixed-income investment-grade bond mutual funds and $1,087 of fixed-income high-yield bond mutual funds. This would take you back to your original percentage allocation.

In the example provided, rebalancing is being done once a year, always taking you back to your original asset-allocation model percentages. Once again, this is a systematic approach that allows you not only to stay within your risk tolerance profile but also to sell a portion of your holdings after they have increased in value and to purchase a portion of your holdings that have decreased in value. The added benefit to this is that you are using a disciplined approach to buy low and sell high for at least a portion of your portfolio.

For many investors, rebalancing once a year is usually sufficient. However, in recent years, due to high volatility in the markets, rebalancing more frequently has become more appropriate. Rather than using a specific date or time frame, it is often better to use a percentage change in your allocation as the trigger point for rebalancing. For example, if any one asset class percentage within your model changes by more than 5% from its original allocation, that would be a trigger point for rebalancing.

Exhibit 9.5 Investment Rebalancing

Example Bond Only Investment Model—Conservative bond Income

	Market Value of Portfolio				% of Portfolio			
	Total	Fixed Income High Yield	Fixed Income Investment Grade	Fixed Income Short Term and Money Market	Total	Fixed Income High Yield	Fixed Income Investment Grade	Fixed Income Short Term and Money Market
Initial Investment	$100,000	$15,000	$35,000	$50,000	100.00%	15.00%	35.00%	50.00%
% Change Year 1		10%	5%	−1%				
Change During Year 1	$2,750	$1,500	$1,750	$(500)				
Year-1 Before Rebalance	$102,750	$16,500	$36,750	$49,500	100.00%	16.06%	35.77%	48.18%
REBALANCE—Year 1	$–	$(1,087)	$(788)	$1,875				
Year 1 After Rebalance	$102,750	$15,413	$35,963	$51,375	100.00%	15.00%	35.00%	50.00%
% Change Year 2		4%	6%	0%				
Change During Year 2	$2,774	$617	$2,158	$–				
Year 2 Before Rebalance	$105,524	$16,029	$38,120	$51,375	100.00%	15.19%	36.12%	48.69%
REBALANCE—Year 2	$–	$(200)	$(1,187)	$1,387				
Year 2 After Rebalance	$105,524	$15,829	$36,933	$52,762	100.00%	15.00%	35.00%	50.00%
% Change Year 3		2%	3%	5%				
Change During Year 3	$4,063	$317	$1,108	$2,638				
Year 3 Before Rebalance	$109,587	$16,145	$38,041	$55,400	100.00%	14.73%	34.71%	50.55%
REBALANCE—Year 3	$–	$293	$314	$(607)				
Year 3 After Rebalance	$109,587	$16,438	$38,355	$54,793	100.00%	15.00%	35.00%	50.00%

One of the major advantages of rebalancing as one of your investment strategies is that it provides you with a disciplined approach to taking profits from some of your winners, allowing you to cash in on those gains. Another advantage to rebalancing is that it allows you to pay close attention to your portfolio; by examining the changes in your investment allocation, you can reevaluate your individual investment choices within each asset class. Finally, rebalancing may smooth out your overall investment rate of return.

Dollar-cost Averaging

The simple fact of investing is that if you could always buy at market lows and always sell at market highs, then you would guarantee yourself a profit and never have a financial worry. Unfortunately, investors and financial advisors have yet to figure out a system to do this consistently. One basic principle of investing is that you must be realistic about what is possible and what is not.

Far too many investors try to predict the market along with their entry and exit points. This strategy typically results in a disappointing overall rate of return. To participate in market gains, you need to be invested in the market during its profitable days. Trying to time the market is a very risky game. Instead, focus on the amount of time you will be invested in the market and not on the timing of your investments. An investment strategy that may help you find the way around these investing pitfalls is *dollar-cost averaging.*

With a dollar-cost averaging investing strategy, you put a certain amount of money into your investment portfolio every month over an extended period. Regardless of market conditions and the ups and downs in the value of your particular investments, you will be committed to purchasing a certain dollar amount each month.

When the individual share price of your investment increases, you buy fewer shares, and when the individual share price of your investment decreases, you buy more shares with the same monetary investment. Therefore, your average cost per share will reflect both the low prices and high prices you paid. This system averages out the overall price per share you ultimately pay.

One of the main advantages of dollar-cost averaging is that you are *not* trying to predict the entry or exit point of your investments. This approach simply puts you into a routine of investing on a regular basis, regardless of market conditions. This investment strategy may also reduce your risk of investing a large sum of money in one investment when the share price may be overvalued.

Another big advantage to utilizing a dollar-cost averaging investment strategy along with a rebalancing strategy is that it may help smooth your investment ride, especially during volatile markets. You will not experience the largest possible gains during a bull market, but you may minimize your losses during a bear market. The simple idea is that the more you do to take the emotions out of investing, the more likely you are to stick to your investment strategy. The ultimate goal, of course, is to return to your original asset allocation model, periodically rebalancing and consistently adding funds to your investment portfolio on a regular basis so that you can pursue your targeted rate of return on your investments over time.

Most people do not realize that when they are contributing to their 401(k) plan at work through each paycheck, they are actually implementing the dollar-cost averaging investment strategy. As we have repeatedly mentioned throughout this book, there is no better way to achieve financial independence than to do it in a tax-efficient manner. Combine these investment strategies with a systematic savings plan that includes paying yourself first, and you will be well on your way to becoming financially independent and creating generational wealth for generations to come.

Inflation and Taxes: The Biggest Drains on Investment Return

Inflation and taxes are perhaps the two biggest drains on your investment returns. Taking these factors into consideration is very important in your journey to achieving financial independence.

The technical definition of inflation is the rise in consumer prices over time. *It is vital to your savings that your investment returns keep pace with the rate of inflation to avoid a true loss of purchasing power.* If the average inflation rate has been 3% and your adjusted after-tax rate of return on your investments is below 3%, you are in fact losing purchasing power and diminishing your wealth.

To accumulate wealth, your investment objective should be to earn a rate of return after taxes that will exceed the prevailing inflation rate. Looking back to the history of the investment markets, the one way to beat inflation is to have some of your money invested in growth-oriented investments. This includes growth stocks, growth mutual funds, growth ETFs, and alternative growth investments.

These vehicles have the potential to deliver returns that outpace inflation over the long term, though they also carry greater risk than other types of investments.

As you select your asset allocation model based on your risk tolerance level, never forget that smart investors always focus on a well-diversified portfolio. Taking on too much risk or too little risk can both be equally damaging to your financial success. You must find your own perfect balance in determining your risk-reward ratio.

You must always consider the tax consequences of your investment when calculating your true rate of return. See Exhibit 9.6 and "Medicaid Surtax on Net Investment Income" in the next section for information on how taxes affect investments.

Under the new tax law, the three capital gains and qualified dividend income thresholds do not align precisely with the ordinary income tax brackets. These preferential tax rate thresholds remain consistent with the structure used prior to the 2018 reforms, though they are now indexed for inflation annually. For 2025, they are applied to maximum taxable income thresholds as follows:

Exhibit 9.6 Long-term Capital Gain and Qualified Dividend Maximum Taxable Income Thresholds

Long-term Capital Gains Rate	Single Taxpayers	Married Filing Jointly	Head of Household	Married Filing Separately
0%	Up to $48,350	Up to $96,700	Up to $64,750	Up to $48,350
15%	$48,351–$533,400	$96,701–$600,050	$64,751–$566,700	$48,351–$300,000
20%	Over $533,400	Over $600,050	Over $566,700	Over $300,000

Please note that if the only thing causing your income to be greater than these amounts is the capital gains or qualified dividends, then only the excess amount of capital gains or qualified dividends are taxed at the next higher capital gains tax rate.

Medicare Surtax on Net Investment Income

Starting in 2013, a 3.8% Medicare surtax, also known as the Net Investment Income Tax (NIIT), was imposed on net investment income for single or head of household taxpayers with modified adjusted gross income (MAGI) over $200,000, married couples filing jointly or a qualifying widow(er) with MAGI over $250,000, and married taxpayers filing separately with MAGI over $125,000.

The combined federal maximum tax rate on short-term capital gains could be as high as 40.8% (37% ordinary income tax + 3.8% Medicare surtax).

The combined federal maximum tax rate on long-term capital gains for those in the 20% capital gains tax bracket could be as high as 23.8% (20% + 3.8%).

The combined federal maximum tax rate on long-term capital gains for those in the 15% capital gains tax bracket could be as high as 18.8% (15% + 3.8%).

The combined federal maximum tax rate on long-term capital gains for those in the 0% capital gains tax bracket remains 0%, since the 3.8% Medicare surtax does not apply below the MAGI thresholds.

Cryptocurrency and Its Tax Treatment

Cryptocurrency was introduced more than 15 years ago and has since become a widely discussed and increasingly adopted investment asset. Over the years, investors have flocked in droves to capitalize on its highly speculative value.

Cryptocurrency, such as Bitcoin, is a form of digital currency that is exchanged over the internet for goods and services, through secure transactions. Unlike regular currency, cryptocurrency is not backed by the good faith of any government or precious metal. This means it is only worth what people will pay for it, and it is difficult to regulate. While some believe cryptocurrency is the future of the economy, critics argue that its dubious nature could cause it to collapse at any time.

The IRS first issued guidance in 2014 stating that virtual currency is to be treated as property for tax purposes, not as actual currency. In other words, even though you can use cryptocurrency to buy and sell things, the IRS does not recognize it as legal tender in any jurisdiction. That position was refined in 2023 under IRS Notice 2023–2034. The way your gains or losses are taxed depends on how you're using the virtual currency. If you're holding it as an investment, similar to stocks or bonds, it's considered a capital asset. In that case, any gains or losses from selling or trading it are treated as either short-term or long-term capital gains or losses. On the other hand, if you're using it as inventory in a business or holding it mainly for sale to customers, it's not considered a capital asset. Those transactions are taxed as ordinary income.

Starting in 2025, the IRS requires brokers, including cryptocurrency exchanges and custodial platforms, to report digital asset transactions using a new form called 1099-DA, which covers sales and exchanges of digital assets. These reports will be sent to taxpayers and to the IRS in early 2026. This is a major change: previously, such transactions weren't subject to third-party reporting like they were for other traditional securities. With the new rules in place, most cryptocurrency activity will now be reported directly to the IRS, making accurate reporting on your tax return more important than ever.

Payments for employee or independent contractor services with cryptocurrency are subject to the same reporting requirements as if it were paid in US dollars, including the issuance of W-2 and 1099 forms. Payments may even be subject to backup withholding.

Cryptocurrency is at risk of virtual theft and is not FDIC insured. It is our view that this is not really a currency, since it is not backed by precious metals or any government guarantee. In addition, currency should be a stable and secure way to transact business. Clearly, cryptocurrency does not have any stability in its pricing.

To better take control of this rapidly evolving facet of our economy, the US government is paying particular attention to the reporting of cryptocurrency transactions. The IRS has taken steps to force these privatized cryptocurrency companies to turn over customer records so that unreported transactions can be properly investigated.

In 2025, the Supreme Court declined to hear an appeal in *Harper v. IRS*, which involved the agency's efforts to obtain customer data from Coinbase, one of the largest cryptocurrency platforms. This decision allowed a lower court ruling to stand, giving the IRS access to detailed account records and reinforcing its authority to enforce tax compliance in the crypto space. With this access, the IRS can identify unreported transactions and pursue back taxes where appropriate. By law, you must report all financial transactions, including bartering. If substantial underreporting of income is discovered, the IRS could pursue these cases as criminal charges. The bottom line here is that, if you are performing any transactions with cryptocurrency, you must be sure you are reporting it on your income tax return.

If you do not pay attention to the tax consequences of your investments, you may be paying significantly more in taxes than the law requires. Therefore, you must include tax planning as part of your overall investment and generational wealth strategy. Using an investment approach that takes advantage of tax-smart strategies will potentially help maximize your after-tax rate of return on your investments.

Tax-smart Strategies for Managing Your Investments

Here are several tax facts and strategies that will address your wealth accumulation goals in a powerful and sustainable way. This will be part of your tax-smart roadmap to financial independence. This is how you can transform the tax code into part of your generational wealth code.

- Consider selling some of your investments in stocks, bonds, or mutual funds that have declined in value from when you originally purchased them. To realize these capital losses, you must complete the transaction before December 31. Capital gains can be offset by capital losses to the extent of gains, and an additional $3,000 in capital losses can be used to offset your ordinary income. Any excess loss above this amount can be carried forward to future years.
- You can then buy back these investments after 30 days to avoid the wash sale rules, which would otherwise disallow these losses. The *wash sale rules* prevent you from claiming a loss on a sale of stock if you buy replacement stock within 30 days before or after the sale.
- Stock dividends and stock splits on common stock are usually not taxable, but dividends paid out of current or accumulated earnings of a corporation are, in fact, taxable. Be sure to include only *taxable* dividends on your income tax return.
- Net long-term capital gains are taxed at a preferential federal rate that does not exceed 20%. If you hold an investment for more than a year, you will have the added advantage of long-term capital gains treatment. Long-term capital gains tax rates still remain as they were under the previous tax law, which includes a 0% tax rate, a 15% tax rate, and a 20% tax rate. These rates will apply based on the long-term capital gain and qualified dividend maximum taxable income thresholds. See Exhibit 9.6
- Dividends from most domestic corporations and many foreign corporations are usually treated as qualified dividends. For 2025, qualified dividends will continue to receive favorable tax-rate treatment which includes a 0% tax rate, a 15% tax rate, and a 20% tax rate. These rates will apply based on the long-term capital gain and qualified dividend maximum taxable income thresholds. See Exhibit 9.6.
- The TCJA provides a code section 199A deduction of up to 20% of "domestic qualified business income" for pass-through entity owners and also applies to an individual's aggregate qualified REIT dividends, qualified publicly traded partnership income, and qualified cooperative dividends. The OBBBA has made the provisions of Section 199A permanent.

- Under current law, there is a 3.8% Medicare tax on net investment income for taxpayers whose modified adjusted gross income exceeds certain thresholds: $250,000 for married filing jointly and qualifying widow(er), $125,000 for married filing separately, and $200,000 for single and head of household. This tax, originally introduced under the Affordable Care Act in 2013, remains in effect and applies to interest, dividends, capital gains, rental income, and other forms of net investment income.
- Interest on securities issued by the federal government (such as Treasury bonds, notes, and bills) is fully taxable at the federal level, but it is not subject to state or local income tax.
- Interest from municipal bonds and municipal bond funds are generally triple tax-free if the underlying bonds are from the state or local government where you reside. If the municipal bonds are not from the state where you reside, they will be free of federal tax and may be subject to your state and local tax. If part of your investment objective is to generate tax-free income, you should consider buying municipal bonds. With the Medicare surtax of 3.8% on net investment income, municipal bonds have become even more attractive since they are also exempt from this tax.
- Although raised to $40,000 under the OBBBA, the state and local tax limitation on itemized deductions still makes municipal bonds attractive, particularly those issued in your state, which may be free from both federal state taxes and local taxes. Taxable bonds are now somewhat less disadvantaged than before, but they still don't offer the same tax-exempt benefits as in-state municipal bonds.
- If you take an early withdrawal from a certificate of deposit, you will be able to deduct the full amount of the early withdrawal penalty from your taxable income.
- Capital losses on the sale of property held for personal use, such as your home, are not tax-deductible.
- When evaluating investment and financial decisions, you should consider the after-tax effects of a transaction so that you truly understand your real rate of return when compared to other investment choices.
- Keep an accurate record of all security transactions, along with when you bought them, especially if you purchased securities from the same issuer at different times. By using specific identification, you may be able to control the amount of gain or loss on the sale or part of your investment holdings. You are required to make an adequate identification, typically by giving your broker specific instructions of which securities lot are to be sold. If you use the specific identification method, your broker must provide written confirmation of your instructions, typically in the form of a trade confirmation or account statement. This could potentially allow you to pay significantly less tax by identifying those shares that have the highest cost basis and will result in the least tax.

An Action Plan for Managing Your Investments

1. **Know how tolerant of risk you are and properly determine your ability and willingness to take on risk, before investing.** Your financial net worth, sources of income, and your age play an important role in determining your ability to take on risk. If you know you are the type of person who prefers to "play it safe," then you may need to invest accordingly. Conversely, if you are the type of person who won't lose sleep at night if you lose money in the market, then you are more likely to be comfortable with taking risk. Ultimately, the decision on the proper level of risk to take will be some combination of both your ability and willingness to take risk.
2. **Understand the different types of risk that can affect your investments.** Learn as much as you can about inflation risk, interest rate risk, default risk, market-rate risk, economic risk, and company-specific or industry-specific risk, political risk, and liquidity risk, all of which may influence how well or how poorly your investments perform.
3. **Diversify your investments so that you do not have "all your eggs in one basket."** If you spread your investment dollars among several different asset classes, you may be able to lower your volatility on your overall investment portfolio without sacrificing your return on investment. For example, you might invest some of your money in specific company stocks, bonds, hybrid securities, mutual funds, ETFs, and private investments.
4. **Include an asset allocation by location strategy and rebalance your portfolio as needed** to bring it back to your original asset allocation model.
5. **Do not try to predict the best timing of when to invest; instead, invest regularly with the same amount of money,** whether the market you are investing in is up or down. This is called *dollar-cost averaging*, and this approach helps you develop a routine or habit of investing. It also helps you avoid making emotional decisions about your investments. When you combine this investment approach with the appropriate rebalancing as needed, you are also getting the added benefit of selling a portion of your investments high and buying others at their lows.
6. **Know how taxes and inflation affect the true rate of return on your investments.** At the very least, your returns should exceed the combined impact of both. Consider working with a financial adviser who understands tax-smart investing strategies and can help you maximize the long-term growth of your portfolio.
7. **Understand how cryptocurrency works and how it is taxed.** Unlike traditional currency, it is not backed by the government or by precious metals. Its value is determined solely by what others are willing to pay, and it remains difficult to regulate. Keep in mind that all financial transactions, including those involving cryptocurrency, must be reported to the IRS.

8. **Work with an investment advisor** that has a fiduciary responsibility to you. Please refer to Appendix A, "Selecting a Trusted Advisor."
9. **Work with a tax-advisor and CERTIFIED FINANCIAL PLANNER®** that can provide you with the tax-smart investing advice covered in this chapter. Please refer to Appendix A, "Selecting a Trusted Advisor."
10. **Work with a financial planner** that will provide you with the necessary advice and guidance that includes the 12 critical areas of comprehensive wealth management covered throughout this book.
11. **Use the tax-smart roadmap to financial independence at the end of this chapter to transform the tax code into part of your generational wealth code.**

CHAPTER 10

Preserving Your Estate

In this world nothing can be said to be certain, except death and taxes.
—Benjamin Franklin, Founding Father of the United States

So, you have worked hard, lived within your means, followed the guidance provided in this book, and achieved financial independence. Congratulations! So, what's next? Creating and maintaining generational wealth.

For your whole life, you dreamed of becoming financially independent for the benefit of yourself and your family. Now it is time to turn your attention to preserving your estate so that your loved ones can benefit from your life's hard work and sacrifices. If you do not take the necessary steps to preserve your estate, unintended beneficiaries may receive or take a significant amount of your estate instead. These unintended beneficiaries include the federal and state governments, the state administrator, attorneys, and perhaps even relatives you have not spoken to in decades. The money you may spend today on a qualified estate attorney may save your estate significant dollars in both estate taxes and administrative costs down the road and will ensure that the beneficiaries of your assets are those you intend.

Estate planning can give you peace of mind by ensuring that your family's financial security will continue after your death. It allows you to transfer and dispose of your assets as you see fit, with consideration to your heirs' individual needs. It is important to understand that estate planning is not just for the wealthy. Every adult should have estate planning in place, some of which will be of assistance during life and some of which will come into play after death.

The Federal Gift and Estate Tax System

The federal gift tax and estate tax system is a unified system that works hand in hand with virtually the same rules and tax rates. The main difference between the two is that the gift tax is imposed on the donor for gifts made during his or her lifetime, whereas the estate tax is imposed on the donor based on the value of his or her net estate upon death.

In 2025, the federal estate, gift, and generation-skipping transfer (GST) tax exemptions are $13.99 million for individuals and $27.98 million for married couples, indexed for inflation. Starting in 2026, the exemption will increase to $15 million for individuals and $30 million for married couples and cost of living adjustments will continue annually under the One Big Beautiful Bill Act (OBBBA).

The top federal estate tax rate remains at 40% of the amount above these lifetime exemption amounts. *Lifetime exemption* represents the total amount you can transfer while alive (by gift) or after death (through your estate) that will not be subject to estate or gift tax under this unified system. Depending on your state of residence, there may also be state-level gift and estate taxes to consider, which can add up to an additional 16% tax in states such as Massachusetts or New York.

To ensure you preserve your estate for your intended beneficiaries, it is important to stay on top of the ever-changing rules of the game. You should make certain that your financial advisor is working closely with a trusted tax advisor and your estate planning attorney to ensure that you can take advantage of these tax law changes when they arise.

Legal Documents to Consider for Estate Planning

Regardless of the size of your estate, you should consider addressing your own individual planning issues to preserve your estate and make your wishes known, preferably in writing. We recommend meeting with a qualified estate planning attorney to determine exactly what estate planning documents you should have prepared, based on your particular facts and circumstances. If you have no minor children, if all your assets are held jointly with your spouse, or if you have no significant assets, then your estate may not need to go through probate. If this is the case, or if you are willing to have your assets administered and distributed according to the rules of your particular state, you may not need a will.

If you need a will, it must be prepared in accordance with the laws of your resident state. If you change domicile, or move to another state of residence, your will may still be valid after you move; however, certain provisions may become invalid or may require changes due to the unique laws of your new state of residence. It is always best to update it and to work with an attorney who is familiar with the laws of your current state.

Estate planning should begin with consideration of individual needs, then determination of what legal documents are most appropriate. These may include a health care proxy (or advanced medical directive), a living will, a last will and testament, a durable or nondurable power of attorney, and a HIPAA (Health Insurance Portability and Accountability Act) authorization to allow medical facilities and physicians to share information if you are incapacitated.

As Barry Holt, senior advanced planning solutions consultant at Cetera Financial Group, explains,

> The HIPAA Authorization is critical for everyone. The Advance Healthcare Directive is equally critical for unmarried adult children who should likely allow their parents to have information in the event of incapacity.

To ensure that your assets are distributed to your intended beneficiaries after your death, you may utilize a last will and testament or trust, or some combination of both. These documents will be explained in more detail in this chapter. Please note that the names of some of these documents vary from state to state.

Before discussing the details of estate planning techniques, it is important to understand some of the key legal documents that may be needed in this planning process. An effective estate plan may need to include one or more of these documents that may cover all three phases of your life. Phase I is while you are alive and well, Phase II is in the event that you become disabled, and Phase III is after your death.

To preserve your estate and allow your loved ones to share in your success of becoming financially independent, you will need to address numerous legal forms so that your legacy can be transferred into generational wealth. All the legal forms described in the next sections must be appropriate to your state of residence and may even be modeled after statutory forms specific to that state. The advantage to using a "statutory form" is that it must be accepted, and it will ensure compliance with your wishes, even in an emergency situation.

If you already have an estate plan that includes some of these documents, review them at least annually. You will be surprised how quickly they can become outdated, or even invalid, with unexpected changes that take place throughout your life. You (and your spouse, if you are married) should have your estate plan reviewed at least once every five years by a competent attorney well-versed in estate planning, or sooner if you experience a life-changing event such as a birth of a child or grandchild, death within your immediate family, marriage, divorce, or retirement. This is necessary to ensure that your estate plan remains up to date with both your wishes and the laws that apply in your current state of residence. You should also consider reviewing and updating these documents more frequently in the event of changes to state or federal legislation. Your estate planning attorney should bring any legislative changes to your attention so that you can take the necessary steps to ensure your estate plan is still fulfilling your wishes and minimizing your estate tax exposure.

All the following documents should be drafted by and executed in the presence of a qualified attorney with significant estate planning experience. Online legal services such as LegalZoom, Nolo, or Trust & Will may be tempting to use, but even if they save you some money upfront, in most cases, the legal advice and associated cost of working directly with an attorney should more than pay for itself in the long run.

Preparing Your Will to Distribute Your Assets After Your Death

A will, also called a *Last Will and Testament,* is a written document that provides instructions on how you would like to distribute your assets after death. It is one of the most widely used and basic estate planning documents, and it also addresses many of your wishes and desires after death, including the designation of your executor, the naming of a guardian of minor children, and the distribution of tangible personal property.

It is extremely important to understand that a will only governs assets held solely in your name. Assets that already have named beneficiaries, jointly held property with rights of survivorship, and transfer on death accounts (TOD) are examples that pass to another automatically upon your death as a matter of law. These different types of ownership are discussed later in this chapter. You should be aware that a will becomes effective only upon your death and after it is probated, i.e., goes through the court process and is validated by a judge. You can change your will at any time prior to your death, assuming that you still possess the legal capacity to execute the document.

Creating a Trust for a Specific Beneficiary(ies)

A trust is a legal entity arrangement involving three parties: the *trust maker* (commonly referred to as a trustor, grantor, or settlor), the *trustee* (can be a natural person or an entity such as a trust bank), and the *trust beneficiary*.

There are many types of trusts used for different purposes. Some trusts, called *inter vivos trusts*, or *living trusts*, are created during one's life and are generally revocable during life. These trusts are separate legal entities that can contain provisions relevant during your life and, like a will, spell out how you want your property distributed upon your death. Others, called testamentary trusts, are contained within wills and only take effect upon death. If used properly, a trust can be a very effective estate planning tool that can accomplish such things as avoiding probate, minimizing taxes and postmortem legal fees, protecting assets, and simplifying the distribution of your assets to your intended beneficiaries. Trusts can also hold assets and provide a structured distribution for minors and individuals with disabilities. Trusts let you customize the distribution of your estate with the added advantages of property management. They are covered in more detail later in this chapter.

Designating a Health Care Proxy

A *health care proxy* is a legal document in which you designate an individual to make decisions regarding your health care treatment if you are incapacitated and unable to provide informed consent. This is also known as a *durable power of attorney for health care*. The person you designate can generally make decisions regarding medical facilities, treatments, surgery, and a variety of other health care matters. Much like a durable power of attorney, the health care proxy involves important decisions. Therefore, you should take extreme care when choosing who will make them on your behalf.

As Christina Pasaturo, estate and eldercare planning attorney at Lenza Law Firm, explains,

> You have the right to appoint one individual or multiple people as your health care proxies to make medical decisions on your behalf, though I recommend choosing an odd number if selecting more than one to help prevent disagreements or stalemates during critical times.

A health care proxy provides an individual with control over the type and level of health care the individual will receive, after that individual becomes incapable of making the decision personally because of his or her mental and/or physical state. This proxy provides the most flexibility for a health care agent to make decisions based on the day-to-day conditions of a patient. This document is solely used for health care decisions and should not be confused with the general power of attorney.

The cost of medical treatment is significant, especially when there are prolonged serious medical conditions involved. Making your wishes clear through a health care proxy can help ensure that care aligns with your values and can save your estate considerable expense on unwanted or unnecessary treatments.

Establishing a Living Will

A *living will*, also known as a *directive to physicians* or an *advanced health care directive*, spells out the kinds of life-sustaining treatment you desire in the event you are determined to be at an end-of-life stage or incurably ill with no hope of recovery. It gives doctors and hospitals your instructions regarding the nature and extent of the care you want should you suffer permanent incapacity, such as an irreversible coma or brain damage, or be deemed to be in a persistent vegetative state. This may address life support services of various kinds, from respiratory assistance to feeding tubes.

Unlike a health care proxy, a living will does not appoint an individual to make decisions for you and does not require actions on anyone's part. Instead, the directive provides written instructions directly from you to the attending physician. The decision for or against life support is one that only you should make. That makes the living will a valuable estate planning document.

When people discuss this difficult but necessary topic, many say they would choose not to prolong their lives if they are suffering from a terminal and painful illness. This is especially true if prolonging their lives will wipe them out financially and not allow them to provide for their loved ones. This is a difficult and sensitive topic, and every individual should have the right to make his or her choices known through a living will.

A living will may be used in conjunction with a durable power of attorney for health care. Bear in mind that laws governing the recognition and treatment of living wills vary from state to state. Nonetheless, it is important that you make your wishes known in writing so that loved ones are not burdened with making these difficult decisions on your behalf.

Designating Durable Power of Attorney

A durable power of attorney is a legal agreement that enables you to designate who will make your legal and financial decisions. This document may be necessary to avoid the need for guardianship or conservatorship. Unlike a standard or nondurable power of attorney, durable powers remain valid before and even after you become incapacitated. For this power to be valid, you must have legal capacity and mental competency when you execute the document.

A durable power of attorney appoints a person you designate to act for you in handling financial matters, should you be unable or perhaps unavailable to do so. This power of attorney may include delegating control over all of your assets and belongings, including real property, such as your primary residence and other real estate, bank accounts, securities or investment accounts, and so on. It can be as broad or as restrictive as you desire.

A power of attorney that is not valid on its execution is called a *springing power of attorney* because the powers spring out at some time in the future. Usually, this is prepared for an individual who does not trust giving someone full power of attorney at the time of its execution. A common problem with a springing power of attorney is that, in the event that you need the agent's powers to start upon your incapacity, an agent may not be comfortable accepting the power of attorney until a court order or medical attestation certifies that you are legally incompetent or incapacitated. This is often a very long and costly process, and the power of attorney may not be legally valid at the time you need to use it, thus defeating the purpose of having it executed in the first place.

Any power of attorney should be used only if you have complete trust in the person to whom you are granting the powers. That individual has the capability to misappropriate your assets at any time without your knowledge, which may be illegal in addition to being unethical. Therefore, your decision on which type of power of attorney to execute requires very careful consideration. You should exercise extreme caution when providing someone with this level of control.

The Probate and Administration Process: Why You May Want to Avoid It

Surrogate courts or probate courts are special courts of law that have specific jurisdiction over proceedings related to the settlement of a decedent's estate. If you die and have a will (testate), your will must generally be probated in order to have it legally recognized.

The legal definition of *probate* is "the act of proving that an instrument purporting to be a Last Will and Testament was executed in accordance with legal requirements and of determining its validity thereby." Your estate will go through the *administration process if you die without a valid will.* In this instance, you are considered to have died *intestate,* and the intestacy laws of your state of residence will determine who will receive your assets.

The major problems associated with both probate and administration include high administrative costs, lengthy delays, retention of assets, and court involvement and supervision, not to mention all the added legal and accounting fees. Disgruntled family members and close friends can also pose a problem to probate by contesting the validity of your Will. Probate and administrative costs can typically range from 3% to 7% of the estate's total value, depending on factors such as complexity, state law, and professional fees.

As Christina Pasaturo emphasizes,

> In some states, even if you have a valid will in place, the probate process still legally requires that your next of kin be notified, regardless of your relationship with them.

> This opens the door for estranged relatives, or even those you've never met, to come out of the woodwork seeking a payday or attempting to contest the will, which can drag out the process and increase costs. In fact, I often see cases where the Surrogate's Court mandates hiring a genealogist to track down distant family members, adding significant expense and delays to the administration of the estate.

These are major reasons to avoid going through probate or administration and applying some of the strategies outlined in this chapter can help accomplish this.

If you are a private person and do not look favorably on disclosing your personal finances to others, you should be aware that the proceedings of the probate courts are a matter of public record open to anyone interested in knowing your personal financial affairs. Moreover, if you own real estate in more than one state, more than one probate proceeding may be necessary.

Properly titling your property, naming beneficiaries, and establishing trusts may allow your estate to pass to your heirs without having to go through the probate or administration processes. Spending a few thousand dollars on estate planning while you are alive can ultimately save your beneficiaries a significant amount of money, headaches, and delays. Also, this process may allow you to be in complete control over the distribution of your estate after your death.

Estate Planning Strategies That Keep You in Control After Your Death

If you want to maintain control of the distribution of your estate after your death, there are several planning strategies you may want to implement while you are alive. Each of these provides a different degree of control over distribution, and each has different pros and cons. You need to understand how your property will be distributed when you die with or without a will, some form of joint ownership, beneficiary-designated contractual agreements, or a trust.

Understanding how each of these estate planning strategies works and interacts with one another is essential to properly controlling the distribution of your estate after your death. If you do not take all these facts into consideration during the estate planning process, the results could be dramatically different than what you had intended.

What Happens to Your Estate When You Have a Will and When You Do Not

As mentioned, when someone dies without a will, that is called dying *intestate*. When that happens, the laws of your state will determine how the assets are distributed. These laws are generally based on your family tree, or genealogy.

When a blood relative or living descendent cannot be located, the state may then be entitled to take ownership of all your estate; this is the common law doctrine known as *escheat*, which originated in the Roman Empire and was later established as a key part of the English feudal system in 1066. If you have not implemented any estate tax planning strategies and you do not have a will, you are going to have the least control over the distribution of your assets and the fulfillment of your last wishes.

Having a will is the most basic estate planning strategy, especially if you are not willing to implement any other strategies. Another essential reason to have a will is if you have minor children. If both parents die at the same time (for example, in a car accident or plane crash), it is best if you have already directed in advance who will care for your children.

As Barry Holt explains,

> In most states, these documents are referred to as a Guardianship Directive for Minor Children, which if properly drafted and executed, are typically honored by the respective court of competent jurisdiction.

You would not want any of your family members fighting over legal custody of your children. Avoiding potential family conflicts over child custody will not only eliminate the expensive legal process, but it will be more likely that family members will work in harmony in looking out for your children's best interests.

With the exception of individuals with minor children, the following represents situations where a will may not be necessary:

- If you have no assets in your individual name (for example, if all your assets are either jointly held or are in the name of a trust for others) or if all the assets in your name have designated beneficiaries other than your estate (for example, if you have a named beneficiary for your life insurance or IRA account), then all of your assets will be transferred by operation of law. In these cases, you may not need to retain an estate attorney to draft a will, but at a bare minimum you can consider a dot com solution (i.e., Trust & Will), which would be better than dying intestate.

- If you want to leave your assets to your beneficiaries in the same proportion as predetermined by your state's laws, you may not need a will to accomplish this. In this case, if you die with or without a will, your individual beneficiaries will receive the same inheritance. Note, however, that without a will, you will not have a say in who your legal representative will be. Therefore, a will is necessary when your wishes are different from your state's predetermined (default) allocations or when you want complete control over the settling of your estate.

By having a properly drafted will, you can decide who will ultimately inherit your assets. You can also choose your executor and set up any trusts that you may want to have in force after death. The *executor* is someone you appoint in your will to carry out your last wishes, as outlined in your testament.

Generally, the only people who can contest (dispute) a will are people who would be entitled to receive a certain percentage of your estate if you die without a will. For example, if you are a widow or widower and have three living children, your three children would equally receive your estate, under all state intestacy laws (provided you do not have a trust naming someone else to receive some or all of your assets). However, suppose you execute a will and decide to exclude one of your children. When you pass away and the will is offered for probate, the excluded child has standing to contest the will because he or she will be receiving less than he or she would have received under the intestacy laws (namely one-third of the estate).

However, it is important to remember that someone who has standing to contest a will cannot contest the will on the grounds that he or she does not like its terms. Instead, that person must allege and prove in court that the will was not properly executed in accordance with the formal requirements of the state, or that the person (e.g., you) did not have the requisite capacity to make the will at the time of its execution.

As Christina Pasaturo explains,

> In some states, when a will is drafted by an attorney and its execution is supervised by that attorney, there is a legal presumption that the will was properly executed in accordance with statutory requirements, making it more difficult to challenge during probate. This presumption shifts the burden to those contesting the will to prove that proper formalities were not followed.

If someone contests the will and is successful, then the will is declared void and the estate will be distributed in accordance with the state intestacy laws or in accordance with the provisions of an earlier will, if you had one.

Many states have begun recognizing electronic wills that are created, signed, and stored digitally, provided they meet specific legal requirements. These may include the use of secure electronic signature technology, witness participation either in person or via approved video conferencing, and storage of the will in a secure electronic repository. While electronic wills can offer convenience, traditional paper wills remain the most widely accepted nationwide. If you are considering an electronic will, consult an attorney who is familiar with the laws of your state to ensure that the document is valid and enforceable.

What Happens to Your Estate When You Have Beneficiary-designated Contractual Agreements

Yet another estate planning strategy to control your assets after death is through a *contractual agreement by beneficiary designation.* For example, if you have a retirement plan through your employer, an IRA, life insurance, or an annuity contract, you can and should designate a beneficiary. The rights to the proceeds from these contracts will automatically pass to the individual(s) you designate as your beneficiary. Using a designated beneficiary on these contracts typically has the added benefit of avoiding probate on those specific assets.

Alternatively, you can also designate your estate as the beneficiary, if you want the asset to be transferred in accordance with your will. Unfortunately, this makes these assets subject to probate; therefore, it is generally best to avoid this choice, if possible. It is extremely important to review these contracts to make sure your beneficiary designations reflect your current wishes because these contractual agreements supersede the intentions you state in your will.

What Happens to Your Estate When You Have a Trust

Perhaps the most flexible estate planning strategy that allows you to control your assets before and after your death is creating a trust. A trust can be created while you are alive (called an *inter vivos trust*) or after your death through your will (called *a testamentary trust*). A trust can give you the maximum control over the distribution of your estate after your death because the terms of a trust provide the trustee with your specific instructions.

A trust can have the added advantage of using the services of professional asset managers, who can protect your assets in the event of your incapacity. When a trust is set up properly, you can use it as a mechanism to significantly reduce your gift and estate tax liabilities. Later in this chapter, the many estate planning strategies that can be implemented with a trust will be covered in detail. When evaluating whether a trust strategy is appropriate for you, you should consider the upfront costs and ongoing administrative and professional fees to maintain it.

Using a Planned Gifting Strategy

For 2025, the gift tax exclusion is $19,000 per year. This means that you can make a gift in this amount to anyone, and to as many people as you like, every calendar year, and that money will not be subject to gift tax or included in your taxable estate. Furthermore, it will not be subtracted from your lifetime exemption of $13.99 million for 2025 ($15 million for 2026). This amount can be increased to $38,000 per year if a nondonor spouse agrees to split the gift. This can be a great way to transfer assets to children, grandchildren, and other intended heirs while you are still alive. Ultimately, this will reduce the taxable value of your estate and your ultimate estate tax liability at the same time.

In theory, if you and your spouse want to gift $38,000 to 10 people this year, you could reduce your estate by $380,000. Based on the 2025 federal estate flat tax rate of 40%, you would save your estate $152,000, assuming you would have a taxable estate upon death. With a properly structured lifetime gifting program, you could significantly reduce and in some cases completely eliminate any potential estate tax liability.

Two of the most overlooked exceptions to the gift tax exclusion limitation have to do with tuition and medical payments, specifically:

1. Any qualified tuition payments made on behalf of a donee beneficiary (for example, your child or grandchild) are not considered a gift if you make the payment directly to the educational institution.
2. Any medical payments made on behalf of a donee beneficiary are also not considered a gift if you make the payment directly to the medical provider.

Therefore, you can pay an unlimited amount of someone's college tuition directly to the school and still be permitted to give an additional $19,000 directly to the donee beneficiary without affecting your lifetime exemption. Thus, you may want to consider paying your children's and grandchildren's tuition directly to the institution, as one of your valuable estate planning tools.

Ownership of Property and How It's Transferred After Death

A critical part of the estate planning process revolves around how the ownership of property (including real estate and any other assets you hold title to) is treated and ultimately how it is transferred to your beneficiaries. In fact, the way you hold title to your property will take precedence over provisions contained in other documents, such as your will. Many times, people may execute a will with the intention of leaving some of their property to individuals, yet those individuals do not receive what was intended by the decedent because all decedent's property was jointly held with others.

For example, here is a very common scenario where a decedent's wishes may be overwritten by operation of law. A parent (often a widow or widower) may have joint bank accounts with only one of his or her children, for convenience purposes. This is usually done with a child who is the primary caregiver for that parent or who handles the parent's banking. The parent makes a will leaving all of his or her assets equally to his or her children. When the parent passes away, those bank accounts become the legal property of the child that had joint ownership over them. Therefore, the legal title of the account passes by operation of law and supersedes the intention of the parent as stated in the will.

For this reason, it is extremely important for you to verify the ownership of property and how it is held. You can either gain or lose significant tax benefits, depending on how you structure the ownership of your property. The following are the four basic forms of legal ownership to property. Understanding the differences between them can have a considerable impact on how your estate assets are ultimately transferred.

Individual Ownership

Individual ownership occurs when one person owns a 100% interest in a property. For example, if you own a piece of real estate, a bank account, or a brokerage account and your name is designated as the only owner, this would be considered individual ownership. Through an estate, ownership is passed in accordance with a will or by the laws of intestacy. The complete value is included in the gross taxable estate of the decedent.

When two or more persons own property, it is said to be held *concurrently*. There are several types of concurrent ownership, including *tenancy in common, joint tenancy*, and *tenancy by the entirety*.

Tenancy in Common

Tenancy in common is the most common type of concurrent ownership in property. In this context, *tenant* means *owner* (not *renter*, as it does in everyday language). Each tenant (*owner*) has the right to convey his or her interest in the property. This means every owner has equal rights to use and enjoy the entire property, even if their ownership shares are unequal. Importantly, each owner's share can be sold, transferred, or left to heirs. When one of the tenants (*co-owners*) dies, that tenant's interest passes to his or her heirs or by will to someone else. With this type of property ownership, each owner has an undivided fractional share of the property.

For example, suppose you own a house with your husband, and the deed to your house is held by tenancy in common. If your husband dies, his share of the house does not automatically transfer to you. Instead, his ownership interest becomes part of his estate and will pass to his heirs under his will or by state intestacy laws. This can mean that you end up co-owning the property with his heirs rather than becoming the sole owner. To ensure that ownership automatically passes to the surviving co-owner, the property would need to be held as "joint tenants," which is explained in the next section.

Joint Tenancy

Joint tenancy exists when two or more persons share equal, undivided whole interests in the property. The key feature of joint tenancy is the right of survivorship, whereby, upon the death of one of the joint tenants, his interest is automatically passed to the others by operation of law and cannot be transferred in accordance with a will or trust document.

An added benefit of joint tenancy is that it avoids probate with respect to this asset. Anyone can share joint interests, but there are additional tax benefits when this arrangement is shared between a husband and wife, which is known as a *qualified joint tenancy*. Under qualified joint tenancy, half of the property is included in the first decedent's estate. Because of this, the surviving spouse obtains a stepped-up basis on the first decedent's half of the property. A *stepped-up basis* allows the beneficiary to value the property at the decedent's date of death for tax purposes, and this value is used to determine gain or loss upon the eventual sale of the asset. Quite simply, the cost for determining gain or loss is based on the property's value after death rather than on what the decedent actually paid for it. If any nonspouses participate in joint ownership, the entire value of the property is includable in the decedent's estate, reduced only to the extent that the estate can prove that the surviving tenant contributed to the cost of the property in proportion to his or her share.

Community property, which applies only in certain states (Arizona, California, Idaho, Louisiana, Nevada, New Mexico, Texas, Washington, and Wisconsin), offers an even greater tax advantage. At the death of the first spouse, the entire property (not just half) receives a full step-up in basis to its fair market value. This can eliminate capital gains tax on appreciation that occurred during the couple's ownership when the surviving spouse, or subsequent heirs, later sells the property.

Tenancy by the Entirety

Tenancy by the entirety is another form of concurrent ownership, like joint tenancy, but it can only be created between spouses. In states recognizing tenancy by the entirety, when a married couple owns real property, the presumption is that it is held as a tenancy by the entirety.

To own property as tenants in common, the married couple would have to specifically state their wishes as such. Neither spouse can convey his or her interest without the express consent of the other.

One of the main advantages to this type of joint ownership is that it offers protection from creditors. A creditor generally cannot place a lien against property held under tenancy by the entirety in a state where both spouses must act together. Therefore, this property may be exempt under bankruptcy proceedings if only one of the spouses is the debtor of the creditor. Neither party can alienate or encumber the property individually, so that upon the death of one spouse, it is inherited by the surviving spouse.

In the event of a divorce, it becomes a tenancy in common, since tenancy by the entirety could only exist between spouses. Tenancy by the entirety is recognized in a limited number of states (approximately half of US states and the District of Columbia). Check with your attorney to see if your state allows this form of joint ownership; it may be vital to maintaining your financial independence in the event creditors try to put a claim against your property.

Amount Includable in the Estate and the Stepped-up Basis

The amount includable in the estate of a decedent is based on his or her percentage of ownership. It is important to remember that the beneficiary can be chosen by the decedent, except in the case of joint tenancy or tenancy by the entirety, in which the surviving tenants automatically inherit the interest of the decedent.

There are major tax benefits to the beneficiary of property from an estate. The beneficiary of the property interest receives a stepped-up basis, as of the fair market value on the date of death or the alternative valuation date (six months later, if elected and applicable under IRS rules). The beneficiary may be able to avoid or minimize capital gains tax on the sale of this asset because their cost basis is increased to this estate valuation.

Here is a common scenario of the benefit from this stepped-up basis: a widow or widower passes away while owning real property. The children inherit the property either through a will or through administration (if there is no will, as described at the beginning of this chapter). The house is valued at $750,000, and the children sell it within a year for $750,000, with closing fees of $30,000. In this example, the children will collectively realize a $30,000 loss on their personal tax returns. If this asset is the only asset in the estate, it will not be subject to estate taxes, and the beneficiaries still receive the stepped-up basis. They not only receive the property free of estate tax but may also be able to get an income tax deduction from the costs of selling the property.

Reasons for Creating a Trust

As mentioned earlier, perhaps the most flexible estate planning strategy that allows you to control your estate before and after death is creating a trust. A trust can take effect while you are alive (an *inter vivos* trust) or after death through your will (a *testamentary* trust). A trust can give you maximum control over the distribution of your estate after death because the terms of a trust will provide the trustee with your specific instructions.

A trust is a powerful legal instrument designed to safeguard and manage your assets while ensuring both current and future beneficiaries are protected. There are three key parties involved in the creation of a trust.

- The first party is the *trustor*, sometimes called the *settlor or grantor of the trust,* which is the individual who establishes and funds the trust.
- The second party is the trustee, which can be a person or an institution. The trustee is entrusted to hold legal title to property in order to administer it for the benefit of the beneficiary in accordance with the trust document.
- The third party is the *beneficiary* (or beneficiaries), who eventually receive 100% distribution of the trust *corpus.* (The trust corpus refers to all property transferred to a trust. For example, if a trust is funded with $100,000 in cash, that money is considered the trust corpus.)

All trusts can be specifically defined and classified after asking the following questions.

1. Was the trust created during an individual's lifetime or upon his death?
   - If the trust was created to be effective during an individual's lifetime through a separate legal document (a trust document), it is considered an *inter vivos trust.*
   - If the trust was created to take effect after death within a Last Will and Testament, it is considered a *testamentary trust.*

2. Can the trust be changed, altered, amended, or revoked by the trustor?
   - If the answer to this question is yes, then this is considered a *revocable trust.*
   - If the answer to this question is no, then this is considered an *irrevocable trust.*
3. For federal income tax purposes, how is the trust classified and taxed?
   - Grantor trust
   - Simple trust
   - Complex trust
4. How does the trust define income?
   - A trust document's definition of income is considered its accounting income, and this can be different than the tax law definition of income. These definitions can have a significant impact on distributions and taxation to both the trust and the beneficiaries.

A living trust (inter vivos) is a trust that is set up during your lifetime and takes effect when you transfer assets into the trust. It can be either revocable or irrevocable. A living trust can be used to transfer legal titles to property, including cash, stocks, and real estate, and can provide a means to manage these assets during your lifetime. Although these asset transfers change the legal title, you (as the creator or grantor) can retain income from the assets throughout your lifetime. With a revocable living trust, you generally retain control and decision-making authority over the assets, while an irrevocable living trust typically limits or eliminates your ability to control the assets after transfer.

These types of trusts are frequently used as a substitute for a will because the trust usually terminates upon the death of the grantor and the trust documents dictate who the beneficiaries of the assets will be. You can also select the person you want as the trustee, which could include yourself in a revocable living trust, to carry out the instructions set out in the trust document. You can name successor trustees to take over if and when you can no longer act as the trustee. Last but not least, a living trust helps you avoid and minimize the administrative expenses, delays, and publicity involved with probate, because these trust assets transfer by operation of law.

In contrast, a *testamentary trust* is a trust created through a will and only takes effect when you die. With these trusts, the legal title to the assets does not transfer until your death. There is no separate legal trust document; it is created by a clause in your will. One of the pitfalls of a testamentary trust is that it will *not* avoid probate because the trust can be created only through the probate of a will.

Family relationships have become an increasingly significant factor in estate planning. Many families worry about how their heirs will handle an inheritance and whether they have the maturity or discipline to manage it wisely. Concerns often center on issues such as substance abuse, reckless spending habits, unstable marriages, or the influence of a child's spouse.

As Christina Pasaturo points out,

> For young couples with children, creating a living trust is a smart and practical step, as it allows their assets to be marshaled into the trust and easily managed; so that if, God forbid, the worst should happen, the guardians and trustees they've carefully chosen will have immediate access to those assets, without court delays, to care for and support their children. Depending on how the trust is drafted, those same trustees may also be able to access and manage the funds if the parents are still alive but become gravely injured or incapacitated, ensuring continuity and stability during a difficult time.

These are just some of the situations where trust planning can be an effective tool. By placing assets in a trust, you can establish clear terms that control how and when a beneficiary will receive those assets. This allows you to guide and protect your heirs well beyond your lifetime. Because these matters are deeply personal, it is important to address them openly with your financial advisor and estate planning attorney.

Revocable and Irrevocable Trusts

Most trusts are *revocable* (in other words, you retain full control); if you create a revocable trust, you can serve as the trustee, make future changes, and even terminate the trust. On the other hand, if the trust is irrevocable, you give up a certain degree of control; therefore, changes and termination are dependent on the terms of the trust and sometimes can be very difficult to make.

When you transfer assets into a revocable trust, the transfer is not considered a completed gift. As a result, you do not have to file a gift tax return, which is required when a gift exceeds $19,000 in any given year (as of 2025). However, upon the death of the trustor (you, as the creator of the trust), the assets of a revocable trust are included in your taxable estate. They are considered part of your estate because you retained beneficial ownership and control of those assets. While revocable trusts do not minimize estate taxes, they do avoid probate or administration, since trust assets pass to your beneficiaries in accordance with the trust document you created.

Living trusts allow you to control the distribution of your estate, and certain trusts may help reduce or avoid some of the taxes and fees imposed on your estate after your death. When you establish a revocable living trust, you are permitted to be the trustor, the trustee, and the beneficiary of that trust. By setting up a living trust, you transfer ownership of selected assets from yourself to the trust. You are no longer the legal owner of the assets you placed in your trust. Your trust is now the legal owner, even though as the trustee, you maintain complete control of these assets during your lifetime.

A-B Trusts

One of the most common types of living trusts is an *A–B trust,* also known as a *bypass trust* or *credit shelter trust.* Historically, these trusts were designed to ensure that both spouses could fully use their estate tax exemptions by dividing assets into two trusts upon the death of the first spouse: the "A" trust (survivor's trust), which holds the surviving spouse's share, and the "B" trust (deceased spouse trust), which holds the deceased spouse's share. Although the federal "portability" law now allows the surviving spouse to use any unused portion of the deceased spouse's *federal* estate tax exemption without the need for an A–B trust, many couples still choose this structure for reasons such as *state* estate tax planning, protecting assets for children, and maintaining control over the ultimate distribution of wealth.

The surviving spouse retains full control of his or her own trust ("A" trust). He or she can also receive income from the deceased spouse's trust ("B" trust) and may withdraw principal for health, support, or maintenance as needed. Upon the death of the second spouse, the assets of both trusts pass directly to the heirs and avoid probate.

With the enactment of the 2010 Tax Relief Act, federal "portability" was introduced, enabling a surviving spouse to claim the unused estate tax exemption of the deceased spouse, reducing the benefit of an A-B trust for federal purposes. That portability remains in effect for 2025; a late portability election may still be made up to five years after the first spouse's death.

It is critically important to note that many states have their own estate or inheritance tax laws you will need to consider. Most of these states do not adopt the federal concept of portability (however, Maryland and Hawaii do allow portability of their state estate tax exemption). Therefore, if you are married and leave all your assets to your surviving spouse in a state without portability, he or she will only be able to use his or her own state exemption, and your unused exemption will be permanently lost.

Although A-B trusts may not be as beneficial for federal tax purposes as they were in the past, they should still be fully utilized by married couples, especially if they live in states that impose their own estate tax without portability. Furthermore, a trust provides you with the ability to shelter the appreciation of assets placed in the trust. It may also protect these assets from creditors and allow you to preserve the state estate tax exemptions for both you and your spouse.

How a Trust Is Taxed

How a trust is classified and taxed for federal income tax purposes depends on the type of trust involved. When determining which type of trust would be most suitable to meet your financial objectives, it is important to understand how different trusts are taxed.

For federal income tax purposes, there are three types of trusts:

1. **Grantor trust:** For income tax purposes, the trust is treated as if it does not exist. All income in a grantor trust is reported on the trustor's personal income tax return as if the trust was never created. All revocable trusts are considered grantor trusts and are taxed in this manner. Some irrevocable trusts are treated as grantor trusts when the terms of the irrevocable trust creates a grantor trust for income tax purposes.

2. **Simple trust:** All income must be distributed and is taxed at the income beneficiary level. Even if the income is not properly distributed, it can be deemed distributed for tax purposes.
3. **Complex trust:** The trustee has certain discretion and can either distribute or not distribute the income to the beneficiaries. Any income not distributed to the beneficiaries is taxed at the trust level and at the trust's tax rate. The trustee has up to 65 days after the close of the trust year to make a distribution, which would be considered made during the previous tax year.

A complex trust is taxed in a manner similar to personal individual income taxation, except the tax rates are compressed and the trust is subject to the maximum tax rate at a much lower threshold. Income earned by a trust will either be taxed at the trust level or at the income beneficiary level. A trust is permitted to take an income distribution deduction against the trust income for all income that is properly distributed from the trust.

Under current law, the following are the tax brackets on income taxable to the trust and estates in 2025:

- 10% on taxable income up to $3,150
- 24% on taxable income over $3,150 but not over $11,450
- 35% on taxable income over $11,450 but not over $15,650
- 37% on taxable income over $15,650

In addition to the above income tax, a trust or estate must pay a 3.8% Medicare tax on net investment income under the Patient Protection and Affordable Care Act. The tax is imposed on the lesser of "undistributed net investment income" or excess of adjusted gross income over the dollar amount at which the highest tax bracket begins, which would be the excess of $15,650 for 2025.

Transfers with Retained Life Interests

When assets are transferred and the transferor retains the use and enjoyment of the transferred asset for the remainder of his or her life, the rules of Internal Revenue Code Section 2036 apply. This is most common when individuals transfer real property to their children and retain a "life estate" interest in the property for themselves.

This simple transfer is fairly common, as it accomplishes the following benefits to estate planning:

- This asset avoids probate or administration of your will when you die, as the property is already titled in your children's name.
- By retaining the "life estate," the IRS still considers the assets owned by you for estate tax purposes, meaning your children will generally be entitled to a stepped-up basis at your death. Without the "life estate," the transfer may be considered an outright gift, and your children would not be entitled to a stepped-up basis.
- The life estate also protects you in case of a dispute between you and your children because it keeps you from being disturbed or evicted from the property. Even in the best families, children may get divorced, predecease their parents, or have conflicts that may impact their decision to try to remove you from your house.

Caution should be exercised, however, in transferring real property to children, even when reserving a life estate interest. First, the transfer would be deemed irrevocable, meaning you would need the consent of the transferee(s) should you decide that you want the property back. Secondly, by titling your property in another's name, it will become vulnerable to that person's life events, such as divorce, bankruptcy, lawsuits, and even death. This is another reason why some people are choosing to title real estate in an irrevocable trust. Since, with this type of transfer, ownership does not vest in the transferee until your death, the property is not subject to the listed vulnerabilities.

Split-interest Trusts

Certain trusts are established with the stipulation that there will be an *income beneficiary* as well as a *remainder beneficiary for the assets transferred into the trust.* A remainder beneficiary of a trust is entitled to the principal of the trust outright after the interest of the prior beneficiary has been terminated. These types of trusts are referred to as *split-interest trusts* and include the following:

- Grantor-retained income trust (GRIT)
- Grantor-retained annuity trust (GRAT)

- Grantor-retained unitrust (GRUT)
- Qualified personal residence trust (QPRT)

The major advantage of establishing these split-interest trusts include the following:

- You (as the trustor) continue to control the income for a set period.
- There is an objective discount in the value of the gifted asset at the time the gift is made, based on the value of the retained interest.
- All future growth of the asset remains outside of the taxable estate of the trustor (transferor).

These three points are critical components of several sophisticated estate planning techniques. The value of the gift can be significantly reduced by the value of the retained interest by the transferor. Because the value of the gift is significantly reduced by implementing this strategy, you can minimize and, in certain cases, eliminate the gift tax consequence of the transfer. If someone makes a gift of a future interest in a property and retains the right to use that property for a period, they are deemed to have given only a partial interest.

For example, let us assume you gave a gift of stock with a current fair market value of $500,000 to a trust, but you retained the right to all income generated by this gift for a set period of 20 years. You will need to determine the present value of this future gift to be completed 20 years from now. The IRS allows you to use the present value of this future gift of $500,000, 20 years from now, which is discounted based on the applicable IRS long-term interest rate. For the purpose of our example, we will assume that the IRS long-term interest rate has been set at 5% at the time of the gift.

Therefore, the future value (FV) of the gift is set at $500,000, the applicable long-term interest rate (i) is equal to 5%, and the number of periods (n) is equal to 20. At this point, you would turn to Chapter 12, "The Time Value of Money," Exhibit 12.4 "PV Factor of a Sum Certain." Go to the 5% column, and then go down the row for 20 years, to find the factor of 0.37689.

In other words, based on the present value factor table, the IRS will allow you to objectively discount the value of this gift from $500,000 to $188,445 ($500,000 × 0.37689). This technique will allow you to transfer $500,000 to the trust for the benefit of your beneficiaries and will only use up $188,445 of your lifetime exclusion. Therefore, if you ultimately have a taxable estate upon death, you have reduced your taxable estate by $311,555 ($500,000 – $188,445). Assuming the estate tax rate upon your death is 40%, this will result in a reduction of your estate tax liability by $124,622 ($311,555 × 40%). In addition, any future appreciation in the value of this $500,000 stock will not be included in your estate.

The only catch is that you (the transferor) must live beyond the 20-year period established by this trust. If you die before the completion of this gift (which, in this example, is 20 years), the full value of the stock as of your date of death will be included in your estate. That would defeat the whole purpose of establishing split-interest trust. Therefore, the biggest pitfall in using this technique is that the trust must terminate before you die. If it does not, the trust assets are valued as a part of your estate, and these assets will be included as of the date of death value.

To highlight the significance of this estate planning technique, let us assume that the $500,000 is worth $2 million on your date of death, which is 21 years after the stock was transferred into the trust. One of the major advantages of transferring property out of your estate while you are alive is that all future capital appreciation will avoid being included in your estate valuation upon your death. Once again, this is a powerful technique for minimizing your estate tax liability and maximizing the amount passed on to your heirs. Let us assume that your estate would have been subject to the estate tax rate of 40%; this technique would have reduced the ultimate federal estate tax liability by $724,622 ($2,000,000 – $188,445 = $1,811,555 × 40%).

This is a somewhat complex estate tax planning technique, but a very effective one for preserving your estate and ultimately maximizing the amount you pass on to your loved ones. This is yet another powerful tool to create and maintain generational wealth. Please note that the tax planning technique known as a split-interest has been significantly limited by the creation of Internal Revenue Code Section 2702.

You should consult with an experienced estate tax attorney and financial planner to determine whether using a split-interest trust would be beneficial to you. These are advanced estate tax planning techniques and can only be properly used with the guidance of an estate tax attorney that specializes in these matters.

The "Charitable" Trust

Charitable trusts are created when you have a charitable intent and would also like to accomplish the following:

- Maintain control of principal or income for a period
- Potentially receive an immediate charitable deduction during your lifetime
- Potentially eliminate capital gains tax on appreciated assets
- Potentially eliminate or reduce estate taxes

These types of trust include the following:

- Charitable lead annuity trust (CLAT)
- Charitable lead unitrust (CLUT)
- Charitable remainder unitrust (CRUT)
- Charitable remainder annuity trust (CRAT)

Charitable lead and charitable remainder trusts operate similarly to the split-interest trusts discussed earlier. The key distinction is that the benefits are divided between charitable and noncharitable beneficiaries. The present value calculations and the estate reduction benefits are comparable, with the added advantage of receiving a charitable deduction.

In a *charitable remainder trust* (CRAT or CRUT), your spouse, children, or other beneficiaries receive income from the trust for a specified term, and the remaining assets ultimately pass to a qualified charitable organization under Section 501(c)(3) of the Internal Revenue Code.

Conversely, in a *charitable lead trust* (CLAT or CLUT), the charity receives income from the trust for a set number of years, and the remaining assets are then distributed to your heirs or other noncharitable beneficiaries.

Although using one of the charitable trusts just discussed is an effective strategy, most people fulfill their charitable goals by simply giving cash or checks. Such contributions entitle you to a tax deduction in the year of the gift, provided you have a receipt or acknowledgment from the charity.

However, rather than donating cash, you can use more sophisticated gifting techniques that not only benefit the charitable organization but, if structured properly, can significantly reduce your income and estate taxes. Both you and the charity can benefit even more when your gift consists of highly appreciated property, such as stocks, real estate, or other investments.

If you own property that has increased in value and wish to make a charitable gift, you can maximize the benefit on both sides. By transferring the property directly to a qualified charity, you may receive an income tax deduction equal to the property's fair market value, and the charity can sell the asset without paying capital gains tax. This approach allows you to avoid recognizing the capital gain yourself while still receiving a larger charitable deduction, essentially allowing you to make the gift with pre-tax dollars.

When you combine a charitable trust with the donation of appreciated assets, both you as the donor and the charity as the recipient can achieve maximum benefit.

To qualify for these tax advantages, your contribution must be made to a qualified charitable organization. To meet IRS requirements, the organization must

- be organized in the United States;
- operate exclusively for charitable, religious, educational, scientific, or literary purposes;
- not participate in political or legislative activities;
- be formally recognized by the IRS as a Section 501(c)(3) organization.

In addition to these entities, contributions to veterans' organizations, certain fraternal societies, volunteer fire departments, and civil defense organizations may also qualify for tax-deductible treatment.

Using a Trust to Further Increase the Benefits of Charitable Gifting

There are several different gifting strategies available for planned giving, which include giving an outright gift to charity or setting up a charitable trust. Each has its own pros and cons, summarized in Exhibit 10.1.

Donor advised funds are designed for individuals who want to make a charitable contribution today, receive an immediate tax deduction, and retain flexibility in deciding when and where the funds ultimately benefit. With a donor advised fund, your

Exhibit 10.1 The Pros and Cons of Various Gifting Strategies

Gifting Strategy	Pros	Cons
Outright Gift	• Income tax-deductible in year of gift	• No retained interest or control after gifted
Donor Advised Funds	• Provides immediate tax deduction and allows tax-free growth while giving flexibility to choose charities later	• Once contributed, funds are irrevocable and may have administrative fees that reduce grantable dollars
Charitable Lead Trust	• Provides a current income stream to charity for a set term • Current income tax deduction (if structured as a grantor CLT) • Transfers assets at a future discounted value, reducing gift/estate taxes	• Charitable gift is irrevocable • Grantor CLT: with current income tax deduction, future income is taxable to the donor • Nongrantor CLT: no upfront income tax deduction • Donor gives up the use of income generated throughout the life of the trust
Charitable Remainder Unitrust	• Current income tax deduction • Avoids capital gains tax on appreciated property and reduces estate taxes	• Charitable gift irrevocable • Qualified appraisal commonly required • Complex administration and setup
Charitable Remainder Annuity Trust	• Current income tax deduction • Avoids capital gains tax on appreciated property • Fixed income stream	• Fixed payment is not limited to the net amount of trust income • Qualified appraisal commonly required • Complex administration and setup

contribution is placed into an account managed by a sponsoring organization, and you may recommend grants to your favorite public charities over time.

Historically, this has allowed taxpayers to group their charitable giving into years where they get the most tax benefit out of their donations. If you usually make regular contributions to multiple organizations, or you would like to simplify your giving while maximizing potential tax benefits, you may be an ideal candidate for a donor advised fund. Since starting in 2026, charitable donations will be subject to a 0.5% of AGI floor, donating to a donor advised fund in 2025 can be an ideal tax savings strategy since this stricter limitation will not apply.

When you contribute to a donor advised fund, you receive a charitable deduction based on the type of your contribution, whether cash, securities, or other appreciated assets. The assets in the fund can then be invested, allowing for potential tax-free growth, which may increase the ultimate amount available to distribute to your charities. Although the contribution is irrevocable, you maintain advisory privileges, meaning you can recommend how the funds are granted and when.

A donor advised fund allows you to centralize your charitable giving, simplify recordkeeping, and maximize tax benefits while still supporting the causes you care about over time. This could be a highly efficient and cost-effective alternative rather than establishing your own private foundation to meet your charitable, long-term goals.

Charitable lead trusts are designed for individuals who would like to see their charity benefit immediately from their gift. With a charitable lead trust, your gift can have an immediate benefit to your charity, and it may entitle you to benefit at the same time. If you usually make outright contributions to your charity, and you generally sell an appreciated investment and give all or some of the money to charity, you may be a perfect candidate to benefit from using a charitable trust.

With a charitable lead trust, you are actually gifting the asset's income to the charity, not gifting the actual asset. Your deduction will be based on the rate of return the charity can reasonably expect to receive, the duration of the trust, and the IRS valuation tables used in calculating the value of the gift. After the income from the gifted assets goes to the charity, the charity will then continue to receive distributions throughout the life of the trust. You can establish the life of the trust for a set number of years or for an individual's lifetime, including your own. Once this period has expired, the trust will terminate, and the remaining assets will be paid to you or your beneficiaries. If, during your lifetime, you are interested in increasing your gifts to charity as well as your tax benefits, a charitable lead trust may enable you to accomplish your goals. With a charitable lead trust, you can also pass an appreciated asset on to your heirs with little or no estate taxes.

Charitable remainder trusts allow you or your beneficiaries to receive payment of a specified amount annually, and at the end of the trust period, the designated charity receives the remainder assets. You can receive either a percentage (*charitable remainder unitrust*) of the value of the trust or a fixed amount (*charitable remainder annuity trust*). The trustee can sell off the highly appreciated assets gifted to the trust and then reinvest the proceeds to generate income and avoid capital gains tax. This strategy may allow you to both rebalance your investment portfolio without the typical tax consequences and shift your investments to high income-generating assets, which will improve your cash flow. Furthermore, you may also be eligible for a current year income tax deduction on the calculated present value of the remainder interest that will ultimately go to the charity at a future date. Although the gift to the trust is irrevocable, you do have control over which charity will eventually receive this gift.

Other Trusts and Related Strategies

Although the following trusts are beyond the scope of this book, we felt it would be useful to include a summary of them here. These strategies can be powerful tools, but whether they are appropriate for you and your family must be carefully evaluated with the guidance of an experienced estate planning attorney and financial planner.

- **Intentionally Defective Grantor Trust (IDGT):** Designed to move appreciating assets out of your taxable estate while you, as the grantor, continue paying the income taxes. This reduces your taxable estate without additional gift tax while allowing the trust assets to grow tax-free for your beneficiaries, an especially effective strategy for highly appreciating assets.
- **Spousal Lifetime Access Trust (SLAT):** Removes assets from your estate for tax purposes but still allows your spouse to access trust income or principal. This provides the dual benefit of reducing estate taxes while maintaining indirect access to funds, making SLATs a flexible option for married couples seeking both tax efficiency and financial security.
- **Dynasty Trust:** Built to preserve and grow wealth across multiple generations while minimizing estate, gift, and generation-skipping transfer taxes. By holding assets in a trust long-term, families can shield wealth from creditors, divorce settlements, and other risks, while supporting children, grandchildren, and beyond.
- **Qualified Terminable Interest Property Trust (QTIP):** Provides lifetime income to a surviving spouse while preserving the principal for other beneficiaries, often children from a prior marriage. This structure ensures the spouse is financially cared for while also guaranteeing that the remaining assets are distributed according to the grantor's wishes, making QTIPs especially valuable in blended family situations.

Summing Up What You Need to Know About Trusts

You must choose a trustee wisely and clearly state your intentions in the trust document. The beneficiary will ultimately assume ownership of the trust assets, even if this does not happen for decades. During the period in between, the trustee is in charge of controlling the assets in the trust and complying with the instructions in the trust document. Choosing someone who knows how to handle financial matters and will carry out your intentions is critically important to the successful utilization of these trust strategies. Trusts are highly complicated instruments that must strictly conform to tax rules and regulations, so you must consult with an experienced estate tax attorney and a financial planner before implementing these strategies.

Benefit from a Family Limited Partnership

If you own a family business, rental property, or a farm, you may have some additional estate planning hurdles to deal with down the road. If you are "hard asset rich" but cash poor, your family may be faced with liquidity problems upon your death, when it comes time to pay estate taxes. The federal government requires your executor or administrator to pay your estate tax liability within nine months of your date of death. Your family members may have no intention to sell any of the property you left behind for them, but they may be forced to do so to pay the estate taxes. The key goal of any estate planning strategy is to minimize estate taxes and to provide the necessary liquidity when the time comes. The main objective is to preserve the estate and to allow your family to continue to own and operate the family business, rental property, or farm.

The formation of a *family limited partnership* is another estate planning strategy to use in these situations. A family limited partnership is typically established as a separate legal entity to hold and manage a family business or investment property; it may also open up the opportunity to use various other estate and income tax planning strategies.

The family limited partnership agreement provides control to the parent and divides the right to the income, including future appreciation in value, among family members, in an attempt to provide financial and tax benefits to the overall family. These family partnerships typically commence by creating and transferring assets into a general limited partnership. As the parent, you can then start the process of gifting limited partnership interests (noncontrolling interests) to your children. You would continue to hold the general partnership interest (controlling interest), which makes the parent the partner with full control. The children would have no control as limited partners. You would continue to maintain and exercise complete control, even after your children become majority partners, so long as you remain the sole general partner. As limited partners, your children would share in the income of the family limited partnership in proportion to their ownership interests, which have been established through your gifts.

This estate tax planning strategy allows you to provide your children with an ownership interest while you are alive, while also allowing you to reduce your future estate tax liability with the added benefit of a succession plan for your family-owned business, property, or farm. You will be able to gift limited partnership interests to your children over time, which will allow you to take full advantage of the $19,000 annual gift tax exclusion for 2025 (or $38,000 if you are married and elect to split gifts) without giving them control of the money or property. If that was not reason enough, your children may also benefit by having their share of the income from this family limited partnership taxed at their potentially lower income tax rate.

The full value of the partnership interests transferred to your children while you are alive will escape inclusion in your taxable estate, including any appreciation in value after the date of transfer. This is a very powerful estate planning strategy if you can take advantage of it.

Irrevocable Life Insurance Trust

An *irrevocable life insurance trust* (ILIT) is another estate planning strategy that can be set up to hold life insurance policies, preventing the proceeds from being included in your taxable estate.

One of the key features of an ILIT is that it allows you to keep the life insurance death benefit out of the value of your estate. You (as the trustor) can make annual gifts to the trust in order for the trustee to pay for the life insurance premiums on your life that are owned by the trust. These gifts are made annually, up to $19,000 per beneficiary in 2025, which will also serve the purpose of further lowering the estate value and estate tax liability. Therefore, not only does the value of the estate get reduced by the gifts you make each year, but ultimately the entire death benefit will escape estate taxes on your death.

It is very important to note that you never want to own life insurance in your own name if the possibility exists that your estate may be large enough to be subject to estate taxes. The death benefit from life insurance held in your name will be included in your taxable estate. Based on the current federal estate tax rate, the federal government may be entitled to 40% of your death benefit. Although life insurance proceeds are generally not subject to income tax, they can and will be subject to estate taxes if they are owned by you and you have a taxable estate. The death benefit of a life insurance policy is also included in the taxable estate if the policy is transferred to another individual or trust by a decedent within three years before his or her death.

A second-to-die life insurance policy insures two people and pays a benefit after the death of the second spouse. (See Chapter 5, "Insuring Your Health and Life," for more details.)

These premiums are typically much less expensive than premiums for a single life insurance policy because they are based on the life expectancy of both insured spouses. Because the unlimited marital deduction allows assets to pass to the surviving spouse without federal estate taxes, the estate taxes generally do not become an issue until the death of the second spouse. When the estate assets pass out of the marriage to the heirs, this is when you normally incur the estate tax liability. Thus, a second-to-die survivorship life insurance policy could pay a benefit at the time when your family really needs it, to pay estate taxes.

Once again, you must seek out a qualified estate attorney and financial advisor to not only set this up properly, but also to administer the trust, because there are strict guidelines that must be followed each year. The cost and availability of life insurance depend on several factors such as your age, health, and the type and amount of insurance coverage you want to purchase. Before implementing a planning strategy involving life insurance, it is sensible to make sure that you are insurable.

Spousal "Portability" of the Exclusion

The 2010 Tax Relief Act revived the estate tax after it was eliminated at the end of 2009. One of its most significant changes was creating spousal "portability" of the lifetime exclusion, which was made permanent with the American Taxpayer Relief Act of 2012. If the first spouse to die does not fully use his or her exclusion, then the surviving spouse may inherit the decedent spouse's unused exclusion and may therefore be entitled up to an inflation adjusted $30 million lifetime exclusion (as of 2026) upon his or her death.

The spousal portability is generally only available if an election is made by the executor or administrator on a timely filed IRS Form 706 for the first spouse to die. If this form is not filed and the election is not made, the surviving spouse will be limited to only his or her $15 million (as of 2026) exclusion. Therefore, even if an estate tax return is not required to be filed upon the death of the first spouse, the surviving spouse and the executor should consider filing and making this election to preserve the full amount of the exclusion made available under spousal portability rules. Although the election must generally be made on a timely filed 706, a late election can be made up to five years after the date of death. A 706 must be filed within this time frame, and "Filed pursuant to Rev Proc 2022–2032" must be written on the top of the form.

If the surviving spouse remarries, he or she can only take advantage of portability rules once. This rule prevents an estate from taking advantage of the spousal portability exclusion more than once because of multiple marriages.

How to Estimate Your Expected Federal Estate Tax Liability

Estate taxes are an important concern in distributing your estate because the money your estate pays in taxes will not be available to your heirs. Each estate is allowed a federal estate tax exemption and a certain amount that can pass tax-free, either through lifetime gifts or after death. By implementing some of the strategies covered in this chapter, you should be able to preserve more of your estate for the benefit of your loved ones, creating and maintaining generational wealth. If the total value of your estate is less than the applicable exemption amount at the time of your death, no federal estate taxes will be due.

We encourage you to use the *What's My Potential Estate Tax?* calculator, available at www.ventotaxandwealth.com under the Resources > Calculators & Tools section to calculate the amount of estate taxes you may owe based on today's estate tax exemption and rates. Be sure to use your statement of financial position (as discussed in Chapter 3), and do not forget to add the death benefit of any life insurance held in your name when determining your net worth for this calculation. You should use this calculator to estimate the approximate amount of federal estate taxes that would be required to be paid based on the current tax laws.

Paying Your Estate Tax Liability

Estate planning requires you to implement strategies to minimize taxes and to plan how your family will pay them when the time comes. As mentioned, estate taxes are generally due nine months after the date of death and are to be paid with cash. There are just a few options when it comes to how your executor will pay the estate taxes upon your death, including:

- Using your current savings and liquid investments
- Borrowing the money
- Liquidating hard assets, such as selling real estate
- Using life insurance proceeds

If the first three options are not appealing or practical, then you should consider implementing the strategies discussed earlier regarding irrevocable life insurance trusts (ILITs). Paying estate taxes could present a challenge to the executor and your survivors. It is therefore essential to put a plan in place that will include how the ultimate estate taxes will be paid. You must put this plan of action in place while you are still alive; otherwise, your executor and survivors may be forced to liquidate your assets at bargain prices to meet this time-sensitive estate tax obligation.

State Inheritance and Estate Taxes

An *inheritance tax* is a state-level tax imposed on the beneficiaries who receive assets from a deceased person. It is distinct from the *estate tax*, which is levied on the decedent's estate before any distributions are made. Both estate and inheritance taxes are governed by the laws of the state where the decedent resided or where the property is located, not by the beneficiary's state of residence. Each beneficiary subject to an inheritance tax must file a return and report their inherited amount in accordance with that state's tax rules. Because inheritance tax laws vary from state to state, each jurisdiction sets its own rates, exemptions, and filing thresholds. As a result, certain beneficiaries may be fully or partially exempt from paying inheritance tax depending on the relationship to the decedent, the value of the inheritance, and the specific provisions of the applicable state law.

The following jurisdictions impose their own estate tax, in addition to federal estate tax: Washington, DC; Maine; New York; Rhode Island; Connecticut; Illinois; Minnesota; Washington; Oregon; Maryland; Vermont; Massachusetts; and Hawaii.

The states of Pennsylvania, Kentucky, Nebraska, New Jersey, and Maryland impose an inheritance tax on beneficiaries who receive an inheritance from a deceased person. The state of Maryland is the only state that imposes both a state estate tax and inheritance tax. You should check with your state tax department for more details if you live in one of the jurisdictions listed.

We recommend going to your resident state's department of taxation website and checking out what the state inheritance and estate taxes are that may apply in your situation. You can, of course, also ask your estate attorney, tax advisor, and financial planner to provide you with further guidance on this.

Asset Protection and Long-term Care

Throughout Chapter 10, we have been discussing various strategies available to you to preserve your estate and to create and maintain generational wealth for your beneficiaries. While the steps you decide to take in this regard are largely within your control, one thing that is not is whether you or your spouse will ultimately require long-term care. With average life expectancy increasing over time, the likelihood of needing assistance with activities of daily living as we age has increased significantly. The type of long-term care an individual may need, whether it be institutional care in a nursing home, assisted living, or home care may be unknown, but what is certain is that the cost of care in any of these settings could wipe out your entire savings.

Therefore, by seeking the advice of an eldercare attorney and financial planner knowledgeable in this area, you can take the steps necessary to minimize the out-of-pocket expense to you (and, therefore, to your estate), should you or your spouse ever need long-term care. This will allow you to protect the generational wealth you've built.

It is important to understand that there is a drastic difference between short-term rehabilitative care and long-term care. Private health insurance or Medicare typically provide coverage (of varying degrees depending on your plan) for short-term rehabilitation after an accident, surgical procedure, or prolonged hospitalization. If, however, your need for rehabilitative care extends beyond the short-term, most health insurance coverage and Medicare benefits will cease. For 2025, Medicare continues to provide coverage for up to 100 days of skilled nursing facility care per benefit period if eligibility requirements are met, with only the first 20 days fully covered. Beyond that, substantial daily copayments apply. Without planning, this can quickly deplete your assets.

One method of minimizing out-of-pocket expenses for long-term care is to purchase long-term care insurance. For more details regarding long-term care insurance, please refer to Chapter 5, "Insuring Your Health and Life."

For those who may not qualify for long-term care insurance, or if the premiums required are cost-prohibitive, another option is to consult an elder law attorney to discuss what steps may be taken to qualify you or your spouse for having long-term care paid for through state administered Medicaid. Since Medicaid is a combined federal and state program, the specific rules of eligibility for Medicaid for long-term care purposes and the programs available vary greatly from state to state.

Despite these variations, with the guidance of an experienced eldercare attorney, you may be able to establish eligibility for Medicaid by transferring your personal use and investment assets out of your name at least five years before the need for long-term care arises. More importantly, depending on the laws in your state, there may be additional transfers and planning techniques that can be implemented even within the five-year look-back period to reduce or eliminate the loss of assets while still allowing you to qualify for Medicaid coverage for long-term care.

Earlier in this chapter, we referred to a legal entity known as an irrevocable trust. Use of this kind of trust is quite common in Medicaid eligibility planning because it allows for the transfer of assets into the trust to gain protected status from future long-term care expenses. The trustor (you) can continue to benefit from the use and occupancy of real estate titled in an irrevocable trust during life and can even receive income generated from trust assets.

After five years, however, the assets titled in the irrevocable trust will not be counted in Medicaid eligibility, nor will they be reachable to pay for the cost of long-term care if handled properly.

Utilizing an irrevocable Medicaid Asset Protection Trust is frequently preferable to transferring assets to children or other individuals because it eliminates vulnerability of these assets during the trustor's life, ensures handling of the assets in accordance with the trustor's wishes (as opposed to decisions made by children), and mandates that any ownership interest in the assets does not vest in the trustor's beneficiaries until his or her death.

Estate planning, including that for the purpose of long-term care, must be tailored to your individual needs. Inaction can be a costly and burdensome mistake. As discussed throughout this chapter, it is important to develop your estate plan with your estate and eldercare planning attorney to ensure your goals are met throughout your lifetime and generational wealth is passed on to your loved ones.

If you do not pay attention to the tax consequences of preserving your estate, your estate may have to pay significantly more in taxes than the law requires, thereby reducing the amount your loved ones will ultimately inherit. Therefore, you must include estate tax planning as part of your overall estate preservation and generational wealth strategy.

Tax-smart Strategies for Preserving Your Estate

Here are several tax facts and strategies that will address your wealth accumulation goals in a powerful and sustainable way. This will be part of your tax-smart roadmap to financial independence. This is how you can transform the tax code into part of your generational wealth code.

- As of January 1, 2025, the federal estate and gift tax exemption has increased to $13.99 million per individual and $27.98 million for married couples, meaning that only amounts exceeding these thresholds are subject to the federal estate tax at a rate of 40%.
- Under the OBBBA, the exemption will permanently increase beginning January 1, 2026, to $15 million per individual (and $30 million for married couples), with future amounts indexed for inflation starting in 2027.

(*continued*)

(*continued*)

- If you give your child or any other individual an interest-free or below-market interest loan, you can limit or even completely avoid imputed interest by the IRS, as long as the total outstanding loan balance owed to you by this individual does not exceed $100,000 and tax avoidance is not the principal purpose of this loan.
- When you sell property that you inherited, you are automatically given a holding period of more than one year (long-term capital gain treatment). Generally, you will also receive a step-up in basis to the fair market value of the property as of the date of death. This step-up in basis completely eliminates the income tax on the sale of most inherited properties. With a step-up in basis, the cost for determining gain or loss is based on the property's value at death and not based on what the decedent actually paid for it.
- When you sell property received as a gift, your cost basis generally depends on both the donor's original cost and the property's fair market value (FMV) at the time of the gift. If the FMV was higher than or equal to the donor's basis, you use the donor's basis plus any portion of gift tax paid that is attributable to the property's appreciation to determine gain or loss. If the FMV was lower, you use the donor's adjusted basis to calculate gain, the FMV at the date of the gift to calculate loss, and no gain or loss is recognized if the sale price falls between those two values.
- Before an anticipated sale, making gifts of appreciated property to a family member who is in a lower tax bracket can reduce the overall income tax to be paid by the family as a whole.
- You can give gifts throughout your lifetime and receive an exemption for the first $13.99 million of taxable gifts in 2025 ($15 million in 2026); this is in addition to the $19,000 annual gift to any number of people per year. These gifts will not be subject to gift tax to you and can be received on a tax-free basis by the recipient.
- You can make annual gifts of $19,000 (2025) to any number of persons, typically children or grandchildren, without incurring a gift tax. If a husband and wife both engage in gifting, they can jointly give away $38,000 per year per recipient without incurring a gift tax. Over several years, the amount of money that can be transferred to beneficiaries can be substantial, thereby reducing the size of the taxable estate and the ultimate estate tax liability.
- You can pay an unlimited amount of someone's college tuition directly to the school and still be permitted to give an additional $19,000 directly to the donee beneficiary without affecting your lifetime exemption. Therefore, you may want to consider paying your children's and grandchildren's tuition directly to the institution as one of your valuable estate planning tools.

- You can pay an unlimited amount of someone's medical expenses directly to the hospital and still be permitted to give an additional $19,000 directly to the donee beneficiary without affecting your lifetime exemption.
- Gifts and inheritances you receive are not taxable at the federal level, but distributions taken from an inherited traditional IRA or qualified plan are taxable. In addition, with an inherited nonqualified annuity, a portion (earnings above original basis) of the distributions may be taxable.
- A gift or inheritance will be subject to income tax if, in fact, it is a payment for services rendered.
- By establishing an ILIT, you can reduce the size of your taxable estate each year, while providing your beneficiaries with a larger inheritance. Each year that you give a gift to the ILIT, it lowers your taxable estate. The trust then buys life insurance for the benefit of your beneficiaries. When you die, the life insurance proceeds are kept outside of the estate (owned by the trust). Then, these proceeds would not be subject to estate tax and of course they are also income tax free to your beneficiaries.
- As a married person, you may be able to use the marital deduction that allows the passing spouse to transfer an unlimited amount of assets to the surviving spouse free from estate and gift tax.
- Under the American Taxpayer Relief Act of 2012, the portability between spouses of the lifetime estate tax exemption was made permanent. For 2025, the exclusion is $13.99 million per individual. Any unused portion of the deceased spouse's exemption can be transferred to the surviving spouse, effectively doubling the exemption to $27.98 million for a married couple. Beginning January 1, 2026, the OBBBA increases the exclusion to $15 million per person (and $30 million per couple), indexed for inflation, making this higher level permanent.
- The spousal "portability" is only available if an election is made by the executor or administrator on a timely filed IRS Form 706, for the *first spouse to die*. If this form is not filed and the election is not made, the surviving spouse will be limited to only his or her $15 million exclusion. Therefore, even if an estate tax return is not required to be filed upon the death of the first spouse, the surviving spouse and the executor should consider filing and making this election to preserve the full amount of the exclusion that was made available under spousal "portability" rules.
- Although the portability election must generally be made on a timely filed Form 706, a late election can be made up to five years after date of death. A 706 must be filed within this time frame, and "Filed pursuant to Rev Proc 2022–2032" must be written on the top of the form.

An Action Plan for Preserving Your Estate

1. **Decide which legal documents you need** to ensure that you and your estate are taken care of properly. Most people should have a will. You may also want to have a living will, a health care proxy, a durable power of attorney, and advance health care directive. You may want to set up one or more revocable or irrevocable trusts. These documents could ensure that your wishes are followed, should you become incapacitated and unable to make decisions for yourself, or even worse, pass away.
2. **Keep in mind that if you die without a will, your estate will be distributed according to the relevant laws in the state where you reside.** Generally, these laws follow your family tree, but distributions may be made in a proportion that is not what you would have wanted. Keep in mind that these distribution rules vary state by state.
3. **Take advantage of planned gifting strategies** that can help you prevent losing some of the value of your estate-to-estate taxes. For example, in 2025, you can gift up to $19,000 (to as many people as you want) each year, which achieves two benefits. First, you can give money or other property up to $19,000 per year directly to your family or friends and an unlimited amount to charities while you are alive. Second, by lowering the value of your estate, your estate taxes will be reduced, assuming you have a taxable estate.
4. **Understand the difference between various types of property ownership:** Individual ownership, tenancy in common, joint tenancy, and tenancy by the entirety each have a different effect on who ultimately inherits that property upon your death.
5. **Understand the reasons and benefits of creating a trust.** This is perhaps the most flexible estate planning tool that allows you to control your assets both before and after your death.
6. **Take advantage of the benefits provided by establishing a Family Limited Partnership (FLP).** A FLP is typically established to hold and manage a family business or investment property. It may also open the door to opportunities to use various other estate and income-tax planning strategies.
7. **Utilize an ILIT if you are a high-net worth individual** to take advantage of the income and estate tax benefits. An ILIT is another powerful estate planning tool that can be established to hold life insurance policies preventing the death benefits from being included in your taxable estate.

8. **Married couples should take advantage of spousal "portability" upon the death of the first spouse** to maximize the lifetime exclusion. If the first spouse to die does not fully use their lifetime exclusion, then the surviving spouse may inherit the decedent spouse's unused exclusion amount. Therefore, the surviving spouse's estate could be entitled to up to an annually inflation adjusted $30 million lifetime exclusion (as of 2026) upon his or her death.
9. **Estimate your expected federal estate tax liability.** Use the *What's My Potential Estate Tax?* calculator, available at www.ventotaxandwealth.com under the Resources > Calculators & Tools section to calculate the amount of estate taxes you may owe based on today's estate tax exemption and rates.
10. **Prepare for your executor to pay your estate tax liability.** Estate taxes are generally due nine months after the date of death and are to be paid with cash. This will leave your executor with the following options: your current savings and liquid investments, borrowing the money, liquidating hard assets (such as real estate), or utilizing life insurance proceeds, preferably owned through an ILIT.
11. **Determine if you live in a state that imposes a state-level inheritance or estate tax.** If so, you may want to consider moving to a more tax-friendly state while you are among the living.
12. **Consider putting an asset protection strategy in place to meet your long-term care needs.** This could include utilizing long-term care insurance or establishing an Irrevocable Medicaid Trust. Five years after titling these assets to this trust, they will not be counted as Medicaid eligible and therefore will not be lost to a Medicaid lien.
13. **If you have a significant estate, you must meet with an experienced estate attorney, tax advisor, and financial planner** to implement some of the advanced estate tax-smart strategies covered in this chapter. See Appendix A, "Selecting a Trusted Advisor."
14. **Work with a tax-advisor and CERTIFIED FINANCIAL PLANNER®** that can provide you with the tax-smart advice covered in this chapter. Please refer to Appendix A, "Selecting a Trusted Advisor."
15. **Work with a financial planner** that will provide you with the necessary advice and guidance that includes the 12 critical areas of comprehensive wealth management covered throughout this book.
16. **Use the tax-smart roadmap to financial independence to transform the tax code into part of your generational wealth code.**

CHAPTER 11

Investing in Real Estate

Ninety percent of all millionaires become so through owning real estate.
—Andrew Carnegie, Industrialist and Philanthropist

For generations, real estate has been viewed as a cornerstone of the American Dream. It represents more than just a place to live. It symbolizes stability, control, and the potential for long-term financial growth. As CPAs and CERTIFIED FINANCIAL PLANNER®, we have worked with countless individuals who have used real estate to accelerate their journey to financial independence. With the appropriate tax-smart real estate investing strategies, real estate can be a powerful wealth-building tool that may help you achieve financial independence and create generational wealth for your family.

Like many aspects of financial planning, real estate is not a one-size-fits-all solution. Some people achieve financial independence through investing in real estate by owning and holding rental properties throughout their lifetime. Others may buy fixer-uppers and then flip them for a quick profit. Still, others leverage alternative real estate investments that require less hands-on management but offer compelling long-term potential. When selling highly appreciated real estate, those who have experienced significant appreciation may face substantial tax consequences, unless they utilize tax-smart strategies such as the Section 1031 exchange to defer the realization of these gains. The truth is, real estate can play a role in almost every financial plan, whether it is your primary focus or just one of many tools in your broader investment portfolio.

However, real estate is not without its risks. Far too many people have rushed into the real estate market without proper planning, only to find themselves overwhelmed by debt, unexpected expenses, or market fluctuations. Others have failed to fully understand the tax implications of buying, holding, or selling property. They miss opportunities to protect their gains and reduce their obligations. That is why this chapter is not about flipping houses or chasing get-rich-quick schemes. It is about taking a thoughtful and disciplined approach to real estate investing, one that is grounded in financial fundamentals and guided by clear tax-smart real estate investing strategies.

Over the following pages, we will explore how real estate can support your journey to financial independence and creating generational wealth. You will learn about the different types of real estate investments, the financial and tax benefits associated with each, and how to evaluate opportunities based on your personal goals and risk tolerance. Most importantly, we will show you how to integrate real estate into your overall wealth plan so that it works in harmony with the other financial strategies discussed throughout this book.

If used wisely, real estate is not just an asset. It is a pathway to financial independence, to stability, and to a future where your money is working for you, and at the same time can help you create and maintain generational wealth. As always, our goal is to help you and your family reach that future with clarity, confidence, and control.

The Power of Leverage: Using Other People's Money to Build Wealth

If you ask any successful real estate investor what helped them get started and grow their portfolio, one of the first words you will likely hear is leverage. And for good reason. Leverage is one of the most powerful tools available to real estate investors. It allows you to use someone else's money, typically a bank or lender, to purchase income-producing assets that you would not otherwise be able to afford on your own.

Think about this for a moment. In most areas of your financial life, you are encouraged to stay out of debt and avoid borrowing money. This is certainly sound advice when it comes to high-interest consumer debt, credit cards, or unnecessary personal loans. However, in the world of real estate, the rules are a little different. When structured responsibly and for the right purpose, borrowing money can actually accelerate your path to financial independence.

Let us say you have $100,000 saved and are considering how to invest it. You could purchase $100,000 worth of stock or mutual funds, which would give you full ownership and any appreciation or dividends those investments may produce. Alternatively, you could use that same $100,000 as a 20% down payment on a $500,000 rental property. In doing so, you now control an asset five times the size of your original capital outlay. If the property appreciates in value, generates rental income, and offers tax benefits, all those gains are earned on the full $500,000, even though you only invested $100,000 of your own money. This use of *leverage* (borrowing to increase your exposure) can also be achieved in securities through margin investing, but real estate typically allows for more stable and longer-term financing.

That is the power of leverage. It magnifies your potential return on investment by allowing you to benefit from the performance of a much larger asset base. Real estate is one of the few investment vehicles where this kind of leverage is not only available but commonly and sustainably used. Banks are generally willing to lend significant amounts of money for real estate because the property itself serves as collateral. As long as you maintain a good credit history, sufficient income, and a manageable debt-to-income ratio, you can access financing that opens the door to properties far beyond your personal savings.

One of the most overlooked aspects of leverage is the long-term wealth it can generate through equity buildup. Each time you make a mortgage payment, a portion of that payment goes toward reducing the principal balance of your loan. Over time, this creates equity (ownership in the property) that grows in value as the loan is paid down. Combine that with appreciation in property value, and the effect is exponential. In essence, your tenants are helping you build wealth by paying down your mortgage for you. Meanwhile, you continue to benefit from any increase in the property's value and the tax deductions available for mortgage interest, property taxes, and depreciation.

But leverage is not magic, and it is not risk-free. When used improperly, it can magnify losses just as easily as it can magnify gains. If the market declines or if you fail to generate enough rental income to cover your mortgage payments, taxes, insurance, and maintenance, you may find yourself in financial trouble. This is especially true if you overextend yourself or take on more properties than you can manage.

For this reason, you should always be conservative and strategic when using leverage. The goal is not to own as many properties as possible, but to own the right properties, with the right financing, and a clear plan for cash flow and long-term growth. You need to evaluate each opportunity with care. Ask yourself whether the property is likely to appreciate over time. Look closely at the local market, the condition of the property, and the potential rental income. Calculate your expenses conservatively and always assume there will be vacancies and unexpected costs along the way.

We also recommend working closely with qualified professionals such as a financial advisor, a tax advisor, and a knowledgeable real estate attorney and broker. They can help you evaluate loan terms, understand tax implications, and structure your investment in a way that supports your broader financial plan. Remember, real estate investing is not a standalone strategy. It should fit into your overall wealth management plan, supporting your goals for retirement, tax efficiency, and financial independence.

To be clear, we are not suggesting that you go out and buy property with nothing down or take on debt you cannot afford. That kind of thinking led to the housing crisis of 2008, and we have seen how devastating the consequences can be. However, when used prudently, leverage can be one of the most effective ways to build wealth through real estate. It allows you to scale your investments, increase your cash flow, and accelerate your journey to financial independence, creating generational wealth for you and your family.

Equity Recycling: Borrowing Against Equity to Expand Your Portfolio

Once you have purchased your first investment property and have built up some equity, one of the most effective ways to continue growing your real estate portfolio is through a strategy known as *equity recycling*. This approach allows you to use the accumulated equity in one property to help finance the purchase of another. You do not need to save for a new down payment all over again. Equity recycling has helped many experienced investors grow their wealth in a responsible and tax-smart way.

Equity is the difference between what your property is worth and what you still owe on it. For instance, if you purchased a rental property for $400,000 with a $300,000 mortgage and the property has appreciated to $500,000 while you have paid down the mortgage to $250,000, you now have $250,000 in equity. That is a significant financial resource. When structured carefully, it can be tapped to fund additional investments.

This equity can be accessed in several ways. The most common include a cash-out refinance, a home equity loan, or a home equity line of credit. Each of these methods allows you to borrow against the equity you have built and use the proceeds for another property purchase. By doing so, you are effectively recycling the equity. Rather than letting that value sit passively in the property, you are putting it back to work to grow your portfolio.

This is not about draining all value from your current investment. It is also not about taking reckless financial risks. Equity recycling, when used properly, is a strategic move. It allows you to continue investing in income-producing properties while still holding on to your original asset. You are not selling, which means you do not trigger capital gains taxes. Instead, you are using a financial tool that gives you liquidity without generating immediate tax obligations.

The tax treatment is one of the main reasons this strategy is so effective. Loan proceeds are not considered income and are therefore not taxable. This means you can unlock the value of your investment without increasing your tax liability. If the property you acquire with that borrowed equity also appreciates and generates rental income, the long-term benefits can be substantial.

To share a real-world example: a client of ours purchased a small multifamily property for $600,000 and put down 20%. Within five years, the property appreciated to $750,000, and he paid down part of the mortgage. At that point, he had close to $300,000 in equity. Instead of selling the property, he refinanced and took out $150,000 in cash. He then used that cash as the down payment on another property. As a result, he now owns two income-producing properties that are both appreciating in value. He was able to do this without depleting his savings or exposing himself to unnecessary risk.

Of course, this strategy requires careful planning and financial discipline. Any funds you borrow will come with monthly repayment obligations. These must be covered by your rental income or other stable sources. You must also retain sufficient equity to meet loan-to-value requirements and avoid becoming overleveraged. Lenders typically require that you maintain at least 20% to 25% equity in the property after refinancing. This helps ensure that you and the lender are protected if market values decline.

Interest rates, fees, and loan structures vary. This is why we strongly recommend working with experienced mortgage professionals who can help you compare options and choose the one that fits your long-term plan. Equity recycling is not something to attempt casually. It must be executed with care and a full understanding of your personal financial situation.

To summarize, equity recycling allows you to unlock the potential of your existing assets and use that value to expand your real estate holdings. It is a practical, tax-efficient approach to portfolio growth. Rather than starting from scratch each time you want to invest, you can use the momentum you have already created to build further.

Depreciation: The Phantom Deduction Driving Tax-deferred Growth

Of all the tax benefits available to real estate investors, one of the most powerful and least understood is *depreciation*. Commonly referred to as a *phantom deduction*, depreciation allows you to reduce your taxable income without spending any money. It is one of the most effective tools for driving tax-deferred growth and accelerating your journey toward financial independence.

Depreciation is based on a simple idea. The government recognizes that physical assets such as buildings wear out over time. Even if your property is appreciating in market value, the structure itself is assumed to have a limited useful life. For residential rental property, the IRS allows you to depreciate the building over 27.5 years. For commercial property, the period is 39 years. This means you can deduct a portion of the building's value from your taxable income each year, even though the property may be increasing in value and generating positive cash flow.

Let us say you purchase a residential rental property for $500,000. Of that amount, let's assume $100,000 is allocated to the land and $400,000 to the structure. Land cannot be depreciated, but the IRS does allow you to depreciate the structure. In this example, you can divide that $400,000 value assigned to the structure by 27.5 years, resulting in an annual depreciation deduction of approximately $14,545. That is a real tax deduction you can use to offset your rental income, even though you have not spent that amount out of pocket.

This is where the concept of the phantom deduction becomes so powerful. You are claiming a tax benefit for a theoretical loss in value that does not reduce your net worth. Your property may be appreciating year after year and generating reliable rent, yet the IRS still allows you to take a deduction for depreciation. This reduces your taxable income and, as a result, lowers the amount of tax you owe.

Over time, these deductions can lead to substantial tax savings. If your rental income is offset by depreciation and other property-related expenses, your taxable income from the property may be reduced to zero or may even reflect a paper loss. These losses can be especially useful for high-income individuals. Depending on your level of participation in the management of the property, you may be able to apply them to offset passive income or, in some cases, even nonpassive income.

Depreciation does come with a trade-off. If you sell the property at a gain, the IRS requires you to recapture the depreciation you claimed. This is known as *depreciation recapture*, and it is subject to tax at a maximum rate of 25%. However, with the right planning, you may be able to defer or even eliminate this tax. For example, by completing a 1031 exchange and reinvesting your gains into another property, you can postpone both capital gains and depreciation recapture taxes. We will discuss the use of 1031 exchanges in further detail later in this chapter.

This is where depreciation supports long-term strategy. You reduce taxes while you own the property and have options to defer them further when you sell. In addition to 1031 exchanges, thoughtful estate planning may allow you to avoid capital gain and depreciation recapture taxes entirely (see Chapter 10). For example, when a property is inherited, it usually receives a step-up in basis. This adjustment often eliminates both the capital gain and the accumulated depreciation recapture, giving heirs a clean slate for future ownership or sale. This is a game changer when it comes to creating and maintaining generational wealth that can endure.

There are also ways to enhance the value of depreciation through cost segregation studies. These studies break down the property into various components such as appliances, fixtures, and finishes. Items like these may qualify for accelerated depreciation schedules, which can range from 5 to 15 years. This front-loads your deductions and delivers greater tax savings during the earlier years of ownership.

You can also take advantage of this strategy when making capital improvements to your building by asking your contractor to break down these improvements into its various components. Be sure to provide this information to your tax advisor to take advantage of accelerated depreciation.

Depreciation is a rare advantage in the tax code. It allows you to reduce your taxes without reducing your cash flow. You are not writing a check to get this deduction. It is embedded in the investment itself. Every real estate investor needs to understand how depreciation works and how it fits into a broader tax-smart financial plan.

In our experience working with clients, we have seen the difference this can make. Strategic use of depreciation has allowed many individuals to retain more of their rental income, reinvest more aggressively, and compound their wealth over time. It is not just about what the property earns on paper. It is about what you actually keep in your pocket.

Estate Planning and Wealth Transfer: The Power of the Step-up in Basis

For many real estate investors, the journey toward financial independence does not end with their own retirement. A well-structured real estate portfolio can serve as a legacy, one that benefits children, grandchildren, or charitable causes for decades to come. One of the most powerful tools for preserving that legacy is the step-up in basis. This provision in the tax code allows heirs to receive inherited property with a new cost basis equal to its fair market value at the time of the original owner's death.

To understand its significance, consider an investor who purchased a property years ago for $300,000. By the time of their passing, the property has appreciated to $700,000. Under the step-up in basis rule, the cost basis for the heir is adjusted to $700,000. If the heir sells the property shortly after inheriting it, and the sale price is also $700,000, there is no capital gains tax due. The $400,000 of appreciation that occurred during the original owner's lifetime is never taxed. This allows for a clean transfer of wealth without the burden of deferred taxes.

This benefit is especially meaningful in real estate because properties are often held for long periods and can accumulate substantial appreciation. Without the step-up, families might face large tax bills when trying to transfer or liquidate real estate holdings. With the step-up, those taxes are largely eliminated, making real estate one of the most efficient assets to pass down across generations. It's important to note, however, that while the step-up in basis can eliminate capital gains and depreciation recapture taxes, it does not eliminate potential estate taxes (see Chapter 10, "Preserving Your Estate").

Another advantage is that this tax reset does not require the heirs to sell the property. They can choose to keep it, collect rental income, and enjoy the benefits of a fresh start in terms of depreciation deductions.

Step-up and Depreciation Reset

When an heir inherits a property and receives a step-up in basis, the depreciation schedule is also *reset*. This means that even if the property has already been fully depreciated by the original owner, the new owner can begin depreciating it again, based on the stepped-up value. It is a fresh opportunity to use the phantom deduction and reduce taxable income without making any actual cash outlay.

This reset is not a temporary tax deferral. It often results in the complete elimination of prior potential tax liabilities related to appreciation and depreciation recapture. The deferred taxes that the original owner would have owed are wiped away. The new owner starts fresh, both from a capital gains perspective and from a depreciation standpoint. This is why the combination of the step-up in basis and depreciation reset is so valuable in estate planning.

Families who plan ahead can use this strategy to preserve wealth across multiple generations. It allows for uninterrupted income from rental properties, continued tax efficiency, and greater flexibility in deciding when or whether to sell inherited assets. By working with a qualified estate planning attorney and a tax advisor, investors can structure their holdings to maximize these benefits and align them with their broader financial goals.

Real estate is not just about cash flow or appreciation. It is also one of the most strategic tools available for transferring wealth with minimal tax consequences. The step-up in basis, combined with a new depreciation schedule, can transform a lifetime of tax deferral into permanent tax savings. It ensures that your legacy is not just preserved but protected and passed on with clarity and intention. For all these reasons, investing in real estate is perhaps the most effective generational wealth building strategy.

How Real Estate Builds Wealth Over Time: Proven Case Studies

One of the best ways to understand the long-term value of real estate investing is to study what has worked in the real world. While financial theories and tax strategies provide a solid foundation, it is real-life examples that bring those principles into focus. They show how consistent execution, patient decision-making, and tax-smart planning can transform an initial investment into a powerful source of wealth.

In this section, we will look at two investors who approached real estate with different strategies but shared the same goal: financial independence. One took a hands-on approach from the start, while the other transitioned from active management to passive income in retirement. Both paths reveal how real estate can serve you at different stages of life, and how aligning your strategy with your values and circumstances can make all the difference.

Case Study 1: The Active Investor's Journey

Lenny was a 34-year-old engineer in private practice when he made his first move into real estate. He purchased a duplex in a neighborhood that was beginning to see new development and revitalization. By living in one unit and renting out the other, he was able to offset most of his housing costs while learning the fundamentals of property management. This approach, often referred to as house hacking, gave him valuable experience and helped him build confidence as a real estate investor.

Over the next eight years, Lenny steadily expanded his real estate portfolio. He purchased three additional multifamily properties, each time applying lessons learned from his earlier investments. He handled basic renovations himself, worked with trusted contractors for larger projects, and developed systems for managing tenants and maintenance. Lenny took a proactive approach by regularly reviewing the performance of each property, adjusting rents based on market conditions, and reinvesting much of his cash flow.

With guidance from his CPA and CFP®, Lenny took advantage of every available tax benefit. He claimed depreciation, deducted operating expenses, and used cost segregation studies on larger properties to accelerate deductions. As his equity grew, he used refinancing strategies to access capital and fund new purchases, all while maintaining conservative loan-to-value ratios to avoid excessive risk.

By age 46, Lenny owned six well-maintained, cash-flowing properties. The income from these properties allowed him to reduce his hours at the engineering practice and was able to spend more time with his family. His real estate plan was built not on speculation, but on consistent savings, disciplined reinvestment, and a clear understanding of how taxes and financing strategies worked together. Real estate provided him with financial freedom and the ability to design a life on his own terms.

Case Study 2: Transitioning to Passive Real Estate Income

Ruby, age 62, had been managing two small apartment buildings for more than 20 years. The properties provided steady monthly income, appreciated in value, and became a significant part of her retirement plan. But after two decades of dealing with tenant issues, property maintenance, and administrative tasks, she was ready for a more simplified lifestyle.

Ruby consulted her financial advisor and tax professional to develop an exit strategy that would preserve the value of her investments without creating a large tax liability. She decided to sell both properties and complete a 1031 exchange. The proceeds were reinvested through Delaware Statutory Trusts (DSTs), which offered her access to institutional-quality properties managed by professional firms. These trusts gave her monthly income, tax deferral, and asset class and geographical diversification, all without the burdens of direct ownership.

The transition brought Ruby several benefits. Her income stream remained consistent, her new investments qualified for depreciation deductions because of additional leverage, and she eliminated the stress of active management. She also simplified her estate planning by holding the DST interests within her revocable trust, which made it easier to pass them on to her heirs without probate complications.

Ruby's story illustrates how real estate investing can adapt over time. The strategy that works in your 30s or 40s may need to evolve as you approach retirement. With thoughtful planning and the right team in place, Ruby was able to shift from active to passive ownership while preserving the wealth she had built.

These case studies demonstrate that there is no single formula for real estate success. The active approach requires time, effort, and a willingness to learn through direct experience. The passive model focuses on delegation, diversification, and long-term planning. Both can work well when supported by careful financial planning and sound tax strategies.

Real estate is not just about accumulating properties. It is about making intentional decisions that reflect your goals, financial situation, and desired lifestyle. Whether you are starting out, growing your holdings, or preparing for retirement, real estate can be a powerful vehicle for lasting wealth and independence. The key is to plan ahead, work with trusted professionals, and keep your long-term vision in focus.

Choosing the Right Entity to Hold Business or Investment Properties

Since we are talking about building wealth over time, it is important to discuss a simple step you can take to protect your overall personal assets against liability in the event something goes seriously wrong with your property. We almost always recommend holding your business or investment real estate through a *limited liability company* (LLC). Look at this as an added insurance policy.

Owning investment real estate through an LLC offers several key advantages over holding it in your personal name or as part of a general partnership. Most importantly, an LLC provides a layer of legal protection by separating your personal assets from potential liabilities related to the property. If a tenant sues or a legal issue arises, your personal wealth is generally shielded.

Although C corporations provide comparable liability protection, LLCs offer more flexible tax treatment by allowing income and losses to pass directly to the owners, avoiding the double taxation typically associated with C corporations.

Unlike general partnerships, which expose each partner to full liability for the actions of the other, an LLC protects each member from the missteps or debts of co-owners. For investors focused on long-term wealth building and asset protection, an LLC is often the most tax-smart and liability-conscious way to structure real estate ownership.

1031 Exchanges: The Tax-deferred Transfer Tool

One of the most powerful advantages in the real estate investor's toolkit is the Section 1031 exchange. Named after a section of the Internal Revenue Code, this strategy allows investors to defer capital gains taxes when they sell an investment or business-use property and use the proceeds to acquire another qualifying property. This creates an opportunity to grow wealth faster, preserve equity, and continually reposition assets without the drag of immediate taxation upon sale of your property.

For individuals building toward financial independence, a 1031 exchange is not just a tax break. It is a core strategy that supports portfolio growth, risk management, and long-term wealth preservation. To use it properly, however, you must understand the rules, timelines, and types of exchanges available. What follows is a closer look at the evolution of this strategy and the most common structures used by today's investors.

Brief History on 1031 Exchanges

The origins of Section 1031 go back to the Revenue Act of 1921, which introduced the idea that exchanging similar properties should not be treated the same as selling one asset and buying another. Lawmakers recognized that when a property owner swaps one property for another of like kind, no economic gain is realized in the traditional sense. This principle eventually gave rise to what we now know as the 1031 exchange.

For more than 100 years, investors have used this provision to roll profits from one property into another without triggering capital gains and depreciation recapture taxes. Over time, the rules have evolved. The 2017 Tax Cuts and Jobs Act narrowed the eligibility criteria, limiting exchanges to real property only. Exchanges of machinery, equipment, vehicles, artwork, collectibles, patents and other intellectual property, and intangible business assets generally no longer qualify. Even with those restrictions, the modern 1031 exchange remains a cornerstone of tax-smart real estate investing.

Understanding this history helps investors appreciate not only the opportunity that a 1031 exchange provides, but also the care and compliance required to use it successfully. This is not a loophole. It is a well-established and widely accepted method for building long-term wealth.

Simultaneous Exchanges

A *simultaneous exchange* occurs when the sale of your relinquished property and the purchase of your replacement property happen at the exact same time. Both transactions close on the same day; the transfer of properties, additional funds if any, and ownership are coordinated in a single, seamless process. While this structure sounds straightforward, it is often the most logistically challenging to execute.

Simultaneous exchanges are rare because they require perfect alignment between multiple parties. Both buyers and sellers must be ready to close at the same time, and the transfer of property and any additional funds must be handled without error. Even a brief delay can disqualify the exchange, resulting in immediate tax consequences.

That said, this structure still works well in tightly controlled transactions, such as when the buyer and seller are related entities or when both properties are managed by the same advisor or intermediary. For most investors, however, the more flexible structures that follow offer better options.

How the 1031 Exchange Process Works When It's Not a Simultaneous Exchange

Successfully completing a 1031 exchange as a tax-deferral strategy requires careful timing, proper documentation, and coordination with a team of experienced professionals. While the underlying concept is straightforward (selling one property and reinvesting the proceeds into another without paying immediate taxes), the actual execution involves a series of precise steps. Understanding how the process works will help you to avoid costly mistakes and to make informed decisions.

Step 1: Engage a Qualified Intermediary The first and most important requirement is to work with a *qualified intermediary* (QI). This third-party facilitator is responsible for holding the proceeds from the sale of your relinquished property and managing the transfer into your replacement property. If you take possession of the funds at any point during the process, even temporarily, the transaction will be disqualified, and all deferred taxes will become immediately due.

Your QI must be involved before the sale of your property is completed. They will help draft the necessary exchange documents, ensure funds are handled properly, and provide guidance on timelines and identification requirements. It is not enough to decide after the sale that you want to do an exchange; the structure must be in place beforehand.

It is important to note that the qualified intermediary needs to be a disinterested third-party to the exchange and cannot be involved in the exchange in any other capacity other than as the QI.

Step 2: Sell the Relinquished Property Once the exchange documents are in place, you can proceed with the sale of your original investment property. The closing is handled as it normally would be, except that the proceeds are transferred directly to the qualified intermediary. These funds are held in a secure escrow account until you are ready to complete the acquisition of your replacement properties.

Step 3: Identify Replacement Properties Within 45 Days After the sale closes, the IRS gives you 45 calendar days to formally identify potential replacement properties with your QI. You can identify one of the following:

1. Up to three replacement properties without regard to value
2. More than three properties as long as the total fair market value of all the properties you identify combined does not exceed 200% of the property you sold
3. More than three properties that have a combined value in excess of 200% of the property you sold, and you must acquire 95% or more of the properties you identify (very rarely used)

To properly identify properties, you must submit a written list to your QI before the end of the 45-day window. This list must clearly describe the properties by name and location. Once this list is submitted, you are limited to purchasing only the properties on that list, so careful planning and backup options are important.

Step 4: Complete the Acquisition Within 180 Days After identifying your properties, you must complete the purchase within 180 days from the date the relinquished property was sold. This is a hard deadline. If the transaction is not completed in time, the exchange fails, and the taxes on the original sale become due.

Step 5: Comply with Value, Equity, and Debt Replacement Requirements To receive full tax deferral under Section 1031, you must reinvest all the net proceeds from the sale, and this must buy you real estate that is equal to or greater than the value of the real estate you sold. This means if you had debt on your relinquished property at the time of sale, then you need to replace that debt. You can do so by adding cash to the investment or taking out a new loan. If you do not reinvest the full amount or replace the debt, the difference will be considered taxable boot and will be subject to capital gains and depreciation recapture taxes.

Delayed Exchanges

By far the most common 1031 exchange is the delayed exchange. This structure allows you to sell your existing property first, then purchase a new property within a set timeline. You must, of course, follow the five strict steps just described and to help you visualize the related timeline, I've included Exhibit 11.1.

Exhibit 11.1 180 Day Timeline

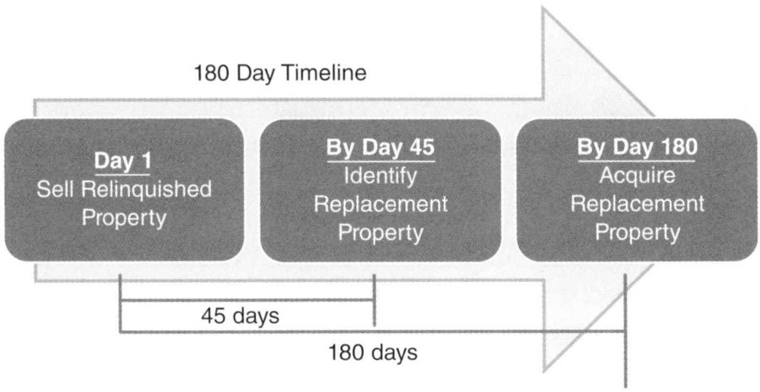

The delayed exchange is popular because it gives you time to search for the right replacement asset while still preserving your ability to defer taxes. You are not under pressure to find a buyer and seller at the same time, which adds flexibility and reduces stress. Still, this type of exchange comes with strict deadlines and documentation requirements. If you miss these requirements, the exchange is disqualified, and the full gain becomes taxable.

That is why it is critical to begin planning a delayed exchange before your initial property goes under contract. Work with your tax advisor, attorney, realtor, and qualified intermediary early in the process. Search for potential replacement properties well in advance. Have backup options, in case your preferred deal falls through. And be sure that your replacement property meets or exceeds the value of the property you sold. These details can make the difference between a successful deferral and an unexpected tax bill.

Reverse Exchanges

A reverse exchange flips the typical sequence. Instead of selling your old property first, you acquire the new property before selling the original one. This structure is useful in competitive markets where desirable properties do not stay on the market for long. It allows you to act quickly without losing the opportunity to defer taxes.

Because you cannot hold both properties in your name at the same time, a reverse exchange requires a qualified intermediary to take temporary title to one of the properties. This is done through a special-purpose entity. You then have 180 days to complete the sale of your relinquished property and transfer ownership of the replacement property into your name.

Reverse exchanges are more complex and typically more expensive to structure. They involve additional legal and administrative steps and must comply with strict IRS guidelines. However, they can be an excellent solution when timing is critical or when the replacement property must be secured before your original property can be sold.

For investors with substantial equity or those seeking to make a strategic move quickly, a reverse exchange may be the best option. Just be sure to involve experienced professionals from the outset. This is not a structure to navigate alone.

Construction or Improvement Exchanges

Sometimes the ideal replacement property does not exist yet or is not in ready-to-rent condition. In those situations, a construction or improvement exchange may be appropriate. This structure allows you to use your exchange funds to purchase a property and make capital improvements to it, provided those improvements are completed within the 180-day exchange window.

The catch is that all improvements must be completed, and the total purchase price of the property, plus improvements, must meet or exceed the value of the relinquished property. Any shortfall is considered boot and that portion would then become immediately taxable. Furthermore, the qualified intermediary must hold title to the property during the improvement period, and the improvements must be in place before the title can be transferred to you.

This type of exchange offers flexibility and customization, especially for investors who want to reposition or upgrade their assets. It can be used to build new structures, modernize existing properties, or convert spaces for new uses. However, it requires detailed planning, reliable contractors, and close coordination with your intermediary and legal team. The clock starts ticking the moment the initial sale is complete, and every improvement must be completed on schedule within 180 days to qualify.

Drop and Swap Strategy

It is important to understand that the same individual or entity that owns a property must also be the one completing the exchange and making the investment into the replacement property. For example, if the property is owned by Sally, then Sally is the one who carries out the exchange and reinvests in the replacement property. If the property is owned by "Sally, Jane, and Bob" LLC, then the LLC itself must be the taxpayer completing the exchange, and it is the LLC that acquires the replacement property. Courts look carefully at who, in substance, is the exchanger, which is why documentation and title vesting matter.

This rule is straightforward when all the partners agree to move in the same direction. The situation becomes more complicated when some partners want to exchange, and others do not. Suppose that Sally and Jane want to pursue a 1031 exchange while Bob wants to cash out. In this case, they may consider a strategy commonly known as a *drop and swap*. This involves restructuring ownership before the sale so that Bob receives a direct interest in the property as a tenant in common, while the LLC entity continues to hold its share. Once that step is complete, the property is owned partly by the LLC and partly by Bob individually. When the property is sold, Bob can take his proceeds directly while the LLC completes the exchange with its portion.

The process of a drop and swap is not simple and requires careful planning. The IRS and the courts will examine whether the ownership changes were made in good faith and whether the property interests were held for investment purposes, not merely to set up an exchange. Substantive factors carry real weight. Deeds should be recorded, sale documents should identify the actual tenants in common as sellers, each owner should bear their share of benefits and burdens, and separate qualified intermediaries should be engaged for those who will exchange. Timing and intent are critical, but there is no fixed federal seasoning period that automatically qualifies the transaction. Recent authorities have even approved a same day drop and swap in a state forum where the formalities were respected, although that decision is not binding for federal tax purposes. A conservative approach is to complete the ownership change well in advance of the sale and to make the facts show real ownership, not just paperwork.

Many investors have heard of the so-called *two-year rule* and assume it applies to drop and swap transactions, but that is not the case. The confusion stems from two unrelated tax authorities that both mention a two-year period. The first is the related-party exchange rule under Section 1031(f), which requires both related parties to hold their exchanged properties for two years or risk disqualification. The second is Revenue Procedure 2008–2016, which provides a two-year safe harbor for dwelling units to demonstrate that they are held for investment rather than personal use. Neither rule directly applies to drop and swaps, yet both reinforce the broader principle that time and intent matter when proving a property was held for investment.

For that reason, many tax professionals recommend allowing a "seasoning" period between the *drop* (when ownership shifts from an entity to its members) and the *swap* (the subsequent exchange). Although not legally required, holding the property for one to two years after the drop can help demonstrate a genuine investment intent and strengthen the taxpayer's position if the transaction is ever reviewed by the IRS.

The strategy generally requires the involvement of an attorney experienced in real estate and partnership law, along with tax professionals who can help ensure the structure will withstand scrutiny. The IRS has specifically added questions to partnership returns that flag distributions of tenancy in common interests, which underscores the need to get the form and the substance right.

It is also important to note that this technique is typically available with partnership or LLC ownership structures that are taxed as partnerships. It is generally not feasible when a property is owned by a corporation, whether a C corporation or an S corporation, because a distribution of appreciated property to shareholders triggers corporate-level gain recognition. In those cases, the corporate entity must complete the exchange itself, and individual shareholders cannot simply drop out to do their own exchange without tax cost.

When executed properly, a drop and swap can give co-owners the flexibility to pursue different goals. Some can exchange into new investment property to continue building wealth on a tax-deferred basis, while others can take their share of the proceeds outright. Because of the complexity and potential challenges, this strategy should always be approached with advanced preparation and professional guidance.

Delaware Statutory Trusts (DSTs)

For many real estate investors, the goal is not simply to accumulate wealth, but to eventually simplify their financial lives. As real estate investors approach retirement or reach a stage where hands-on property management becomes less appealing, they begin to look for alternatives that allow them to maintain income, tax efficiency, and long-term growth. The *Delaware Statutory Trust,* more commonly known as a DST, offers just that. It provides a structured, IRS-approved way to invest passively in institutional-grade real estate, all while preserving the ability to defer taxes through a 1031 exchange.

DSTs are not widely understood by many real estate investors, yet they have become one of the most important tools available for any accredited investor looking to transition from active to passive real estate ownership. They combine the income potential and tax benefits of direct ownership with the ease of managed investments. When structured correctly, DSTs also create powerful estate planning advantages, offering a pathway to multigenerational wealth transfer without the logistical complications of managing individual properties.

In this section, we will examine the legal framework of DSTs, the key benefits they provide for passive investors, and the risks and limitations that every investor should consider before participating. This section is designed to help you determine whether a DST fits within your broader tax-smart strategy and long-term financial plan.

Accredited Investors

It is important to note that DST offerings are considered private placements regulated by the Securities and Exchange Commission (SEC). As a result, they are typically available only to *accredited investors.*

An accredited investor is defined as someone who meets at least one of the following criteria:

- Individuals who have a net worth exceeding $1 million, excluding the value of their primary residence.
- Individuals who have earned income exceeding $200,000 in each of the past two years (or $300,000 jointly with a spouse) and reasonably expect the same in the current year.
- Individuals who hold certain financial licenses, such as Series 7 (General Securities Representative), Series 65 (Investment Adviser Representative), or Series 82 (Private Securities Offerings Representative).

- Individuals who are knowledgeable employees of a private fund (such as executive officers, directors, trustees, general partners, or advisory personnel).
- Trusts, LLCs, corporations, and family offices can also be considered accredited if they meet specific asset or knowledge-based thresholds (typically $5 million in assets or all equity owners are accredited).

Accreditation ensures that investors have the financial sophistication and risk tolerance required for complex, nonpublic investment offerings. Before considering a DST or any similar investment, be sure to consult with your financial advisor or tax professional to confirm whether you meet the qualifications and to determine whether such an investment aligns with your overall strategy.

Structure and Legal Framework

A DST is a legally recognized entity formed under Delaware law, although the real estate it owns may be located anywhere in the United States. Investors purchase fractional interests in the trust, which holds title to underlying properties. Each investor is considered a beneficial owner and receives a proportional share of the income, tax deductions, and appreciation generated by the properties.

DSTs are governed by a trust agreement that defines the responsibilities of the plan sponsor, the management structure, and the terms under which the property will be operated and eventually sold. The sponsor is responsible for all decisions relating to leasing, maintenance, financing, and compliance.

This legal structure was solidified by IRS Revenue Ruling 2004-86. According to that ruling, as long as the DST is structured properly and investors do not participate in day-to-day operations, the investment qualifies as a direct real estate interest. This allows investors to use proceeds from a 1031 exchange to purchase DST interests without triggering capital gains or depreciation recapture taxes.

DSTs are typically used to acquire high-value properties such as Class A apartment complexes, commercial buildings, medical centers, or industrial warehouses. By pooling resources, the DST can access assets that would otherwise be beyond the reach of individual investors. Each participant benefits from the scale, professional oversight, and potential stability of these institutional-grade investments.

Benefits of DSTs for Passive Investors

One of the primary advantages of DSTs is the ability to earn passive real estate income without the burden of active management. This makes them especially attractive to seasoned investors who have spent decades dealing with tenants, repairs, and regulatory requirements and are now looking for a more simplified way to stay invested in the real estate market.

It is also an extremely attractive option for business owners who have sold their business, along with the related real estate. As an example, if you own a dental practice along with the related real estate office, when you sell your practice, if you also sell the office building, then the real estate portion of the sale can be separated and 1031 exchanged.

The following are 10 of the main benefits of completing your 1031 exchange through a DST.

1. **No management responsibilities:** DSTs are managed by experienced real estate property management firms that handle all aspects of property operations. This includes finding and managing tenants, collecting rent, handling maintenance issues, and preparing financial reports. Investors can step away from the day-to-day responsibilities while still benefiting from real estate rental income and potential capital appreciation.
2. **Access to institutional quality property:** By investing through a DST, individuals gain access to properties that would normally be limited to institutional investors. These may include assets such as properties leased to national tenants on long-term contracts, multifamily, build-to-rent communities, student housing, senior living facilities, self-storage facilities, and many other institutional-grade properties, which can help reduce vacancy risk and income volatility.
3. **Limited personal liability:** Loans are nonrecourse to investors. The DST is the sole borrower, and the investor does not have to apply or qualify for a mortgage.
4. **Lower minimum investments:** DSTs can accommodate minimum investments of $100,000 or more, where if you are buying a property directly, you'd have to come up with significantly more. If you acquired property to manage on your own but did not invest the full amount held through the qualified

intermediary, you can also eliminate the boot by investing the excess cash into a DST.

5. **Diversification opportunities:** Because many DSTs have relatively low minimum investment thresholds, investors can spread their capital across multiple properties and markets. This helps reduce risk by avoiding overconcentration in any one location or property type. This provides investors with both geographical and real estate asset class diversification.

   For example, a balanced approach might include a multifamily DST for steady cash flow, an industrial DST for growth potential tied to e-commerce and logistics, and a medical office DST for low turnover and long-term leases with creditworthy tenants. This approach can help maintain stability while still positioning part of your portfolio for future appreciation. It also provides a hedge against regional economic downturns by spreading exposure across different parts of the country.
6. **Estate planning:** Because DST interests are clearly defined and titled, they are easy to include in estate plans. They can be held within a revocable as well as irrevocable trust, distributed according to a will, or transferred to heirs through a beneficiary designation.

   Upon the death of the owner, DST interests may receive a step-up in basis if structured correctly. This will provide the beneficiary with the immediate tax benefit through additional depreciation and will eliminate the deferred tax liability as of the date of death which they can take advantage of once the DST property is sold. This is where tax deferral becomes complete tax avoidance, since neither the deceased taxpayer nor their beneficiaries will have to pay capital gains or depreciation recapture tax upon sale of the DST property.
7. **Ease of identification and investing:** Given the strict 45-day deadline post-property sale to identify a replacement property when executing a 1031 exchange, many investors find it extremely challenging to complete an exchange on their own. It is not easy to find a quality investment property in just 45 days! This is another way DSTs benefit investors. Because the DST structures are already in place, investors do not have to worry about finding a property on their own and can invest the proceeds right away.

8. **Insurance policy:** For investors looking to acquire their own property to manage, they can always identify one or more DSTs as one of their fallback options. This keeps their options open during days 46 through 180. If they have issues closing on the acquisition of the property they originally wanted to acquire, they can opt to invest in the DST instead.

   The bottom line is that if you are an investor looking to do a 1031 exchange yourself, it is highly recommended to at least identify a DST as one of your properties during the 45-day ID window to keep your options open and to help ensure you don't get stuck paying the taxes.
9. **Consistent monthly income:** Most DSTs are designed to provide predictable distributions on a monthly or quarterly basis. These distributions represent the investor's share of the net rental income collected from the property after expenses. This steady cash flow can be a valuable income source, particularly for those in or near retirement.
10. **Swap until you drop:** Every DST comes with a specific business plan with the intention of increasing net cash flow and increasing the value of the underlying property so it can be sold off within 5–10 years. Each time the underlying DST property is sold, the investor has the option to take some or all the cash and pay the associated taxes, complete a 1031 exchange into a property they wish to own and manage directly, or reinvest through another DST. Ultimately, the swap until you drop strategy allows you to continue to do 1031 exchanges until you pass away, allowing not only you, but your beneficiaries, to completely avoid capital gains and depreciation recapture tax on the property.

Risks and Limitations of DSTs

While DSTs offer many benefits, they also come with limitations that should be considered carefully. These investments are not suitable for everyone and should be evaluated within the context of your broader financial goals.

1. **Lack of investor control:** DST investors have no decision-making authority. All property management, leasing, and sale decisions are handled by the sponsor. If you are used to managing your

own properties or prefer to be involved in operational decisions, this lack of control may be viewed as a disadvantage.
2. **Illiquidity:** DSTs are long-term investments with holding periods that typically range from 5–10 years. There is no public market for reselling interests, and early redemption is usually not possible. Investors must be comfortable with having their funds locked in for an extended period.
3. **Fee structure:** DSTs involve multiple layers of fees, including acquisition fees, management fees, and sponsor compensation. These fees can impact overall returns. It is important to work with a trusted advisor who can help you evaluate the fee disclosures and compare offerings from different sponsors.
4. **Market and operational risk:** As with any real estate investment, DSTs are subject to market fluctuations, tenant defaults, rising interest rates, and unexpected maintenance issues. While professional management can help reduce risk, no investment is immune to economic cycles or sector-specific challenges.
5. **Income variability:** As with all real estate investing, there is no guarantee of consistent monthly income, since this would be contingent on market conditions, occupancy rates, and the risk of escalating costs. Investors should be prepared for the possibility that distributions may fluctuate or be reduced during periods of economic stress or higher-than-expected expenses.

For investors seeking passive income, tax deferral, and simplified estate transfer, DSTs can be a powerful planning tool. When used thoughtfully and in consultation with qualified professionals, they can provide an income-producing alternative to traditional real estate investing. As with any investment, careful evaluation, due diligence, and alignment with your long-term goals are essential.

Utilizing a DST with a 1031 Exchange

For many real estate investors looking to transition into a more passive role, the combination of a 1031 exchange and a DST offers an exceptional opportunity.

In practice, many investors use DSTs as the replacement property in a 1031 exchange when they are ready to exit active ownership. Instead of buying another single property and managing it on their own, they reinvest in one or more DSTs that meet the like-kind requirement. This not only meets the IRS rules for a tax-deferred exchange, but it also transforms the nature of the investment. What was once a hands-on real estate business, now becomes a passive income stream, still backed by tangible real estate assets.

Satisfies Debt Requirements for Replacement Through a DST

To avoid taxable gains in a 1031 exchange, investors must also replace any debt they may have had on the property they sold. DSTs can accommodate this requirement in several ways. Some DSTs come with pre-arranged nonrecourse debt, which allows you to assume your pro rata share of the trust's loan. Others may be offered as all-cash investments; in which case you will need to invest more of your own funds or use additional DSTs to reach the replacement debt value required.

Plan Sponsor Ongoing Reporting

Once the exchange is complete, the DST sponsor will provide regular reports on the performance of the property, including income distributions, tax documents such as Form 1099 or K-1 equivalents, and annual financial summaries. You will also receive updates on any major events that may have occurred during that period.

This structure provides transparency, oversight, and consistency, making it an ideal solution for those seeking a passive investment that still maintains many of the benefits associated with direct property ownership.

Professional Guidance Is Essential

While the benefits of DSTs within a 1031 exchange can be significant, achieving those benefits requires careful planning and professional execution. This is not a process to handle on your own. The rules governing 1031 exchanges are strict, and the financial implications of getting it wrong can be substantial.

Not all DSTs are created equal. Sponsors vary widely in experience, reputation, and investment philosophy. Before committing to any DST, take time to review the sponsor's background, the terms of the offering, the lease structures, and the projected cash flow and capital appreciation. Evaluate the asset type, tenant mix, financing arrangements, and geographic location. Look closely at the fee structure, including acquisition costs, management fees, and exit costs, to understand how they will impact your returns. For this reason, working closely with a team of professionals is essential.

Your team should include a qualified intermediary, who manages the technical execution of the exchange and ensures compliance with all IRS requirements. You should also work with a financial advisor who understands your broader goals and can help evaluate which DST offerings align best with your needs. Your CPA plays a critical role as well, helping you analyze how the transaction affects your tax situation and making sure the structure supports your overall financial strategy.

Utilizing a 1033 Exchange with Involuntary Conversions

There are times when the sale of real estate is not a choice but the result of events completely outside of our control. A flood, fire, hurricane, or even government condemnation can destroy or take away property that an investor never intended to sell. When that happens, the owner may receive insurance proceeds, disaster relief payments, or a condemnation award. Under normal circumstances, if the amount received is greater than the property's adjusted basis, the excess is treated as a taxable gain.

Fortunately, the tax law provides relief through a 1033 exchange. This provision is specifically designed for these involuntary conversions. Rather than being forced to recognize the gain right away, an investor can defer it by reinvesting the proceeds into replacement property within the time limits set by the IRS. The key is that the full amount received must be rolled into the new property. When done properly, the tax that would otherwise be due is postponed, and the basis of the destroyed or condemned property carries over into the new property.

One of the main advantages of 1033 over 1031 is that no intermediary is required. The insurance proceeds or condemnation award can be paid directly to the investor, who then uses the funds to purchase the replacement property. The rules also provide more flexibility in what qualifies as replacement property. It must be similar or related in service or use, which is a looser standard than the strict like-kind requirement under 1031.

Investors also enjoy a longer time frame. In most cases, it is two years from the end of the tax year of the conversion. For business or investment property, the window extends to three years, and when a federally declared disaster is involved, the IRS often grants additional time.

The bottom line is that a 1033 exchange can be an invaluable tax-smart strategy for real estate investors who experience an involuntary conversion. It allows them to turn an otherwise devastating event into an opportunity to rebuild without the immediate burden of capital gains and depreciation recapture tax.

Exhibit 11.2 will provide you with a side-by-side comparison of the major differences between a 1031 Exchange and 1033 Exchange.

Exhibit 11.2 1031 Exchanges Versus 1033 Exchanges

Feature	1031 Exchange (Voluntary)	1033 Exchange (Involuntary)
Triggering Event	Voluntary sale or exchange of investment or business property	Involuntary conversion such as destruction, theft, seizure, condemnation, or natural disaster
Type of Proceeds	Proceeds from sale of property	Insurance proceeds, disaster relief payments, or condemnation awards
Tax Deferral Requirement	Proceeds must be reinvested in like-kind property	Proceeds must be reinvested in property "similar or related in service or use"
Intermediary Required	Yes, must use a qualified intermediary to hold and transfer proceeds	No intermediary required. Investor can directly receive and reinvest proceeds
Time Frame to Reinvest	45 days to identify replacement property; 180 days to close	Two years from the end of the tax year of the conversion (three years for business or investment real estate). Extensions possible in federally declared disaster areas
Flexibility	Strict rules and deadlines. Limited flexibility	More flexibility in property type, timing, and process
Example of Use	Investor sells an apartment building and reinvests in a shopping center.	Investor's rental home was destroyed by a hurricane. Insurance proceeds reinvested into another rental property to defer gain.

Leveraging a 1033 Exchange with a DST

One of the most effective ways to carry out a 1033 exchange, especially for investors who prefer a passive and professionally managed option, is to reinvest in a DST. Under the Internal Revenue Code, DSTs qualify as replacement property for real estate taken through condemnation.

In the case of property destroyed by a natural disaster, a DST may also qualify if it is considered "similar or related in service or use" to the property that was lost. For owner-investors, the IRS looks at factors such as the type of property, the business risks involved, and the level of management required. As a result, a DST will often be an appropriate fit when the destroyed property was already held as a relatively passive rental or investment property.

This feature makes DSTs particularly appealing following an involuntary conversion. The process of losing property to condemnation or casualty can be disruptive and stressful, and many owners do not want to reenter the demands of direct property management. A DST allows you to preserve the tax-deferral benefit of 1033 while transitioning away from the responsibilities of active ownership.

The mechanics of a 1033 exchange also make DSTs more accessible than 1031 exchanges. There is no need to use a qualified intermediary, and there are no 45-day or 180-day deadlines. Instead, you have two years from the end of the tax year of the conversion, or three years for business and investment property, to identify and acquire replacement property. In federally declared disaster areas, the IRS may grant additional time. See Exhibit 11.2 for a side-by-side comparison of a 1031 versus a 1033 exchange.

For property owners facing condemnation, destruction, or any form of forced sale, a 1033 exchange provides a critical opportunity to protect wealth and avoid unnecessary taxation. When combined with a DST, it becomes a powerful strategy that blends tax efficiency, investment simplicity, and long-term planning. The rules in this area are precise, and professional guidance is essential, but with the right planning this approach can turn a challenging situation into a renewed path toward financial independence.

Passive Income Generators: What They Are and When to Use Them

As you move further along your journey to financial independence, you will begin to shift your focus from accumulating wealth to generating reliable income from the wealth you have built. That is where *passive income generators*, often referred to as PIGs, enter the picture. These are investment vehicles tied to real estate or real estate-backed assets, specifically structured to provide steady, predictable income to investors who no longer want the demands of direct property ownership.

The name may sound informal, but the concept is foundational to effective retirement and legacy planning. PIGs are designed to deliver cash flow without the ongoing responsibilities associated with managing tenants, coordinating repairs, or overseeing property finances. For those transitioning into retirement, reducing their work hours, or planning their estate, PIGs can provide the stability and tax efficiency needed to maintain a comfortable lifestyle while preserving long-term financial goals.

The most common types of PIGs include DSTs, triple-net lease properties, and certain private real estate income funds. These structures are typically overseen by experienced managers and supported by contracts or leases that define how and when income is distributed. The underlying real estate is often leased to creditworthy tenants on long-term agreements, which helps create a reliable revenue stream for investors.

One of the main advantages of PIGs is the ability to generate passive income that is often partially or fully sheltered from taxes using noncash deductions such as depreciation. This tax efficiency increases the net value of the income you receive. For individuals who have spent years building equity in real estate, the ability to transition that equity into an income-producing asset without triggering a major tax event can be both strategic and liberating.

The primary objective of a PIG is not growth through speculation. Instead, the focus is on consistency, preservation of capital, and dependable monthly or quarterly payments. This makes PIGs especially well-suited for retirees who need predictable cash flow to cover living expenses or for high-net-worth individuals who want to reduce volatility in their investment portfolios.

Incorporating PIGs into your financial strategy requires a thoughtful analysis of your personal goals, liquidity needs, and tax profile. For example, if your priority is stable monthly income, you might consider a diversified basket of triple-net lease properties backed by national retailers. If you are more focused on simplicity and estate efficiency, a DST might be the right choice, particularly if you are completing a 1031 or 1033 exchange and want to maintain your tax deferral while removing yourself from active management responsibilities.

For real estate investors who incur operating losses, it is important to understand how the Passive Activity Loss Rules under Internal Revenue Code Section 469 may affect your ability to claim those losses. If your modified adjusted gross income is $100,000 or less, you may be eligible to deduct up to $25,000 in passive real estate losses annually against your other income. However, once your income exceeds $100,000, this benefit begins to phase out and is completely eliminated at $150,000. Losses that cannot be deducted due to these income limits are not lost but are instead suspended and carried forward into future years, available to offset future passive income or gain from the sale of a passive investment.

This is where PIGs can play a strategic role. If you have accumulated suspended real estate losses that you have not been able to use because of income limitations, investing in a PIG can allow you to unlock their value. The income generated by the PIG is considered passive income and can be offset by these previously unusable losses. This can result in tax-free income, which enhances your cash flow while simultaneously drawing down your suspended losses. This approach not only makes tax-efficient use of your existing investment history but also integrates seamlessly with a broader strategy of simplification and diversification.

It is important to remember that not all PIGs are created equal. Some may offer higher returns but come with higher risks, more complex structures, or limited access to your principal. Others may prioritize capital preservation and liquidity but generate lower yields.

When used correctly, passive income generators can serve as a cornerstone of your retirement income plan. They allow you to convert illiquid, actively managed real estate into streamlined, tax-efficient income that supports your lifestyle and long-term financial goals. Whether you are looking to simplify, stabilize, or pass on your wealth, PIGs offer a way to keep your money working for you, even as you scale back your own day-to-day involvement.

Qualified Opportunity Zone Funds

Qualified Opportunity Zone Funds (QOZFs) represent one of the most innovative and potentially rewarding tools in the real estate investment landscape for those seeking to defer capital gains and support long-term tax-free growth. Originally created as part of the Tax Cuts and Jobs Act (TCJA) of 2017 and reestablished with the One Big Beautiful Bill Act (OBBBA) of 2025, these funds are designed to encourage investment in economically distressed communities across the United States. In return for providing capital to these areas, investors receive a series of valuable tax incentives.

QOZ 1.0. (TCJA) Applicable for Investments Through December 31, 2026

At its core, the *Qualified Opportunity Zone* program lets you reinvest capital gains from the sale of many types of assets into designated census tracts that were nominated by governors and certified by the Treasury Department. These zones are identified using federal low-income community criteria that capture areas with elevated poverty and lower median family income. A total of 8,764 zones were designated across the states, the District of Columbia, and the territories.

The near-term benefit is tax deferral. If you reinvest an eligible capital gains in a Qualified Opportunity Fund within 180 days of recognizing that gain, you can defer the tax on that amount until the end of 2026 under the original framework. The regulations also provide flexible 180-day timing rules for pass-through K-1 gains, capital gains dividends from Regulated Investment Companies and Real Estate Investment Trusts, and installment sales.

The long-term benefit is the opportunity to eliminate tax on future appreciation. If you hold your Qualified Opportunity Zone investment for at least 10 years, you may elect to step up your basis to fair market value at the time of sale so that the appreciation on that fund investment is excluded from federal capital gains.

Most investors access the rules through a QOZF, a corporation or partnership that self-certifies on IRS Form 8996 and must hold at least 90% of its assets in Qualified Opportunity Zone property.

QOZFs differ from 1031 exchanges in several helpful ways. Only the amount of gain needs to be reinvested in QOZF to qualify. You do not have to replace the entire gross sales price or match prior debt as you would in a typical like-kind exchange. There is no 45-day identification period, and you are not required to use a QI. The 180-day window and the requirement to invest through a properly structured QOZ still apply.

QOZ 2.0. (OBBBA) Applicable for Investments After December 31, 2026

On July 4, 2025, Congress enacted the OBBBA, Public Law 119-21. The law made the Opportunity Zone framework a permanent part of the code and revised several key mechanics for new investments beginning in 2027.

- **Recognition timing:** For amounts invested in a Qualified Opportunity Zone after December 31, 2026, the inclusion date for the originally deferred gain moves to the earlier of the date you sell the fund investment or the date that is five years after you make the fund investment. This creates a rolling five-year deferral window for new investments.

- **Basis increases:** If you hold a post-2026 fund investment for at least five years, your basis in that fund interest increases by 10% of the deferred gain before the five-year inclusion date applies. The law also creates a special category for qualified rural opportunity funds that receive a 30% basis increase at the five-year mark.
- **Ten-year exit:** The 10-year rule that allows you to exclude appreciation on a QOZ investment remains in place. Under the new statute, the basis step-up election is clarified with a fair market value basis at sale and a 30-year outside date if there is no sale.
- **Designations and substantial improvement:** New QOZ designations made after enactment run for 10 years from an applicable start date, and the prior rule for certain contiguous tracts was removed. For projects in rural zones, the substantial improvement threshold for existing structures may be met at 50% of adjusted basis rather than 100%.
- **Reporting:** The statute adds detailed annual information reporting for funds and underlying QOZ businesses, which increases transparency and compliance requirements.

Example Under the Post-2026 Rules

Samantha bought stock for $10,000 in 2013. On February 18, 2027, she sells for $110,000 and recognizes a $100,000 capital gain. She invests $100,000 of gain in a QOZF by August 17, 2027, which is within 180 days. She holds the fund investment until 2038 and then sells this QOZF project. Her share of the sale proceeds is $180,000.

Tax result under QOZ 2.0:

- **Deferral:** Samantha defers tax on the $100,000, 2027 stock gain until the earlier of a sale of her fund interest or the date five years after her investment. If she continues to hold onto the QOZF investment, the deferred gain will be included in her 2032 tax year under the five-year rule.
- **Five-year basis increase:** Because she has had QOZF for at least five years, she receives a 10% basis increase on the deferred gain. Her recognized gain in 2032 is reduced to $90,000 for federal tax purposes.
- **Ten-year exclusion:** Because she has had QOZF investment for more than 10 years, she may elect to step up her basis to

fair market value on exit. The appreciation inside the fund from her entry value to her final value is excluded from federal capital gains. In this example, the $180,000, 2038 proceeds from the fund are received without additional federal capital gain tax on the appreciation and she does not have to recapture any depreciation that she benefited from throughout the holding period.

Only the recognized gain needs to be invested. You can retain your original cost basis from the asset you sold because basis is not taxable. You still must invest through a properly organized and self-certified QOZF and meet the 90% asset test at the fund level. The familiar 180-day timing rules for when gains become eligible continue to apply through the new regulations. Finally, the new statute adds reporting and tracking that your fund and its underlying businesses will need to satisfy.

Private Real Estate Placements: Access to Institutional-grade Deals

Private real estate placements provide individual investors with access to large-scale, professionally managed properties that were once available only to institutions and ultra-high-net-worth individuals. These investments provide access to the private real estate market, even for investors who are not selling an existing property. These opportunities are typically offered through limited partnerships or limited liability companies and are structured as Regulation D offerings under federal securities law.

By investing in a private placement, you can own a fractional interest in assets such as apartment complexes, industrial parks, medical centers, or mixed-use developments. These deals are often sponsored by experienced real estate firms that manage the property, execute the business plan, and distribute income to investors based on their ownership share.

What makes private placements appealing is the opportunity to participate in projects with strong income potential and long-term appreciation. The properties are usually stabilized or undergoing value-add improvements, and they are often located in markets with high growth potential. Because the investments are pooled, you benefit from the scale and expertise of a professional sponsor without having to take on management responsibilities yourself.

However, private placements are illiquid, long-term commitments. Most come with a minimum investment threshold, typically ranging from $100,000 to $250,000, and a holding period of 5 to 10 years. They are best suited for accredited investors who have a clear long-term plan and who are comfortable trying to tie up capital in exchange for income and growth.

When selected carefully and incorporated into a diversified real estate portfolio, private placements can be a valuable way to enhance returns, reduce operational burdens, and access investment opportunities that are not available on public markets.

Real Estate Investment Trusts

Not everyone is in a position to purchase and manage physical properties or participate in private real estate offerings. But that doesn't mean they have to miss out on the income, growth, and diversification benefits that real estate can offer. For many investors, *Real Estate Investment Trusts* (REITs) provide a practical way to participate in the real estate market without the responsibilities of direct ownership.

A REIT is a company that owns, operates, or finances income-producing real estate. To qualify as a REIT under federal law, it must meet strict criteria, including the requirement to distribute at least 90% of its taxable income to shareholders each year. These regular distributions are often appealing to income-focused investors and can provide a reliable stream of cash flow, an essential ingredient in achieving financial independence.

There are two ways to classify REITs. The first is based on how they are accessed:

- **Publicly Traded REITs:** Listed on major stock exchanges and can be bought and sold like any other stock. They offer liquidity, transparency, and easy access for everyday investors.
- **Public Nontraded REITs:** Registered with the SEC but do not trade on exchanges. While they are less liquid and often have higher fees, they may offer more consistent valuations during market volatility.
- **Private REITs:** Not publicly registered and are typically available only to accredited investors. These are usually offered through financial professionals as part of a broader investment strategy.

The second way to categorize REITs is by what they invest in:

- **Equity REITs:** Own and manage real estate such as apartment buildings, shopping centers, office complexes, and more. They earn income primarily through rent.
- **Mortgage REITs (mREITs):** Invest in mortgages and mortgage-backed securities. Their income comes from the interest on these loans.
- **Hybrid REITs:** Combine both equity and mortgage strategies.

From a tax planning standpoint, REITs can complement other real estate strategies in a diversified portfolio. Although they don't offer tax deferral like 1031 exchanges and QOZFs, many REIT dividends qualify for the 20% Qualified Business Income (QBI) deduction under current law. This can reduce the tax burden on income and help maximize after-tax returns.

REITs also play an important role in building passive income, a key component of financial independence. The regular cash flow they provide, combined with the potential for long-term capital appreciation, makes them an effective tool for investors seeking to reduce their reliance on earned income over time. And because they're accessible through traditional brokerage accounts, REITs can be easily integrated into retirement plans, taxable portfolios, or income strategies.

Whether used as a standalone investment or in conjunction with other real estate holdings, REITs offer a tax-smart, low-maintenance way to put your money to work in real estate.

How the IRS Classifies Real Estate Investors

Before you can fully understand how real estate income and losses affect your tax return, you need to know how the IRS classifies your involvement in rental real estate. The tax treatment of your income or losses depends not on what kind of investor you are in general terms, but on how the IRS views your level of participation in real estate activities under Internal Revenue Code Section 469. These classifications determine whether and how you can deduct real estate losses from other income sources, and they are central to building a tax-smart financial strategy.

The IRS generally places rental real estate activities into one of three treatment categories:

1. Passive participation (the default)
2. Active participation (allows limited deductions)
3. Real estate professional status (allows full deductions)

While these are not official "investor types" in the IRS code, they are the key categories used by tax professionals when applying the passive activity loss rules. Each classification carries different thresholds, limitations, and planning opportunities. Understanding where you fall, and how to structure your involvement, can help you reduce your tax liability and optimize your investment results.

Active Participation Versus Passive Activity

The IRS treats all rental real estate activity as passive by default. This means that, unless you qualify for a specific exception, you generally cannot deduct losses from rental properties against your nonpassive income such as wages, salaries, or business income. For many casual investors, this means that real estate losses generated by depreciation or operating costs are suspended and carried forward into future years. Those losses can only be used to offset passive income or recognized when the property is sold in a fully taxable transaction.

A valuable exception exists, however, for investors who meet the criteria for active participation. If you own at least 10% of the rental property and make management-level decisions such as approving tenants or authorizing repairs, you may qualify to deduct up to $25,000 in real estate losses each year against your ordinary income. This benefit is subject to an income limitation: it begins to phase out once your modified adjusted gross income (MAGI) exceeds $100,000 and is fully eliminated when your income reaches $150,000. Losses not used due to this income limitation are carried forward and may be applied against future passive income.

From a tax planning perspective, these rules create distinct strategies for different income levels. If your income is below the threshold and you are actively managing your property, claiming the $25,000 deduction can provide meaningful annual tax savings.

In contrast, higher-income investors who cannot benefit from this deduction may choose to invest in PIGs such as DSTs or triple-net lease properties. These investments generate passive income that can be offset by suspended passive losses, allowing you to realize cash flow with minimal or no tax liability.

The key takeaway is that the IRS does not simply look at whether you own property; it considers how involved you are in managing it, how much income you earn, and how your income is derived. Structuring your investments with these rules in mind allows you to capture available deductions, defer taxable income, and create a more efficient long-term income plan.

Real Estate Professional Status

If your real estate involvement goes beyond part-time investing or occasional management, you may be able to qualify as a *real estate professional.* This is a distinct classification under Section 469(c)(7) of the tax code that allows eligible individuals to treat rental real estate as a nonpassive activity. Unlike passive or active participants, real estate professionals are not subject to the $25,000 maximum loss rule or its income-based limitations. This makes the classification one of the most powerful tools available to individuals who are deeply involved in real estate and looking to maximize tax efficiency.

To qualify, the IRS requires that you meet two specific criteria each year:

1. You must spend more than 750 hours during the tax year participating in real property trades or businesses in which you materially participate.
2. More than 50% of your total working hours must be spent in those same qualifying real estate activities. These include development, redevelopment, construction, reconstruction, acquisition, conversion, rental, leasing, management, and brokerage.

If you are employed in another full-time profession, meeting these standards becomes extremely difficult unless real estate is your primary occupation. Both tests must be met annually, and time spent on investment analysis or portfolio review generally does not count toward the required hours.

Qualifying as a real estate professional offers a fundamentally different tax treatment from passive or active participation. Passive investors cannot use real estate losses to offset nonpassive income such as wages, business profits, or capital gains. Active participants may deduct up to $25,000 in losses against other income, but only if their modified adjusted gross income is below $100,000 and they meet certain involvement thresholds. By contrast, real estate professionals face no income limit and no $25,000 cap. If you meet the criteria, and materially participate in your rental activity, all losses are fully deductible, which can dramatically reduce your overall tax burden, especially in otherwise high-income years.

Because of the substantial tax benefits at stake, the IRS often scrutinizes claims of real estate professional status. Audit risk is significantly higher in this area, particularly for individuals who hold other full-time jobs or cannot produce detailed documentation.

To protect yourself, it is essential to maintain accurate, contemporaneous records. These should include time logs, calendars, and supporting documents that detail what you did, when you did it, and how it related to your real estate activity. Acceptable documentation may also include emails, repair orders, lease documents, and notes from property management tasks. If you own multiple properties, you may file an election with your tax return to treat all rental activities as one for the purpose of meeting the material participation requirement.

Strategically, the best approach to qualifying as a real estate professional is to be both intentional and methodical. If real estate is your primary occupation, track your hours diligently throughout the year. If you are working toward qualification, consider reducing your hours in nonreal estate work or increasing your direct involvement in your properties. Couples filing jointly can leverage the rule that only one spouse needs to qualify, which can be especially beneficial when one spouse manages the real estate full-time while the other works outside the home.

When supported by credible documentation and aligned with your actual work activity, the real estate professional classification can transform your tax profile (see Exhibit 11.3). It allows you to convert paper losses, especially those generated through depreciation, into real-time tax savings. Used correctly, it turns your real estate holdings into a flexible tool for income management, wealth building, and accelerated financial independence.

Exhibit 11.3 Real Estate Investor Classifications at a Glance

IRS Classification	Participation Standard	Deductible Loss Limit	Income Limit	Can Offset Nonpassive Income?	Audit Risk	Key Planning Strategy
Passive Participant	No material participation	None (losses suspended)	Not Applicable	No	Low to Moderate	Use passive losses against passive income or future gains
Active Participant	10% ownership and active decision-making	Up to $25,000 per year	Phases out between $100–150k MAGI	Yes (within limits)	Moderate	Claim $25k offset against nonpassive income if eligible and under income threshold
Real Estate Professional	>750 hours and >50% of working time in real estate	Unlimited (if materially participating)	None	Yes	High	Track hours and elect aggregation if needed

Best Practices and Pitfalls to Avoid as a Real Estate Investor

Real estate can be one of the most rewarding components of a financial independence plan, but it also comes with risks. Like any powerful tool, it must be used wisely. Over the years, we have seen clients succeed through careful planning and disciplined execution. We have also seen people make costly mistakes because they overlooked key fundamentals or acted on emotion rather than strategy. In this section, we will cover the essential best practices every real estate investor should follow and highlight the most common pitfalls to avoid.

- **Start with a clear plan:** Before you purchase a property or invest in a real estate fund, take the time to define your objectives. Are you looking for long-term growth, steady income, tax benefits, or estate planning advantages? Different strategies serve different purposes. Your goals should guide your decisions about property type, location, financing, and management structure.
- **Build the right team:** Successful real estate investing is rarely a solo effort. You need the support of experienced professionals who understand the tax code, legal structures, market dynamics, and property management. This includes a qualified CPA, a real estate attorney, a knowledgeable real estate broker, and, when needed, a financial advisor who can help align your real estate decisions with your broader financial plan.
- **Maintain adequate reserves:** One of the most common reasons investors get into trouble is a lack of liquidity. Always keep a cash reserve for unexpected expenses, vacancies, or market downturns. Do not assume your property will generate perfect cash flow every month. Conservative planning creates resilience and gives you the ability to weather temporary setbacks.
- **Understand the tax implications:** Real estate offers valuable tax advantages, but those benefits depend on how your investment is structured and managed. Know how depreciation, mortgage interest, cost segregation studies, and 1031 exchanges work. Be aware of potential exposure to depreciation recapture or state-specific tax rules. Ignorance is costly. Knowledge allows you to capture opportunities and protect your gains.

- **Review your portfolio regularly:** Markets change. So do your personal goals and financial needs. Make it a habit to review your real estate holdings at least once a year. Assess performance, cash flow, property condition, and the role each asset plays in your overall strategy. If something no longer serves your goals, be willing to pivot. That might mean selling, refinancing, or transitioning to a more passive structure.

Now, let's look at a few of the most common mistakes real estate investors make and how to avoid them.

- **Overleveraging:** Borrowing can help you grow your portfolio, but too much debt can create vulnerability. Use leverage carefully and understand your debt coverage ratios. Never stretch your finances so thin that one vacancy or interest rate increase puts your investment at risk.
- **Chasing appreciation without fundamentals:** Buying a property just because you believe it will go up in value is speculation, not investing. Look for strong fundamentals: solid cash flow, good location, stable tenant demand, and manageable expenses. Appreciation should be the bonus, not the foundation.
- **Neglecting due diligence:** Always inspect before you invest. That means reviewing title reports, getting professional inspections, analyzing rent rolls, studying market trends, and confirming zoning and permit history. Rushing into a deal without full information can lead to expensive surprises.
- **Failing to plan for exit:** Every investment should include a plan for how and when you might exit. Will you sell, exchange, pass the property to heirs, or refinance for income? Without an exit plan, you may miss opportunities for tax efficiency or wealth transfer. Think ahead and keep your options open.

With the right discipline and support, real estate can be a reliable and transformative part of your financial independence journey. Stick to the fundamentals, stay informed, and treat every investment like a business. These best practices will help you build wealth steadily and avoid the missteps that cause others to fall short. The goal is not just to invest in real estate, but to invest with clarity, confidence, and long-term success in mind.

Real Estate Investment Checklists and Evaluations

Even the most experienced investors benefit from structure and discipline. Real estate can involve high stakes, long timelines, and complex decisions. Using checklists helps ensure that nothing critical is overlooked and that each investment aligns with your goals, risk tolerance, and tax strategy. In this final section, we provide tools to help you evaluate opportunities methodically and make informed decisions at every stage of the process.

These checklists are designed for practical use. You can refer to them when evaluating a new property, conducting due diligence, or considering a transition to a more passive investment structure. They are also helpful for conversations with your advisors, giving you a shared framework to assess risks, opportunities, and next steps.

Following are three core checklists: one for evaluating a direct real estate investment, one for preparing for a 1031 or 1033 exchange, and one for selecting a passive investment such as a DST, private placements, or REITs.

Direct Real Estate Investment Checklist

- Have I clearly defined my investment goals (income, expected appreciation, tax benefits, etc.)?
- Does this property align with my short-term and long-term financial plan?
- Have I verified cash flow projections, including realistic vacancy rates and expenses?
- Have I reviewed property condition reports and estimated capital improvements?
- Have I conducted a market analysis to assess local demand, pricing trends, and employment conditions?
- Am I prepared to manage this property, or have I secured a reliable management firm?
- Do I have sufficient liquidity for closing costs, repairs, and reserves?
- Have I reviewed all legal documents including title, zoning, and any liens?
- How does this property complement or diversify my existing portfolio?
- What is my exit strategy for this investment?

1031/1033 Exchange Preparation Checklist

- Have I consulted my CPA and legal team before initiating the sale of my property?
- Have I engaged a qualified intermediary to handle the funds if using a 1031 exchange?
- Do I understand the timeline requirements (45-day identification and 180-day close for 1031; up to two or three years for 1033)?
- Have I identified like-kind replacement properties that meet IRS criteria?
- Am I matching or exceeding the value and debt of my relinquished property?
- Have I evaluated DSTs, private placements, or other passive options for reinvestment?
- How will this exchange affect my tax position this year and in future years?
- Is this reinvestment aligned with my cash flow needs and estate planning objectives?

Passive Real Estate Investment Evaluation Checklist

- Is the sponsor or manager experienced and reputable?
- Have I reviewed detailed offering documents including fee structures and distributions?
- Is the underlying asset type aligned with my investment objectives?
- Does the investment provide adequate income for my needs?
- What is the minimum investment and expected holding period?
- What are the liquidity limitations and exit options?
- Have I reviewed tax implications, including projected depreciation and reporting format?
- Does this investment provide geographic or sector diversification within my portfolio?
- Have I evaluated the risk disclosures and stress-tested assumptions?
- How does this passive investment support my financial independence goals?

These checklists are not meant to replace professional advice, but to enhance it. They bring clarity and consistency to your decision-making process and help ensure that your investments remain aligned with your broader vision. Whether you are just beginning or refining a long-standing portfolio, these tools can guide you toward smarter, more strategic real estate decisions. Keep them close, revisit them often, and use them as part of your ongoing path to financial independence and creating and maintaining generational wealth.

Integrating Real Estate into Your Financial Planning and Generational Wealth Strategy

Throughout this chapter, we have explored how real estate can serve as a flexible, powerful, and tax-smart tool on your journey to financial independence and creating and maintaining generational wealth. Whether you are just starting out, actively expanding your portfolio, or transitioning into a more passive approach, real estate offers opportunities to generate income, preserve wealth, and create a lasting legacy. The key is to approach it with intention, discipline, and a clear plan that supports your personal vision and financial goals.

Real estate is not a one-size-fits-all investment. Some investors find success managing their own rental properties, while others prefer the hands-free approach of professionally managed structures such as DSTs. Some use 1031 exchanges to build wealth over time, while others take advantage of QOZFs or 1033 exchanges to manage the tax impact of unique events. The common thread among all these strategies is that they can be tailored to match your goals, your timeline, and your tolerance for risk and involvement.

When integrated properly into a broader financial plan, real estate becomes more than just another asset. It becomes a way to align your money with your values, your time with your purpose, and your future with your vision. It offers a level of control that few other investment classes can match, along with tangible benefits like cash flow, tax deferral, and portfolio diversification.

But like all powerful tools, real estate must be managed wisely. This means understanding the rules, following a thoughtful investment process, and seeking guidance when needed. It means not just reacting to market trends but making proactive choices that support your long-term financial health.

Most importantly, real estate must fit into your life in a way that enhances your freedom, not adds unnecessary stress. For some, that might mean remaining actively involved and personally managing each property. For others, it might mean selling appreciated assets and reallocating into passive income generators that require little day-to-day oversight. There is no right or wrong answer, only the strategy that best supports your version of financial independence.

As you reflect on your own journey to financial independence, consider how real estate can serve your broader goals. Can it provide the income you need in retirement? Can it offer opportunities for tax savings or wealth transfer? Can it help you fund other life priorities such as education, charitable giving, or travel? Real estate, when used intentionally, can do all these things and more.

Your plan should be as dynamic as the markets in which you invest. Review it regularly. Update it as your circumstances change. And never forget that the ultimate goal is not just to accumulate properties, but to create a life that reflects what matters most to you.

With appropriate guidance, a solid strategy, and a commitment to making informed decisions, real estate can help you move confidently toward your financial goals and live with greater clarity and control. That is what financial independence is all about and being able to do the same for your family by creating generational wealth.

If you do not pay attention to tax consequences while managing real estate, you may be paying significantly more in taxes than the law requires. Therefore, you must include tax planning as part of your overall real estate investing and generational wealth strategy. Using a financial planning approach that takes advantage of tax-smart strategies could maximize your ability to build wealth while establishing your real estate portfolio.

Tax-smart Strategies for Investing in Real Estate

Here are several tax facts and strategies that will address your wealth accumulation goals in a powerful and sustainable way. This will be part of your tax-smart roadmap to financial independence. This is how you can transform the tax code into part of your generational wealth code.

- Accelerate deductions through depreciation and cost segregation studies. Depreciation allows you to recover the cost of a property over time, reducing taxable income each year. Cost segregation goes a step further by identifying components of a property that can be depreciated over shorter periods. By accelerating these deductions, you improve your cash flow and reinvestment ability during the most active years of your real estate journey.

- Defer capital gains using 1031 exchanges. When you sell a property at a gain and reinvest the proceeds into another like-kind property, a properly executed 1031 exchange lets you defer both capital gains and depreciation recapture taxes. This strategy allows your capital to grow tax-deferred, which can compound your investment returns and support long-term growth without the drag of immediate taxation.
- Utilize 1033 exchanges for involuntary conversions. When property is taken through eminent domain or lost to a natural disaster, Section 1033 allows you to defer the gain if the compensation is reinvested into similar property. With longer timelines and greater flexibility compared to a 1031, this lesser-known strategy can provide tax relief during a difficult transition.
- Recycle equity to expand your portfolio tax-free. If your property has appreciated in value, you can often refinance it and pull out capital without triggering a taxable event. This recycled equity can then be used to fund new acquisitions, increasing your overall portfolio size and income potential without selling and recognizing gains.
- Qualify as a real estate professional to deduct full losses. If real estate is your primary occupation and you meet IRS requirements for hours and participation, you may qualify as a real estate professional. This classification removes income limits and the $25,000 cap on real estate loss deductions against non-passive income. Proper documentation and strategic involvement can transform paper losses into real tax savings.
- Use PIGs to unlock suspended losses. If you have accumulated real estate losses that you have not been able to deduct due to income limits, consider investing in passive income generators such as DSTs or triple-net lease properties. These investments produce passive income that can be offset by suspended losses, creating tax-free cash flow.
- Shift to passive income while maintaining tax advantages through DSTs, which allow you to transition out of active management while continuing to enjoy tax-deferred status and rental income. This is especially useful in retirement or when simplifying your life and estate. A DST can serve as a bridge between wealth preservation and lifestyle freedom, providing hands-free real estate ownership without losing important tax benefits.
- Maximize step-up in basis and depreciation reset in estate plans. When real estate is passed to heirs, it typically receives a step-up in basis, eliminating capital gains and depreciation recapture on prior appreciation. Inherited properties also begin a new depreciation schedule based on the fair market value as of the date of death. These provisions can significantly reduce tax burdens and simplify wealth transfer.
- Explore QOZFs for long-term, tax-free growth. By reinvesting capital gains into a QOZF, you can defer taxes on the initial gain and eliminate taxes on the appreciation of the new investment if held for at least 10 years. While QOZF

(*continued*)

(*continued*)

are not suitable for everyone, they offer one of the few paths to complete capital gains elimination.

- Review how you hold property. Whether real estate is held in your personal name, an LLC, a trust, or as joint ownership, the structure has implications for taxes, liability, and estate planning. The right structure depends on the type of property, your financial goals, and your need for protection or flexibility.
- Preserve liquidity to support your plan. Tax strategies are only effective if your cash flow remains strong. Always maintain reserves for unexpected expenses, vacancies, or economic downturns. Adequate liquidity ensures that you can protect your portfolio and continue investing strategically.
- Reassess regularly to stay ahead of changes. Tax laws, market conditions, and personal goals evolve over time. Make it a point to review your real estate holdings and planning strategies annually. Small adjustments can result in significant tax savings and performance improvements over the long run.
- Take advantage of the QBI deduction on REIT dividends. Many REITs pay dividends that qualify for a 20% deduction under the current QBI provisions. This can lower the effective tax rate on REIT income, making it a tax-efficient way to generate passive cash flow. REITs favorable tax treatment and hands-off structure make them a valuable tool in a diversified, tax-aware real estate strategy, especially for investors focused on liquidity and retirement income.

An Action Plan for Investing in Real Estate

1. **Use real estate to accelerate your journey to financial independence.** With the most appropriate tax-smart real estate investing strategies, real estate can be a powerful wealth-building tool that may help you achieve financial independence and create generational wealth for you and your family.
2. **Clarify your financial objectives for real estate.** Determine what you want each property or investment to accomplish. Whether your focus is income, appreciation, legacy planning, or diversification, having clear goals will guide your decision-making and help you select the right tools and structures.
3. **Utilize other people's money to build wealth.** Leverage is one of the most powerful tools available to real estate investors. It allows you to use someone else's money, typically a bank, to purchase income-producing assets that you would not otherwise be able to afford on your own.
4. **Borrow against equity to expand your portfolio.** This approach allows you to use the accumulated equity of one property to help finance the purchase of another. Equity recycling has helped many experienced investors grow their wealth in a responsible and tax-smart way.

5. **Utilize the Phantom Deduction (depreciation) to drive tax-deferred growth.** Of all the tax benefits available to real estate investors, one of the most powerful and least understood is depreciation. It is one of the most effective tools for driving tax-deferred growth and accelerating your journey to financial independence.
6. **Utilize the power of the step-up in basis rules as part of your estate planning and generational wealth transfer.** A well-structured real estate portfolio can serve as a legacy, one that benefits your children, grandchildren, or charitable causes for centuries to come.
7. **Make sure you choose the right legal entity to hold your business or investment real estate property.** We almost always recommend holding business or investment real estate through an LLC. This is not only an added insurance policy against lawsuits but could also be a powerful tool in minimizing income tax if there are two or more partners through the PTET program if applicable.
8. **Take full advantage of the 1031 Exchange rules as a tax deferral tool when selling business or investment, real estate.** This may create an opportunity to grow wealth faster, preserve equity, and continually reposition assets without the drag of immediate taxation upon the sale of your property.
9. **You may consider a DST as one possible option for completing a 1031 Exchange and transitioning toward a more passive real estate investment approach.** A DST can provide a structured, IRS-approved method for fractional ownership in institutional-grade real estate. This option may help investors reduce active management responsibilities while maintaining tax-deferral benefits, but it is not the only pathway and should be evaluated based on individual goals and suitability.
10. **Utilize a 1033 Exchange with involuntary conversions.** There are times when the sale of real estate is not a choice, but the result of events that are completely outside of our control. Fortunately, the tax law provides relief with a 1033 Exchange. This provision is specifically designed for those involuntary conversions.
11. **Use PIGs to simplify your real estate ownership and to take advantage of suspended losses.** These structures can provide monthly cash flow, preserve tax deferral, and align your investments with your retirement or estate planning goals.
12. **You may consider a QOZF as one possible option for pursuing tax deferral on eligible capital gains** and, if certain requirements are met, potential long-term tax benefits. QOZFs provide a structured, IRS-defined method for investing in designated opportunity zones with the goal of encouraging economic development. This strategy may offer tax advantages for some

(continued)

(continued)

investors, but it is not appropriate for everyone and should be evaluated carefully based on your individual circumstances, investment objectives, and risk tolerance.

13. **Take advantage of the opportunity to access institutional-grade deals through private real estate placement offerings**. They provide individual investors with access to large-scale professionally managed properties once available only to institutional and ultra-high net worth individuals.
14. **Consider adding REITs to your investment portfolio.** For many investors, REITs provide a practical way to participate in the real estate market without the responsibility of direct ownership.
15. **Understand how the IRS classifies real estate investors** and that you are utilizing one that is most appropriate for you. These classifications range from passive activity to active participation to real estate professional status, which can come with significantly more tax benefits.
16. **Implement best practices and avoid the pitfalls that apply to being a real estate investor.** Real estate investing can be one of the most rewarding components of a financial independence plan, but it also comes with many risks. Like any powerful tool, it must be used wisely.
17. **Fully utilize the real estate investment checklist and evaluations** provided in this chapter: evaluating direct real estate investments, preparing for a 1031 or 1033 exchange, and selecting a passive real estate investment.
18. **Build a professional support team.** Collaborate with a financial advisor, a tax-smart real estate CPA, and a real estate attorney. These experts can help ensure that your investments are compliant, efficient, and aligned with your long-term vision. They can also help you respond to new opportunities or risks as they arise. See Appendix A, "Selecting a Trusted Advisor."
19. **Use the tax-smart roadmap to financial independence to transform the tax code into part of your generational wealth code.**

CHAPTER 12

The Time Value of Money

Compound interest is the eighth wonder of the world. He who understands it, earns it...he who doesn't...pays it.

—Albert Einstein, Father of Modern Physics

One of the most important concepts for becoming financially independent and accumulating generational wealth is understanding the *time value of money*. By far, the most valuable asset we have is time, yet it is often taken for granted and not fully appreciated until later in life.

The time value of money formulas are highly complex mathematical equations, beyond the scope of this book. You can simplify this process by purchasing a financial calculator, or even better, by downloading an app that gives you access to one free of charge. This tool can perform these calculations for you. In fact, in the business world, owning a financial calculator is a necessary tool to succeed. Rather than turning this into a complicated chapter that feels like a calculus class, we will share simple examples and financial tables to make this concept easy to understand.

Before we get started, we would like to define the most basic interest formula:

$$I = P \times R \times T$$

I = Interest calculated
P = Principal
R = Annual interest rate
T = Time period covered in the interest calculation (number of months out of 12)

For example, if you have \$100,000 and are earning 5% interest over one year, the components of the formula would be P = \$100,000, R = 5%, and T = 1 year. Therefore, \$100,000 × 5% × (12/12) 1 year = \$5,000. This represents the most basic calculation of interest.

After 1 year, your principal would now be worth \$105,000, which is the original \$100,000 plus \$5,000 in interest.

In year 2, you would have P = \$105,000, R = 5% and T = 1 year. Therefore, \$105,000 × 5% × (12/12) 1 year = \$5,250. As a result, in year 2, your original \$100,000 increased its earning power by \$250 with all other factors remaining the same.

With each year that passes, the earning power increases: this is referred to as the *power of compounding*. You can truly appreciate this over time because the outcome can be astonishing.

The Rule of 72

Before we describe how to use the financial tables provided in the following pages, we would like to explain the *Rule of 72*, which helps you estimate how long it will take to double your money. Of course, the answer depends on your interest rate (rate of return). Simply divide the assumed rate of return into 72. For example:

- If your assumed rate of return is 10%, divide 10 into 72, which equals 7.2 years.
- If your assumed rate of return is 5%, divide 5 into 72, which equals 14.4 years.

So, for the purpose of this example, let us assume a rate of return of 10% per year and a starting point of \$25,000. Based on the Rule of 72 (see Exhibit 12.1), here's how that amount will increase:

- In 7.2 years, that \$25,000 will double to \$50,000.
- In 14.4 years, it will double once again to \$100,000.
- In 21.6 years, it will double once again to \$200,000.
- In 28.8 years, it will double once again to \$400,000.
- In 36 years, it will double once again to \$800,000.
- In 43.2 years, it will double once again to \$1.6 million.

This mathematical formula is a shortcut that approximates and simplifies the concept of the time value of money and does not represent any particular investment product. Most people are

Exhibit 12.1 Rule of 72

Annual Rate of Return	Years to Increase Your Investment					
	2 times	4 times	8 times	16 times	32 times	64 times
1%	72.00	144.00	216.00	288.00	360.00	432.00
2%	36.00	72.00	108.00	144.00	180.00	216.00
3%	24.00	48.00	72.00	96.00	120.00	144.00
4%	18.00	36.00	54.00	72.00	90.00	108.00
5%	14.40	28.80	43.20	57.60	72.00	86.40
6%	12.00	24.00	36.00	48.00	60.00	72.00
7%	10.29	20.57	30.86	41.14	51.43	61.71
8%	9.00	18.00	27.00	36.00	45.00	54.00
9%	8.00	16.00	24.00	32.00	40.00	48.00
10%	**7.20**	**14.40**	**21.60**	**28.80**	**36.00**	**43.20**
11%	6.55	13.09	19.64	26.18	32.73	39.27
12%	6.00	12.00	18.00	24.00	30.00	36.00
13%	5.54	11.08	16.62	22.15	27.69	33.23
14%	5.14	10.29	15.43	20.57	25.71	30.86
15%	4.80	9.60	14.40	19.20	24.00	28.80
16%	4.50	9.00	13.50	18.00	22.50	27.00
17%	4.24	8.47	12.71	16.94	21.18	25.41
18%	4.00	8.00	12.00	16.00	20.00	24.00
19%	3.79	7.58	11.37	15.16	18.95	22.74
20%	3.60	7.20	10.80	14.40	18.00	21.60

astonished when they truly understand the power of compounding and how powerful the time value of money can be.

Trump Accounts and the Time Value of Money

To emphasize how important it is to start saving at a young age, we're going to provide you with the following example, where we can combine the new Trump Accounts under the One Big Beautiful Bill Act, with the power of compounding, starting at birth. (Refer to Chapter 8, "Planning for Retirement," for more details of how this new savings vehicle works).

If you were to establish a Trump Account for your child and fund it with $5,000 from birth to age 17 (for 18 total annual contributions), and if that account earned a 10% annual rate of return, your child would have accumulated $227,996 in retirement assets at that young age.

If your child then decides to roll these funds over to a Traditional IRA account and never puts another penny of their own money into the account again, by the time the child reaches age 65, assuming a continued annual rate of return of 10%, your child will have accumulated $22,119,541 in retirement assets! This means that giving your child a $5,000 gift per year, for 18 years, turns $90,000 into more than $22,000,000 throughout the full 65-year period with compounding.

When we first went through this calculation, we had to check our math over and over again. We just could not believe that saving $5,000 per year over 18 years could accumulate to over $22,000,000 over a 65-year period through the power of compounding, having assumed an average rate of return of 10% per year.

In Chapter 8, we discussed the retirement equation to help you achieve financial independence. Now that you have a better understanding of the time value of money, you can appreciate even more the importance of starting to save now rather than later. Achieving the highest rate of return within your risk tolerance (Chapter 9, "Managing Your Investments") is a critical component of this equation. Starting early and appreciating your most valuable asset, time, will give you a tremendous advantage in achieving your financial goals.

To do your own financial calculations and determine what it will take to achieve your own financial independence and generational wealth, you need to understand how the following four financial tables work (Exhibits 12.2–12.5).

Future Value Factor of a Sum Certain

The future value (FV) factor of a sum will determine how large a single sum would become at the end of a specified period if the amount invested earns a specified interest rate (rate of return) with compounding each period. Please refer to Exhibit 12.2, "FV Factors of a Sum," as we take you through this example. The purpose of Exhibit 12.2 is to determine the future dollars you will have based on your *investment today* over time at an assumed interest rate (rate of return).

For example, if you invested $10,000 today at a 7% return per year, after 20 years, you would have $38,700. You determine this by looking at Exhibit 12.2, finding the row for 20 years, then moving

Exhibit 12.2 FV Factors of a Sum

The purpose of this table is to determine the future dollars you will have based on your investment today over a defined period at an assumed interest rate (rate of return).

Insert		Your Calculation
%	Step 1	Insert your expected annual return on your investment.
	Step 2	Insert the amount of years of your investment.
	Step 3	Using the table, identify the correct interest column, and insert the result for the row that has the correct number of years.
$	Step 4	Insert your investment amount today.
$	Step 5	Multiply the factors in steps 3 and 4. This is your future dollars.

Year	1%	2%	3%	4%	5%	6%	7%
1	1.010	1.020	1.030	1.040	1.050	1.060	1.070
2	1.020	1.040	1.061	1.082	1.103	1.124	1.145
3	1.030	1.061	1.093	1.125	1.158	1.191	1.225
4	1.041	1.082	1.126	1.170	1.216	1.262	1.311
5	1.051	1.104	1.159	1.217	1.276	1.338	1.403
6	1.062	1.126	1.194	1.265	1.340	1.419	1.501
7	1.072	1.149	1.230	1.316	1.407	1.504	1.606
8	1.083	1.172	1.267	1.369	1.477	1.594	1.718
9	1.094	1.195	1.305	1.423	1.551	1.689	1.838
10	1.105	1.219	1.344	1.480	1.629	1.791	1.967
11	1.116	1.243	1.384	1.539	1.710	1.898	2.105

(Continued)

Exhibit 12.2 (*Continued*)

Year	1%	2%	3%	4%	5%	6%	7%
12	1.127	1.268	1.426	1.601	1.796	2.012	2.252
13	1.138	1.294	1.469	1.665	1.886	2.133	2.410
14	1.149	1.319	1.513	1.732	1.980	2.261	2.579
15	1.161	1.346	1.558	1.801	2.079	2.397	2.759
16	1.173	1.373	1.605	1.873	2.183	2.540	2.952
17	1.184	1.400	1.653	1.948	2.292	2.693	3.159
18	1.196	1.428	1.702	2.026	2.407	2.854	3.380
19	1.208	1.457	1.754	2.107	2.527	3.026	3.617
20	1.220	1.486	1.806	2.191	2.653	3.207	**3.870**
21	1.232	1.516	1.860	2.279	2.786	3.400	4.141
22	1.245	1.546	1.916	2.370	2.925	3.604	4.430
23	1.257	1.577	1.974	2.465	3.072	3.820	4.741
24	1.270	1.608	2.033	2.563	3.225	4.049	5.072
25	1.282	1.641	2.094	2.666	3.386	4.292	5.427
26	1.295	1.673	2.157	2.772	3.556	4.549	5.807
27	1.308	1.707	2.221	2.883	3.733	4.822	6.214
28	1.321	1.741	2.288	2.999	3.920	5.112	6.649
29	1.335	1.776	2.357	3.119	4.116	5.418	7.114
30	1.348	1.811	2.427	3.243	4.322	5.743	7.612
31	1.361	1.848	2.500	3.373	4.538	6.088	8.145
32	1.375	1.885	2.575	3.508	4.765	6.453	8.715

33	1.389	1.922	2.652	3.648	5.003	6.841	9.325
34	1.403	1.961	2.732	3.794	5.253	7.251	9.978
35	1.417	2.000	2.814	3.946	5.516	7.686	10.677
36	1.431	2.040	2.898	4.104	5.792	8.147	11.424
37	1.445	2.081	2.985	4.268	6.081	8.636	12.224
38	1.460	2.122	3.075	4.439	6.385	9.154	13.079
39	1.474	2.165	3.167	4.616	6.705	9.704	13.995
40	1.489	2.208	3.262	4.801	7.040	10.286	14.974
41	1.504	2.252	3.360	4.993	7.392	10.903	16.023
42	1.519	2.297	3.461	5.193	7.762	11.557	17.144
43	1.534	2.343	3.565	5.400	8.150	12.250	18.344
44	1.549	2.390	3.671	5.617	8.557	12.985	19.628
45	1.565	2.438	3.782	5.841	8.985	13.765	21.002

Year	8%	9%	10%	12%	15%	20%	25%
1	1.080	1.090	1.100	1.120	1.150	1.200	1.250
2	1.166	1.188	1.210	1.254	1.323	1.440	1.563
3	1.260	1.295	1.331	1.405	1.521	1.728	1.953
4	1.360	1.412	1.464	1.574	1.749	2.074	2.441
5	1.469	1.539	1.611	1.762	2.011	2.488	3.052
6	1.587	1.677	1.772	1.974	2.313	2.986	3.815
7	1.714	1.828	1.949	2.211	2.660	3.583	4.768
8	1.851	1.993	2.144	2.476	3.059	4.300	5.960
9	1.999	2.172	2.358	2.773	3.518	5.160	7.451

(*Continued*)

Exhibit 12.2 ***(Continued)***

Year	8%	9%	10%	12%	15%	20%	25%
10	2.159	2.367	2.594	3.106	4.046	6.192	9.313
11	2.332	2.580	2.853	3.479	4.652	7.430	11.642
12	2.518	2.813	3.138	3.896	5.350	8.916	14.552
13	2.720	3.066	3.452	4.363	6.153	10.699	18.190
14	2.937	3.342	3.797	4.887	7.076	12.839	22.737
15	3.172	3.642	4.177	5.474	8.137	15.407	28.422
16	3.426	3.970	4.595	6.130	9.358	18.488	35.527
17	3.700	4.328	5.054	6.866	10.761	22.186	44.409
18	3.996	4.717	5.560	7.690	12.375	26.623	55.511
19	4.316	5.142	6.116	8.613	14.232	31.948	69.389
20	4.661	5.604	**6.727**	9.646	16.367	38.338	86.736
21	5.034	6.109	7.400	10.804	18.822	46.005	108.420
22	5.437	6.659	8.140	12.100	21.645	55.206	135.525
23	5.871	7.258	8.954	13.552	24.891	66.247	169.407
24	6.341	7.911	9.850	15.179	28.625	79.497	211.758
25	6.848	8.623	10.835	17.000	32.919	95.396	264.698
26	7.396	9.399	11.918	19.040	37.857	114.475	330.872
27	7.988	10.245	13.110	21.325	43.535	137.371	413.590
28	8.627	11.167	14.421	23.884	50.066	164.845	516.988
29	9.317	12.172	15.863	26.750	57.575	197.814	646.235
30	10.063	13.268	17.449	29.960	66.212	237.376	807.794

31	10.868	14.462	19.194	33.555	76.144	284.852	1,009.742
32	11.737	15.763	21.114	37.582	87.565	341.822	1,262.177
33	12.676	17.182	23.225	42.092	100.700	410.186	1,577.722
34	13.690	18.728	25.548	47.143	115.805	492.224	1,972.152
35	14.785	20.414	28.102	52.800	133.176	590.668	2,465.190
36	15.968	22.251	30.913	59.136	153.152	708.802	3,081.488
37	17.246	24.254	34.004	66.232	176.125	850.562	3,851.860
38	18.625	26.437	37.404	74.180	202.543	1,020.675	4,814.825
39	20.115	28.816	41.145	83.081	232.925	1,224.810	6,018.531
40	21.725	31.409	45.259	93.051	267.864	1,469.772	7,523.164
41	23.462	34.236	49.785	104.217	308.043	1,763.726	9,403.955
42	25.339	37.318	54.764	116.723	354.250	2,116.471	11,754.944
43	27.367	40.676	60.240	130.730	407.387	2,539.765	14,693.679
44	29.556	44.337	66.264	146.418	468.495	3,047.718	18,367.099
45	31.920	48.327	72.890	163.988	538.769	3,657.262	22,958.874

across to the 7% column per year to obtain the factor of 3.870. Multiply the current single sum of $10,000 by the future value factor of 3.870: ($10,000 × 3.870) = $38,700.

For comparison purposes, if you use the same assumptions but are fortunate enough to generate a 10% return on your money, you will end up with $67,270 after the same 20-year period. If you look at Exhibit 12.2, the intersection of 20 years at 10% shows an FV factor of 6.727. This extra 3% return over a 20-year period with compounding results in an additional $28,570 in earnings. This example highlights the importance of aiming for the highest possible rate of return within your risk tolerance over the long run.

FV of an Annuity Factor

The FV of an annuity factor would determine the future value of a stream of equal payments made at regular intervals over a specified period, if the amount invested earns a specified interest rate (rate of return) with compounding each period. Please refer to Exhibit 12.3, "FV of an Annuity Factor," as we take you through this example. The purpose of Exhibit 12.3 is to determine the future dollars you will have based on your *annual investment* over a defined period at an assumed interest rate (rate of return).

For example, if you invested $5,000 annually at a 5% return per year, after 25 years, you would have $238,635. To determine this, look at Exhibit 12.3, find the row for 25 years, then move across to the 5% column per year to obtain the factor of 47.727. Multiply the annual investment of $5,000 by the FV annuity factor of 47.727: ($5,000 × 47.727) = $238,635.

For comparison purposes, if you use the same assumptions but are fortunate enough to generate a 10% return on your money, you will end up with $491,735 after the same 25-year period. Later in Exhibit 12.3, the intersection of 25 years at 10% shows an FV annuity factor of 98.347. This extra 5% return over a 25-year period with compounding results in an additional $253,100 in earnings. This example highlights the importance of aiming for the highest possible rate of return within your risk tolerance over the long run.

Exhibit 12.3 FV of an Annuity Factor

The purpose of this table is to determine the future dollars you will have based on your annual investment over a defined period at an assumed interest rate (rate of return).

Insert		Your Calculation
%	Step 1	Insert your expected annual return on your investment.
Years	Step 2	Insert the amount of years of your investment.
	Step 3	Using the table, identify the correct interest column, and insert the result for the row that has the correct number of years.
$	Step 4	Insert your annual investment amount.
$	Step 5	Multiply the factors in steps 3 and 4. This is your future dollars.

Year	1%	2%	3%	4%	5%	6%	7%
1	1.000	1.000	1.000	1.000	1.000	1.000	1.000
2	2.010	2.020	2.030	2.040	2.050	2.060	2.070
3	3.030	3.060	3.091	3.122	3.153	3.184	3.215
4	4.060	4.122	4.184	4.246	4.310	4.375	4.440
5	5.101	5.204	5.309	5.416	5.526	5.637	5.751
6	6.152	6.308	6.468	6.633	6.802	6.975	7.153
7	7.214	7.434	7.662	7.898	8.142	8.394	8.654
8	8.286	8.583	8.892	9.214	9.549	9.897	10.260
9	9.369	9.755	10.159	10.583	11.027	11.491	11.978
10	10.462	10.950	11.464	12.006	12.578	13.181	13.816
11	11.567	12.169	12.808	13.486	14.207	14.972	15.784

(*Continued*)

Exhibit 12.3 ***(Continued)***

Year	1%	2%	3%	4%	5%	6%	7%
12	12.683	13.412	14.192	15.026	15.917	16.870	17.888
13	13.809	14.680	15.618	16.627	17.713	18.882	20.141
14	14.947	15.974	17.086	18.292	19.599	21.015	22.550
15	16.097	17.293	18.599	20.024	21.579	23.276	25.129
16	17.258	18.639	20.157	21.825	23.657	25.673	27.888
17	18.430	20.012	21.762	23.698	25.840	28.213	30.840
18	19.615	21.412	23.414	25.645	28.132	30.906	33.999
19	20.811	22.841	25.117	27.671	30.539	33.760	37.379
20	22.019	24.297	26.870	29.778	33.066	36.786	40.995
21	23.239	25.783	28.676	31.969	35.719	39.993	44.865
22	24.472	27.299	30.537	34.248	38.505	43.392	49.006
23	25.716	28.845	32.453	36.618	41.430	46.996	53.436
24	26.973	30.422	34.426	39.083	44.502	50.816	58.177
25	28.243	32.030	36.459	41.646	**47.727**	54.865	63.249
26	29.526	33.671	38.553	44.312	51.113	59.156	68.676
27	30.821	35.344	40.710	47.084	54.669	63.706	74.484
28	32.129	37.051	42.931	49.968	58.403	68.528	80.698
29	33.450	38.792	45.219	52.966	62.323	73.640	87.347
30	34.785	40.568	47.575	56.085	66.439	79.058	94.461
31	36.133	42.379	50.003	59.328	70.761	84.802	102.073
32	37.494	44.227	52.503	62.701	75.299	90.890	110.218

33	38.869	46.112	55.078	66.210	80.064	97.343	118.933
34	40.258	48.034	57.730	69.858	85.067	104.184	128.259
35	41.660	49.994	60.462	73.652	90.320	111.435	138.237
36	43.077	51.994	63.276	77.598	95.836	119.121	148.913
37	44.508	54.034	66.174	81.702	101.628	127.268	160.337
38	45.953	56.115	69.159	85.970	107.710	135.904	172.561
39	47.412	58.237	72.234	90.409	114.095	145.058	185.640
40	48.886	60.402	75.401	95.026	120.800	154.762	199.635
41	50.375	62.610	78.663	99.827	127.840	165.048	214.610
42	51.879	64.862	82.023	104.820	135.232	175.951	230.632
43	53.398	67.159	85.484	110.012	142.993	187.508	247.776
44	54.932	69.503	89.048	115.413	151.143	199.758	266.121
45	56.481	71.893	92.720	121.029	159.700	212.744	285.749

Year	8%	9%	10%	12%	15%	20%	25%
1	1.000	1.000	1.000	1.000	1.000	1.000	1.000
2	2.080	2.090	2.100	2.120	2.150	2.200	2.250
3	3.246	3.278	3.310	3.374	3.473	3.640	3.813
4	4.506	4.573	4.641	4.779	4.993	5.368	5.766
5	5.867	5.985	6.105	6.353	6.742	7.442	8.207
6	7.336	7.523	7.716	8.115	8.754	9.930	11.259
7	8.923	9.200	9.487	10.089	11.067	12.916	15.073
8	10.637	11.028	11.436	12.300	13.727	16.499	19.842
9	12.488	13.021	13.579	14.776	16.786	20.799	25.802

(*Continued*)

Exhibit 12.3 ***(Continued)***

Year	8%	9%	10%	12%	15%	20%	25%
10	14.487	15.193	15.937	17.549	20.304	25.959	33.253
11	16.645	17.560	18.531	20.655	24.349	32.150	42.566
12	18.977	20.141	21.384	24.133	29.002	39.581	54.208
13	21.495	22.953	24.523	28.029	34.352	48.497	68.760
14	24.215	26.019	27.975	32.393	40.505	59.196	86.949
15	27.152	29.361	31.772	37.280	47.580	72.035	109.687
16	30.324	33.003	35.950	42.753	55.717	87.442	138.109
17	33.750	36.974	40.545	48.884	65.075	105.931	173.636
18	37.450	41.301	45.599	55.750	75.836	128.117	218.045
19	41.446	46.018	51.159	63.440	88.212	154.740	273.556
20	45.762	51.160	57.275	72.052	102.444	186.688	342.945
21	50.423	56.765	64.002	81.699	118.810	225.026	429.681
22	55.457	62.873	71.403	92.503	137.632	271.031	538.101
23	60.893	69.532	79.543	104.603	159.276	326.237	673.626
24	66.765	76.790	88.497	118.155	184.168	392.484	843.033
25	73.106	84.701	**98.347**	133.334	212.793	471.981	1,054.791
26	79.954	93.324	109.182	150.334	245.712	567.377	1,319.489
27	87.351	102.723	121.100	169.374	283.569	681.853	1,650.361
28	95.339	112.968	134.210	190.699	327.104	819.223	2,063.952
29	103.966	124.135	148.631	214.583	377.170	984.068	2,580.939
30	113.283	136.308	164.494	241.333	434.745	1,181.882	3,227.174

31	123.346	149.575	181.943	271.293	500.957	1,419.258	4,034.968
32	134.214	164.037	201.138	304.848	577.100	1,704.109	5,044.710
33	145.951	179.800	222.252	342.429	664.666	2,045.931	6,306.887
34	158.627	196.982	245.477	384.521	765.365	2,456.118	7,884.609
35	172.317	215.711	271.024	431.663	881.170	2,948.341	9,856.761
36	187.102	236.125	299.127	484.463	1,014.346	3,539.009	12,321.952
37	203.070	258.376	330.039	543.599	1,167.498	4,247.811	15,403.440
38	220.316	282.630	364.043	609.831	1,343.622	5,098.373	19,255.299
39	238.941	309.066	401.448	684.010	1,546.165	6,119.048	24,070.124
40	259.057	337.882	442.593	767.091	1,779.090	7,343.858	30,088.655
41	280.781	369.292	487.852	860.142	2,046.954	8,813.629	37,611.819
42	304.244	403.528	537.637	964.359	2,354.997	10,577.355	47,015.774
43	329.583	440.846	592.401	1,081.083	2,709.246	12,693.826	58,770.718
44	356.950	481.522	652.641	1,211.813	3,116.633	15,233.592	73,464.397
45	386.506	525.859	718.905	1,358.230	3,585.128	18,281.310	91,831.496

Present Value Factor of a Sum

The present value (PV) factor of a sum helps you determine the current value of a single sum to be paid at a specified date in the future, if the amount invested earns a specified interest rate (rate of return) by compounding each period. Please refer to Exhibit 12.4, "PV Factor of a Sum," as we take you through this example. The purpose of this table is to determine the *present investment* needed to reach a future amount of dollars over time at an assumed interest rate (rate of return).

For example, if you wanted $100,000 in 20 years, how much would you need to invest today at a 5% interest rate (rate of return) per year? To determine this, look at Exhibit 12.4, find the row for 20 years, then move across to the 5% column per year to obtain the factor of 0.37689. Multiply the future amount of dollars needed of $100,000 by the PV factor of 0.37689: ($100,000 × 0.37689) = $37,689. Therefore, if you would like to have $100,000 in 20 years and expect to earn a 5% return, you would need to invest $37,689 today.

You can verify this by cross-checking with the FV factors from Exhibit 12.2. If you look back to Exhibit 12.2, year 20, rate of return 5%, you will find an FV factor of 2.653. If you multiply $37,689 by 2.653, you get the same $100,000 with a small rounding difference. This not only confirms these calculations but also proves that the PV and FV factors have an inverse relationship with one another.

It is important to note that the PV factor is used to find the PV of a future payment by discounting it at a specific rate, and this factor is always less than one when interest rates are positive. In contrast, the FV factor is used to find the FV of a present amount and is always greater than one.

As Clint Brookshire, CFP®, Avantax Community Leader at Cetera Financial Group explains:

> The power of compounding is critical when considering the present value of future expenses. For example, if you anticipate needing $120,000 for education in 18 years, and you assume a 6% annual return compounded annually, you would need to invest about $42,000 today. This illustrates how starting early can make long-term goals more achievable, but actual results depend on investment performance, inflation, and other factors.

Exhibit 12.4 PV Factor of a Sum

The purpose of this table is to determine the present investment needed for a future amount of dollars over a defined period at an assumed interest rate (rate of return).

Insert		Your Calculation
%	**Step 1**	**Insert your expected annual return on your investment.**
Years	**Step 2**	**Insert the amount of years of your investment.**
	Step 3	**Using the table, identify the correct interest column, and insert the result for the row that has the correct number of years.**
$	**Step 4**	**Insert your future investment amount.**
$	**Step 5**	**Multiply the factors in steps 3 and 4. This is your present value.**

Year	1%	2%	3%	4%	5%	6%	7%
1	0.99010	0.98039	0.97087	0.96154	0.95238	0.94340	0.93458
2	0.98030	0.96117	0.94260	0.92456	0.90703	0.89000	0.87344
3	0.97059	0.94232	0.91514	0.88900	0.86384	0.83962	0.81630
4	0.96098	0.92385	0.88849	0.85480	0.82270	0.79209	0.76290
5	0.95147	0.90573	0.86261	0.82193	0.78353	0.74726	0.71299
6	0.94205	0.88797	0.83748	0.79031	0.74622	0.70496	0.66634
7	0.93272	0.87056	0.81309	0.75992	0.71068	0.66506	0.62275
8	0.92348	0.85349	0.78941	0.73069	0.67684	0.62741	0.58201
9	0.91434	0.83676	0.76642	0.70259	0.64461	0.59190	0.54393
10	0.90529	0.82035	0.74409	0.67556	0.61391	0.55839	0.50835
11	0.89632	0.80426	0.72242	0.64958	0.58468	0.52679	0.47509

(Continued)

Exhibit 12.4 ***(Continued)***

Year	1%	2%	3%	4%	5%	6%	7%
12	0.88745	0.78849	0.70138	0.62460	0.55684	0.49697	0.44401
13	0.87866	0.77303	0.68095	0.60057	0.53032	0.46884	0.41496
14	0.86996	0.75788	0.66112	0.57748	0.50507	0.44230	0.38782
15	0.86135	0.74301	0.64186	0.55526	0.48102	0.41727	0.36245
16	0.85282	0.72845	0.62317	0.53391	0.45811	0.39365	0.33873
17	0.84438	0.71416	0.60502	0.51337	0.43630	0.37136	0.31657
18	0.83602	0.70016	0.58739	0.49363	0.41552	0.35034	0.29586
19	0.82774	0.68643	0.57029	0.47464	0.39573	0.33051	0.27651
20	0.81954	0.67297	0.55368	0.45639	**0.37689**	0.31180	0.25842
21	0.81143	0.65978	0.53755	0.43883	0.35894	0.29416	0.24151
22	0.80340	0.64684	0.52189	0.42196	0.34185	0.27751	0.22571
23	0.79544	0.63416	0.50669	0.40573	0.32557	0.26180	0.21095
24	0.78757	0.62172	0.49193	0.39012	0.31007	0.24698	0.19715
25	0.77977	0.60953	0.47761	0.37512	0.29530	0.23300	0.18425
26	0.77205	0.59758	0.46369	0.36069	0.28124	0.21981	0.17220
27	0.76440	0.58586	0.45019	0.34682	0.26785	0.20737	0.16093
28	0.75684	0.57437	0.43708	0.33348	0.25509	0.19563	0.15040
29	0.74934	0.56311	0.42435	0.32065	0.24295	0.18456	0.14056
30	0.74192	0.55207	0.41199	0.30832	0.23138	0.17411	0.13137
31	0.73458	0.54125	0.39999	0.29646	0.22036	0.16425	0.12277
32	0.72730	0.53063	0.38834	0.28506	0.20987	0.15496	0.11474

33	0.72010	0.52023	0.37703	0.27409	0.19987	0.14619	0.10723
34	0.71297	0.51003	0.36604	0.26355	0.19035	0.13791	0.10022
35	0.70591	0.50003	0.35538	0.25342	0.18129	0.13011	0.09366
36	0.69892	0.49022	0.34503	0.24367	0.17266	0.12274	0.08754
37	0.69200	0.48061	0.33498	0.23430	0.16444	0.11579	0.08181
38	0.68515	0.47119	0.32523	0.22529	0.15661	0.10924	0.07646
39	0.67837	0.46195	0.31575	0.21662	0.14915	0.10306	0.07146
40	0.67165	0.45289	0.30656	0.20829	0.14205	0.09722	0.06678
41	0.66500	0.44401	0.29763	0.20028	0.13528	0.09172	0.06241
42	0.65842	0.43530	0.28896	0.19257	0.12884	0.08653	0.05833
43	0.65190	0.42677	0.28054	0.18517	0.12270	0.08163	0.05451
44	0.64545	0.41840	0.27237	0.17805	0.11686	0.07701	0.05095
45	0.63905	0.41020	0.26444	0.17120	0.11130	0.07265	0.04761

Year	8%	9%	10%	12%	15%	20%	25%
1	0.92593	0.91743	0.90909	0.89286	0.86957	0.83333	0.80000
2	0.85734	0.84168	0.82645	0.79719	0.75614	0.69444	0.64000
3	0.79383	0.77218	0.75131	0.71178	0.65752	0.57870	0.51200
4	0.73503	0.70843	0.68301	0.63552	0.57175	0.48225	0.40960
5	0.68058	0.64993	0.62092	0.56743	0.49718	0.40188	0.32768
6	0.63017	0.59627	0.56447	0.50663	0.43233	0.33490	0.26214
7	0.58349	0.54703	0.51316	0.45235	0.37594	0.27908	0.20972
8	0.54027	0.50187	0.46651	0.40388	0.32690	0.23257	0.16777
9	0.50025	0.46043	0.42410	0.36061	0.28426	0.19381	0.13422

(*Continued*)

Exhibit 12.4 ***(Continued)***

Year	8%	9%	10%	12%	15%	20%	25%
10	0.46319	0.42241	0.38554	0.32197	0.24718	0.16151	0.10737
11	0.42888	0.38753	0.35049	0.28748	0.21494	0.13459	0.08590
12	0.39711	0.35553	0.31863	0.25668	0.18691	0.11216	0.06872
13	0.36770	0.32618	0.28966	0.22917	0.16253	0.09346	0.05498
14	0.34046	0.29925	0.26333	0.20462	0.14133	0.07789	0.04398
15	0.31524	0.27454	0.23939	0.18270	0.12289	0.06491	0.03518
16	0.29189	0.25187	0.21763	0.16312	0.10686	0.05409	0.02815
17	0.27027	0.23107	0.19784	0.14564	0.09293	0.04507	0.02252
18	0.25025	0.21199	0.17986	0.13004	0.08081	0.03756	0.01801
19	0.23171	0.19449	0.16351	0.11611	0.07027	0.03130	0.01441
20	0.21455	0.17843	0.14864	0.10367	0.06110	0.02608	0.01153
21	0.19866	0.16370	0.13513	0.09256	0.05313	0.02174	0.00922
22	0.18394	0.15018	0.12285	0.08264	0.04620	0.01811	0.00738
23	0.17032	0.13778	0.11168	0.07379	0.04017	0.01509	0.00590
24	0.15770	0.12640	0.10153	0.06588	0.03493	0.01258	0.00472
25	0.14602	0.11597	0.09230	0.05882	0.03038	0.01048	0.00378
26	0.13520	0.10639	0.08391	0.05252	0.02642	0.00874	0.00302
27	0.12519	0.09761	0.07628	0.04689	0.02297	0.00728	0.00242
28	0.11591	0.08955	0.06934	0.04187	0.01997	0.00607	0.00193
29	0.10733	0.08215	0.06304	0.03738	0.01737	0.00506	0.00155
30	0.09938	0.07537	0.05731	0.03338	0.01510	0.00421	0.00124

31	0.09202	0.06915	0.05210	0.02980	0.01313	0.00351	0.00099
32	0.08520	0.06344	0.04736	0.02661	0.01142	0.00293	0.00079
33	0.07889	0.05820	0.04306	0.02376	0.00993	0.00244	0.00063
34	0.07305	0.05339	0.03914	0.02121	0.00864	0.00203	0.00051
35	0.06763	0.04899	0.03558	0.01894	0.00751	0.00169	0.00041
36	0.06262	0.04494	0.03235	0.01691	0.00653	0.00141	0.00032
37	0.05799	0.04123	0.02941	0.01510	0.00568	0.00118	0.00026
38	0.05369	0.03783	0.02673	0.01348	0.00494	0.00098	0.00021
39	0.04971	0.03470	0.02430	0.01204	0.00429	0.00082	0.00017
40	0.04603	0.03184	0.02209	0.01075	0.00373	0.00068	0.00013
41	0.04262	0.02921	0.02009	0.00960	0.00325	0.00057	0.00011
42	0.03946	0.02680	0.01826	0.00857	0.00282	0.00047	0.00009
43	0.03654	0.02458	0.01660	0.00765	0.00245	0.00039	0.00007
44	0.03383	0.02255	0.01509	0.00683	0.00213	0.00033	0.00005
45	0.03133	0.02069	0.01372	0.00610	0.00186	0.00027	0.00004

PV of an Annuity Factor

The PV of an annuity factor helps you determine the current value of a stream of equal payments made at regular intervals over a specified period, if the amount invested earns a specified interest rate (rate of return) by compounding each period. Please refer to Exhibit 12.5, "PV on an Annuity Factor," as we take you through this example. The purpose of this table is to determine the present investment needed to receive *equal future annual cash receipts* over time at an assumed interest rate (rate of return).

For example, if you want to receive $25,000 annually for 25 years, how much would you need to invest today at a 4% interest rate (rate of return)? To determine this, look at Exhibit 12.5, find the row for 25 years, then move across to the 4% column per year to obtain the factor of 15.62208. Multiply the annual amount you want to receive, $25,000 by the PV annuity factor of 15.62208: ($25,000 × 15.62208) = $390,552. Therefore, if you would like to receive $25,000 per year over the next 25 years and expect to earn a 4% return, you would need to invest $390,552 today.

For comparison purposes, if you use the same assumptions but are fortunate enough to generate a 10% return on your money, you will only need $226,926. Later in Exhibit 12.5, the intersection of 25 years at 10% shows a PV annuity factor of 9.07704. This additional 6% return over 25 years with compounding allows you to receive the same $25,000 annual annuity payment, with an investment of $226,926. This means you would be able to invest $163,626 less ($390,552 minus $226,926) and still generate the same annual annuity payment. This example highlights the importance of aiming for the highest possible rate of return within your risk tolerance over the long run.

Summing Up the Time Value of Money and the Power of Compounding

Having a solid understanding of the tables in this chapter is essential for calculating and budgeting your way to financial independence and creating and maintaining generational wealth. With the time value of money and the power of compounding, you can map out

Exhibit 12.5 PV of an Annuity Factor

The purpose of this table is to determine the present investment needed to have equal future annual cash receipts over a defined period at an assumed interest rate (rate of return).

Insert		Your Calculation
%	**Step 1**	**Insert your expected annual return on your investment.**
Years	**Step 2**	**Insert the amount of years of your investment.**
	Step 3	**Using the table, identify the correct interest column, and insert the result for the row that has the correct number of years.**
$	**Step 4**	**Insert your annual cash receipts you want to receive.**
$	**Step 5**	**Multiply the factors in steps 3 and 4. You need to invest this amount.**

Year	1%	2%	3%	4%	5%	6%	7%
1	0.99010	0.98039	0.97087	0.96154	0.95238	0.94340	0.93458
2	1.97040	1.94156	1.91347	1.88609	1.85941	1.83339	1.80802
3	2.94099	2.88388	2.82861	2.77509	2.72325	2.67301	2.62432
4	3.90197	3.80773	3.71710	3.62990	3.54595	3.46511	3.38721
5	4.85343	4.71346	4.57971	4.45182	4.32948	4.21236	4.10020
6	5.79548	5.60143	5.41719	5.24214	5.07569	4.91732	4.76654
7	6.72819	6.47199	6.23028	6.00205	5.78637	5.58238	5.38929
8	7.65168	7.32548	7.01969	6.73274	6.46321	6.20979	5.97130
9	8.56602	8.16224	7.78611	7.43533	7.10782	6.80169	6.51523
10	9.47130	8.98259	8.53020	8.11090	7.72173	7.36009	7.02358
11	10.36763	9.78685	9.25262	8.76048	8.30641	7.88687	7.49867

(Continued)

Exhibit 12.5 (*Continued*)

Year	1%	2%	3%	4%	5%	6%	7%
12	11.25508	10.57534	9.95400	9.38507	8.86325	8.38384	7.94269
13	12.13374	11.34837	10.63496	9.98565	9.39357	8.85268	8.35765
14	13.00370	12.10625	11.29607	10.56312	9.89864	9.29498	8.74547
15	13.86505	12.84926	11.93794	11.11839	10.37966	9.71225	9.10791
16	14.71787	13.57771	12.56110	11.65230	10.83777	10.10590	9.44665
17	15.56225	14.29187	13.16612	12.16567	11.27407	10.47726	9.76322
18	16.39827	14.99203	13.75351	12.65930	11.68959	10.82760	10.05909
19	17.22601	15.67846	14.32380	13.13394	12.08532	11.15812	10.33560
20	18.04555	16.35143	14.87747	13.59033	12.46221	11.46992	10.59401
21	18.85698	17.01121	15.41502	14.02916	12.82115	11.76408	10.83553
22	19.66038	17.65805	15.93692	14.45112	13.16300	12.04158	11.06124
23	20.45582	18.29220	16.44361	14.85684	13.48857	12.30338	11.27219
24	21.24339	18.91393	16.93554	15.24696	13.79864	12.55036	11.46933
25	22.02316	19.52346	17.41315	**15.62208**	14.09394	12.78336	11.65358
26	22.79520	20.12104	17.87684	15.98277	14.37519	13.00317	11.82578
27	23.55961	20.70690	18.32703	16.32959	14.64303	13.21053	11.98671
28	24.31644	21.28127	18.76411	16.66306	14.89813	13.40616	12.13711
29	25.06579	21.84438	19.18845	16.98371	15.14107	13.59072	12.27767
30	25.80771	22.39646	19.60044	17.29203	15.37245	13.76483	12.40904
31	26.54229	22.93770	20.00043	17.58849	15.59281	13.92909	12.53181
32	27.26959	23.46833	20.38877	17.87355	15.80268	14.08404	12.64656

33	27.98969	23.98856	20.76579	18.14765	16.00255	14.23023	12.75379
34	28.70267	24.49859	21.13184	18.41120	16.19290	14.36814	12.85401
35	29.40858	24.99862	21.48722	18.66461	16.37419	14.49825	12.94767
36	30.10751	25.48884	21.83225	18.90828	16.54685	14.62099	13.03521
37	30.79951	25.96945	22.16724	19.14258	16.71129	14.73678	13.11702
38	31.48466	26.44064	22.49246	19.36786	16.86789	14.84602	13.19347
39	32.16303	26.90259	22.80822	19.58448	17.01704	14.94907	13.26493
40	32.83469	27.35548	23.11477	19.79277	17.15909	15.04630	13.33171
41	33.49969	27.79949	23.41240	19.99305	17.29437	15.13802	13.39412
42	34.15811	28.23479	23.70136	20.18563	17.42321	15.22454	13.45245
43	34.81001	28.66156	23.98190	20.37079	17.54591	15.30617	13.50696
44	35.45545	29.07996	24.25427	20.54884	17.66277	15.38318	13.55791
45	36.09451	29.49016	24.51871	20.72004	17.77407	15.45583	13.60552

Year	8%	9%	10%	12%	15%	20%	25%
1	0.92593	0.91743	0.90909	0.89286	0.86957	0.83333	0.80000
2	1.78326	1.75911	1.73554	1.69005	1.62571	1.52778	1.44000
3	2.57710	2.53129	2.48685	2.40183	2.28323	2.10648	1.95200
4	3.31213	3.23972	3.16987	3.03735	2.85498	2.58873	2.36160
5	3.99271	3.88965	3.79079	3.60478	3.35216	2.99061	2.68928
6	4.62288	4.48592	4.35526	4.11141	3.78448	3.32551	2.95142
7	5.20637	5.03295	4.86842	4.56376	4.16042	3.60459	3.16114
8	5.74664	5.53482	5.33493	4.96764	4.48732	3.83716	3.32891
9	6.24689	5.99525	5.75902	5.32825	4.77158	4.03097	3.46313

(Continued)

Exhibit 12.5 (*Continued*)

Year	8%	9%	10%	12%	15%	20%	25%
10	6.71008	6.41766	6.14457	5.65022	5.01877	4.19247	3.57050
11	7.13896	6.80519	6.49506	5.93770	5.23371	4.32706	3.65640
12	7.53608	7.16073	6.81369	6.19437	5.42062	4.43922	3.72512
13	7.90378	7.48690	7.10336	6.42355	5.58315	4.53268	3.78010
14	8.24424	7.78615	7.36669	6.62817	5.72448	4.61057	3.82408
15	8.55948	8.06069	7.60608	6.81086	5.84737	4.67547	3.85926
16	8.85137	8.31256	7.82371	6.97399	5.95423	4.72956	3.88741
17	9.12164	8.54363	8.02155	7.11963	6.04716	4.77463	3.90993
18	9.37189	8.75563	8.20141	7.24967	6.12797	4.81219	3.92794
19	9.60360	8.95011	8.36492	7.36578	6.19823	4.84350	3.94235
20	9.81815	9.12855	8.51356	7.46944	6.25933	4.86958	3.95388
21	10.01680	9.29224	8.64869	7.56200	6.31246	4.89132	3.96311
22	10.20074	9.44243	8.77154	7.64465	6.35866	4.90943	3.97049
23	10.37106	9.58021	8.88322	7.71843	6.39884	4.92453	3.97639
24	10.52876	9.70661	8.98474	7.78432	6.43377	4.93710	3.98111
25	10.67478	9.82258	**9.07704**	7.84314	6.46415	4.94759	3.98489
26	10.80998	9.92897	9.16095	7.89566	6.49056	4.95632	3.98791
27	10.93516	10.02658	9.23722	7.94255	6.51353	4.96360	3.99033
28	11.05108	10.11613	9.30657	7.98442	6.53351	4.96967	3.99226
29	11.15841	10.19828	9.36961	8.02181	6.55088	4.97472	3.99381
30	11.25778	10.27365	9.42691	8.05518	6.56598	4.97894	3.99505

31	11.34980	10.34280	9.47901	8.08499	6.57911	4.98245	3.99604
32	11.43500	10.40624	9.52638	8.11159	6.59053	4.98537	3.99683
33	11.51389	10.46444	9.56943	8.13535	6.60046	4.98781	3.99746
34	11.58693	10.51784	9.60857	8.15656	6.60910	4.98984	3.99797
35	11.65457	10.56682	9.64416	8.17550	6.61661	4.99154	3.99838
36	11.71719	10.61176	9.67651	8.19241	6.62314	4.99295	3.99870
37	11.77518	10.65299	9.70592	8.20751	6.62881	4.99412	3.99896
38	11.82887	10.69082	9.73265	8.22099	6.63375	4.99510	3.99917
39	11.87858	10.72552	9.75696	8.23303	6.63805	4.99592	3.99934
40	11.92461	10.75736	9.77905	8.24378	6.64178	4.99660	3.99947
41	11.96723	10.78657	9.79914	8.25337	6.64502	4.99717	3.99957
42	12.00670	10.81337	9.81740	8.26194	6.64785	4.99764	3.99966
43	12.04324	10.83795	9.83400	8.26959	6.65030	4.99803	3.99973
44	12.07707	10.86051	9.84909	8.27642	6.65244	4.99836	3.99978
45	12.10840	10.88120	9.86281	8.28252	6.65429	4.99863	3.99983

your own formula for financial success. These tables will help you answer the following essential questions:

1. How much will my current investment account be worth (Exhibit 12.2) based on an assumed rate of return at a particular point in time?
2. If I invest a fixed amount annually, how much will it be worth (Exhibit 12.3) based on an assumed rate of return at a particular point in time?
3. How much will I need to invest today (Exhibit 12.4) based on an assumed rate of return so that I can have a certain amount of dollars at a future date?
4. How much will I need to accumulate (Exhibit 12.5) in my investment account based on an assumed rate of return so I can receive an annual annuity payment starting at a particular point in time for a fixed number of years?

You should reread this section until you fully understand how these formulas and calculations work. Take time to go through different "what-if" scenarios and use these tables to answer the previous four questions based on your particular facts and circumstances. These tables and calculations are essential tools in planning for retirement as well as creating and maintaining generational wealth for your family.

The time value of money and the power of compounding are clearly one of the most powerful tools in creating and maintaining generational wealth. The more generations involved, the more powerful they become. The formulas and calculations provided in this chapter are the secret combination of the generational wealth code. Use them wisely and encourage your family to do the same. This will build a family legacy that can endure for many generations to come.

APPENDIX A

Selecting a Trusted Advisor

Perhaps one of the most important decisions you will need to make in your pursuit of financial independence is the selection of a trusted advisor. This trusted advisor will be your life coach, who will be there for you during good times and bad times and whose primary goal will be to help you achieve your long-term financial objectives. This trusted advisor should be a financial planner who can analyze your financial status and assist you in setting up and implementing a financial program to achieve your ultimate goals of financial independence and generational wealth. Developing a close relationship is critical to your overall success because your advisor should understand you and have a clear picture of your financial goals and dreams. This trusted advisor and his or her team must be able to provide you with comprehensive wealth management services that include financial planning, tax preparation and planning, investment advising, risk management, education planning, retirement planning, and estate planning services.

The best place to start is by asking your friends and family if they can recommend a trusted advisor with whom they have worked well. Before meeting with financial planners, you should do some research about their backgrounds, including their education and other relevant credentials. A good place to start would be visiting their websites and the licensing board website for whatever credentials they hold.

You should meet and interview a few financial planners who can meet your needs. When meeting with them, consider the following 10 questions:

1. Do you have confidence in the person who referred you to this advisor?
2. What education and credentials does this advisor hold to make him or her qualified to advise you? (Read through the qualifications of trusted advisors listed later, and decide what is most important to you.)
3. What is the compensation model for the advice and service: fee-based, hourly, or commission? (Fee-based is a percentage of your money under management, hourly is based on time charges, and commission is transaction based.)
4. What are the financial advisor's areas of expertise, and does this line up well with your needs? (Wealth management issues go hand-in-hand with the areas of expertise.)
5. What standard of care will this advisor be held to: fiduciary or a suitability standard? (These terms are described in the next section.)
6. What is the extent of services that will be provided: is it transactional or is it truly a trusted advisor relationship? (Transactional means compensation is based on commissions.)
7. Is the financial decision-making customized to you, or does the advisor take a one-size-fits-all approach? One-size-fits-all is not appropriate. An 18-year-old individual's goals and risk tolerance are much different from an 80-year-old retiree's.
8. Does the financial advisor provide tax advisory services such as tax planning and preparation that are integrated into your overall financial planning?
9. What is the organizational structure of the advisor's firm: will you be dealing directly with the same advisor or a junior member of the team?
10. What is the financial advisor's philosophy and approach to handling risk? Does this advisor make you comfortable?

There are more than 200 designations, or credentials, in the financial service industry, with many more being created each year. It is very important to understand the difference between these designations so that you can narrow down your search to those who are the most qualified and suitable to meet your needs. This appendix provides you with a description of the designations that are most respected and recognized in the financial industry. They are subdivided into the following categories: financial planners, tax advisors, investment advisors, insurance advisors, and attorneys.

The Difference Between Suitability and Fiduciary Standards

The *suitability standard* requires a client to receive recommendations that are suitable, or appropriate, to the individual's particular circumstances. Under the suitability standard, financial professionals are not required to put the client's best interests first. Financial professionals are also not obligated to disclose conflicts of interest.

This standard is less rigorous than the *fiduciary standard,* which requires financial professionals to act in the best interests of their clients. They are required to disclose conflicts of interest. The fiduciary standard also requires that financial professionals do not maximize their own compensation ahead of their clients' best interests.

The fiduciary standard has traditionally applied only to certain financial professionals and industries, such as Registered Investment Advisors (RIAs) and CERTIFIED FINANCIAL PLANNER® professionals. Several years ago, the Department of Labor made an effort to expand this higher standard of care. On June 9, 2017, a rule went into effect that increased the number of advisors required to act in a fiduciary capacity. While this was a positive development, the rule was limited in scope. It applied only to retirement accounts and did not extend to all types of investments or financial advice.

To further enhance investor protections, on June 30, 2020, the Securities and Exchange Commission implemented Regulation Best Interest, commonly referred to as Reg BI. This rule raised the bar for broker-dealers by requiring that they act in the best interest of their clients when making investment recommendations. However, Reg BI still fell short of the full fiduciary obligation. It improved transparency and addressed certain conflicts of interest, but it did not require all financial professionals to place the client's interest ahead of their own at all times.

When evaluating who you should rely on to guide you through your life journey to financial independence, it is critically important to understand what standard of care they are held to. Ask them directly whether they are required by law to act in your best interest and whether they are obligated to disclose any potential conflicts. Your financial future depends on having someone who puts your interests first, every time.

Financial Planners

The title *financial planner* frequently refers to a financial advisor who develops and implements a comprehensive wealth-management plan based on your needs analysis. This includes your long-term financial goals, together with issues pertaining to investments, estate planning, tax planning, risk management, education planning, and debt management. Many financial service providers refer to themselves as *financial planners,* but quite often, they do not consider a client's overall financial situation. A true financial planner should address all these issues because they are interrelated, and quite often, how you deal with one will have a direct effect on the others. When choosing a financial planner, make sure you are receiving comprehensive service and not simply being sold on one particular product or service.

CERTIFIED FINANCIAL PLANNER®

CERTIFIED FINANCIAL PLANNER® (CFP) is perhaps the most widely recognized credential in the financial planning industry. These advisors must pass a comprehensive financial planning exam and the rigorous certification requirements that are administered by the CFP® Board.

The CFP® exam consists of two three-hour sessions given in a single day, with a total of 170 multiple-choice questions that test the candidate's ability to apply financial planning knowledge to real-life situations. Prospective CFP® candidates must also complete at least three years of professional experience and earn a bachelor's degree from an accredited college or university either before or within five years after passing the exam. The academic requirements for certification include courses covering insurance, estate, retirement, education, tax, and investment planning, as well as ethics and the financial planning process.

CFP®s must abide by a code of ethics that includes adhering to a fiduciary standard as well as complying with specific practice principles. Most CFP®s are also investment advisors, but not all investment advisors are CFP®s. Financial planners may be fee-only or fee-based. For a more detailed description, visit cfp.net.

Chartered Financial Consultant®

The Chartered Financial Consultant (ChFC®) designation was originally created by the life insurance industry. Today, it is awarded by the American College of Financial Services and is recognized as a comprehensive credential in financial planning. The ChFC® designation requires the same core courses as the CFP® designation, plus two additional elective courses that tend to focus on specialized areas such as behavioral finance, planning for nontraditional families, divorce, and special needs planning. There is no comprehensive board exam required for this credential. Those who earn this qualification are considered knowledgeable in financial planning matters and are considered to have the ability to provide appropriate financial advice.

To be eligible for this designation, the applicant must already have a minimum of three years of relevant work experience in the financial service industry. It is also highly recommended that applicants have a degree connected to finance or business before applying, because that will make the course of study easier to master. For a more detailed description, visit theamericancollege.edu.

Tax Professionals

Tax professionals include those licensed or authorized by their state and/or the Internal Revenue Service (IRS), who have advanced training and are knowledgeable on the tax law. They are retained in order to legally minimize the client's tax burden and assist them in being compliant with the law.

Certified Public Accountant

The certified public accountant (CPA) designation is the oldest and most respected financial credential in the United States. This designation has long been widely recognized by the public as the definitive credential of tax expertise. CPA requirements vary by state, but generally a CPA needs 150 semester hours of undergraduate level courses that cover accounting, auditing, and business law, plus a bachelor's degree or higher in order to sit for the Uniform CPA Examination.

As of 2024, the CPA exam was updated to reflect the profession's evolving demands. The new structure includes three core sections: auditing and attestation, financial accounting and reporting, and regulation. In addition, candidates choose one discipline-specific section, which may include topics such as financial data analysis, IT systems and controls, or advanced tax planning. This updated format, introduced through the CPA Evolution Initiative, ensures that future CPAs are well prepared for a more specialized and technology-focused financial environment.

A CPA is always an accountant, but not all accountants are CPAs. CPAs handle a variety of jobs and tasks. They offer income tax preparation and advice for a range of clients including individuals, small businesses, and corporations. To maintain their license, every three years CPAs must take 120 hours of continuing education courses in order to stay abreast of changes in their profession.

Many states have a second tier of accountant qualification, usually entitled public accountant (PA) or licensed public accountant (LPA). The majority of states have closed the designation of PA to new entrants, however, with only four states continuing to offer this designation.

Certain CPAs who are interested in specializing in financial planning can also obtain a personal financial specialist (PFS) designation, which is offered by the American Institute of Certified Public Accountants. To qualify, CPAs must be members in good standing and complete the additional educational and testing requirements. For a more detailed description, visit aicpa.org.

Enrolled Agent

Enrolled Agents (EAs) provide a very important service to the general public. An EA is an individual designation provided by the IRS. It is one of the few designations that signifies a concentration of proficiency in the field of taxation. Unlike CPAs, who may or may not provide tax services, all EAs specialize in taxation.

To become an EA, individuals must pass the Special Enrollment Examination (SEE), a comprehensive three-part test administered by the IRS. The exam covers individual and business tax returns, as well as representation, ethics, and IRS procedures. Candidates must complete all three parts within a designated time frame. Unlike other financial exams, the SEE does not include accounting or auditing topics.

EA status is awarded by the IRS to individuals who meet its requirements, including a background check to ensure compliance with tax laws. Individuals who earn this designation must adhere to ethical standards and are required to complete 72 hours of continuing education credits every three years to maintain this status.

EAs are granted the same privilege as attorneys and CPAs, who have the authority to represent clients before the IRS, with a properly executed IRS Form 2848 Power of Attorney and Declaration of Representative. For a more detailed description, visit irs.gov.

Investment Professionals

An investment advisor is defined by the Investment Advisers Act of 1940 as a "person or firm that, for compensation, is engaged in the act of providing advice, making recommendations, issuing reports or furnishing analyses on securities, either directly or through publications."

In 2010, the Dodd-Frank Act amended certain provisions of the Investment Advisers Act of 1940 by delegating to the states the responsibility for regulating investment advisors who have under $100 million of assets under management. This amendment to the Act increased the threshold above which all investment advisors must be registered with the Securities and Exchange Commission (SEC), from $30 million to $100 million under management. This means that state securities regulators now have the primary authority over a substantial number of investment advisors who were previously subject to primary regulation by the SEC.

Registered Investment Advisor

Registered investment advisors (RIAs) are either registered with the SEC or the state securities agency in the state where they have their principal place of business. As of current regulations, firms managing $100 million or more in assets must register with the SEC, while those managing less typically register with their state securities authority.

Investment advisors are prohibited from providing advice known to be deceitful or fraudulent. They are also prohibited from acting as a principal on their own accounts by buying and selling securities between themselves and their clients without proper disclosure and consent. Investment advisors have a fiduciary duty to their clients, which holds them to a much higher standard. This means they have a fundamental obligation to provide not only suitable investment advice, but they are always obligated to act in the client's best interests and not their own.

Most investment advisors charge either a flat fee for their services or a percentage of the assets under management. Some advisors now offer alternative fee models such as annual fees, hourly billing, or subscription-based pricing. These models are becoming more common and may appeal to clients with less complex needs or smaller portfolios.

On average, fee-based advisors charge between 1% and 1.5% of the assets under management per year for providing ongoing investment advisory services, and they do not charge commissions. In many cases, fee percentages decline as the value of the portfolio increases, a structure known as tiered pricing. Larger accounts may be charged 0.75% or even lower, depending on the advisor and level of service provided.

This compensation structure typically limits potential conflicts of interest between the investment advisors and their clients. The advisor will generally get paid more as the client's asset base grows from the advisor's recommendations because the advisor's fees are based on assets under management. This is a significant difference when compared to transactional compensation (commissions), as is usually the case with a stockbroker.

RIAs are normally established by individuals or small investment firms that are independent of the larger financial services firms. They are also commonly known as financial advisors, asset managers, money managers, portfolio managers, investment counselors, or investment managers.

The SEC and state security regulators do not make any recommendation or endorsement of any investment advisor; in fact, if one is registered, it simply means that the investment advisor has fulfilled all of the necessary requirements for registration. For a more detailed description, visit sec.gov.

Chartered Financial Analyst®

The Chartered Financial Analyst (CFA®) designation is considered to be one of the most elite and difficult credentials to obtain in the investment management industry and is widely recognized around the world as the gold standard for professionals in investment analysis and portfolio management. The academic requirements and standards for this designation are second only to that of a CPA. This designation requires three years of coursework that covers a range of topics and disciplines, such as technical and fundamental analysis, financial accounting, portfolio theory and analysis, as well as a strong emphasis on ethics, professional standards, and fiduciary responsibility. In addition to the exams, candidates must complete at least 4,000 hours of qualified work experience, completed in a minimum of 36 months. Those who earn this designation frequently become portfolio managers or analysts for a variety of financial institutions. For a more detailed description, visit cfainstitute.org.

Investment Advisor Representative

Individuals who work for investment advisory companies and whose main responsibility is to provide investment-related advice are referred to as investment advisor representatives (IARs). IARs are only permitted to provide advice on topics on which they have successfully passed the appropriate examinations and are properly licensed. Most IARs are required to pass the Series 65 exam or an equivalent combination of licensing exams. Some professional designations, such as the CFP or ChFC, may also satisfy certain licensing requirements.

An IAR is also required to be registered with the appropriate state authorities. Many IARs hold either the CFP or ChFC designations, to increase their credibility and financial knowledge. For a more detailed description, visit finra.org.

Stockbroker

A stockbroker is a legal term that refers to an investment professional who buys and sells securities on behalf of clients. Stockbrokers are regulated by state securities commissioners and by the SEC. They are also subject to oversight by the Financial Industry Regulatory

Authority, which is an industry self-regulatory body. They are also registered with state securities regulators.

Under Regulation Best Interest (Reg BI), broker-dealers are required to act in the best interest of their retail customers when making investment recommendations. This standard includes obligations related to disclosure, care, conflicts of interest, and compliance.

Stockbrokers are also legally referred to as *registered representatives*. They may also call themselves *financial consultants* or *investment consultants*. They can also call themselves *financial advisors* if they are advisory registered. For a more detailed description, visit finra.org.

Insurance Professionals

Before we get into the specialized designations for insurance professionals, it is important to understand the difference between an insurance agent and an insurance broker.

Insurance Agents

Insurance agents are insurance professionals who serve as a liaison between an insurance company and the insured. Insurance agents have an administrative responsibility, which relates to the timely and accurate processing of forms, premium payments, and the related paperwork. An agent does not have a duty or responsibility to conduct a thorough examination of your finances or to make certain that you have been provided proper coverage. As the insured person, it is *your* responsibility to make sure you have purchased the necessary coverage.

Insurance agents can be captive or independent. A captive agent is an agent who works for only one company and, therefore, sells policies provided by only one insurance company. In contrast, an independent agent is one who works for many insurance providers and can provide a comparison of different insurance policies and providers.

Insurance Brokers

An insurance broker is required to have a broker's license, which normally means the broker will have additional educational qualifications and broader experience than an insurance agent. Brokers typically provide a variety of different insurance products to meet your needs. Most states require insurance brokers to have a higher duty of responsibility to their clients than an agent. Brokers have the duty to analyze your particular situation and secure the proper and adequate coverage that you may require. Typically, brokers will charge an administrative fee, or the premium payments may be higher to reflect this higher level of service.

Chartered Life Underwriter®

The Chartered Life Underwriter (CLU®) designation was originally created by the life insurance industry. This is a professional designation for individuals who wish to specialize in life insurance and estate planning. Individuals must complete four required courses and one elective course, each concluding with a two-hour, 100-question examination to receive the designation. The courses required to earn this professional designation are offered through the American College. There is no comprehensive board exam required for this credential. For a more detailed description, visit theamericancollege.edu.

Chartered Property Casualty Underwriter®

The Chartered Property Casualty Underwriter (CPCU®) is respected as the premier designation in property-casualty insurance. This designation is offered by the Institutes, formerly known as the Insurance Institute of America. This program provides a broad understanding of the property-casualty insurance industry and focuses on the legal, financial, and operational aspects of risk management and insurance. This designation requires the completion of eight courses of intensive academic study, but as with the CLU® and the ChFC®, no comprehensive board examination is required. For a more detailed description, visit theinstitutes.org.

Attorneys

To become a lawyer, you must have an undergraduate degree and then successfully complete three years of law school to earn a law degree. After law school, generally you must pass a bar examination in the state where you will be practicing law.

Tax Attorney

Tax attorneys are lawyers who have advanced education and training in tax law. Tax attorneys typically get involved with high-level tax matters, which may require a legal opinion or legal representation with the IRS or tax courts. Tax attorneys can negotiate settlements on your behalf and are trained to analyze complicated tax matters, allowing them to formulate a plan for resolving your problem and settling your case. Tax attorneys are most qualified to do the following:

- Represent someone in lawsuits with the IRS
- Represent someone in criminal IRS investigations
- Represent someone accused of tax fraud against a taxpayer
- Represent someone in income tax audits and appeals before the IRS
- File estate-related tax returns and representation in estate tax audits
- Assist with business start-ups, mergers, and acquisitions that involve complex structures
- Handle employee payroll tax issues and disputes
- Advise on international business transactions and related tax treaties

Estate and Elder Law Attorneys

An attorney who specializes in estate and elder law typically has an expertise in trust, estate, and/or Medicaid planning. These attorneys will work very closely with financial planners and will draft and execute the legal documents required as part of the overall financial planning process. These attorneys are experts in drafting wills, health care proxies, powers of attorney, and trust documents. Many of these attorneys also handle transactions that involve a family business and real estate.

Some of these attorneys refer to themselves as *elder law attorneys* and will have an added level of expertise in Medicaid planning for assisted-living or nursing-home care. They can provide an asset protection plan for clients who may need long-term care. They may also represent individuals in both contested and uncontested guardianship actions.

APPENDIX B

101 Ways to Save $20 or More per Day

Here is a list of 101 ways you could save $20 or more. That may not sound like a lot of money to you, but watch how that $20 can grow:

- If you tuck away that extra $20 into a savings account *every week*, at the end of the year, *you will have $1,040.*
- If you are 30 years old and invest that additional $1,040 for 35 years (until you are 65) at an 8% rate of return, *you will have $179,209.*
- If you can save $20 or more *per day* ($7,300 per year) for 35 years at an 8% rate of return, *you will have $1,257,914.*

It is pretty astonishing that as little as $20 per day has the potential of accumulating to more than $1 million over 35 years. With that said, becoming a millionaire is within almost any hard-working American's reach. All you need is the desire, willingness, discipline, and information provided throughout this book to help get you there.

Working together with your entire family, you could easily adopt several of these savings strategies, allowing each of you to set aside a minimum of $20 or more *per day.* Your family finances should be discussed and shared with your entire family so that a cooperative commitment to financial responsibility is established. Ultimately, each of you should set a goal of becoming financially independent and creating and maintaining generational wealth.

Use the *How Compound Interest Works* calculator, available at www.ventotaxandwealth.com under the Resources > Calculators & Tools section, to determine just how quickly and easily you can accumulate a million dollars or more based on an assumed initial balance, annual savings, annual increase in contributions, number of years, and rate of return. You could also use Exhibit 12.3, "FV on an Annuity Factor," to calculate this amount.

Chapter 3 showed you how to prepare your own statement of cash flow and to analyze this statement with your family to improve and increase your discretionary cash flow. The additional cash flow provided through these cost-saving strategies should be added to your investment assets, which will lead you to financial independence. Sit down with your family and plan your goals. Save money by planning which expenses are necessary and unnecessary (needs vs. wants) and use the internet to find cheaper alternatives to the items that remain in your budget.

Regardless of your income level, you can find ways to save money by cutting costs. My parents were Italian immigrants who barely spoke English, my mother was a seamstress in a sweatshop, and my father cut hair in a barber shop, and they were able to achieve financial independence within their lifetime and established their family's generational wealth code. If they were able to reach financial independence with their limited resources, there is absolutely no excuse for you not to be able to do the same. You just must be willing to make some adjustments to your standard of living, and we truly don't believe this will affect the quality of your life.

If you have made a firm commitment to saving for the future, or if you are simply looking for ways to save even more, the following list of 101 basic money-saving tips can help you achieve your goals. These tips are designed to help you find the extra money needed to begin or strengthen your savings plan. They are presented in the same order as the statement of cash flow shown in Exhibit 3.2 in Chapter 3 for ease of use together.

Housing

1. Reduce your cable bill by dropping premium channels, negotiating with your provider, or switching to basic service. Better yet, consider canceling cable entirely and switching to low-cost streaming services like Netflix, Hulu, Disney+, or free options such as Pluto TV and Tubi.

2. Buy older cell phone models and hold on to them as long as they work for you. Always buying the newest model can cost you thousands over time and is usually not necessary.
3. Bundle your cell phone, internet, and home entertainment services to reduce monthly costs. If you have a cell phone and rarely use your landline, consider eliminating it altogether to avoid paying for what you don't need.
4. Buy generic or store-brand products.
5. Clean your house yourself. If you must use a cleaning service, consider having them come every other week or once a month.
6. Learn to do simple home repairs yourself such as shampooing rugs, unclogging a sink, and mowing your lawn. Try to avoid calling expensive plumbers, gardeners, and handymen, if possible.
7. Install a smart thermostat like Nest or Ecobee to reduce energy costs and check for local utility rebates or grants that can help cover the cost of energy-efficient upgrades.
8. Replace incandescent bulbs with CFLs, halogen incandescent, or LEDs, which use up to 80% less energy and last much longer. To save even more, turn off lights when you leave a room and unplug electronics you rarely use.
9. Never let the hot water run in the sink or shower unless you are actually using it and try to cut your time in the shower by half to significantly reduce your hot water use and cost.
10. Ensure that your home, especially your attic, is sufficiently insulated. If the insulation in your attic is less than 6 inches thick, you are under-insulated. Insulation that is 12 inches thick can lower your heating and cooling costs by 25% each year. If you rent your home, consider installing draft stoppers or thermal curtains.
11. Installing an alarm system, smart smoke detectors, and water sensors can reduce your homeowner's insurance premiums. Many insurers offer discounts for proactive safety measures that lower the risk of damage or loss.
12. Installing ceiling fans can help cut air conditioning costs.
13. Clean out the coils in your refrigerator every six months to keep it running efficiently. Having only one refrigerator in your home will cut energy costs as well.

14. Always run full loads in your dishwasher and washer. Half-loads waste water, detergent, and energy. Wait until the machine is full to get the best value from every cycle.
15. You can save up to 14% or more on your energy bill by upgrading to a tankless or solar water heater.
16. If you're paying for a storage unit, go through the contents and ask yourself whether you really need to keep what's inside. Sell, donate, or discard unused items, and if possible, eliminate the storage unit altogether and store items more efficiently at home.
17. Shut the doors and close the vents in rooms you rarely use, like guest bedrooms or formal living spaces. This helps your heating and cooling systems run more efficiently and can reduce your utility bills.
18. If you rent your home, before accepting a rent increase, speak with your landlord about keeping your rent stable. Highlight your on-time payment history and offer to sign a longer lease in return for a reduced or unchanged rate. Many landlords are open to negotiation, especially with reliable tenants.

Transportation

19. Reduce commuting costs by using public transportation, school buses, or joining a carpool. If other options don't work, ride-sharing apps like Uber may still be cheaper than taxis.
20. Use apps like GasBuddy or Upside to track down the lowest gas prices in your area and earn cash back at participating stations.
21. Practice smart driving habits by regularly checking your tire pressure and staying on top of routine maintenance. These simple steps can improve fuel efficiency and extend the life of your vehicle. If your car has an eco-driving mode, use it whenever possible. And if it does not, remember to turn off the engine when idling for more than a minute.
22. Avoid driving over 55 miles per hour to save gas.
23. Bundle your auto and homeowners' insurance with the same carrier to receive a multipolicy discount. Many companies offer lower rates when you keep all your coverage in one place.

24. Ask your insurance provider about available discounts for safe driving, low mileage, antitheft devices, good grades, or having multiple vehicles on the same policy.
25. Consider increasing your deductibles to lower your monthly premiums. Just be sure you have enough in savings to cover the higher out-of-pocket cost if you need to file a claim.
26. Wash your own car. You can save anywhere from $5 to $30 on an expensive car wash, and you can usually do it just as well, if not better, on your own.
27. Buying a used car can be much less expensive than a car that is brand new.
28. If you have a car that you rarely use, consider selling it to save on insurance and maintenance costs.
29. Join local or regional EV (electric vehicle) owner communities. These often offer group discounts on insurance, charging stations, or accessories, and help identify free public charging options.
30. Join organizations such as AAA, USAA, and AARP for discounts on car repairs, auto insurance, travel, car rentals, shopping, and entertainment. These companies also offer limited free roadside assistance. Whenever getting work done on your car, booking travel or buying tickets, ask if they accept discounts for members.

Family Risk Management

31. Buy term life insurance early to lock in lower premiums while you're healthy. Use online tools to compare quotes and choose a coverage length that fits your long-term needs.
32. Before getting a life insurance policy, check with your employer's human resources department to find out if your company offers this coverage to employees. Companies typically get these policies at a much cheaper rate than an individual can.

Food

33. Skip the daily coffee run and brew coffee at home for pennies per cup. Invest in a good travel mug and consider making your own lattes, protein shakes, or smoothies to save hundreds per year.
34. Brown-bag your lunch and your kids' lunches too.

35. Never throw out good food. Use leftovers for tomorrow's lunch or reheat for the next day's dinner.
36. Buy in bulk from warehouse clubs like Sam's Club and Costco or online platforms like Boxed and Thrive Market. Bulk items such as rice, canned goods, and cleaning supplies often cost far less per unit.
37. Use store rewards cards to access sales, special discounts, and extra perks. Many grocery chains also offer dual-purpose programs that provide both grocery and gas savings.
38. Invest in a water filter pitcher or a faucet attachment instead of buying bottled water. You'll save money, reduce plastic use, and always have clean water on hand.
39. Plan your weekly shopping using supermarket circulars to buy groceries that are on sale.
40. Many grocery stores charge for plastic bags. Keeping a few cloth or foldable bags on hand prevents unnecessary charges and helps the environment.
41. Eat at least one vegetarian meal per week. It is not only healthier, but also cheaper.
42. If you frequently eat out or order in, try limiting it to once a week, or even once a month. Learn to cook your favorite restaurant meals at home for a fraction of the cost and enjoy the added benefit of healthier, customized options.
43. When eating out with your spouse or friends, share a meal. Portions are usually much more than you should be eating anyway so you will eat less and save money.
44. Take advantage of restaurant coupons and early bird specials.
45. Make your own baby food with fresh fruits and vegetables.
46. Buy your favorite type of wine from a less expensive winery. For example, purchasing a California wine may be less expensive than a French wine, but just as tasty. Buy the cheaper brands of liquor, Scotch, gin, vodka, and so forth, especially if you use a mixer.
47. Consider cutting down your alcohol consumption, or even better, stop drinking altogether. This not only saves you money but also lowers your risk of severe health issues.
48. Planning your meals can save you money and time. When grocery shopping, you will know exactly what you need to buy so there is no excess food thrown out at the end of the week.

Personal Care

49. Do not throw out torn clothing or broken items; instead, mend or repair.
50. Invest in high-quality, durable basics. Well-made wardrobe staples last longer and reduce the need for constant replacement.
51. Buy clothing that can be hand or machine washed to avoid dry cleaning costs.
52. Hang your clothes to dry instead of using a dryer. This saves money on your utility bills as well as wear and tear on your clothing.
53. Buy clothes at discounted brand name stores, such as Marshalls, T.J. Maxx, and so forth. You can also check out resale or vintage stores.
54. Try coloring your hair at home with over-the-counter hair dyes instead of professionally. If you want to have your hair colored professionally, extend the time between colorings with over-the-counter touch-ups.
55. Do your own manicures and pedicures.
56. Switch to reusable personal care products such as washable cotton pads, safety razors, or menstrual cups. These products cut recurring costs and are environmentally friendly.
57. Evaluate your gym or club memberships. If you rarely use them, cancel and explore free alternatives like walking, running, biking, or online workout videos. You can also find neighborhood walking groups or join community fitness events at no cost.
58. When cleaning out your closet, sell your clothing or donate it to receive a tax deduction.

Entertainment

59. Instead of paying full price for a movie in theaters, wait a few weeks and rent it on streaming for a fraction of the cost.
60. Rotate one streaming service per month instead of subscribing to several at a time.
61. Explore free community events like concerts, movie nights, and workshops through your town, local libraries, or schools. Many communities offer a rich calendar of no-cost entertainment year-round.

62. Use your library card to access free streaming and reading apps like Libby, Kanopy, and Hoopla. You can borrow movies, audiobooks, eBooks, and more, completely free.
63. Support your local community theater, where you can often see high-quality shows for a fraction of what you would pay for a professional show.
64. Cancel physical subscriptions in favor of digital access. Most newspapers, magazines, and learning platforms offer online versions, often for free or at a reduced rate.
65. Review your recurring subscriptions every three months and cancel anything you no longer use.
66. Host celebrations at home or in a local park instead of renting expensive venues. Bake your own cake, limit the guest list, and skip the party favors. Use digital invitations and choose simple, meaningful activities over costly entertainment. A thoughtful, low-cost party can be just as memorable without the financial hangover.

Loan Payments

67. Call your credit card company and ask for a lower interest rate, especially if you have a strong payment history. Many will reduce your APR or waive fees to keep you as a customer.
68. If you are not paying off your credit cards each month, stop using them. Destroy them or store them in a safe place to eliminate temptation.
69. Pay off your credit card debt using either the snowball (smallest balance first) or avalanche (highest interest first) method. Even a 1% monthly interest on an $8,000 balance adds up to more than $20 a week in interest alone.
70. Avoid unnecessary bank fees by switching to a no-fee online bank like SoFi, Ally, or Chime. These accounts often offer better interest rates, no minimums, and mobile tools to track your finances.

Taxes

71. Use the tax-smart strategies provided at the end of each chapter in this book to minimize your biggest expenditure, which is taxes.

Gifts and Donations

72. Do not donate money when you cannot afford it. Instead of donating money, donate your time or items that you no longer need.
73. If you want to make a big impact for your charity but don't have the means to make a large gift, see if your company will make a gift match. You can make the same impact for half the cost.
74. You don't need to spend a lot on birthday or holiday gifts. Thoughtful gestures like handwritten notes, homemade treats, or shared experiences often carry more meaning than anything you can buy in a store.

Professional Fees and Legal Obligations

75. Do not view accounting, legal, financial planning, and investment advisory fees as an expense. If your advisor is not saving you many times the cost of their fee, then it's time to look for someone else. Make sure you are securing your professional services from a trusted advisor who can meet your professional needs (see Appendix A).

Child Care and Other Expenses

76. Buy children's toys, books, and clothes through secondhand sources like Facebook Marketplace, consignment shops, or local parenting swap groups. You can also save by rotating toys through a local toy library or borrowing big-ticket baby gear instead of buying new.
77. Ask family and friends for hand-me-down clothes that their children have outgrown.

Pet Care and Other Expenses

78. Shop online or use auto-ship programs from Chewy or Amazon to save on pet food and supplies. Many offer discounts on repeat deliveries and let you schedule items based on your pet's needs.
79. Maintain your pet's hygiene at home. Brush their teeth using baking soda and a soft cloth or invest in an affordable pet

toothbrush. You can also groom them yourself with a clipper set, saving on salon costs.

80. Avoid buying expensive bedding or toys for pets. Use old blankets for bedding; make play toys out of old clothes or boxes. Stuff catnip toys with bulk catnip. The animals will not know the difference.
81. Check with your local animal shelter to see if they provide annual pet vaccinations for free or for a minimal fee.
82. Use virtual vet services like Pawp or Fuzzy for 24/7 advice, emergency triage, and routine care questions. These services often cost less than a single office visit and can prevent unnecessary trips to the vet.
83. Consider pet insurance to protect against high vet bills. Unexpected veterinary emergencies can cost thousands. Pet insurance helps cover the cost of accidents, illnesses, and sometimes routine care.
84. If you or your child is yearning for a pet, choose an animal from a shelter. It is not necessary to spend thousands on a special breed, and shelters are usually overrun with animals that need loving homes. Many shelters sponsor a Clear the Shelters Day, where pet adoptions are free.

Personal Expenses

85. Use digital loyalty accounts and browser extensions. Many retailers now offer their own digital coupons or member discounts. Sign up for these programs to receive exclusive pricing. You can also install tools like PayPal or Honey, which automatically apply coupon codes at checkout.
86. Enable price-drop alerts directly through retailer sites. Most online stores now offer built-in tools to notify you when prices fall on items in your cart or wish list.
87. Disable in-app purchases on mobile devices to avoid unnecessary charges. Whether it's your child playing games or you making quick buys, turning off purchases or requiring a password can help prevent impulse spending.
88. Travel during low-demand seasons. Airfare and hotels tend to be much more expensive in the summer and around school holidays. Consider traveling in the off-season to find better deals, smaller crowds, and more flexibility.

89. Use Google Flights or Hopper to track airfare. These tools let you monitor prices over time and notify you when to buy. Flights departing on Tuesdays, Wednesdays, or sometimes Saturday are often cheaper.
90. Bundle your flight, hotel, and rental car through travel deal sites or airline vacation portals to unlock significant savings. Packages often cost less than booking each component separately and may include extras like free breakfast, room upgrades, or bonus points.
91. Check if your company offers travel discounts. Depending on where you work, they can sometimes offer better deals on travel and activities than you would get through big-name travel sites.
92. When renting a car, don't pay for rental insurance. Check with your auto insurance provider or credit card company, which probably will already cover your rental.
93. If you don't absolutely need a more expensive rental car model, reserve a cheaper model and request a free upgrade at the rental desk, if available.
94. Consider vacation rentals instead of hotels. Sites like Airbnb or Vrbo often offer more space, kitchens, and better value, especially for families or group travel. Always compare total cost including cleaning and service fees.
95. Book a rental space or hotel suite that includes a kitchen and bring your own groceries and alcohol. Since eating at restaurants for every meal can be extremely expensive, especially in tourist areas, choosing to cook throughout your vacation can save a considerable amount.
96. Consider a "staycation." Avoid the cost of travel and lodging by spending your vacation finding fun or relaxing things to do in your own area. Explore nearby parks, beaches, museums, and landmarks that you may have overlooked before.
97. Use a travel rewards credit card for your everyday purchases to accumulate points or miles. Over time, these rewards can be redeemed for flights, hotel stays, or other travel expenses, helping you significantly cut vacation costs without changing your spending habits.
98. Planning a trip around where your loved ones live can cut lodging costs significantly. Staying with family or friends not only saves money on accommodations, but also gives you access to local tips, home-cooked meals, and free amenities.

99. Booking a tour with a group can often be a cheaper and safer option when traveling internationally.
100. If you want full freedom when traveling abroad, consider backpacking and staying at hostels. However, be sure to always do your research and make safety a priority.
101. Know cultural differences where you're traveling. Some countries expect you to bargain for the best price. Others don't expect you to give tips for service. Not knowing these nuances could cost you more than you may realize!

APPENDIX C

Basic Concepts and Definitions of Various Types of Taxes

In the United States, taxes are imposed on individuals and corporations by the federal government, most state governments, and many local (or municipal) governments. These taxes include income tax, property tax, sales tax, payroll tax, estate tax, gift tax, excise tax, tariffs, customs duties, licensing fees, occupational taxes, and various other user-based fees. Some of these taxes are paid directly, while others are embedded in the cost of goods and services.

Federal Income Taxes

At the federal level, the Internal Revenue Code (IRC) imposes income tax on individuals, corporations, estates, and trusts. Income subject to tax includes almost all income from whatever source derived. US citizens and resident aliens are taxed on worldwide income but may be eligible for a foreign tax credit if foreign taxes were paid on the same income. In addition, income earned from services performed outside the United States may be fully or partially excluded from taxable income, subject to the foreign earned income exclusion (FEIE), which is currently capped at $130,000 for tax year 2025.

The tax is based on taxable income (as defined in the IRC) multiplied by progressive tax rates, from 10% up to 37%, while corporations are taxed at a flat rate of 21%.

Since 2018, following the 2017 Tax Cuts and Jobs Act, the US corporate tax system shifted from a worldwide system to a territorial system. This change ended US tax on foreign profits that are accumulated but not repatriated after 2017.

As an individual, you may reduce your taxable income by taking a standard deduction or certain itemized deductions, such as home mortgage interest, state and local taxes (subject to the SALT cap), charitable contributions, and qualifying medical expenses. Widespread tax credits are also available, some of which are refundable.

In 2025, the current federal tax rates range from 10% to 37% of taxable income.

State Income Taxes

In the United States as of 2025, 41 states and many localities impose an income tax on individuals; 44 states and many localities impose a tax on the income of corporations. Tax rates vary by state and locality, and they may be flat or graduated. State and local income taxes are imposed in addition to federal income tax and are determined under state law. Most states conform to many federal concepts and definitions, including defining income and business deductions. Some states have alternative measures of taxable income, or alternative taxes, especially for corporations.

States imposing an income tax generally tax all income of corporations organized in the state and individuals residing in the state. Taxpayers from another state are subject to tax only on income earned in the state or apportioned to the state. Businesses are subject to income tax in a state only if they have sufficient connection to the state.

Estate and Gift Taxes

Estate and gift taxes in the United States are imposed by the federal and some state governments. An *estate tax* is an excise tax levied on the right to pass on property at death. (Here, "property" means any personal property, including real estate, as well as cars, jewelry, furniture, investments, and other assets.)

The estate tax is imposed on the estate, not the beneficiary. A few states impose an *inheritance tax* on recipients of bequests. *Gift taxes* are levied on the giver (donor) of property transferred for less than its fair market value. An additional *generation-skipping transfer (GST) tax* is imposed by the federal and some state governments on transfers to grandchildren or further descendants.

Taxable gifts are those that exceed the annual exclusion. For 2025, the annual exclusion is $19,000 per donor per donee. The taxable amount of an estate is the gross fair market value of all property owned at the date of death (the *gross estate*), plus lifetime taxable gifts, minus liabilities, costs of administration (including funeral expenses), and allowable deductions. State estate taxes are deductible, with limitations, in computing the federal taxable estate. Bequests to charities reduce the taxable estate.

The federal lifetime exemption for estate, gift, and GST taxes is $13.99 million per individual in 2025 ($27.98 million for married couples). Estates exceeding that exemption are taxed at 40% at the federal level. Life insurance proceeds, if owned by the decedent, are included in the gross estate.

Estate tax applies to all property owned wholly or partly by a citizen or resident at death, to the extent of their interest in the property. Whether a person has sufficient interest for the tax is determined under applicable state property laws. Most property is subject to estate tax, including jointly owned assets and certain lifetime transfers made within three years of death.

Taxable values of estates and gifts are determined at fair market value. For publicly traded assets, values are based on market listings; other property is appraised. Monetary assets are valued at face amount unless another value is clearly established. Life insurance proceeds are included if the decedent owned the policy or retained incidents of ownership.

Payroll Taxes

Payroll taxes are the taxes an employer withholds and pays on behalf of its employees and are based on the wages or salary of the employee. Payroll taxes are imposed by the federal and most state governments. Revenues from these taxes are used to fund such programs as Social Security, Medicare, unemployment compensation, workers' compensation, and health care.

In the United States, payroll taxes are assessed by the federal government, all 50 states, the District of Columbia, and numerous cities. These taxes are imposed on employers and employees and on various compensation bases. They are collected and paid to the taxing jurisdiction by the employers. Most jurisdictions imposing payroll taxes require reporting quarterly and annually.

Income Tax Withholding

Federal, state, and local withholding taxes are required in those jurisdictions imposing an income tax. Employers must withhold the tax from wages paid to their employees in those jurisdictions. Computation of the amount of tax to withhold is performed by the employer, based on representations by the employee regarding his or her tax status on IRS Form W-4. Amounts of income tax withheld must be paid to the taxing jurisdiction, and they are available as refundable tax credits to employees. Income taxes withheld from payroll are not final taxes, merely estimated prepayments. Employees must still file income tax returns and self-assess tax, claiming amounts withheld as payments.

Social Security and Medicare Taxes

Federal Social Security taxes are imposed equally on employers and employees, consisting of a tax of 6.2% of wages up to an annual wage maximum of $176,100 for 2025, and a tax of 1.45% of total wages for Medicare. To the extent an employee's portion of the 6.2% tax exceeds the maximum by reason of multiple employers, the employee is entitled to a refundable tax credit on filing an income tax return for the year.

Employees and the self-employed are required to pay an additional 0.9% Medicare tax on their earned wages and self-employed income in excess of limits based on filing status ($250,000 for married filing jointly, $200,000 for single, head of household, or qualifying widow(er), or $125,000 for married filing separately). This 0.9% surtax applies upon filing your personal tax return, in addition to any Medicare tax already withheld.

Unemployment Taxes

Employers are subject to unemployment taxes by the federal and all state governments. The tax is a percentage of taxable wages with a cap, which varies by jurisdiction and by employer's industry and experience rating. Some states also impose unemployment, disability insurance, or similar taxes on employees.

At the federal level, under the Federal Unemployment Tax Act (FUTA), employers pay 6.0% on the first $7,000 of each employee's annual wages for 2025. Most employers qualify for a credit of up to

5.4%, reducing the effective FUTA rate to 0.6%. However, employers in states with outstanding federal loans may face credit reductions, increasing their rate above 0.6%.

State unemployment taxes (SUTA) are also employer-paid and vary by state. Each state's taxable wage base must at least match the FUTA base of $7,000, though many states set higher limits, for example, Washington's is $72,800. Rates depend on state formulas, industry, and employer history.

Reporting and Payment

Employers must report payroll taxes to the appropriate taxing jurisdiction in the manner that each jurisdiction requires. Quarterly reporting of income tax withholding and Social Security taxes is required in most jurisdictions, typically via Form 941 (or Form 944 if eligible), due January 31 for the fourth quarter, with remaining quarters due by the last day of the month following the quarter. Employers must also file reports of unemployment tax quarterly and annually with each applicable state, and annually at the federal level via Form 940.

Each employer must provide employees with an annual report on IRS Form W-2 of wages paid and federal, state, and local taxes withheld. Employers must file Copy A (with Form W-3) with the Social Security Administration by January 31, with many states also requiring copy submissions. Failure to file or furnish these on time may incur penalties, beginning at $60 per late or incorrect form and increasing to $130 if over 30 days late, and $330 (or more) after August 1; higher penalties apply for intentional disregard.

Employers must deposit withheld taxes and employer contributions (Social Security, Medicare, income tax) using EFTPS or applicable state systems. Deposit frequency depends on Internal Revenue Service (IRS) schedules (monthly or semiweekly) and state rules.

Severe penalties apply where federal income tax withholding or Social Security taxes are not properly withheld or remitted. The Trust Fund Recovery Penalty can be assessed up to 100% of the unpaid amount from responsible persons.

Medicare Surtax on Net Investment Income

The Patient Protection and Affordable Care Act (2010) provided a new 3.8% Medicare tax surcharge on net investment income (including interest, dividends, capital gains, rental and royalty income, and passive business income). This was the first time in US history that a payroll tax was (and still is) imposed on unearned income (earnings you did not work for). This, too, is above and beyond the Medicare tax imposed on the earned income of employees and the self-employed.

This Medicare tax may be imposed on the net investment income for single and head of household taxpayers with income over $200,000, married couples and qualifying widow(er) with income over $250,000, and married filing separately with income over $125,000.

For individuals, this tax applies to the *lesser* of: (1) an individual's "net investment income" for the tax year, *or* (2) any excess of "modified adjusted gross income" (MAGI) for the tax year over the applicable threshold amount.

For example, if a single taxpayer has $180,000 of wages and received $30,000 in net investment income, their modified adjusted gross income would be $210,000 or $10,000 above the threshold amount. The 3.8% Medicare surtax would apply to the lower of net investment income ($30,000) or the excess of modified adjusted gross income over the threshold amount ($10,000). Therefore, only the $10,000 will be subject to this 3.8% Medicare surcharge for a total of $380.

Property Taxes

Property taxes are most commonly applied to real estate and business property, including interest in land, buildings, and improvements. Ownership interests include legal title and certain other rights to property. Automobile and boat registration fees are a subset of this tax.

Property taxes are imposed on owners by most local governments and many special-purpose authorities. Property tax rules and rates vary widely. These taxes are typically imposed only at the local level, though multiple jurisdictions may tax the same property, such as counties, municipalities, school districts, and special districts.

Property tax is based on the fair market value of the property. The amount of tax is determined annually based on that value on a specific date, often January 1 for the taxable year. Assessment frequency ranges from annually to every few years depending on state law.

The assessment process for property taxes varies by state and sometimes within a state. Each taxing authority determines values and calculates tax based on its rate, expressed as a mill rate or percentage of assessed value. Taxing jurisdictions often use valuation ratios and cap increases as allowed by state law.

Payment times and procedures vary widely. If a property owner fails to pay the tax, the taxing jurisdiction has various remedies for collection, including seizure and sale of the property.

Sales Taxes

Sales taxes are imposed on the price at retail sale of many goods and some services by most states and some localities. Sales tax rates vary widely among jurisdictions, from 0% to more than 10%, and may differ within a jurisdiction based on the particular goods or services taxed. Most jurisdictions exempt food sold in grocery stores, prescription medications, and many agricultural supplies. Generally, coupons and cash discounts are not included in the taxable price.

Sales tax is collected by the seller at the time of sale or remitted as use tax by buyers of taxable items who did not pay sales tax. Sales taxes, including those imposed locally, are generally administered at the state level. States imposing sales tax require retail sellers to register with the state, collect tax from customers, file returns, and remit the tax to the state.

There are no federal sales taxes in the United States.

Excise Taxes

Excise taxes are imposed at the federal and state levels on the manufacture, sale, and/or consumption of a wide variety of goods, including alcohol, tobacco, tires, gasoline, diesel fuel, coal, firearms, telephone service, air transportation, and many other commodities and services. Some jurisdictions require that tax stamps be affixed to goods to demonstrate payment of the tax.

As of 2025, federal excise taxes include 18.4 cents per gallon on gasoline, 24.4 cents per gallon on diesel, $1.01 per pack of cigarettes, and $13.50 per proof gallon on distilled spirits. States also impose excise taxes at varying rates on many of these same items.

Tariffs, Customs, and Duties

The United States imposes tariffs or customs duties on the import of many types of goods from many jurisdictions. The duty is levied at the time of import and must be paid by the importer of record before the goods can be legally entered. Rates of duty vary from 0% to more than 50%, based on the particular goods and country of origin, and the specific tariff regime in effect. Customs duties and tariffs are only imposed by the federal government.

The Trump administration introduced a universal base tariff of 10% on nearly all imports effective April 2025, with country and product specific reciprocal tariffs ranging from 11% to 50%. Steel and aluminum imports are subject to up to 50% tariffs, auto imports 25%, Chinese imports up to 30%, and country specific duties on Canada and Mexico at 25%, although goods compliant with the United States-Mexico-Canada Agreement are exempted. These measures have significantly raised the average US tariff rate, which peaked around 27% in mid-2025 and currently averages approximately 16%.

President Trump is using these high tariffs as negotiating tools for free and better trade deals for the United States. The goal is to pressure trading partners to the table in pursuit of more equitable terms. Hopefully, any high-level tariffs imposed will be negotiated down as agreements are made with other countries.

Customs duties must be paid before goods clear Customs and Border Protection (CBP), the agency responsible for enforcing import laws. Other related fees, including user or license fees, may also apply. Failure to comply with customs rules can result in seizure of goods and civil or criminal penalties, including fines up to twice the value of the goods and potential prison sentences. Imported goods may enter Foreign Trade Zones, where duties are deferred until they leave the zone for domestic consumption.

Licenses and Occupational Taxes

Many jurisdictions within the United States impose taxes or fees on the privilege of carrying on a particular business or maintaining a particular professional certification. Common examples include accountants, attorneys, stockbrokers, barbers, casinos, dentists, doctors, auto mechanics, and plumbers. *Licensing* or *occupational taxes* may be a fixed-dollar amount per year for the licensee, an amount based on the number of practitioners in the firm, a percentage of revenue, or any of several other bases. Persons providing professional or personal services are often subject to such fees. In addition to the tax, other requirements may be imposed for licensure.

In 2025, county-level occupational license fees are common, 87 counties impose fees based on payroll and 70 counties also apply them to net profits. Rates range from 0.5% to 2.5% of payroll or profits, with a median rate around 1%.

All 50 states impose *vehicular license (license plate) fees*. Generally, the fees are based on type, weight, age, or value of the vehicle and are imposed annually or biannually. In 2025, registration fees vary from as low as $8 in Arizona to more than $600 in Oregon for certain vehicles.

All states and the District of Columbia also impose a fee for a driver's license, which generally must be renewed with payment of a fee every few years.

User Fees

Fees are often imposed by the federal or state governments for use of certain facilities or services. For example, fees are often imposed for use of national or state parks, use of certain highways (called *tolls* on toll roads), parking on public streets, and public transportation. Such fees are usually imposed at the time of use.

Administrating Taxes: Collecting and Distributing

Three different entities handle different aspects of taxes:

1. Congress, the Senate, and the president of the United States write and approve federal tax laws.
2. The IRS administers the laws, collects taxes, processes returns, issues refunds, and remits revenues to the US Treasury.
3. The US Treasury is responsible for paying government expenses.

Taxes in the United States are administered by hundreds of tax authorities. At the federal level, there are three main agencies:

1. The Alcohol and Tobacco Tax and Trade Bureau (TTB) administers taxes on alcohol, tobacco, and firearms. TTB is part of the US Department of the Treasury.
2. The IRS administers all domestic taxes. The IRS is a bureau of the US Department of the Treasury.
3. The CBP administers taxes on imports (as mentioned, as part of customs duties). The CBP belongs to the US Department of Homeland Security.

Organization of state and local tax administrations varies widely. Every state maintains a tax administration. A few states administer some local taxes in whole or in part. Most localities also maintain a tax administration or share one with neighboring localities.

Income Taxes: Concepts You Should Know

Under the US tax system, every individual or entity is taxed in some way. This includes every person, company, corporation, or nonprofit organization. (Generally, partnerships and Subchapter S Corporations are not taxed directly by the federal government. Their partners or shareholders pay tax at the personal level on income generated regardless of whether it was distributed to them or not. Furthermore, certain tax deductions and tax credits also flow through directly to the partner's or shareholders' tax return as reported on Form K-1.)

In plain terms: you are taxed based on your income. Income is any money you have earned by working or investing. It includes wages, interest, dividends, profits on investments, and pension distributions; however, it does not include gifts, certain inheritances, and scholarships. Individuals and organizations are responsible for reporting their income and calculating their tax. Some organizations are exempt from tax, but they still are legally required to file a tax return.

The amount of taxes you owe is based on your income. People who earn more income generally pay a higher tax rate than those who earn less; this means that tax rates get progressively higher the more you earn. Conversely, you can reduce your taxes by taking advantage of various tax benefits or, to put it another way, through tax-smart planning. It is up to you to take control of your tax situation.

The federal income tax is usually the largest tax you will have to pay every year. As mentioned, most American families pay about a third of their gross income in taxes, including federal, state, and any applicable local taxes, Social Security taxes, and Medicare tax.

The Tax Cuts and Jobs Act was signed into law on December 22, 2017. It made major changes to the US tax code for both individuals and corporations. In fact, it represented the most significant tax changes in the United States in more than three decades. Most of the changes to individual taxes were originally set to expire after the 2025 tax year. These provisions have now been extended and made permanent through new legislation enacted on July 4, 2025, commonly referred to as the One Big Beautiful Bill Act (OBBBA). This law maintains the individual tax rate structure and many of the key provisions introduced in 2017. However, all tax provisions remain subject to change under future administration and Congress.

General Payment or Withholding of Income Taxes

The US federal and state income tax systems are self-assessing systems. In other words, taxpayers must declare and pay tax, but they are not assessed by the taxing authority. Employers must withhold income tax, as well as Social Security and Medicare taxes from wages. Quarterly payments of estimated taxes are required if taxes are not paid through withholding. Married taxpayers who both work must consider whether they need to increase their withholding because of the graduated tax rates. The tax withholding tables your employer uses do not account for the possibility that the overall family income may fall into a higher tax bracket due to multiple jobs or because your spouse also works.

Progressive Tax Rates

Personal income taxes are figured on a progressive rate: the larger the amount of the taxable income, the higher the rate at which it is taxed. Also, income is taxed in *brackets*. In other words, as income moves from a lower range to a higher range (or bracket), the percentage of tax goes up. The higher rate applies only to the income in that particular bracket, not the entire taxable income (see Exhibit C.1 for more detail). The tax rate for each bracket, whether it is 10%, 24%, or more, is called the *marginal tax rate*. The *total tax liability*, which is calculated by dividing the tax liability by the taxable income, is called the *average tax rate*, and is usually much less.

Filing Status

Taxes depend in part on filing status, which is based on your marital and family situation as of the last day of the tax year (December 31). Filing status affects whether you are required to file an income tax return, the amount of your standard deduction, and your tax rate. If you have a choice (such as married, filing jointly; or married, filing separately), you should calculate your taxes both ways, and choose the status that results in the lower overall tax.

There are five filing statuses:

1. **Single taxpayers:** Unmarried or legally separated from their spouses
2. **Married, filing jointly:** Married couples who combine their income and allowable deductions and file one tax return

3. **Married, filing separately:** Each spouse files a separate return, reporting only his or her income, deductions, and credits
4. **Head of household:** A taxpayer who is unmarried or considered unmarried and pays more than half the cost of maintaining a home for a dependent child or relative
5. **Qualifying widow(er):** A widow or widower with a dependent child

Pay-as-you-go Process

As anyone who has ever received a paycheck knows, our active wages are not the amount we actually receive; instead, our *take-home* pay is composed of our gross wages minus our taxes. By law, you must pay your taxes throughout the year. This is called *pay-as-you-go*. For most people, this means your income taxes are taken out of your paycheck and sent directly to the federal, state, and local governments. At the end of the year, you have paid in a certain amount of money in taxes.

Self-employed persons also prepay their taxes by forwarding part of their income to the IRS four times a year on specified dates. These are called *quarterly estimated tax payments.*

If you paid in more than you owe, the government refunds the amount in excess of what you owed. This is called a *tax refund.* If you have not paid enough to cover what you owe, then you have a balance due. You must pay this amount by April 15 of the following year, or the government may charge you additional interest and penalties on the amount you have not paid.

Federal Withholding Tax Allowances These taxes depend on the level of your earnings and the number of allowances you claim. (These allowances are requested on a form called a W-4, which you fill out at the behest of your employer.) A taxpayer is allowed certain special allowances based on a variety of factors, such as marital status, amount of time worked during the year, large, itemized deductions, and so forth.

Federal Insurance Contributions Act All employed workers (except certain employees of the federal government) must pay taxes under the Federal Insurance Contributions Act (FICA), for old-age benefits, survivors' benefits, disability benefits, and hospital insurance benefits. This tax is commonly known as Social Security (and includes Medicare), and various percentages are allotted to both, depending on current law. The employer pays 50%, and the employee pays 50%. Self-employed people must pay the whole tax, but they can deduct 50% on their tax returns.

Other Withholding Taxes Most states also require income taxes to be withheld, and the rates differ from state to state. Some cities and localities also impose income taxes.

Calculating Your Taxable Income and Liability

Calculating and paying income taxes is an incredibly complex process. It can be a tricky process just to define such concepts as *gross income* as well as the *true income subject to tax* (which is calculated by subtracting certain adjustments and deductions from gross income). Beyond that, the IRC places all sorts of conditions and exceptions on how the idea of *income* can be defined and treated. Nevertheless, it is important that you comprehend the basic definitions of the most important terms, as well as the fundamentals of this process.

Gross Income

Gross income is all the income you receive during the year from whatever source. Personal gross income falls into four general categories:

1. **Active income:** Wages, salaries, bonuses, tips, and commissions, as well as certain business income in which you materially participate.
2. **Portfolio income:** Interest, dividends and profits generated from investments, including savings accounts, stocks, bonds, mutual funds, ETFs, options, and futures.
3. **Passive income:** Income derived from real estate, limited partnerships, and other tax shelters. Losses from passive activities can generally only offset passive income and may need to be carried forward.
4. **Other unearned income:** Income that does not fall under active, portfolio, or passive income, yet is still taxable. This includes but is not limited to Social Security benefits, pension income, gambling winnings, alimony received (post-2018 agreements), canceled or forgiven debt, prizes and awards, jury duty pay, bartering income, and many others. While diverse in source, these types of income must be carefully tracked and properly reported for tax purposes.

Certain income is *tax exempt*, including the following:

- Child-support payments
- Compensation from accident, health, and life insurance
- Gifts and inheritances
- Municipal bond interest
- Scholarships and fellowships (subject to limitations)
- Veteran benefits

In addition, deductions and write-offs in various categories are subject to detailed rules, regulations, and limitations.

Capital gains are the gross income realized when an individual sells an asset (such as a stock, bond, or real estate) for more than its original cost (basis). These gains are taxed at different rates, depending on whether the holding period of the asset is short term or long term. There are also restrictions on how much capital loss can be claimed in a given year (with excess losses carried forward).

Adjusted Gross Income

Several adjustments against your basic gross income are permitted before you reach a number that represents your adjusted gross income. These elements include (with numerous limitations) the following:

- Student loan interest
- IRA deductible contributions
- Self-employed health insurance premiums
- Penalty on early withdrawal of savings
- Alimony paid (if divorced prior to 2019)
- Moving expenses (applies only to active-duty military personnel as of 2018)
- Deductible contributions to a Health Savings Account (HSA) and Archer Medical Savings Account (MSA) that you or your spouse made
- Contributions to a qualified retirement plan for the self-employed or other small-business owner, such as SEP IRA, SIMPLE IRA, or solo 401(k)
- New temporary above-the-line deductions for 2025–2028 under the OBBBA include:
    - Car loan interest up to $10,000 annually for interest paid on new US assembled personal vehicles (first lien only)

- Senior bonus deduction $6,000 for individuals age 65 or older, $12,000 for married couples filing jointly (phased out at higher MAGI)
- Tip income deduction up to $25,000 of reported gross tips for workers who earn and report tip income
- Overtime "half portion" deduction allows deduction of the extra 0.5× portion of time-and-a-half overtime pay
- Universal charitable deduction up to $1,000 per individual and $2,000 per couple (starting in 2026)

Expanded and continuing benefits include increased HSA contribution limits as well as annual inflation-adjusted thresholds for student loan interest, IRA contributions, military moving costs, self-employed retirement plans, and other longstanding AGI adjustments.

All of these adjustments are reported on Schedule 1 of IRS Form 1040 and directly reduce your AGI, which is the baseline figure used for determining eligibility for many deductions, credits, and tax brackets.

The ultimate number reached (after subtracting these adjustments from your gross income) is termed your *adjusted gross income (AGI).*

Deductions: Standard and Itemized

After you have calculated your AGI, you can consider other deductions. You can take the *standard deduction,* which is a fixed amount that depends on your filing status (for 2025 the standard deduction is $15,750 single, $31,500 married filing jointly and surviving spouse, $15,750 married filing separately and $23,625 head of household). Or you can list *itemized deductions,* which allow taxpayers to reduce their taxable income by listing certain personal expenditures, including the following:

- Medical expenses (in excess of 7.5% of AGI)
- State and local income tax or sales tax, real property taxes. (Deductible up to $40,000 for most filers beginning in 2025, increasing 1% per year through 2029. The cap reverts to $10,000 in 2030. A phaseout applies for high-income taxpayers, with the deduction reduced and eventually eliminated above approximately $500,000 in Modified AGI for most filers, although the $10,000 baseline remains available regardless of income. For married filing separate filers, the

deduction is limited to $20,000 and the income phaseout starts at $250,000.)

- Residential mortgage interest (can only be taken on new mortgage debt up to $750,000, down from $1,000,000 prior to 2018. Special rules apply here. Please refer to Chapter 4, "Managing Debt" for more detail.)
- Charitable contributions. (Beginning in 2026, only the portion of donations exceeding 0.5% of AGI is deductible.)

These deductions are usually subject to various restrictions and limitations. Many personal itemized deductions were eliminated beginning in 2018, such as casualty and theft loss (except those attributable to federally declared disasters and now some state declared disasters), tax preparation fees, unreimbursed employee expenses, and other miscellaneous deductions previously subject to the 2% AGI limitation. These eliminations remain in place under current law.

The decision to take a standard or itemized deduction may change from year to year, depending on your particular situation. The standard deduction, which was nearly doubled beginning in 2018, has now been made permanent by the OBBBA. Personal exemptions remain eliminated.

The higher standard deduction continues to simplify the tax reporting and preparation process. Many taxpayers who have itemized in the past may no longer benefit from itemizing given the continued restrictions and the larger standard deduction. This shift has also reduced the need for IRS audits on individual taxpayers, as fewer items require review.

Exemptions

Prior to 2018, exemptions allowed you a deduction from your AGI based on the number of dependents an individual has. For example, in 2017, each exemption allowed the taxpayer a $4,050 deduction. You were able to claim an exemption for yourself, your spouse, and any dependents, including children or other relatives earning less than a certain income. An exemption could have only been claimed by one taxpayer in any given tax year.

The Tax Cuts and Jobs Act of 2017 eliminated personal exemptions starting in 2018. The OBBBA, enacted in 2025, made this elimination permanent.

Calculating and Filing Your Taxes

To estimate the amount of tax you must pay, you now need to address a number of issues:

- The tax rate applicable to your personal income
- Tax credits
- Tax forms and schedules

Tax Rates

To find the amount of your taxable income, you subtract deductions (standard or itemized) from your AGI. Once you know your taxable income, refer to tax rate tables to determine the amount of taxes you owe. Exhibit C.1 shows how you calculate your tax rate at various income levels for each filing status. The Tax Cuts and Jobs Act of 2017 changed the tax brackets as follows: 10%, 12%, 22%, 24%, 32%, 35%, and 37%. Under the OBBBA, these tax rates and bracket structures have been made permanent. Inflation adjustments will continue annually for each bracket.

Alternative Minimum Tax

The Alternative Minimum Tax (AMT) was originally created to ensure that high-income taxpayers paid their fair share of taxes, regardless of how many deductions they were able to claim. Many high-income earners had previously managed to pay very little tax based on the tax breaks that were available to them. Under AMT, these high-income taxpayers are required to calculate their tax in two different ways. First it is calculated under the standard tax system, based on the formula we described earlier. This tax is then recalculated, which eliminates many of their deductions, such as state and local income tax or sales tax, real estate taxes, unreimbursed employee business expenses, and investment-related expenses. This alternative minimum taxable income is then subject to tax at a lower rate. The problem that developed over the years with the AMT exemption was that it was not originally indexed for inflation every year. Over time, the AMT started to affect more and more taxpayers, including the middle class, which was never its targeted group.

As of 2025, the AMT exemption amounts remain at elevated levels originally established by the Tax Cuts and Jobs Act and adjusted

Exhibit C.1 Tax Rate at Various Levels

Table 1: 2025 US Tax Rate Schedule for Individual: Filing Status Is Single

Example: IF you are SINGLE and your taxable income is $92,000 for 2025, your US income tax is					**$ 16,025**
Taxable Income			The Tax Is		
$ 48,475			$ 5,579		
$ 43,525	Multiply by	24%	$ 10,446		
$ 92,000	Total Taxable Income		$ 16,025	Total Tax	

2025 Schedule X: Use if your 2025 filing status is SINGLE

If Taxable Income Is						
Over	But Not Over	Then the Tax Would Be				Taxable Income of the Amount Over
$ —	$ 11,925			10%	MULTIPLIED by	$ —
$ 11,925	$ 48,475	$ 1,193	PLUS	12%	MULTIPLIED by	$ 11,925
$ 48,475	**$ 103,350**	**$ 5,579**	**PLUS**	**22%**	**MULTIPLIED by**	**$ 48,475**
$ 103,350	$ 197,300	$ 17,651	PLUS	24%	MULTIPLIED by	$ 103,350
$ 197,300	$ 250,525	$ 40,199	PLUS	32%	MULTIPLIED by	$ 197,300
$ 250,525	$ 626,350	$ 57,231	PLUS	35%	MULTIPLIED by	$ 250,525
$ 626,350	---------	$ 188,770	PLUS	37%	MULTIPLIED by	$ 626,350

Table 2: 2025 US Tax Rate Schedule for Individual: Filing Status Is Married Filing Jointly or Qualifying Widow(er)

Example: IF you are MARRIED FILING JOINTLY and your combined taxable income is $220,000 for 2025, your US income tax is **$ 38,494**

Taxable Income			The Tax Is	
$ 206,700			$ 35,302	
$ 13,300	Multiply by	24%	$ 3,192	
$ 220,000	Total Taxable Income		$ 38,494	Total Tax

2025 SCHEDULE Y-1: Use if your 2025 filing status is MARRIED FILING JOINTLY or QUALIFYING WIDOW(ER)

If Taxable Income Is						
Over	But Not Over	Then the Tax Would Be				Taxable Income of the Amount Over
$ —	$ 23,850			10%	MULTIPLIED by	$ —
$ 23,850	$ 96,950	$ 2,385	PLUS	12%	MULTIPLIED by	$ 23,850
$ 96,950	$ 206,700	$ 11,157	PLUS	22%	MULTIPLIED by	$ 96,950
$ 206,700	**$ 394,600**	**$ 35,302**	**PLUS**	**24%**	**MULTIPLIED by**	**$ 206,700**
$ 394,600	$ 501,050	$ 80,398	PLUS	32%	MULTIPLIED by	$ 394,600
$ 501,050	$ 751,600	$ 114,462	PLUS	35%	MULTIPLIED by	$ 501,050
$ 751,600	---------	$ 202,155	PLUS	37%	MULTIPLIED by	$ 751,600

(*Continued*)

Exhibit C.1 ***(Continued)***

Table 3: 2025 US Tax Rate Schedule for Individual: Filing Status Is Married Filing Separately

Example: IF you are MARRIED FILING SEPARATELY and your taxable income is $80,000 for 2025, your US income tax is **$ 12,514**

Taxable Income			The Tax Is	
$ 48,475			$ 5,579	
$ 31,525	Multiply by	22%	$ 6,936	
$ 80,000	Total Taxable Income		$ 12,514	Total Tax

2025 SCHEDULE Y-2: Use if your 2025 filing status is MARRIED FILING SEPARATELY

If Taxable Income Is						
Over	But Not Over	Then the Tax Would Be				Taxable Income of the Amount Over
$ —	$ 11,925			10%	MULTIPLIED by	$ —
$ 11,925	$ 48,475	$ 1,193	PLUS	12%	MULTIPLIED by	$ 11,925
$ 48,475	**$ 103,350**	**$ 5,579**	**PLUS**	**22%**	**MULTIPLIED by**	**$ 48,475**
$ 103,350	$ 197,300	$ 17,651	PLUS	24%	MULTIPLIED by	$ 103,350
$ 197,300	$ 250,525	$ 40,199	PLUS	32%	MULTIPLIED by	$ 197,300
$ 250,525	$ 375,800	$ 57,231	PLUS	35%	MULTIPLIED by	$ 250,525
$ 375,800	---------	$ 101,077	PLUS	37%	MULTIPLIED by	$ 375,800

Table 4: 2025 US Tax Rate Schedule for Individual: Filing Status Is Head of Household

Example: IF you are HEAD OF HOUSEHOLD and your taxable income is $60,000 for 2025, your US income tax is **$ 6,860**

Taxable Income			The Tax Is	
$ 17,000			$ 1,700	
$ 43,000	Multiply by	12%	$ 5,160	
$ 60,000	Total Taxable Income		$ 6,860	Total Tax

2025 SCHEDULE Z: Use if your 2025 filing status is HEAD OF HOUSEHOLD

If Taxable Income Is Over	But Not Over	Then the Tax Would Be				Taxable Income of the Amount Over
$ —	$ 17,000			10%	MULTIPLIED by	$ —
$ 17,000	**$ 64,850**	**$ 1,700**	**PLUS**	**12%**	**MULTIPLIED by**	**$ 17,000**
$ 64,850	$ 103,350	$ 7,442	PLUS	22%	MULTIPLIED by	$ 64,850
$ 103,350	$ 197,300	$ 15,912	PLUS	24%	MULTIPLIED by	$ 103,350
$ 197,300	$ 250,500	$ 38,460	PLUS	32%	MULTIPLIED by	$ 197,300
$ 250,500	$ 626,350	$ 55,484	PLUS	35%	MULTIPLIED by	$ 250,500
$ 626,350	---------	$ 187,032	PLUS	37%	MULTIPLIED by	$ 626,350

annually for inflation. For 2025, the AMT exemption is $88,100 for single or head of household filers, $137,000 for married filing jointly, and $68,650 for married filing separately. The income thresholds at which the exemption begins to phase out are $626,350 for individual filers and $1,252,700 for joint filers. These amounts were preserved under the OBBBA for 2025.

However, starting in 2026, the OBBBA resets the phaseout thresholds to their pre-TCJA levels: $500,000 for single and $1 million for joint filers, adjusted for inflation from 2018. Additionally, the AMT exemption phaseout rate increases from 25% to 50%, meaning the exemption will phase out twice as quickly once income exceeds the threshold. While the 2025 rules continue to shield most middle-class taxpayers from AMT liability, the post-2026 structure could result in more high-income households being subject to the AMT unless further reform occurs.

The most significant aspect to the change in the AMT tax is regarding personal itemized deductions under the standard tax system. By far, the reason that the majority of taxpayers were subject to the AMT tax in the past was because of the tax deductibility of state and local income tax, sales tax, property tax, unreimbursed work expenses, and investment expenses subject to the 2% AGI limitation. Since many of these items have now been either minimized or eliminated, the vast majority of taxpayers who were subject to the AMT tax will no longer be subject to this tax going forward. Quite frankly, this is perhaps one of the most significant changes in simplifying our existing income tax code.

"Kiddie Tax"

The "Kiddie Tax" is an IRS rule designed to prevent parents from avoiding higher tax rates by shifting investment income to their children, who are typically in lower tax brackets. The tax applies to the unearned income of certain children once it exceeds a specific threshold.

The "Kiddie Tax" may apply to children under 18, 18-year-olds with limited earned income, and full-time students aged 19–23, depending on their unearned income levels for the tax year. Unearned income includes sources like interest, dividends, capital gains, rents, and royalties, but not wages or salary.

For the 2025 tax year, there are specific thresholds for how unearned income is taxed. The first portion may be tax-free due to the standard deduction, the next portion is taxed at the child's rate, and unearned income above a certain amount is taxed at the parents' marginal tax rate.

The tax can be reported on the child's return or, in some cases involving only interest and dividends below a certain amount, parents can elect to report it on their own return using Form 8814. Earned income is taxed at the child's rate and is an exception to the Kiddie Tax. Certain educational savings earnings, and IRA earnings funded by earned income may also be exempt.

For 2025, the first $1,350 of a child's unearned income is tax-free. The next $1,350 is taxed at the child's own rate. Any unearned income over $2,700 is taxed at the parent's marginal rate. These thresholds are adjusted annually for inflation.

Tax Credits

After determining taxable income and calculating tax liability (i.e., the amount you owe), you may be allowed to take certain *tax credits.* A wide variety of tax credits may reduce income tax at the federal and state levels. Some credits are available only to individuals, such as the child tax credit for each dependent child, the childcare credit, and the earned income tax credit for low-income wage earners. A few credits, such as the foreign tax credit, may be available to all types of taxpayers.

Difference Between a Tax Deduction and a Tax Credit It is important to understand the difference between a tax deduction and a tax credit. A *tax deduction* reduces the amount of income you pay taxes on; a *tax credit* reduces dollar-for-dollar the amount of taxes you pay.

For example, if you have a $1,000 tax deduction from your income, and you are in the 35% tax bracket, you will save $350 ($1,000 × 35%) in taxes. Conversely, if you have a $1,000 tax credit, this amount is deducted, dollar-for-dollar, from your tax liability, and you will save $1,000. Some of these tax credits can only be used to reduce your tax liabilities. Others can be refundable after your tax liability has been reduced to zero.

Tax Forms and Schedules

The IRS requires taxpayers to file their returns using specific tax forms, usually a 1040 form or some variation. The government no longer automatically mails these tax forms to taxpayers. You should go online to www.irs.org to download the necessary forms or publications you need to prepare your tax returns. The vast majority of taxpayers use a paid preparer or an online tax program to file their tax returns.

Other Tax Considerations

As complicated as this process already is, certain other variables may need to be taken into account with regard to personal taxes.

Estimated Taxes

For most people, taxes are taken out of their paychecks by their employers. However, if you work for yourself or otherwise receive income that is not subject to withholding (investments, consulting fees, freelance jobs, etc.), you are required to pay estimated taxes to comply with the IRS *pay-as-you-go* ruling. Estimated taxes must be paid in four installments throughout the year, on April 15, June 15, September 15, and January 15 (of the next tax year). Penalties apply for underpayment or late payment.

Remote Work and Multistate Taxes

If you work remotely from a different state than where your employer is located or if you live in one state and work in another, you may be subject to tax in more than one state. Some states have reciprocity agreements, while others may require separate filings or estimated tax payments. It is important to check the tax rules for both your resident state and your employer's state to avoid underpayment penalties or double state taxation.

April 15

The tax year for personal income tax filers corresponds to the calendar year: January 1 through December 31. Returns must be filed (or extended) no later than April 15 of the year immediately following the tax year, and any balance due must be paid by that date. (This can be done electronically.) Overpayments are refunded; underpayments must be paid to avoid penalties.

Extensions

If needed, you can apply for a filing extension, with a due date of October 15 by filing Form 4868. Extensions apply to filing only. To avoid penalties, you must estimate and pay any tax due by April 15.

(In other words, a tax extension does not give a taxpayer more time to *pay* their taxes; it simply gives the taxpayer more time to file their tax return.)

Amended Returns

If you discover overlooked taxable income or deductions or credits, you may file an amended return, using Form 1040-X, up to three years from the date you filed your original return or two years from when the tax was paid, whichever is later.

Filing on Behalf of Another Taxpayer

If you are managing the affairs of a deceased spouse, elderly parent, or another dependent adult, you may be responsible for filing a return on their behalf. This could involve additional forms such as IRS Form 1310 for claiming a refund due to a deceased taxpayer. Make sure you retain legal authority, such as power of attorney or court appointment, if required, and keep documentation with the return.

Audited Returns

Although the chances of being audited are low, the IRS does review some returns to make sure they have been correctly calculated; this review is called an *audit*. The IRS conducts a few random checks. It also targets high-income earners. In addition, certain items can trigger an audit: a sudden increase in income, returns missing a signature, or itemized deductions that are exceedingly high or higher than previous years or the average of others in the same tax bracket.

The IRS can take three years from the date of filing to audit your return. If it does audit your taxes, the IRS will be looking to see that all income received was properly reported and that any and all deductions were legitimate. As a result, it is imperative that you keep complete and accurate records, and store them for at least three years, or to be on the safe side, for six years.

While the overall audit rate remains low, recent legislative changes, including the OBBBA, continue to modernize the IRS's enforcement priorities. Audit activity is increasingly driven by data analytics and matching technologies, which focus on discrepancies between reported income and third-party sources. For most taxpayers, especially those with wage income and standard deductions, the likelihood of being audited remains extremely low. However, it is more important than ever to ensure that your records are thorough and your filings accurate.

Recordkeeping

You must keep records supporting income, deductions, or credits for at least three years after filing your tax return. In cases where the IRS could claim substantial underreporting of income, you should keep these records up to six years. In fraud or no-return filed cases, you should keep them indefinitely since there is no statute of limitation. Records related to property should be kept until the statute of limitations expires after sale and filing of the related tax return.

About the Authors

John J. Vento, CPA, MBA, CFP® is the founder and Chairman of the Board of *Vento Tax & Wealth Management Group*, which he founded in 1985 in New York City. With more than 40 years of experience, John has built a nationally recognized wealth and tax advisory practice focused on helping individuals, professional practices, and business owners achieve financial independence through strategic, tax-smart planning.

Vento Tax & Wealth Management Group serves more than 250 businesses, as well as over 1,000 individual clients. John is affiliated with Cetera Wealth Services, LLC, a leading broker-dealer, and previously affiliated with Avantax Investment Services, Inc., where he was ranked as one of the elite financial professionals nationwide for 19 consecutive years, managing more than a quarter of a billion dollars in assets as of October 31, 2025. His expertise lies in tax-smart financial planning, investing, and wealth management.

John began his career at KPMG LLP, one of the "Big Four" CPA firms, where he specialized in audits of financial service and health care organizations. He holds a bachelor's degree in business administration with a concentration in public accounting from Pace University and an MBA in taxation from St. John's University. John is a certified public accountant (CPA) licensed in Florida, a CERTIFIED FINANCIAL PLANNER® (CFP)® professional, and holds licenses in both securities and insurance.

John has been featured in leading publications such as *Money Magazine*, *The Wall Street Journal*, and *Forbes*, as well as on major television networks including NY1, CNBC, Fox Business, and Reuters TV. He has served as a keynote speaker for major institutions and conferences across the country, including NYU Langone Health, Mount Sinai Hospital, the NYU School of Dentistry, and the Greater New York Dental Meeting. Additionally, he has served as an adjunct professor at St. Francis College, Wagner College, and St. John's University in New York City, and is a passionate advocate for financial literacy.

Outside of his professional work, John is a proud husband and father of three children, all of whom have followed in his footsteps to become accomplished professionals in the financial service industry. He has demonstrated his commitment to financial literacy as the founder of the Educate the Children Foundation, Ltd. of New York and his outreach programs throughout the New York City public library system.

Coauthor: John J. Vento Jr., CPA, CFP® is the president and managing partner of *Vento Tax & Wealth Management Group*, where he leads the firm's tax and accounting division. With more than a decade of experience at the firm, he brings deep expertise in accounting, finance, and tax planning.

John Jr. began his career at PricewaterhouseCoopers LLP after earning dual degrees in accounting and finance from Quinnipiac University and went on to obtain his CPA designation, CFP® credential, as well as his securities and insurance licenses.

Since joining Vento Tax & Wealth Management Group, he has completed a master's degree in taxation from Rutgers University and now serves as the firm's lead expert on evolving tax laws. His insight and leadership have been instrumental in positioning the firm as a trusted provider of comprehensive tax-smart financial guidance. With his specialization in tax-smart strategies as a CPA and CFP®, John Jr. helps clients turn financial data into actionable strategies that aim to grow and optimize both their business and personal finances.

He is also an accomplished speaker, having presented tax-smart strategies for the American Dental Association and the Greater New York Dental Meeting, and having served as a keynote speaker for *Accounting Today* webinars attended by thousands of CPAs, enrolled agents, and financial planners on the new tax laws under the One Big Beautiful Bill Act.

John Jr. is recognized for his deep technical expertise, a clear understanding of today's evolving tax laws, and a forward-looking perspective that makes his guidance especially valuable for individuals and business owners navigating an increasingly complex financial landscape.

Coauthor: Nicole Vento, CPA, CFP® is a financial advisor at *Vento Tax & Wealth Management Group*, bringing extensive experience from top-tier institutions in the financial services industry. Prior to joining the firm, she developed a strong foundation in wealth management through her tenure as an advisor for JP Morgan Private Bank and her five years at Goldman Sachs, where she served as a sales-trader for ultra-high net worth clients.

Nicole holds dual Bachelor of Science degrees in accounting and finance, as well as a master's degree in accounting, all from Penn State University. She is a CPA, a CFP®, and holds her securities and insurance licenses, reflecting her strong commitment to professional growth and excellence. She has also presented for the American Dental Association and the Greater New York Dental Meeting, where she has spoken on topics such as managing your investments and tax-smart investing strategies.

With a solid background in asset management and investment strategies, along with her designation as a CPA and CFP®, Nicole provides comprehensive, tax-smart financial guidance. Her sharp analytical skills, strong educational foundation, and dedication to client success have earned her recognition as a trusted advisor for individuals seeking to build, preserve, and grow their wealth over the long term.

Coauthor: Christine (Vento) Conway, CPA is a senior vice president and external wholesaler at *Inland Securities Corporation*, where she specializes in real estate investments, including 1031 exchanges, Delaware Statutory Trusts, Qualified Opportunity Zone Funds, and private real estate offerings. Her insights are shaped by years of hands-on experience and a well-earned reputation as a leading expert in tax-smart real estate investing.

Christine holds dual Bachelor of Science degrees in finance and accounting, and a master's degree in accounting, all from Penn State University. She is a CPA and holds multiple security licenses. Her prior experience includes her work at KPMG LLP's Deal Advisory practice, where she supported high-level mergers and acquisitions through complex financial modeling and valuation analysis, as well as her role at Meridian Capital Group, where she played a key role in streamlining operations and facilitating hundreds of commercial real estate transactions.

Christine is a featured speaker at dozens of educational events each year, reaching professionals across the financial, legal, and real estate sectors. With specialized expertise in tax-advantaged real estate strategies and a strong foundation in both accounting and commercial real estate, she is highly regarded for her ability to guide clients and advisors through this complex field. Her technical insight, practical experience, and clear communication have made her a trusted resource for those seeking to maximize the benefits of real estate within a comprehensive wealth management plan.

Disclosures and Disclaimers

While the publisher and the authors have used their best efforts in preparing this work, including a review of the content of the work, neither the publisher nor the authors make any representations or warranties with respect to the accuracy or completeness of the contents of this work and specifically disclaim all warranties, including without limitation any implied warranties of merchantability or fitness for a particular purpose. No warranty may be created or extended by sales representatives, written sales materials or promotional statements for this work. The fact that an organization, website, or product is referred to in this work as a citation and/or potential source of further information does not mean that the publisher and authors endorse the information or services the organization, website, or product may provide or recommendations it may make. This work is sold with the understanding that the publisher is not engaged in rendering professional services. The advice and strategies contained herein may not be suitable for your situation. You should consult with a specialist where appropriate. Further, readers should be aware that websites listed in this work may have changed or disappeared between when this work was written and when it is read. Neither the publisher nor authors shall be liable for any loss of profit or any other commercial damages, including but not limited to special, incidental, consequential, or other damages.

Market risk. *Investments are subject to market risks including the potential loss of principal invested.*

Rule of 72. *The Rule of 72 is a mathematical concept, and the hypothetical return illustrated is not representative of a specific investment. Also, note that the principal and yield of securities will fluctuate with changes in market conditions so that the shares, when sold, may be worth more or less than their original cost.*

Retirement plan general. *Retirement plan withdrawals may be subject to taxation and penalties when withdrawn early.*

SEP IRA. *Money withdrawn from a SEP-IRA (and not rolled over to another plan) is subject to income tax for the year in which an employee receives a distribution. If an employee withdraws money from a SEP-IRA before the age of 59½, a 10% tax penalty generally applies in addition to any regular income tax.*

SIMPLE IRA. *Employees who withdraw funds in a SIMPLE plan before age 59½ may have to pay a 10% additional tax penalty on any withdrawals, in addition to any regular income tax. However, if the withdrawal occurs during the employee's first two years of participation, the tax penalty is increased to 25%, in addition to any regular income tax.*

401(k). *Employees who withdraw funds in a 401(k) plan before age 59½ may have to pay a 10% tax penalty on any withdrawals in addition to any regular income tax.*

Rollover. *Both qualified retirement plans and IRAs typically involve fees, expenses, and services that should be compared when considering a qualified plan rollover.*

CDs. *FDIC insured, CDs offer a fixed rate of return. They do not necessarily protect against a rising cost of living. The FDIC insurance on CDs applies in case of insolvency of the bank but does not protect market value. Other investments are not insured, and their principal and yield may fluctuate with market conditions.*

529 plans. *Investors should consider the investment objectives, risks, charges, and expenses associated with municipal fund securities before investing. This information is found in the issuer's official statement and should be read carefully before investing. Investors should also consider whether the investors or beneficiary's home state offers any state tax or other benefits available only from that state's 529 plan. Any state-based benefit should be one of many appropriately weighted factors in making an investment decision. The investor should consult their financial or tax advisor before investment in any state's 529 plan.*

Where any **hypothetical case studies** *appear: This information is intended to be educational and does not reflect any particular investment or investment needs or scenario of any specific investor.*

Investing risk. *All investing involves risk, including the possible loss of principal. There is no assurance that any investment strategy will be successful.*

Limited Partnerships/DPPs. *Limited partnerships are subject to special risks and individuals must meet specific suitability standards before investing. This is neither an offer to sell nor a solicitation of an offer to buy any security. Such an offer is made by a prospectus only. Prospectuses will be available. Please read it carefully before investing or sending money.*

Risks include the following:

- *May not be suitable for all investors*
- *Redemption may be at more or less than original amount invested*
- *Potential for illiquidity of the DPP units*
- *Special risks of the DPPs underlying investments*
- *No assurance that the stated investment objectives will be met*

Asset allocation. *Asset allocation is an investment strategy that will not guarantee a profit or protect you from loss.*

Diversification. *A diversified portfolio does not assure a profit or protect against loss in a declining market.*

Rebalancing. *Before you rebalance your portfolio, you should consider whether the method of rebalancing you decide to use will trigger transaction fees or tax consequences. Your financial professional or tax advisor can help you identify ways that you can minimize those potential costs.*

Dollar cost averaging. *Because dollar cost averaging involves continuous investment in securities regardless of fluctuating prices, the investor should consider his or her financial ability to continue purchases through periods of falling prices, when the value of their investments may be declining. Dollar cost averaging does not ensure a profit or protect against loss.*

General securities. *The return and principal value of stocks fluctuate with changes in market conditions. Shares when sold may be worth more or less than their original cost.*

Individual Retirement Accounts

Limitations and early withdrawals. Some IRAs have contribution limitations and tax consequences for early withdrawals. For complete details, consult your tax advisor or attorney.

Retirement plans. Distributions from traditional IRAs and employer sponsored retirement plans are taxed as ordinary income and, if taken prior to reaching age 59½, may be subject to an additional 10% IRS tax penalty.

Roth IRA. Converting from a traditional IRA to a Roth IRA is a taxable event. A Roth IRA offers tax-free withdrawals on taxable contributions. To qualify for the tax-free and penalty-free withdrawal or earnings, a Roth IRA must be in place for at least five tax years, and the distribution must take place after age 59½ or due to death, disability, or a first-time home purchase (up to a $10,000 lifetime maximum). Depending on state law, Roth IRA distributions may be subject to state taxes.

Annuities in an IRA. If you are purchasing an annuity to fund any tax-qualified retirement plan (IRA), you should be aware that this tax-deferral feature is available with any investment vehicle and is not unique to an annuity. Carefully consider the features and benefits of the annuity before making the decision to purchase.

Investing in Private Placements *such as DSTs and QOZFs are only available to accredited investors. An accredited investor is defined by the SEC as follows:*

- *Individuals who have a net worth exceeding $1 million, excluding the value of their primary residence.*
- *Individuals that have earned income exceeding $200,000 in each of the past two years (or $300,000 jointly with a spouse) and reasonably expect the same in the current year.*
- *Individuals that hold certain financial licenses, such as: Series 7 (General Securities Representative), Series 65 (Investment Adviser Representative), or Series 82 (Private Securities Offerings Representative).*
- *Individuals who are knowledgeable employees of a private fund (such as executive officers, directors, trustees, general partners, or advisory personnel).*
- *Trusts, LLCs, corporations, and family offices can also be considered accredited if they meet specific assets or knowledge-based thresholds (typically $5 million in assets or all equity owners are accredited).*

Past Performance: *Past performance is not an indication or guarantee of future results.*

Index. *Investors cannot invest directly in indexes. The performance of any index is not indicative of the performance of any investment and does not take into account the effects of inflation and the fees and expenses associated with investing.*

Rates of return *shown are purely hypothetical and do not represent the performance of any individual investment or portfolio of investments. They are for illustrative purposes only and should not be used to predict future product performance. Specific rates of return, especially for extended time periods, will vary over time. There is also a higher degree of risk associated with investments that offer the potential for higher rates of return. You should consult with your representative before making any investment decisions.*

Cost and fees associated with variable insurance. *Before investing, you should consider the costs and fees associated with a variable life insurance policy. Plans are subject to enrollment, maintenance, and administration/management fees, surrender charges, mortality and expense risk charges, and charges for any optional benefits. As with any investment, it's important to fully consider the plan's objectives, risks, charges, and expenses before investing.*

John J. Vento, John J. Vento Jr., and Nicole Vento are financial advisors. *Securities offered through Cetera Wealth Services, LLC, Member FINRA/SIPC. Advisory services offered through Cetera Investment Advisers LLC, a registered investment adviser. Cetera is under separate ownership from any other named entity.*

Cetera Wealth Services, LLC exclusively provides investment products and services through its representatives. Although Cetera does not provide tax or legal advice, or supervise tax, accounting or legal services, Cetera representatives may offer these services through their independent outside business. This information is not intended as tax or legal advice.

Avantax Elite Ranking *for 2006–2025 was issued by Avantax Investment Services, Inc. Criteria: Recognizes financial professionals ranking among the top 150 based on gross dealer concessions. Listing in this publication and/or award is not a guarantee of future investment success. This recognition should not be construed as an endorsement of the financial professional by any client. No compensation was provided directly or indirectly by the recipient for participation or in connection with obtaining or using the third-party rating or award.*

For the endorsements *given by Michael Deluke and Satjit Bhusri, MD, who are clients of the financial advisor, no compensation was provided directly or indirectly. These individuals maintain an ongoing professional relationship with the firm. The endorsements provided by Michael Sincere and Gene Goldman, who are non-clients of the author, were given voluntarily. No compensation—direct or indirect—was provided in connection with these endorsements. Both the author and Gene Goldman are registered through Cetera-affiliated firms, which represents a material conflict of interest because their professional relationship may influence the views expressed in this endorsement. These endorsements do not guarantee future performance or investment success, nor should they be assumed to reflect the experience of other clients or investors. Additional background information about this professional is available on FINRA BrokerCheck: https://brokercheck.finra.org.*

Tax Law Interpretation and Guidance Disclaimer: *The information and strategies presented throughout this book are based on current laws, regulations, and professional interpretations available at the time of writing. Tax laws are subject to change, and new IRS guidance or legislative updates may alter how certain provisions are applied. While we have made every effort to provide accurate and practical advice, it is possible that some interpretations may be revised in the future as additional clarification becomes available. All tax laws discussed throughout this book were sourced through the IRS website,* IRS.gov, *as well as the One Big Beautiful Bill Act.*

Readers are strongly encouraged to consult with their qualified tax advisor or financial professional before implementing any strategy discussed in this book. The examples and guidance are intended to be educational and illustrative but may not be applicable to every situation or reflect the most current legal standards at the time of reading.

Tax and legal disclaimer: *Cetera Wealth Services, LLC exclusively provides investment products and services through its representatives. Although Cetera does not provide tax or legal advice, or supervise tax, accounting or legal services, Cetera representatives may offer these services through their independent outside business. This information is not intended as tax or legal advice.*

Index